DATE DUE

DE 9 '06			

DEMCO 38-296

Generating Jobs

Generating Jobs

How to Increase Demand for Less-Skilled Workers

Richard B. Freeman
Peter Gottschalk

RUSSELL SAGE FOUNDATION

NEW YORK

age Foundation

ldest of America's general purpose founda-
garet Olivia Sage for "the improvement of so-
es." The Foundation seeks to fulfill this man-
emination of knowledge about the country's
political, social, and economic problems. While the Foundation endeavors to assure the
accuracy and objectivity of each book it publishes, the conclusions and interpretations
in Russell Sage Foundation publications are those of the authors and not of the Foundation, its Trustees, or its staff. Publication by Russell Sage, therefore, does not imply
Foundation endorsement.

Library of Congress Cataloging-in-Publication Data

Generating jobs : How to increase demand for less-skilled workers / [edited by]
Peter Gottschalk & Richard Freeman.
    p.   cm.
Includes bibliographical references and index.
ISBN 0-87154-360-5
1. Labor demand—United States. 2. Unskilled labor—Supply and demand—
United States. 3. Wages—Unskilled labor—United States. 4. Manpower policy—
United States.
I. Gottschalk, Peter, 1942– . II. Freeman, Richard B. (Richard Barry), 1943– .
HD5715.2.L32 1998   97-37083
331.12'042'0973—dc21   CIP

The paper used in this publication meets the minimum requirements of American National Standard for Information Sciences—Permanence of Paper for Printed Library Materials. ANSI Z39.48-1992.

Text design by Suzanne Nichols.

RUSSELL SAGE FOUNDATION
112 East 64th Street, New York, New York 10021
10   9   8   7   6   5   4   3   2   1

Contents

Contributors

RICHARD B. FREEMAN is Herbert Ascherman Professor of Economics at Harvard University. He is also director of labor studies at the National Bureau of Economic Research and director of the Program for Discontinuous Economics at the London School of Economics.

PETER GOTTSCHALK is professor of economics at Boston College and research affiliate at the Institute for Research on Poverty at the University of Wisconsin, Madison.

REBECCA M. BLANK is member-nominee at the Council of Economic Advisers, Washington, D.C. and on leave from Northwestern University.

EDWARD M. GRAMLICH is dean of the School of Public Policy at the University of Michigan, Ann Arbor.

COLLEEN M. HEFLIN is research associate at the Poverty Research and Training Center at the University of Michigan, Ann Arbor.

HARRY J. HOLZER is professor of economics at Michigan State University.

SUSAN N. HOUSEMAN is senior economist at the W. E. Upjohn Institute for Employment Research.

LAWRENCE F. KATZ is professor of economics at Harvard University and research associate at the National Bureau of Economic Research.

DOUGLAS L. KRUSE is associate professor at the School for Management and Labor Relations, Rutgers University, and research associate at the National Bureau of Economic Research.

STEPHEN NICKELL is professor of economics at the University of Oxford.

Introduction

Less skilled and low-paid workers—those in approximately the lowest thirty percentiles of the earnings distribution—are in trouble in the United States. Their real wages fell during the 1980s, and their employment prospects have worsened. While workers in the middle parts of the earnings distribution have not fared well, the sharp drop in the rewards to those at the bottom has shocked many economists and analysts. One outcome of the fall in earnings for those at the bottom of the distribution has been that the gap between low-paid and the high-paid workers grew markedly through the 1980s , bringing the United States to levels of inequality not seen since the Great Depression. But lower earnings have not created a job boom for the less skilled. While the employment and hours worked by the less skilled vary cyclically, the trend has been for less skilled men in particular to work fewer hours (Juhn, Murphy, and Topel 1991; Freeman 1995).

There is a wide spectrum of views on the question of what kind of policies might increase the wages and employment of low-paid workers in the United States. Some analysts favor no policy interventions and would leave the position of low-paid workers to the market in the hope that they will respond to adversity by increasing their investment in skills and that employers will respond by increasing their demand for less skilled workers once these workers become cheaper. Some favor private charitable activity to help those in trouble. Others favor restrictions on immigration or trade. Still others endorse increased education and training. There are advocates of increasing the Earned Income Tax Credit and advocates of reducing the capital gains tax to spur investment or of general tax cuts to raise take-home pay. Some favor a policy of encouraging the growth of unionism or other forms of worker organizations that can collectively force employers to increase the pay of low-wage workers. Others want to increase the minimum wage or mandate employer-funded benefits.

In addition, many people favor general policies to maintain a macroeconomic expansion in the hope that strong growth will ultimately "trickle down" to all, so that special policies to aid low-paid and less skilled workers will be unnecessary. Growth through the mid-1990s did not benefit these workers, and we are dubious that "growth, growth, growth" will by itself resolve their economic problems. Not until the rate of unemployment reached 5 percent or less in 1996 to 1997 did the earnings of many low-paid workers begin to pick up. Whether the U.S. economy can maintain unemployment in the range of 4 to 5 percent and avoid a recession that will inevitably reduce the wages and employment of those workers is debatable. In any case, the real earnings of low-paid workers have a long way to go to reach the levels of 1973, much less to restore only the level of disparity between their pay and that of high-paid workers that existed before the increase in earnings inequality. Strong economic growth is probably necessary but not sufficient to improve the earnings of workers in the lower tiers of the earnings and skill distribution in this country. Special measures or policies to help low-paid workers are probably needed if the United States is to share its economic prosperity with these workers.

This book examines a set of policies that have been relatively neglected in discussions of ways to improve the market for less skilled workers: *micro demand-side policies* that seek to induce firms and government agencies to increase their employment of less skilled workers or that seek to raise the pay and benefits of low-skill labor. Some of the demand-side policies we examine are concerned with increasing employment. Others focus on improving the wages and benefits of low-paid workers. Since particular policies target either employment or wages, the researchers who study them often focus on one or the other of these outcomes. But policies that affect demand for labor impact both employment and wages. We contrast these policies to education and training policies that affect the supply of labor.

In years past, analysts and decision makers viewed demand-side policies as important tools to improve the employment situation of workers in trouble. During the Depression the Roosevelt administration created the Public Works Administration (PWA) and the Works Program Administration (WPA) to provide public-sector employment. The Johnson administration initiated affirmative action programs to shift demand toward discriminated groups. The Nixon administration developed the Comprehensive Employment and Training Act (CETA), which included federal funds to support state and local government jobs for low-skill workers; at one point, CETA enrolled one million adult workers and one million youths in summer jobs. The Carter administration experimented with subsidies for employment and short-term compensation programs to provide unemployment insurance to workers whose hours of work were reduced but who were not laid off.

In the 1990s, however, most attention turned from demand-side policies to supply-side policies: job training and schooling to raise labor skills; lower taxes by instituting an Earned Income Tax Credit to raise the take-home pay of the less skilled.[1] But for all their putative virtues, supply-side policies have not been the panacea that many had hoped. It takes a very large investment in skills to restore the 20 to 25 percent loss in real earnings experienced by low-skill Americans.[2] Given the magnitude of the problem, it seemed to us important to look again at the experience with policies that affect the other blade of the market scissors—demand for labor.

Which, if any, demand-side policies have succeeded in raising the employment or earnings of low-skill workers in the past, and which have not succeeded? Regardless of the past success of these policies, what lessons can we draw from them for the development of future programs?

This book contains seven studies that examine the effectiveness of micro demand-side policies—by which we mean policies that affect employers' demand for labor without risking the macro-economic problems of inflation. Even within the boundaries of micro demand policies, the book is selective. The policies examined partly reflect the interests and expertise of the researchers. The book is also selective because some demand-side programs—for instance, increased tariffs that would shift demand from foreign goods to American goods—have such high costs (even without foreign retaliatory tariffs) as to be nearly impossible to justify as cost-effective. For example, Gary Hufbauer and Kimberly Elliott (1994) estimate that the consumer cost of saving a job by tariffs is more than $100,000, with an average of around $170,000. It is hard to imagine circumstances under which the benefits of saved jobs would be worth even the lower end of the cost estimates, so we do not examine this policy.

Most of the policies on which the book reports operated in an economic context different from the 1990s world of inequality. Some of the policies have been tried more extensively in countries besides the United States. It is important to remember that policies that work or do not work in one economic environment or country may work differently in a new setting. Nevertheless, if a policy failed in the past, we would be leery of trying it in the present without at least tailoring it to current circumstances. Similarly, if a policy succeeded in the past, we are more likely to believe that something analogous would work in the present—though, again, we would want to tailor it to fit current realities. To assess the potential for micro demand-side policies to raise the economic position of low-skill and low-paid workers, we must understand both the current problem facing these workers and the effectiveness of policies in the past.

The 1990s Problem

The 1980s to 1990s was an epoch that witnessed a huge rise in earnings inequality in the United States (see Levy and Murnane [1992]), fueled by substantial falls in the real hourly pay of young and less educated workers, particularly men. As these changes have been well documented elsewhere, we simply note four aspects of the problem in the mid-1990s.

First, the wage distribution has become bifurcated in many dimensions. From the 1980s through the mid-1990s, educated, older, and highly paid workers gained in wages relative to less educated, young, and low-paid workers. Figure I.1 shows the change in a commonly used measure of earnings inequality—the earnings of persons at the ninetieth percentile relative to the earnings of persons at the tenth percentile. The value of 2.3 for the 90/10 ratio in 1963 indicates that a male at the ninetieth percentile earned 2.3 times as much as a male at the tenth percentile.

Figure I.1   Difference in Weekly Wages for Male and Female American Workers at the 90th and 10th Percentiles, 1963 to 1993

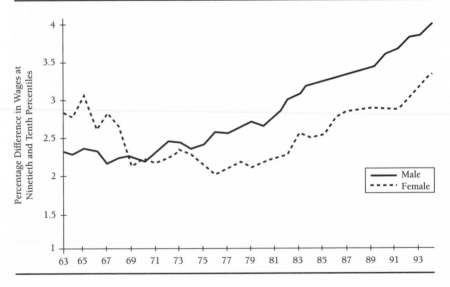

Source: Author's tabulation of the March CPSs.

By this and other metrics, earnings inequality increased from the late 1960s through the mid-1990s. Despite impressive economic and employment growth from the mid-1980s through the mid-1990s, inequality continued to grow.

Second, the rise of inequality was due to falling real earnings for low-paid workers, not to huge gains in real earnings for the more skilled and better paid and smaller gains for others. Some groups enjoyed large increases in pay—CEOs, sports, movie, and TV stars, for instance—but for the most part, real earnings stagnated for men and rose modestly for women. The distribution widened because real earnings fell for a substantial number of low-paid workers, particularly men. The magnitude of decline in the earnings of low-paid workers varies depending on the years covered, the earnings measure, and the price series used to deflate earnings. For young men with less than a high school education and for those in the bottom percentiles of the earnings distribution, the fall in real earnings has been on the order of 15 to 25 percent.

Third, the fall in the hourly pay of the less skilled was accompanied by decreases in the amount of time they were employed over the year. Annual hours employed over the year also became more unequally distributed in the United States. If you were a high-skill and high-paid employee, your wages and hours worked rose, whereas if you were low-skill and low-paid, your wages and hours worked fell. Thus, yearly earnings became even more unequal than hourly pay. And fringe benefits such as private pensions and employer health care coverage also became more unequally distributed, at least among male workers. Almost all skilled and high-paid workers have pensions and health insurance. The unskilled and low-paid were increasingly unlikely to have these benefits.

Fourth, the "rising tide of economic growth that lifts all boats," the historic pattern by which nearly all Americans benefited from rising national income or employment, broke down in the 1980s (see Blank and Blinder [1986] and Danziger and Gottschalk [1995]). Between 1967 and 1979, as figure I.2 shows, poverty varied with the business cycle, falling as income rose and rising in recessions. But in the 1980s, even though median income rose, poverty did not fall. In 1989 the official poverty rate was higher than in 1979, when the median income had been lower and the unemployment rate modestly higher. The pattern of declining poverty during expansions reemerged in the post-1993 expansion. But the tradeoff had dramatically worsened. Even with median income above its 1979 level, poverty rates were a full two points higher.

These aspects of U.S. economic performance have attracted considerable national concern. After all, our history is one of rising earnings

Figure I.2   Median Household Income and Poverty, 1967 to 1996

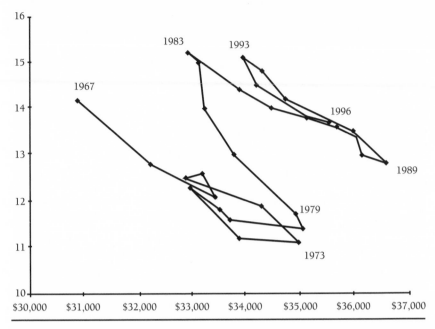

Source: U.S. Dept. of Labor, Bureau of the Census, *Current Population Reports*, series p-60

for all. It is newsworthy when gross domestic product (GDP) grows and many Americans do not enjoy rising incomes. But even as we focus in this volume on the problems of low or declining earnings for low-skill and low-paid workers and possible micro demand-side solutions to those problems, it is important to recall that the American job market has done well along other dimensions. The impressively high level of employment relative to the adult population is the envy of much of the advanced world. More and more women have found work, buttressing family incomes. Many firms have introduced new ways of working with employees and unions that go far beyond the adversarial labor-management relations of the past.

But our focus is not on economic successes but on the problems that have marred these successes. For two decades, if not longer, the benefits of economic progress have been highly concentrated among the skilled and high-paid to the exclusion of many workers on the middle and lower rungs of the earnings distribution. How long this will continue is uncertain. While the economy often changes in surprising ways, no one anticipates a sudden reversal in the job market fortunes of low-paid and less educated workers—hence our examination of possible demand-side policies to redress these problems.

Causes Versus Cures

Why does the rising tide no longer raise all boats? What has caused the problem of rising inequality? Many analysts have examined possible causes (see Danziger and Gottschalk 1995; Blackburn, Bloom, and Freeman 1990; Katz and Murphy 1992). Some attribute the change to declining relative demand for the services of low-skill workers compared to the relative supply of these workers. Many believe the decline in demand for low-skill workers is due to changes in technology associated in large part with computerization. Others argue that a major cause of the shift in demand has been increased international trade and outsourcing. Still others attribute some of the problems of low-skill American workers to the influx of sizable numbers of less skilled immigrants in the 1980s and 1990s. Some analysts stress changes in wage-setting institutions: the decline in unionization and the falling real value of the minimum wage.

This book does not address the question of causality. None of the contributors ask why inequality suddenly burst onto the national scene or why the rate of growth of real earnings fell for so many workers. The problem of causality is certainly important, and it has motivated much research and argumentation. We do not address it, however, because our focus is on potential policy cures to the problem, and causality is largely irrelevant to policy cures. A moment's thought makes this point clear. Assume that the cause of rising inequality is technological change. Would the cure then be to return to 1950s technology? No one would endorse a Luddite policy of smashing machines. If a worker's earnings fall because technology has outmoded his skills, train him and give him a tax cut or subsidy to allow him to have a decent living standard, but do not ban computers or advanced technologies. Just as we cure myopia (a largely genetic disease) with glasses or contact lenses (environmental changes), so too can we cure increased inequality in earnings due to technology, trade, or declining unionization with very different policies.

We note further that in assessing programs that raise the earnings of workers in the lower rungs of the wage distribution, we must weigh the costs of the programs against the benefits of the higher earnings. Virtually every governmental intervention in the market has an efficiency cost. Taxes must be raised, and administrative costs and "deadweight losses" are then incurred as people change their behavior in response to the new taxes. On the other hand, the fact that costs are incurred does not mean that programs should be rejected, but that you, we, the nation must balance the costs against the gains.

Micro Demand-Side Policies

The chapters in this volume cover four types of micro demand-side policies. The first set are those policies that try to lower the cost of employing some groups of workers by offering tax credits or subsidies to employers (Katz) or tax concessions to firms to locate in designated areas (Gramlich and Heflin).

The second type of policy focuses directly on government employment. If the private sector cannot be induced to hire less skilled workers, perhaps government should hire some of them or, more radically, serve as an employer of last resort (Gottschalk).

The third sort of policy changes modes of pay. One such change is to introduce more profit-sharing into wage-setting, a policy that is supposed to induce employers to hire more workers in good times and lay off fewer in bad times (Kruse). A very different change in the mode of pay is to mandate minimum pay or benefits for low-paid workers (Houseman).

The fourth kind of policy focuses on changing the regulations or rules of hiring that can influence firms' employment decisions. One such policy is work-sharing—limiting the hours worked by the currently employed to induce firms to hire more people (Freeman). Another employment regulation is the antidiscrimination law that seeks to shift demand for labor from groups that have benefited from discrimination, notably white males, to groups, notably women, minorities, or older or disabled workers (including white males), that have suffered from discrimination (Holzer). Finally, employers and the law distinguish between part-time and full-time workers, and firms hire some workers on a contingent rather than permanent basis, raising the question of whether changing these regulations or policies might raise the economic position of the low-paid (Blank).

The final chapter presents a broad comparison of the American job market with that of a country with different demand-and-supply policies, Germany (Nickell). This chapter makes it clear that economic differences between countries are related to systemic institutional differences that are not easily altered and reminds us that while micro demand-side policies may improve the economic prospects of some workers, they cannot readily change the overall nature of the U.S. labor market.

Policies to Lower the Cost of Employing the Disadvantaged

The contributors to this book reached certain conclusions on the effectiveness of micro demand-side policies.

1. Wage subsidies to employers to hire disadvantaged workers have succeeded in raising demand for labor for those workers, albeit modestly, and thus deserve consideration in any national policy to restore the economic well-being of low-wage or low-skill workers.

Subsidizing the pay of disadvantaged workers to increase their employability has been part of the antipoverty arsenal since the mid-1970s. Among the most important such programs are the Targeted Job Tax Credit (enacted in 1978 and expired in 1994), which provides tax credits to employers that hire individuals from particular disadvantaged groups, and the Youth Incentive Entitlement Pilot Project (YIEPP), which guaranteed full-time summer jobs and part-time school-year jobs to sixteen- to nineteen-year-olds in selected communities.

Lawrence Katz examines the nation's experience with these and related programs that cover part of the costs of hiring disadvantaged workers. He reports that upwards of 9 percent of economically disadvantaged youths were at one point hired under the Targeted Job Tax Credit, and that the credit appears to have increased employment of the covered group. While many employers were reluctant to use the YIEPP, presumably because the covered workers were stigmatized as risky, enough employers participated so that employment rates rose modestly in covered communities. Katz suggests that if wage subsidies were general—covering, say, all low-wage worker—the stigma might be reduced, and that a tax credit for wage subsidies could play a role in increasing the demand for less skilled workers.

2. Subsidies to employers to locate in particular impoverished areas are not cost-effective. Creating jobs in enterprise zones is expensive, because many of the jobs go to workers from other locales.

The federal government has often targeted jobs programs at specific areas by offering special incentives to businesses to locate in those areas. The Area Redevelopment Act of 1961 and its successor, the Appalachia Act, were designed to break down the barriers of spatial isolation and

encourage firms to locate in particular distressed areas. State governments often compete for business investments, offering incentives for
firms to locate in their area rather than somewhere else.

Edward Gramlich and Colleen Heflin summarize studies that have
shown that moving jobs to disadvantaged workers is very expensive,
roughly $60,000 for each new job; that cost is not quite as high as the
cost of creating jobs through tariffs, but it is likely to exceed any benefits of such job creation. They conclude that the cost of moving jobs to
workers is substantially higher than the costs of alternative mobility
strategies that move workers to jobs.

The lesson from these studies is that subsidy policies should target
disadvantaged people, not disadvantaged areas. Further, to avoid stigmatizing the recipients of subsidies, the broader the group covered by
the subsidy the better. This conclusion is consistent with Western European efforts to lower the cost of hiring low-paid workers by reducing
the payroll tax firms pay for them, shifting the cost of that tax (which
pays for pensions) to taxpayers with higher incomes.

Public Jobs

If private employers cannot be induced to hire less skilled workers, then
perhaps the government should do so as an employer of last resort.

3. Public employment policies can increase the number of workers from
   targeted groups working during the program. These policies are less
   successful at raising future wages.

Public service employment policies that deal directly with joblessness by having the government hire workers in high unemployment
groups have been used in the United States and other countries at various times. U.S. programs, such as the Public Service Employment (PSE)
segment of the Comprehensive Employment and Training Act (CETA)
of the 1970s, have concentrated on particular disadvantaged workers.
Western European programs have been more inclusive.

The effectiveness of public employment programs has been ques-
tioned on the grounds that, rather than creating new jobs for targeted
groups, they simply replace existing jobs with PSE jobs through various
mechanisms—for instance, by substituting those workers for employees
they would otherwise have hired, freeing that money for other purposes.

Peter Gottschalk reviews the U.S. experience with a diverse set of
public-sector job programs, ranging from CETA to the Job Corps to
Community Work Experience Programs (CWEPs) that require welfare

recipients to work. Overall, the programs succeeded in raising employment. The low-skill and disadvantaged workers covered consistently accepted the public-sector low-paid jobs. But the programs had less success in raising the future wages or skills of these workers.

Policies That Change Modes of Pay

4. Profit-sharing is not common among low-skill workers and is unlikely to raise their employment significantly.

Profit-sharing—firms paying part of an employee's wage as an agreed-upon share of profits or net revenues—has desirable economic attributes. It can save jobs in downturns by cutting labor costs as profits fall. It gives firms an incentive to want more workers, since each additional hire spreads profits over more people and thus also reduces the cost of employment. In the 1980s the notion that profit-sharing might alleviate employment problems was popular. Many countries, such as France, have legislated the use of profit-sharing as a mode of pay, and the Japanese, Koreans, and other East Asians use an implicit form of profit-sharing through bonuses (Freeman and Weitzman 1987).

Does profit-sharing increase employment of less skilled workers? Douglas Kruse finds the evidence that the effect is weak at best. First, low-skill workers are currently less likely to be covered by profit-sharing than skilled workers, presumably because their work offers them less chance to influence profits through individual decisions on the job. The primary exception is the worker who receives tips, as in hotels and some restaurants. Second, the rate of displacement from jobs paid under profit-sharing is only marginally lower than under other jobs. Thus, it is unlikely that very much employment gain would result from changing the method of pay. In short, encouraging more profit-sharing does not look as if it would do much to raise the economic well-being of low-wage and low-skill workers.

5. Mandated wages and benefits can increase the compensation of low-paid workers, with little cost in jobs.

A natural way for governments to try to raise the compensation of low-wage workers is through legislation that mandates that firms pay all workers at least a specified minimum wage and provide certain benefits, such as health insurance. Minimum wages are found in virtually all countries, as are public pension programs such as social security funded by payroll taxes. Many countries also use payroll or income taxes to pay for national health insurance. Low-wage workers gain from such policies when their pension or health insurance benefits exceed the taxes they pay.

But mandating minimum benefits or wages is problematic. Increasing one part of a compensation package, such as employer spending on health insurance, induces employers to lower other parts of compensation, shifting the cost of the mandated benefit to workers. The result may very well be a change in the form of pay but not in the overall level. A second problem, most prominently associated with minimum wages, is that mandated increases in pay or benefits that firms cannot shift back to workers make employment more expensive and, thus, can lead firms to cut employment.

Evaluating the evidence on these two problems, Susan Houseman concludes that mandated wages or benefits can raise the compensation of low-paid workers. The link between mandated benefits and wages is not a strong one-to-one relation. The effects of minimum wages on employment have recently been found to be small—often indistinguishable from zero, at least at the low levels of the minimum wage in the United States.

By raising the cost of hiring low-paid workers, mandated wages or benefits operate in the opposite direction from policies that subsidize the employment of those workers. Mandates succeed if elasticities of labor demand for these workers are modest: then the costs can be raised fairly high and few jobs disappear. Subsidies succeed if those elasticities are large: lowering the costs marginally leads to large increases in employment. That wage subsidies have only modest effects in expanding employment and that mandates lead to modest job losses are thus consistent conclusions.[3]

Policies That Change Employment Regulations

Policies that change employment regulations usually have the goal of distributing demand for labor differently—to increase the demand, say, for employees instead of hours, for minorities and women instead of for white men, or for permanent employees instead of for contingent workers. If the policies are targeted at low-employment or low-wage groups, however, they may improve the position of those workers at the expense of workers in more advantaged groups.

6. Work-sharing arrangements negotiated between employers and unions have saved some jobs in Europe and Canada, but these schemes are no panacea for unemployment and have not worked well in the United States, where workers seek overtime and higher earnings rather than more leisure time.

When unemployment rates are high, some people call for sharing the burden of joblessness by lowering the hours of current employees and distributing those hours to the jobless. In the 1970s Congress enacted legislation that allowed states to alter unemployment benefits systems to provide unemployment compensation to workers who worked fewer hours. The idea was to encourage firms to reduce hours rather than to lay off workers over the business cycle. In the 1980s and 1990s some Western European countries, notably France, tried work-sharing schemes to lower unemployment.

Richard Freeman's review of the evidence on work-sharing shows that it works only under limited conditions that are not well met in the United States. Work-sharing saves jobs when workers want additional leisure rather than earnings; when the employed and unemployed have similar skills; and when management and unions work out specific sharing arrangements. When the Mitterand government of France tried to impose work-sharing on the entire economy in the early 1980s, the program resulted in disaster and was abandoned within a year. By contrast, when unions and employers have negotiated work-sharing through collective bargaining, as in Germany, some jobs have been saved in major manufacturing activities.

American workers and firms use the short-time compensation features of the U.S. unemployment benefits system relatively rarely. One reason is that workers whose real wages have stagnated want more work and greater earnings, not more leisure. Another is that firms that offer expensive health insurance policies prefer to spread those fixed costs over more hours worked by employees rather than incur additional costs for new employees. In addition, the skills of workers differ so much that substitution of hours for employees is more difficult than advocates of work-sharing recognize.

7. Equal employment and affirmative action programs have shifted demand toward minorities and women but have not eliminated the disadvantages faced by minorities, owing in part to the concentration of these workers in economically distressed inner cities.

Since many minority and women workers who suffered from labor market discrimination in years past are still less skilled and lower paid than other workers, equal employment laws disproportionately raise demand for this group of less skilled workers. In the 1970s the debate over whether these programs worked was contentious, but as more and more studies examined the programs, their effectiveness became clearer. There was also debate over whether the concentration of minorities in inner cities contributed to their employment problems.[4]

Harry Holzer's review of the evidence supports the claim that existing statutes have in fact opened up jobs for women and minorities, at the expense of white male workers. He also finds evidence for spatial problems for black workers, in the form of substantial discrepancies between the success of minority workers who obtain jobs in suburban locations and the number of applicants. This finding suggests that focusing equal opportunity or affirmative action resources on suburban employers could expand the demand for black workers and raise the employment or wages of these workers.

8. Imposing uniform standards for benefits on all jobs, including contingent work, could raise the costs of nonstandard forms of work and lower the employment opportunities of contingent workers. However, unemployment insurance could be fruitfully extended to part-time workers.

Many "nonstandard workers"—contingent and part-time workers—are low-paid and lack the pension and health benefits of permanent or full-time workers. Thus, one way to improve the economic well-being of the low-paid is to enact regulations forcing employers to give these workers comparable benefits or pay as full-time workers. For instance, regulations could require that part-timers receive certain benefits, such as coverage by unemployment insurance, prorated to their time worked rather than being excluded from those benefits, and that workers in temporary jobs receive the same benefits as permanent employees of hiring firms.

Rebecca Blank argues that such an extension of benefits would raise costs so high as to threaten to eliminate many part-time or contingent jobs. Some workers would clearly benefit from turning nonstandard jobs into jobs with permanent full-time pay or benefits, but many employees prefer contingent work arrangements and many employers find these flexible arrangements beneficial to their businesses. The costs of making contingent or part-time work more expensive could thus very well exceed the benefits of limiting nonstandard work arrangements. In the case of unemployment insurance, however, the logic and evidence suggest room for extending normal workplace benefits to many of the workers hired under nonstandard contracts.

A Comparative Perspective

The final chapter assesses micro demand-side policies that might improve the employment or wages of low-paid or low-skill American workers. It considers why low-paid workers in Germany have enjoyed sizable increases in real earnings in contrast to their American peers and the possible role of a host of policies, including micro demand-side policies, in this difference in outcomes.

9. The major reason for the improved earnings of low-wage German workers compared to falling earnings for low-wage American workers is that German schooling brings all pupils to an acceptable level of achievement. While micro demand-side policies contributed only modestly to Germany's rising wages, a combination of minimum wages and job subsidies raised pay for some of the less skilled in the short run.

One of the most disturbing aspects of the problem of rising inequality and falling real wages for low-paid American workers is that it stands in sharp contrast to the improvement of wages for low-paid workers in many other advanced countries. Europeans often look at U.S. job performance and ask what they can learn to raise job creation and lower unemployment. Stephen Nickell looks at Germany's record of rapidly rising real earnings for low-paid workers and asks what we can do to raise pay for low-paid American workers.

He reports that Germany spends more on subsidized employment or direct government job creation and labor market training programs for those in trouble than the United States does, but he finds these expenditures insufficiently large to explain the greater increase in German real wages for low-skill workers. The fundamental reason for the narrower distribution of earnings in Germany is, he argues, that low-skill Germans have skills closer to the average than do low-skill Americans (or low-skill British workers), a difference that he attributes to the German education and training system.

From this perspective, Nickell argues that micro demand-side policies should be viewed largely as short-term transitional programs to stabilize or improve the position of low-skill and low-paid workers while the nation seeks to upgrade their skills or those of succeeding generations. He favors targeted micro demand-side programs as opposed to across-the-board tax cuts and combinations of programs to minimize undesirable side effects—such as loss of jobs due to mandated benefits.

All told, the studies in this volume show that some demand-side programs could help address the problems of low-skill, low-paid workers, while others do not seem to hold much promise. Tax credits to firms that hire low-wage workers can shift employment toward the disadvantaged workers who fall under these programs; public-sector employment can increase the number of jobs available to less skilled workers; and mandated benefits can improve the earnings of some low-paid workers. But area subsidies, laws to encourage profit-sharing or work-sharing, and limits on flexible contingent work arrangements would be less successful.

Past policies offer no magic micro demand-side solutions to the problems facing people in declining low-wage labor markets, but some programs do make a difference. Moreover, several policies that singly contribute only marginally to raising the employment or earnings of the low-paid can have a larger effect in combination. And substantially larger gains could also result from implementing some of the more carefully designed programs examined in this book. Just as the United States learned from successes and failures in the space program how best to advance in space, just as individual firms learn from their successful and unsuccessful products how best to compete in the market, so too should the nation's economic and labor policy makers and administrators learn from the successes and failures of past micro demand-side policies to develop more effective modes of raising the wages and employment of the low-paid.

Notes

1. Some attention was paid to demand-side policies in the 1990s. The Bush administration outlawed discrimination against the handicapped, and Congress increased the minimum wage. The Clinton administration tried to expand medical insurance coverage and raised the minimum wage.
2. Evaluation studies usually show that government training programs have positive but small impacts on future earnings of adult women, and little impact on the earnings of youth. The amount of training provided was too small to have a large impact on earnings. Even if a program invested the typical $6,000 per recipient and had a 10 percent rate of return, it would raise the earnings of trainees by only $600 per year. Hence, any hope that modest training programs could boost a family out of poverty and into the middle class had to be abandoned. As LaLonde (1995, 159) concludes: "We got what we paid for. Public sector investments and training are exceedingly modest compared to the magnitude of the skills deficiencies that policy makers are trying to address." Heckman (1993) estimates that even if human capital programs had a 10 percent rate of return, restoring the 1979 earnings differentials (between college-educated workers and high school graduates and between high school graduates and high school dropouts) would have cost more than $1,304 billion in 1989.
3. It may be possible to create better outcomes by combining wage subsidies and mandated benefits: the subsidies would permit the employer to pay the mandates without any loss of employment. In this case, the cost of the benefit falls

on taxpayers in general rather than on the firm or persons who consume its product. The firm becomes the conduit of the publicly funded mandated benefit

4. Antidiscrimination laws can increase equity and efficiency. When firms discriminate against women or minorities, they raise the prices of goods to consumers by ignoring a potential supply of labor and thus producing less than could be produced. Effective antidiscrimination laws should lead to higher measured GDP.

References

Blackburn, McKinley, David Bloom, and Richard Freeman. 1990. "The Declining Economic Position of Less Skilled American Men." In *A Future of Lousy Jobs?*, edited by Gary Burtless. Washington, D.C.: Brookings Institution.

Blank, Rebecca M., and Alan S. Blinder. 1986. "Macroeconomics, Income Distribution, and Poverty." In *Fighting Poverty: What Works and What Doesn't*, edited by Sheldon Danziger and Daniel Weinberg. Cambridge, Mass.: Harvard University Press.

Danziger, Sheldon, and Peter Gottschalk. 1995. *America Unequal*. Cambridge, Mass.: Harvard University Press.

Freeman, Richard, 1995. "The Limits of Wage Flexibility to Curing Unemployment." *Oxford Review of Economic Policy* 11(1): 63–72.

Freeman, Richard B., and Martin L. Weitzman. 1987. "Bonuses and Employment in Japan." *Journal of the Japanese and International Economies* 1: 168–94.

Heckman, James. 1993. "Assessing Clinton's Program on Job Training, Workfare, and Education in the Workplace." Working Paper 4428. Cambridge, Mass.: National Bureau of Economic Research (August).

Hufbauer, Gary Clyde, and Kimberly Ann Elliott. 1994. *Measuring the Costs of Protection in the United States*. Washington, D.C.: Institute for International Economics.

Juhn, Chinhui, Kevin M. Murphy, and Robert Topel. 1991. "Why Has the Natural Rate of Unemployment Increased over Time?" *Brookings Papers on Economic Activity* 2(2): 75–142.

Juhn, Chinhui, Kevin M. Murphy, and Brooks Pierce. 1993. "Wage Inequality and the Rise in the Returns to Skill." *Journal of Political Economy* 101 (June): 410–42.

Katz, Lawrence F., and Kevin M. Murphy. 1992. "Changes in Relative Wages, 1963–1987: Supply and Demand Factors." *Quarterly Journal of Economics* 107 (February): 35–78.

LaLonde, Robert J. 1995. "The Promise of Public Sector-Sponsored Training Programs." *Journal of Economic Perspectives* 9 (Spring): 149–68.

Levy, Frank, and Richard J. Murnane. 1992. "U.S. Earnings Levels and Earnings Inequality: A Review of Recent Trends and Proposed Explanations." *Journal of Economic Literature* 30 (September): 1333–81.

Part I

Wage Subsidies and Public Employment

Chapter 1

Wage Subsidies for the Disadvantaged

Lawrence F. Katz

G rowing disparities in the economic fortunes of American families over the past twenty years have been associated with large increases in wage inequality and rising gaps in labor market outcomes between highly skilled workers and those less skilled. The real earnings of many groups of workers, particularly less-educated young men, have fallen since the early 1970s. Much research suggests that a major contributor to these changes has been a substantial decline in the relative demand for the less educated and those who do more routinized tasks compared to the relative supply of such workers (see, for example, Bound and Johnson 1992; Katz and Murphy 1992). The shift in relative demand against the less skilled appears to be driven by both skill-biased technological change—the computer revolution—and the increased internationalization of economic activity. The relative importance of different causes of the decline in demand for the less skilled has been much debated, but the overall trend does not appear likely to reverse itself quickly. In summary, the U.S. labor market has experienced a sustained twist against disadvantaged workers—those who have limited education or skills and/or are from impoverished families and neighborhoods—that has greatly diminished their earnings prospects.

Market incentives for increased educational investments and skill upgrading can play some role in alleviating growing wage inequality. Evidence from U.S. time-series and cross-country studies strongly suggests that rapid expansions of the supply of more educated workers narrow earnings differentials and improve the labor market position of the less skilled (Freeman and Katz 1994). But the process of supply adjustment can take many years, and the many disadvantaged individuals who face financial and informational barriers to pursuing further education and training are likely to be left behind.

This prospect motivates an examination of policies that deal directly with the market shifts that adversely impact less skilled workers by improving their skills and/or stimulating employment opportunities through direct job creation in the public sector or subsidization of their employment in the private sector. Much recent work has evaluated the effectiveness of alternative education and training policies for improving the labor market prospects of the disadvantaged. Increased access to schooling at mainstream educational institutions (high schools, community colleges, and universities) for those from low-income families appears to have a reasonably high payoff (Card 1994). Public-sector-sponsored training programs have a mixed record: the results are strong and positive for disadvantaged adults (particularly adult women), but more disappointing for disadvantaged out-of-school youths (Heckman, Roselius, and Smith 1994; Katz 1994; LaLonde 1995).

Much less research attention has been focused recently on micro demand-side policies to offset the decline in demand for the less skilled. Wage subsidies to private employers have often been proposed by economists as a relatively flexible and efficient method to improve the earnings and employment of the less skilled. In a wage subsidy program, job creation and hiring decisions remain in the hands of private firms but the cost is partially borne by government. Firms are likely to respond to wage subsidies by increasing their utilization of workers in the targeted population. The extent to which this response raises the wages and employment of the targeted group and impacts nonsubsidized workers is an empirical question whose answer depends on the relevant labor demand-and-supply parameters as well as administrative aspects of the design of the subsidy program. The United States has experimented with a variety of tax credit programs to encourage firms to change their hiring patterns, and several demonstration projects using variants of wage subsidies have been evaluated. Most other Organization for Economic Cooperation and Development (OECD) nations also have experience with private-sector employment subsidies.

In this chapter, I first lay out briefly the basic economics of wage subsidies and the issues that arise in the design of alternative forms of wage subsidies. I then review the available evidence on the effectiveness of private-sector wage subsidies as a tool to improve the labor market prospects of less skilled workers, and I provide some new evidence on the employment effects of the targeted jobs tax credit, a targeted wage subsidy program that operated in the United States from 1979 to 1994. Finally, I derive lessons for policy design from past experience with wage subsidies.[1]

I conclude that the probable effects of a general graduated wage subsidy for low-wage or low-skill workers are very uncertain, but that the evidence suggests it is a policy worthy of further experimentation. Stand-alone wage subsidies (or employment tax credits) that are targeted at very specific socioeconomic groups (such as welfare recipients or ex-convicts) appear to be somewhat less effective than more broadly targeted subsidies and may sometimes stigmatize the targeted group. Policies that use an intermediary (such as a public employment agency or nonprofit training organization) to combine job development, job search assistance, training, and wage (or employment) subsidies appear more successful for targeting specific disadvantaged groups.

The Economics and Design of Wage Subsidies

The idea behind employer-side wage subsidies is to reduce the costs to employers of employing the targeted group of workers, thereby stimulating demand for these workers and raising their employment rates and earnings. A substantial literature has examined the analytics of the impacts of wage subsidies on employment and wages in both standard competitive labor market models and models with various types of wage rigidities or other market imperfections that generate structural unemployment (see, for example, Kaldor 1936; Hamermesh 1978; Phelps 1994b; and Snower 1994). Edmund Phelps (1994a, 1997) makes a particularly strong case for wage subsidies for low-wage workers based on equity considerations, the social costs of inefficiently high unemployment, and the possible negative effects of poor labor market performance by the disadvantaged on their neighbors, children, and younger siblings.

The Design of Wage Subsidies

Employer-side wage subsidies (programs that subsidize efforts to create jobs in the private sector) can take a variety of forms (Hamermesh 1978; OECD 1982). A wage subsidy can be applied to all employment, to net changes in employment (a marginal or incremental employment subsidy), or to gross flows into employment arising from new hires or layoffs. Subsidies based on total employment (or often, in practice, on the total wage bill) apply during the entire time a worker is employed with a firm and create "windfalls" to employers on that part of employment that would exist in the absence of the subsidy. True marginal employment subsidies could eliminate these windfalls (and reduce the net costs of job creation/wage increases), but such a policy requires information on what employment levels would be in the absence of the subsidy. Actual incremental employment subsidies can somewhat reduce windfalls by providing subsidies only for employment growth beyond a base employment level, but such policies can create perverse incentives for employment variation and changes in organizational form and can also become administratively quite complex. Many OECD wage subsidy programs are in fact hiring subsidies that provide temporary wage subsidies for selected groups of new hires. Such programs can generate incentives for higher turnover and disproportionately benefit sectors with high turnover and more variable employment. Some U.S. programs have attempted to mitigate these incentives by barring employers who systematically fail to retain subsidized workers. Some OECD nations have attempted to provide subsidies to "struggling" firms to avert layoffs, but such policies can create the moral hazard problem of firms threatening layoffs to gain a subsidy.

Wage subsidies can also be either general or categorical. Categorical subsidies (targeted wage subsidies) are paid on the employment or hiring of only certain categories of workers (for instance, economically disadvantaged youth, public assistance recipients, the disabled, dislocated workers, the long-term unemployed). Targeted wage subsidies are often motivated by a desire to affect the composition of employment; they aim program benefits at specific groups of workers whose employment opportunities are viewed as particularly in need of improvement. But targeting on the basis of sociodemographic categories that employers may view negatively can stigmatize participating job seekers and limit employer interest in the program. If categorical subsidies succeed in expanding employment opportunities for target-group members, one must worry about the horizontal equity of potentially displacing workers with similar labor market prospects who are not eligible for the program. General wage subsidies with caps on the amount of subsidy per worker or with a graduated structure may be able to increase the incentives for employing low-wage workers without the stigmatizing potential of categorical programs.

Two other considerations in the design of wage subsidies are the geographic extent of the subsidies and the administrative operation of the program. Wage subsidies can either operate nationally or be restricted to certain regions or local labor markets. Place-based targeting based on location of residence may be less stigmatizing than targeting on the basis of demographic groups. Place-based subsidies may largely serve to redistribute employment levels across areas, having small impacts on aggregate employment opportunities for the targeted groups if firm and/or worker migration is significant in response to labor market incentives. Subsidies can be run through the tax system (employment tax credits, as in the new jobs tax credit and the targeted jobs tax credit), thus reducing administrative burdens but providing incentives only to firms with positive tax liabilities (although they can be designed with generous loss carryovers). Subsidies can also be directly paid to employers, a procedure that may require new information and an administering agency.

In a simple Coasian world without transaction costs or imperfect information, it should not matter whether wage subsidies are provided to employers or equivalent earnings supplements are provided to workers. There are many reasons, however, why the side of the market in which the subsidy is provided could matter in practice. For example, employee earnings supplements (such as the earned income tax credit) may allow better targeting on the basis of family income without the stigma of sociodemographic targeting in categorical employer subsidies. When wages are rigid because of a binding minimum-wage law or other impediments to wage adjustment, employee-side wage supplements are more effective in raising take-home earnings, and employer-side subsidies more effective at increasing employment. Choosing which side of the market to place a subsidy may depend on the decision maker one is directly trying to affect. Employer-side hiring subsidies for targeted groups are more likely to be salient and to affect recruiting patterns toward those groups, while employee-side wage supplements or reemployment bonuses may have a greater impact on worker search behavior.

The Simple (Partial-Equilibrium) Analytics of Wage Subsidies

An employer-side wage subsidy for low-wage workers shifts out the labor demand curve for low-wage workers. In a situation of structural unemployment in which the effective supply of labor is infinitely elastic (figure 1.1a), a (proportional) wage subsidy (s) does not affect the wages of low-wage workers but expands their employment in proportion to the (absolute value of the) elasticity of labor demand for low-wage workers. More generally the impact on wages and employment of the targeted group depends on the effective wage elasticities of labor demand and labor supply for the group (figure 1.1b). The impact of a proportional wage subsidy (s) for low-wage workers on the employment (L) and wages (W) of low-wage workers starting from a point of zero subsidy is given by the standard formulas:

Figure 1.1   Partial-Equilibrium Impact of a Wage Subsidy (*s*) on the Low-Wage Labor Market

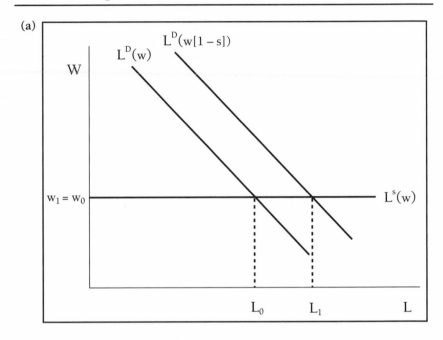

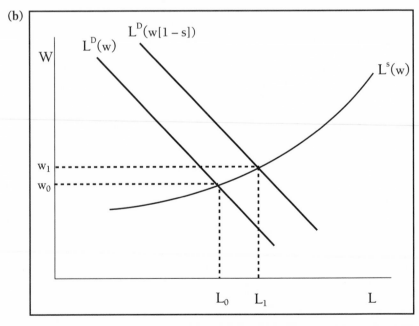

(1.1) $$\frac{d \ln L}{ds} = \frac{\eta \, \epsilon}{\eta + \epsilon}$$

(1.2) $$\frac{d \ln W}{ds} = \frac{\eta}{\eta + \epsilon}$$

where η is the absolute value of the labor demand elasticity for low-wage labor and ϵ is the effective labor supply elasticity. Thus, the greater the effective labor supply elasticity, the greater the effect of a wage subsidy on employment and the smaller the effect on wages. More elastic labor demand implies larger wage and employment effects of a subsidy. The impact of an actual wage subsidy depends not only on the relevant labor supply-and-demand parameters but also on design issues such as administrative costs, whether the subsidy stigmatizes eligible groups, and the extent to which employers are aware of the program.

There is much uncertainty about the magnitude of the relevant labor supply and labor demand elasticities for quantitatively assessing the probable impact of a wage subsidy on low-wage or low-skill workers in the U.S. labor market. Most research suggests at least fairly substantial positive labor supply elasticities for low-wage workers. Chinhui Juhn, Kevin M. Murphy, and Robert Topel (1991) interpret the decline in employment rates for low-wage adult U.S. males in the 1980s as a reflection of a downward shift in labor demand for less skilled workers combined with a stable labor supply curve. Their estimates (based on both cross-section and time-series variation) of the gross wage elasticity of the labor supply of low-wage men (those in the bottom quintile of the wage distribution) range from 0.3 to 0.4. Many studies conclude that labor supply elasticities for teenagers and low-wage women are likely to be at least as large as these estimates for low-wage men, although Robert Moffitt (1992) argues for lower wage elasticities of around 0.2 for single female household heads.

There is even less consensus on the relevant labor demand elasticity for low-wage workers. The empirical labor demand literature that attempts to estimate labor demand elasticities using "exogenous" supply shifts concludes that own-wage elasticities are particularly high for less skilled workers in the range of -0.5 or even greater in magnitude (Hamermesh 1993). But much of the literature estimating the impact of minimum wages on low-wage (particularly teenage) employment suggests small to negligible adverse employment impacts, which may imply that the demand for low-wage labor is quite inelastic (Card and Krueger 1995). One possible reconciliation of these findings is the "dissipation effect" of estimated minimum-wage effects. Since a minimum-wage increase does not change the wages of many teenage workers, the percentage increase in the total labor costs of employing teenagers rises by less than the percentage increase in the minimum wage. Thus, standard elasticities of a minimum-wage increase on teenage employment-population ratios of -0.05 to -0.20 could be consistent with labor demand elasticities for teenagers in the -0.10 to -0.60 range (since Card and Krueger's estimates suggest that average teenage wages appear to rise proportionately by one-third to one-half as much as increases in the minimum wage). Furthermore, if employers have some wage-setting power in low-wage labor markets, as in certain efficiency wage models and search models, then even exogenous minimum-wage increases cannot easily be used to estimate labor demand elasticities for low-wage labor (Manning 1995). Increases in total labor costs may be less than proportional to observed wage increases since, for example, turnover costs may be reduced by a higher minimum wage. Administrative burdens and lack of employer awareness of some targeted wage subsidies suggest the "effective labor demand elasticity" in response to such a wage subsidy may be lower than for an "equivalent" wage decline.

My best guess at "reasonable" parameters for simulating the probable medium-term impact of a general wage subsidy for U.S. low-wage workers is a labor supply elasticity of approximately 0.4 and a labor demand elasticity of approximately -0.5. Translating these guesses into equations 1.1 and 1.2 yields the prediction that a general 10 percent wage subsidy for low-wage workers will expand their employment by approximately 2 percent and increase their hourly wages by approximately 5 to 6 percent. Thus, wage subsidy evaluations that focus only on employment effects may miss the possibly larger effect of such policies on the wages of the targeted group. But, as I noted earlier, substantial uncertainty surrounds these predictions, and "reasonable" choices of elasticities based on existing evidence can lead to very different estimates. If the labor demand elasticity were -0.1 (as suggested by the minimum-wage literature) and the labor supply elasticity 0.4, then a 10 percent subsidy will produce a 0.8 percent increase in employment and a 2 percent increase in wages. If the labor supply elasticity is much larger, as may be the case for groups facing substantial structural unemployment (such as disadvantaged inner-city teenagers), then it is reasonable to focus more on employment effects. This wide range of scenarios suggests that a possibly more fruitful approach to assessing the effectiveness of a wage subsidy policy is to examine the outcomes observed in past attempts at using wage subsidies and in demonstration projects designed to test alternative employment-subsidy strategies.[2]

The U.S. Experience with Wage Subsidies

The United States has experimented over the past three decades with various forms of categorical wage subsidies to increase private employment opportunities for the disadvantaged and with an incremental employment tax credit as part of a fiscal stimulus package. The three major efforts have been the new jobs tax credit, the targeted jobs tax credit, and some aspects of Title II of the Job Training Partnership Act of 1983. Two early attempts were the contract component of the Job Opportunities in the Business Sector (JOBS) program, a late 1960s–early 1970s effort to train and hire disadvantaged workers, and the Work Incentive Tax Credit (WINTC) program, a 1970s subsidy paid on the wages of AFDC recipients enrolled in the work-incentive program.

The JOBS program started as a voluntary effort by the National Alliance of Business (NAB) to place young and less-educated workers from impoverished backgrounds in private employment. To assist NAB in placing participants, the federal government offered contracts that reimbursed businesses for part of the costs of employment ($3,200 per placement on average). Despite this fairly large hiring subsidy and much publicity, surprisingly few of the employers who cooperated with NAB and accepted placements (those employing about one-third of the JOBS enrollees) took advantage of it (Hamermesh 1978). The JOBS program provided subsidies to approximately ninety-three thousand positions at its peak in 1971; it was eliminated with the introduction of the Comprehensive Employment and Training Act (CETA) in 1973.

Data from the WINTC program indicate low utilization: no more than 20 percent of the WIN individuals known to have entered employment during the year were ever claimed by firms as tax credits (O'Neill 1982). The JOBS and WINTC experiences suggest some reluctance on the part of employers to hire under a highly targeted subsidy that requires paperwork not normally part of the hiring process.

New Jobs Tax Credit

The United States has tried one noncategorical employment subsidy, the new jobs tax credit (NJTC), which was in effect from mid-1977 to the end of 1978. Its main objective was countercyclical—to spur private employment expansion and speed up the recovery that was already under way.

The relatively simple idea was to provide a tax credit of 50 percent of the first $4,200 of wages per employee for increases in employment of more than 2 percent over the previous year. But the NJTC was complicated by attempts to close loopholes and limit the share of tax benefits accruing to large employers (Ashenfelter 1978). Subject to various limitations, the NJTC entitled employers to a tax credit equal to 50 percent of the excess of wages covered by federal unemployment insurance tax (FUTA) over 102 percent of FUTA wages (the first $4,200 of annual wages paid to each employee summed over all employees on the payroll at any time during the year) for the previous year. The total credit could not exceed $100,000 for any one firm (a maximum of approximately forty-seven employees), so that no marginal incentives were provided for large growing firms.

The NJTC was not explicitly targeted at any sociodemographic group. But because it applied only to the first $4,200 of wages per employee (a maximum credit of $2,100), it provided a greater relative incentive for the hiring of low-wage, more disadvantaged, and part-time labor than for the hiring of high-wage and full-time labor. While the NJTC was a marginal credit affecting "incremental" hirings rather than a wage subsidy covering all employment, the maximum allowable credit implies that the NJTC provided only a lump sum credit and no marginal wage subsidy to firms with planned employment growth, in the absence of the NJTC, greater than the employment growth subsidized by the credit. Contracting firms also faced no marginal change in incentives. The credit's employment incentives may also have been limited by its complexity.

The NJTC appears to have been fairly widely claimed on corporate tax returns especially in 1978, although it is unclear the extent to which firms were aware of the credit at the time they were making employment decisions. The Treasury estimates that the direct reduction in tax revenues arising from the NJTC was $5.7 billion for 1977 and 1978 combined (U.S. Departments of Labor and Treasury 1986). Bishop (1981) estimates that at least 1.1 million employees were subsidized in 1977, and at least 2.15 million in 1978.

Two studies have attempted to evaluate the effects of the NJTC on employment growth. Jeffrey Perloff and Michael Wachter (1979) use data from a large employer survey to compare the 1976 to 1977 employment growth of firms that knew about the NJTC to that of firms unaware of the NJTC. Only 34 percent of the firms in their sample knew of the program, although almost all large firms did. They find (from employment growth regressions with controls for firm size, one-digit industry, region, and tax filing status) that firms that knew about the credit increased employment by over 3 percent more than similar firms that were ignorant of the program. The proportional increase in employment from knowledge of the program decreased with firm size, a finding consistent with the lower likelihood that the NJTC would produce marginal employment incentives for large firms. Nevertheless, one should be somewhat critical of these results, since firms with growing employment had a much greater incentive to learn about the program and knowledge of the tax code may be correlated with other characteristics of more successful, growing firms.

John Bishop (1981) estimates labor demand equations in which employment is related to a measure of employer awareness of the NJTC, current and lagged output, and current and lagged measure of wages and other inputs using time-series data for the construction, wholesale, and retail trade industries. His estimates imply that the NJTC increased employment in construction and retail from 150,00 to 670,000 (equivalent to an economywide employment increase of 0.2 to 0.8 percent) over the mid-1977 to mid-1978 period. While it may be difficult to sort out the effects of the NJTC from other cyclical factors affecting the economy, the evidence suggests that a temporary, noncategorical, incremental employment subsidy has some potential for stimulating employment growth.

Targeted Jobs Tax Credit

The targeted jobs tax credit (TJTC) was enacted in 1978 to replace the NJTC and remained in effect during almost all of the 1979 to 1994 period.[3] The program offered a tax credit to employers hiring certified target-group individuals. The groups targeted by the TJTC have varied over time but have included economically disadvantaged youths, public assistance and SSI recipients, Vietnam-era veterans, certain ex-convicts, and disabled individuals undergoing vocational rehabilitation. The TJTC originally provided a tax credit amounting to 50 percent of first-year and 25 percent of second-year wages, up to $6,000, for employers who hired individuals certified as members of a target group. Those individuals could attain Employment Service vouchers to give to employers to allow them to receive the credit. The TJTC appears to have been utilized mainly by large firms in the retail and service sectors that contracted with management assistance companies to review the eligibility of all new hires and arrange for the Employment Service to voucher retroactively and certify those found eligible (Lorenz 1995).

The federal government increasingly restricted eligibility and reduced the value of the credit starting in the mid-1980s. The tax credit for the second year of employment was eliminated in late 1986, and the subsidy rate for the first year of employment was simultaneously reduced to 40 percent for the first $6,000 of qualified wages. The age range for eligible economically disadvantaged youth was reduced from eighteen to twenty-four years to eighteen to twenty-two years starting on January 1, 1989. The real value of the maximum credit declined by 75 percent over the course of the program. Table 1.1 illustrates that the number of TJTC-certified workers (number of jobs receiving a tax credit from the TJTC) reached a peak of 622,000 in 1985 and then declined to 364,000 in 1992 in the face of program changes. A recent survey of TJTC-certified workers indicates that the median duration of a TJTC job was six months in the early 1990s (U.S. Department of Labor 1994). This finding suggests that the stock of indi-

Table 1.1 Targeted Jobs Tax Credit (TJTC) Certifications and the Employment of Economically Disadvantaged Youth, 1984 to 1992 (in Millions)

| | TJTC Certifications | | Employment of Disadvantaged Youth | | |
Year	Total	Disadvantaged Youth	18–22	23–24	Total Eligible
1984	.563	.328	1.454	.649	2.103
1985	.622	.367	1.452	.624	2.076
1986	.242	.144	1.264	.617	1.881
1987	.598	.349	1.213	.562	1.776
1988	.497	.282	1.200	.550	1.750
1989	.452	.231	1.281	.477	1.281
1990	.445	.219	1.204	.502	1.204
1991	.428	.225	1.181	.513	1.181
1992	.364	.191	1.174	.541	1.174

Sources: Numbers of TJTC certifications are from U.S. House of Representatives (1993, 1073) and from unpublished tabulations provided by the U.S. Department of Labor, Employment and Training Administration. Data on certifications for 1984 and 1985 cover fiscal years (October of the previous year to September of the listed year); data for 1986 cover October 1985 to December 1986; data for 1987 to 1992 cover calendar years. The low number of certifications in 1986 partially reflects the suspension of the program from January to late October 1986.

Notes: I tabulated employment levels of economically disadvantaged youth from the March current population surveys using CPS basic sampling weights. Economically disadvantaged status for each individual aged eighteen to twenty-four in the March CPSs from March 1984 to March 1992 was imputed using the available information on family income in the previous calendar year and family structure combined with information on the relevant lower income living standard level by geographic region and metropolitan area of residence. Residents of Alaska and Hawaii are excluded from the employment totals. Economically disadvantaged individuals aged eighteen to twenty-four were eligible for the TJTC during the 1984 to 1988 period; eligibility was restricted to those aged eighteen to twenty-two from 1989 to 1992.

viduals in TJTC jobs at a point in time was approximately half the total number of TJTC certifications in a year. Thus, the TJTC may have subsidized approximately 0.4 percent of private employment at its peak in 1985. Tax expenditures on the TJTC were approximately $500 million (in 1991 dollars) in the mid-1980s, declining to $245 million in 1991 (U.S. Office of Management and Budget 1992). Thus, the TJTC paid approximately $570 per starting participant in 1991 ($245 million divided by 428,000 participants). The mean TJTC worker earned approximately $5.00 per hour and worked close to thirty hours per week in 1992 (U.S. Department of Labor 1994). Thus, the TJTC appears to have reduced employer wage costs by approximately 15 percent for the typical TJTC participant in a job of six months' duration in the early 1990s.

The TJTC has played a modest labor market role for disadvantaged youths and welfare recipients, who together accounted for more than 80 percent of the total tax credits. Economically disadvantaged youth represented the majority of TJTC certifications throughout the life of the program. Table 1.1 provides a comparison of the level of TJTC certifications and an estimate of the number of employed economically disadvantaged youths for whom firms could theoretically collect the TJTC.[4] The estimates in the table imply that from the mid- to late-1980s approximately 9 percent of economically disadvantaged youth who were eligible and employed had been hired under the credit. This take-up rate is a bit higher than the rate of under 5 percent estimated by Dave O'Neill (1982) for the first year of program operation.

The TJTC may have been underutilized because of regulatory burden and lack of support for the program by its administering agencies, the Department of Labor and the state Employment Services. Alternatively, a stigma may attach to the targeted workers whose employment the government seeks to advance. The stigma hypothesis gains support from the results of a controlled experiment conducted in Dayton, Ohio, in 1980 to 1981 to test the effectiveness of two targeted wage subsidy plans (Burtless 1985). Welfare (AFDC and general assistance) recipients, all eligible for the TJTC, were randomly assigned to three groups. The first group received vouchers that could be presented to prospective employers for direct cash rebate subsidies. Members of the second experimental treatment group were given tax credit vouchers that allowed prospective employers to receive either the WIN tax credit or the TJTC. Participants in these first two groups were encouraged to distribute explanatory material about the wage subsidies (tax credits) to employers they contacted during their job search. Members of the third group, while technically eligible for the WIN or TJTC tax credits, received no vouchers and were not informed of their eligibility for these programs. The striking result of this experiment was that job seekers given experimental vouchers in both treatment groups were significantly less likely to find employment than were job seekers without vouchers. One interpretation is that vouchers indicating eligibility for a targeted wage subsidy but also indicating that the individual was a welfare recipient were more of a stigma than a help in finding a job. Kevin Hollenbeck and Richard Willke (1991) report that in a similar random assignment experiment conducted by the Wisconsin Department of Health and Social Services the target-group members (welfare recipients, ex-offenders, and the handicapped), who were trained to announce their eligibility for the TJTC to employers, also fared worse than the controls. It is unclear whether the results from these two studies from the early 1980s for welfare recipients are transferable to the largest TJTC group, economically disadvantaged youth.

Several nonexperimental studies have attempted to estimate the impacts of the TJTC on the earnings and employment of eligible workers and on net job creation, but the sources of identifying information have not been very persuasive. Hollenbeck and Willke (1991) find greater regional availability and usage of the TJTC is associated with positive labor market impacts for nonwhite male youths and small negative impacts on other eligible race/sex groups, but the results are fairly sensitive to specification choice. Edward Lorenz (1988) finds positive impacts of the TJTC on earnings in the year the credit is received, but the control group of those vouchered and not obtaining TJTC jobs is likely to bias him toward finding positive results. John Bishop and Mark Montgomery (1993) use a survey of thirty-five hundred private employers from the early 1980s to determine whether use of the TJTC alters a firm's employment level and/or whom the firm hires. They compare hiring patterns and employment growth in firms that do and do not use the TJTC. They conclude that each subsidized hire generates between 0.13 and 0.3 new jobs to a participating firm and that program use induces shifts in employment toward workers under age twenty-five. But they do not present a convincing solution to the endogeneity of TJTC usage arising from the likelihood that fast-growing firms and those using the youth labor market are simply more likely to use the TJTC.

Evaluating the Effect of TJTC Eligibility on the Employment of Disadvantaged Youth

Legislative changes in the eligibility rules and generosity of the TJTC may provide a more plausible and exogenous source of variation to use in identifying the impacts of the TJTC on the labor market outcomes of the target groups. A major change occurred on January 1, 1989, when economically disadvantaged youths aged twenty-three to twenty-four were made ineligible for the TJTC while those aged eighteen to twenty-two maintained their eligibility. Table 1.1 shows that the number of TJTC certifications for economically disadvantaged youths fell by more than 50,000 from 1988 to 1989 and averaged 93,000 less per year in 1989 to 1990 than in 1987 to 1988. This 30 percent decline in certifications for disadvantaged youth from 1987 to 1988 to 1989 to 1990 is similar to the share of total employment of disadvantaged youth of individuals aged twenty-three to twenty-four.

An analysis of the employment rates of disadvantaged individuals aged twenty-three to twenty-four before and after this legislative change can help us assess the employment impacts of the TJTC. If the TJTC buoyed the employment of these youths, then its removal should have lowered the employment of disadvantaged youths aged twenty-three to twenty-four in 1989 to 1990 relative to their employment in earlier years. But other factors (such as business cycle conditions) are also likely to have caused changes in employment of young adults over this period, and it is critical to account for these. One useful approach is to compare the employment experience of disadvantaged twenty-three- to twenty-four-year-olds with the employment experiences of other twenty-three- to twenty-four-year-olds over the same time period. The gap in the before/after change in employment rate of disadvantaged twenty-three- to twenty-four-year-olds to others aged twenty-three to twenty-four provides a differences-in-differences estimate of the impact of TJTC eligibility on the employment of the target group. This differences-in-differences estimate does not take into account non-TJTC factors that differentially affect the labor market prospects of disadvantaged and nondisadvantaged workers. Since disadvantaged eighteen- to twenty-two-year-olds (who remained covered by the TJTC after 1988) and disadvantaged twenty-five- to twenty-nine-year-olds (who were never eligible) were not affected by the legislative change, the changes in their employment rates relative to those of nondisadvantaged individuals of the same age provide an estimate of the magnitude of non-TJTC factors differentially affecting the employment of disadvantaged young workers over this period. Subtracting the differences-in-differences estimate of disadvantaged-specific employment factors for the "placebo" groups (eighteen- to twenty-two- and twenty-five- to twenty-nine-year-olds) from the differences-in-differences estimate for the "experimental" group (twenty-three- to twenty-four-year-olds) yields a differences-in-differences-in-differences (DDD) estimate of the employment effect of the TJTC on disadvantaged youth

aged twenty-three to twenty-four. This DDD estimate adjusts the simple
before/after change in employment of the group losing TJTC eligibility
for general labor market trends affecting young workers and for those
specifically affecting economically disadvantaged individuals.

Such an analysis also requires a designation of the appropriate before and after periods. The macroeconomic environment was reasonably
stable in the period surrounding the legislative change from early 1987
to early 1990. TJTC rules were unchanged during 1987 and 1988. The
TJTC was much more generous in the period prior to 1986, and the program expired at the beginning of 1986 with uncertainty concerning its
reauthorization prior to late 1986, when it was retroactively reauthorized. The labor market for disadvantaged youth was affected in the period after March 1990 by increases in the federal minimum wage in April
1990 and April 1991 and by a recession that could have substantially
changed the composition of individuals imputed to be economically disadvantaged. Thus, I focus on 1987 to1988 as the before period and 1989
to 1990 as the after period.

Table 1.2 presents estimates calculated from the March current population surveys (CPSs) of the employment rates of disadvantaged and
nondisadvantaged youths and young adults from 1984 to 1992 for the
experimental group (those aged twenty-three to twenty-four) and the
two placebo groups (those aged eighteen to twenty-two and twenty-five
to twenty-nine). The employment rate of disadvantaged twenty-three-
to twenty-four-year-olds is lower in 1989 to 1990 than in 1987 to 1988,
while, in contrast, the employment rate for nondisadvantaged twenty-
three- to twenty-four-year-olds increased over this period. Table 1.3
shows that these employment rate patterns imply a simple differences-
in-differences estimate of a marginally statistically significant $-.030$, indicating a decline of 3 percentage points in the employment of disadvantaged to nondisadvantaged twenty-three- to twenty-four-year-olds
after elimination of eligibility for the TJTC of this age group. Tables 1.2
and 1.3 show that similar declines in the relative employment of the economically disadvantaged did not occur for those aged eighteen to
twenty-two and twenty-five to twenty-nine. Figure 1.2 further illustrates
that the gap in employment rates between nondisadvantaged and disadvantaged twenty-three- to twenty-four-year-olds expanded relative to
the analogous two control groups in the 1989 to 1990 period versus the
1987 to 1988 period. The DDD estimate (presented in table 1.3) comparing the change in the gap in employment rate for disadvantaged and
nondisadvantaged individuals in the experimental group with the average of the change in the two placebo groups from 1987 to 1988 to 1989

Table 1.2   Employment Rates for Economically Disadvantaged and Nondisadvantaged Young Adults, Aged 18 to 29 Years, 1984 to 1992

	18 to 22 Years Old		23 to 24 Years Old		25 to 29 Years Old	
Year	Disadvantaged	Nondis-advantaged	Disadvantaged	Nondis-advantaged	Disadvantaged	Nondis-advantaged
1984	.361	.631	.425	.779	.421	.798
	(.010)	(.005)	(.017)	(.006)	(.011)	(.004)
1985	.381	.642	.422	.783	.408	.811
	(.010)	(.005)	(.017)	(.006)	(.012)	(.004)
1986	.365	.643	.456	.804	.412	.820
	(.010)	(.005)	(.018)	(.006)	(.012)	(.004)
1987	.365	.647	.455	.806	.424	.824
	(.011)	(.005)	(.019)	(.006)	(.012)	(.004)
1988	.367	.644	.429	.821	.423	.836
	(.011)	(.005)	(.019)	(.006)	(.012)	(.004)
1989	.397	.657	.412	.825	.419	.836
	(.012)	(.005)	(.020)	(.007)	(.013)	(.004)
1990	.391	.644	.435	.825	.434	.839
	(.012)	(.005)	(.019)	(.007)	(.013)	(.004)
1991	.378	.629	.400	.797	.413	.829
	(.012)	(.005)	(.019)	(.007)	(.012)	(.004)
1992	.349	.644	.448	.781	.391	.826
	(.011)	(.005)	(.020)	(.007)	(.012)	(.004)

Notes: Employment rates by economically disadvantaged status and age group are estimates from the March CPSs for 1984 to 1992 based on current employment status for March of each year. Each observation is weighted by its CPS basic sampling weight. Cell sample sizes vary from 599 to 11,442. Standard errors are in parentheses.

Economically disadvantaged status for each individual aged eighteen to twenty-nine in the March CPSs from 1984 to 1992 was imputed using the available information on family income in the previous calendar year and family structure combined with information on the relevant LILSL by geographic region and metropolitan area of residence. Residents of Alaska and Hawaii are excluded from the samples.

to 1990 implies that the TJTC boosted the employment rate of disadvantaged twenty-three- to twenty-four-year-olds by 0.043 (with a standard error of 0.020).

This basic DDD estimate fails to account for changes in the composition of the treatment groups (the disadvantaged) and control groups (the nondisadvantaged) that could affect their employment rates. A simple regression framework allows one to adjust the DDD estimates for changes in the observed individual characteristics. The regression equa-

Table 1.3　Differences-in-Differences-in-Differences (DDD) Estimates of the Impact of Targeted Jobs Tax Credit (TJTC) Eligibility on Employment Rates

	Employment Rates		
	Before 1987–1988	After 1989–1990	Time Difference
Experimentals, 23–24-year-olds			
Disadvantaged	.442	.423	−.019
	(.013)	(.014)	(.019)
Nondisadvantaged	.814	.825	.012
	(.004)	(.005)	(.006)
Disadv./nondisadv.	−.372	−.402	
difference	(.012)	(.012)	
Difference-in-difference			−.030
			(.017)
Placebos, 18–22- and 25–29-year-olds			
Disadvantaged	.390	.410	.019
	(.006)	(.006)	(.009)
Nondisadvantaged	.748	.755	.006
	(.002)	(.002)	(.003)
Disadv./nondisadv.	−.358	−.345	
difference	(.006)	(.006)	
Difference-in-difference			.013
			(.008)
DDD estimate			−.043
			(.020)
Adjusted DDD estimate			−.034
			(.019)

Notes: Cells contain mean employment rates for the identified group and time period from the March CPSs for 1987 to 1990. Standard errors are in parentheses. Each observation is weighted by its CPS basic sampling weight. The DDD estimate is the difference-in-difference from panel A minus that in panel B. Economically disadvantaged status for each individual aged eighteen to twenty-nine in the March CPSs was imputed using the available information on family income in the previous calendar year and family structure combined with information on the relevant LILSL by geographic region and metropolitan area of residence. Residents of Alaska and Hawaii are excluded from the samples

The adjusted DDD estimate is the coefficient on the third-order interaction term of a time period (before/after) dummy with an age-group dummy (age twenty-three to twenty-four equals 1) and a disadvantaged status dummy in an individual-level employment regression of the form given by equation 1.3 covering all eighteen- to twenty-nine-year-olds for pooled March CPS data covering 1987 to 1990. The other covariates included are three individual-year dummies; a disadvantaged-status dummy; eleven age dummies; two dummies for the interaction of age group (eighteen to twenty-two and twenty-five to twenty-nine) with disadvantaged status; a before/after dummy interacted with disadvantaged status; two interactions of age group and the before/after dummy; dummy variables for sex, marital status, and race; four education-group dummies; interactions of the sex dummy with the race, marital status, and education dummies; interactions of the before/after dummy with the education, race, and sex dummies; fifty state dummies; and eight dummies for interactions of the before/after dummy with census-division dummies. The sample size for the regression is 103,600. The regression was estimated using CPS basic sampling weights.

Figure 1.2   Differences in Employment Rates Between Nondisadvantaged and Disadvantaged Youth, 1984 to 1992

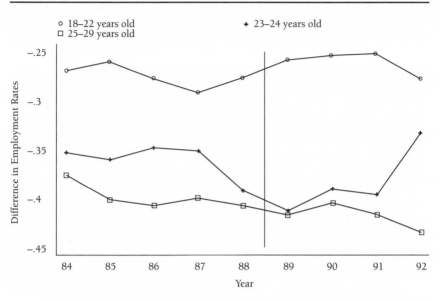

tion—a linear probability model for employment (E)—is estimated on pooled March CPS data from 1987 to 1990 for individuals aged eighteen to twenty-nine:

$$(1.3) \quad E_{it} = \alpha + \beta_0 X_{it} + \beta_1 DIS_{it} + \beta_2 \tau_t + \beta_3 AGED_{it} + \beta_4(DIS_{it} * \tau_t)$$
$$+ \beta_5(DIS_{it} * AGED_{it}) + \beta_6(AGED_{it} * \tau_{it})$$
$$+ \beta_7(DIS_{it} * \tau_t * AGED_{it}) + \epsilon_{it}$$

where i indexes individual, t indexes time, α and the βs are the parameters to be estimated, X is a vector of observable covariates (for example, years of schooling, race dummies, marital status, region), DIS is a dummy variable taking on a value of 1 for disadvantaged individuals, τ equals 1 in 1989 to 1990 and 0 in 1987 to 1988, $AGED$ equals 1 for those aged twenty-three to twenty-four and 0 otherwise, and ϵ is an error term. The coefficient on the third-level interaction term (β_7) captures variation in employment specific to the disadvantaged (relative to the nondisadvantaged) in the experimental age group (relative to the placebo age groups) in the after period (relative to the before period). This provides an adjusted DDD estimate of the effect of the TJTC on the employment of disadvantaged twenty-three- to twenty-four-year-olds. The bottom row of table 1.3 presents the adjusted DDD estimate from a specification of the form of equation 1.3, including a substantial number of demographic controls, state dummy variables, and region-specific trends. The adjusted DDD estimate indicates a decline of 3.4 percentage points (or 7.7 percent) in employment associated with removal of eligibility from the TJTC. Since wage costs were reduced approximately 15 percent on average by the TJTC in this period, a 7.7 percent employment effect suggests an own-wage labor demand elasticity of -0.5 (under the restrictive assumption that the labor supply of the affected group was effectively infinite).

A decline of 3.4 percentage points in the employment rate for economically disadvantaged twenty-three- to twenty-four-year-olds in 1989 represents a decline of 39,000 jobs relative to a base of possibly 100,000 annual certifications for this group in 1987 to 1988. Employment durations for certified twenty-three- to twenty-four-year-olds were likely to have been a bit longer than for the typical younger TJTC recipient. My crude guess at the typical TJTC job duration for twenty-three- to twenty-four-year-olds is nine to twelve months. This implies a (point-in-time) stock of approximately 75,000 to 100,000 jobs that received the TJTC. The adjusted DDD estimate suggests that 40 to 52 percent of the jobs receiving TJTC subsidies reflected net employment additions for economically disadvantaged twenty-three- to twenty-four-year-olds at a cost of approximately $1,500 (1991 dollars) per net job created.

There are reasons to be cautious in interpreting these DDD estimates of the employment effects of the TJTC. Figure 1.2 and table 1.2 suggest that the relative decline in the employment of disadvantaged twenty-three- to twenty-four-year-olds started in 1988, a year before elimination of TJTC eligibility for this group. Thus, other unmeasured factors differentially affecting disadvantaged twenty-three- to twenty-four-year-olds could be present.[5] But the elimination in 1987 of TJTC subsidy for a second year of employment could have been more important for twenty-three- to twenty-four-years-olds, who are likely to have more stable labor force attachment than eighteen- to twenty-two-year-olds. Thus, the TJTC does appear to have had modest positive employment effects on economically disadvantaged young adults.

Temporary Wage Subsidies for On-the-Job Training Under JTPA Title II

The Job Training Partnership Act (JTPA) replaced CETA as the major federally sponsored employment and training program for the disadvantaged in 1983. JTPA, unlike CETA, has no provision for adult public service employment, but it does emphasize on-the-job training (OJT) and provide temporary wage subsidies of 50 percent of wages for up to six months of employment to encourage firms to hire and train JTPA participants. Employers receiving wage subsidies under JTPA are expected to provide long-term employment opportunities for OJT participants, and employers that exhibit a pattern of failing to retain OJT participants lose eligibility for future subsidies. Wage subsidies under JTPA have been most important for economically disadvantaged adults (who are not public assistance recipients), since this group has not been eligible for the TJTC. In 1993, JTPA Title II (excluding the summer youth employment program) enrolled about 550,000 new participants, of whom 310,000 were adults, and approximately 18 percent of the adult JTPA Title II participants received on-the-job training (U.S. Department of Labor 1995).

Thirty-month follow-up results from the National JTPA Study, a large-scale, random assignment evaluation of JTPA Title II, provide estimates of the impacts of JTPA services on the earnings of JTPA enrollees (Bloom et al. 1994). Twenty thousand JTPA applicants at sixteen sites were randomly assigned to either a treatment group that could use JTPA services or a control group that could not use JTPA services but could make use of non-JTPA training and education services. Prior to randomization, the applicants (both treatments and controls) were classified by local JTPA staffs into service strategy groups. Thus, one can estimate the impact on future earnings of a strategy focused on OJT by examining differences in outcomes between treatments and controls for whom OJT was the recommended strategy. (Since many of the treatment group members were enrolled in job search assistance [JSA] while searching for a subsidized OJT position or an unsubsidized job, they were designated the OJT/JSA subgroup.) The OJT/JSA service strategy group included the most "job-ready" JTPA eligibles, approximately 39 percent of applicants.

The National JTPA Study findings indicate that JTPA has substantial and sustained positive effects on earnings for adults enrolled in a service strategy that emphasizes placement in subsidized OJT positions with private employers (Bloom et al. 1994). The OJT/JSA strategy is estimated to increase the earnings of adult women by a highly statistically significant 15 percent ($2,292) and those of adult men by a marginally significant 10 percent ($2,109) over thirty months. Positive program impacts on earnings are present both during the six months of program participation and in the first two post-program years. In fact, both men and women in the OJT/JSA strategy group showed statistically significant earnings gains of more than $1,000 (17 percent for women and 13 percent for men) in the second post-program year. The OJT/JSA service strategy for adults appears to have substantial net benefits for both enrollees and society even aside from possible sustained impacts on earnings beyond the thirty months so far analyzed in the National JTPA Study (Bloom et al. 1994). Unfortunately, the JTPA evaluation indicates that this same strategy has no impacts on the earnings or employment prospects of out-of-school disadvantaged youth.

A mixed strategy providing job search assistance, job development, and a temporary wage subsidy seems to be a successful approach to making substantial improvements in the earnings of disadvantaged adults (particularly adult women). But, like other nonintensive strategies that have been evaluated, it does not appear very effective for out-of-school youth from poor families. The JTPA evaluation provides estimates of the marginal impacts of JTPA services above the impacts of non-JTPA training services available to control group members. The OJT wage subsidy was a more important marginal service for adults than for youths since economically disadvantaged youth eligible for JTPA in the control group were eligible for a wage subsidy from the TJTC. Thus, the importance of a temporary wage subsidy may explain the more positive program impacts for adults than youth. The extent to which the positive JTPA impacts on participants come at the expense of displacement effects on other workers cannot be determined from the JTPA evaluation.

Evaluations of U.S. Wage Subsidy Demonstration Projects

Further information on the likely effectiveness of private-sector employment subsidies can be gleaned from evaluation studies of several U.S. demonstration projects that tested the effectiveness of policies with wage subsidy components in improving the employment and earnings of disadvantaged youth, AFDC recipients, and unemployment insurance recipients.

Youth Incentive Entitlement Pilot Project

The Youth Incentive Entitlement Pilot Project (YIEPP) demonstration was active from late 1978 to early 1981; it guaranteed full-time summer jobs and part-time school-year jobs to disadvantaged youth aged sixteen to nineteen in selected communities provided that they stayed in school (Farkas et al. 1982; U.S. Department of Labor 1995). All the jobs offered paid the minimum wage. The project directly created jobs in the public and nonprofit sectors and also offered 100 percent wage subsidies to private-sector for-profit firms to encourage them to hire disadvantaged in-school youth. Thus, the YIEPP represented a saturation job creation program that attempted to induce both private- and public-sector employers to hire in-school youth in poor neighborhoods. Twenty-nine percent of the program jobs were with private, for-profit employers, the largest category of which were in retail trade.

The program does appear to have increased substantially the earnings and employment rates of youths in the treatment communities relative to those in four "comparable" cities used as control sites (Farkas et al. 1982, 1984). School-year employment rates doubled from about 20 percent to 40 percent, while summer employment rates increased from about 35 percent to 45 percent. Minority employment rates under YIEPP were raised to those of whites in the same areas. School-year earnings were estimated to have increased by 46 percent to 161 percent in the different years of operation of the program, and summer earnings were raised by approximately 50 percent. Most of the in-program earnings gains arose from increases in employment rates and hours worked per week rather than from higher wages; this is not surprising since the program funded only minimum-wage jobs. Private-sector employment increased by 18 percent (representing an increase of 3.1 percentage points in the employment-population ratio) on average during the operation of the program. While the employer take-up rate was low, substantial wage subsidies combined with job development efforts by an intermediary did substantially expand private employment for difficult-to-employ poor youth. Comparisons of the treatment effect on private-sector employment with the total number of private-sector jobs subsidized implies a 50 percent displacement rate for YIEPP private-sector job slots: it took two private-sector slots to expand employment of YIEPP participants by one.

Despite the linkage of employment opportunities to school enrollment, the YIEPP did not appear to increase the school enrollment rate of eligible youth. Nevertheless, the YIEPP does suggest the importance of demand-side barriers to employment of poor minority youth and the potential for mixed public-private employment creation efforts to improve the situation. Furthermore, Farkas et al. (1984) find a positive and statistically significant post-program overall weekly earnings effect of 39 percent (and a modest but statistically insignificant 5 percent increase in hourly wages) in the year following program termination.

Subsidized Employment for AFDC Recipients

Several evaluations suggest that subsidized employment combined with training and other support services appears to be a promising and particularly effective strategy to improve the earnings of adult female AFDC recipients. The strongest positive earnings impacts of the OJT/JSA service strategy in the JTPA Title II evaluation were found for adult female AFDC recipients (U.S. Department of Labor 1995). Similarly, state work-welfare demonstrations in New Jersey and Maine that emphasized on-the-job training with subsidized wages showed earnings impacts of more than $1,000 per year (Gueron and Pauly 1991). The National Supported Work Demonstration (NSW) of the late 1970s provided single parents who were long-term welfare recipients with extensive support services and twelve to eighteen months of subsidized employment on projects (sheltered workshops) directly developed and managed by the demonstration's operators. A random assignment evaluation of the NSW found large in-program annual earnings increases during the period of subsidized employment of more than $6,000 (300 percent) on average. Earnings increases of more than 20 percent were apparent in the first two post-program years, and substantial earnings impacts of more than $400 per year remained in the sixth through eighth post-program years (Gueron and Pauly 1991; Couch 1992).

The Homemaker-Home Health Aide (HHHA) demonstrations of the mid-1980s provided "job-ready" AFDC recipients with four to eight weeks of training and up to twelve months of subsidized employment under close supervision as home health aides with private and quasi-public nursing homes and home health care agencies. The HHHA demonstrations were implemented with a random assignment design in seven states and, unlike the NSW, made substantial use of subsidies for employment with private-sector employers operating in a "real" market (Bell and Orr 1994). The HHHA demonstrations produced significant earnings gains for participants in five out of the seven states in which they were carried out. The earnings gains averaged around $2,000 annually in the first two years of the program, and gains of approximately $500 annually were sustained during the fourth to fifth years after exit from the program (U.S. Department of Labor 1995). Stephen Bell and Larry Orr (1994) estimate positive net social benefits in six of the seven states that experimented with HHHA.

Thus welfare-to-work programs that combine training, job development, employment subsidies to private-sector employers, and support services appear to be a cost-effective route to producing substantial and sustained earnings increases for AFDC recipients. But the low earnings base for this population implies that such programs by themselves do not produce earnings gains large enough to move such families out of poverty. Furthermore, the extent to which modest-sized demonstration projects that emphasize subsidized employment can be successfully implemented on the scale necessary for a work program associated with the currently popular time-limited welfare proposals is very much an open question.

Wage Subsidies for Job Losers

Many recent random assignment experiments have evaluated alternative approaches to improving the reemployment prospects of U.S. unemployment insurance (UI) recipients. Some evidence on the effectiveness of hiring subsidies for UI recipients can be extracted from the Illinois reemployment bonus experiments (Woodbury and Spiegelman 1987).

In the employer bonus experiment, a random sample of UI claimants were told that their next employer would qualify for a cash bonus of $500 if they, the claimants, found a job within eleven weeks of filing the UI claim and if they retained that job for four months. Participation in the experiment was voluntary for the treatments. About one-third of the subjects refused to take the subsidy voucher offered to them. The participation rates were lower for higher skilled workers, suggesting that the vouchers were perceived to have a stigmatic effect. Under the assumption that the treatment had no effect on those not participating (not accepting the vouchers), the availability of the wage subsidy reduced the weeks of insured employment by approximately one week on average and reduced UI benefits paid over the benefit year by a modest, marginally statistically significant amount (Dubin and Rivers 1993). The number of employer bonuses claimed were quite small (only 3 percent of the sample), and the impacts of the employer hiring bonus were smaller than the estimated effects of a claimant bonus treatment in which the UI recipient could earn the $500 bonus and did not have to provide any information about the bonus to an employer. The employer subsidy appears less powerful than the claimant reemployment bonus in speeding up reemployment. Nevertheless, Bruce Meyer (1995) reports mixed results concerning the impacts of reemployment bonuses in a series of other experiments and is skeptical about the efficacy of a permanent reemployment bonus program.

Experiences of Other OECD Countries with Employer Subsidies

OECD countries have experimented with a variety of subsidies for private-sector employment, although few formal evaluations of the impacts of non-U.S. programs have been performed.[6] Many countries implemented marginal (incremental) employment subsidies of some type during the 1970s. Canada operated an employment tax program from 1978 to 1981 that was similar to the U.S. NJTC. Surendra Gera (1987) estimates that the job creation and net costs per job created under this Canadian program were quite similar to estimates for the NJTC. Evaluations of 1970s marginal employment subsidies in other countries are not terribly convincing; they are typically based on surveys that ask employers whether they altered their behavior in response to the subsidy. The OECD (1982) concludes that, on the basis of this type of evidence, marginal employment subsidies can be a reasonably efficient employment-promoting device on a temporary basis during a recovery.

More recently, many OECD nations have attempted to use wage subsidies to spur the employment of targeted groups, particularly the long-term unemployed and unemployed youth. The OECD (1993) concludes from the existing evaluations that targeted recruitment subsidies are likely to have substantial displacement effects and large deadweight losses, but none of the studies summarized are particularly compelling. A careful nonexperimental evaluation of two Dutch wage subsidy schemes for the long-term unemployed suggests that they may have increased reemployment rates for the long-term unemployed by up to 10 percent, but at the cost of substantial displacement of the employment of other workers (de Koning 1993). Further evaluations of the variety of private-employment subsidy programs being implemented outside the United States could greatly increase our understanding of the efficacy of wage subsidies.

Conclusion

Despite the substantial experience of advanced nations with private-sector employment subsidies, the probable impacts of such policies are highly uncertain because of the lack of formal evaluation evidence. Table 1.4 summarizes the characteristics and estimated impacts of the major U.S. wage subsidy programs and demonstrations targeted at the economically disadvantaged. The current evidence suggests that wage subsidies combined with training and job development are effective in improving the earnings and employment of disadvantaged adults, particularly welfare (AFDC) recipients. Stand-alone targeted wage subsidies appear to be hampered by stigma and low employer utilization when the eligible groups are those with negative connotations for employers. But some new evidence presented in this chapter indicates that the targeted jobs tax credit may have modestly improved the employment rates of

Table 1.4 Major U.S. Wage Subsidy Programs and Demonstration Projects for the Disadvantaged

Program	Description	Estimated Impacts
New jobs tax credit (NJTC), 1977–1978	A noncategorical, incremental employment subsidy that provided a 50% tax credit for wages of up to $4,200 per employee for increases in employment of more than 2% over the previous year.	Evidence suggests the NJTC modestly expanded aggregate employment (by 0.2% to 0.8%) from mid-1977 to mid-1978, with the impact concentrated in construction and retail trade.
Targeted jobs tax credit (TJTC), 1979–1994	A categorical wage subsidy that provided a tax credit to employers hiring certified target-group individuals. Target groups included economically disadvantaged youth and AFDC recipients.	Estimates from legislative changes in TJTC eligibility rules suggest up to a 7% positive impact on employment of disadvantaged young adults. Random assignment evaluations for welfare recipients suggest job searchers are less likely to find jobs when they are encouraged to inform employers of eligibility.
Job Training Partnership Act (JTPA), Title II, 1983–present	The on-the-job-training (OJT) component of JTPA, Title II, provides a temporary wage subsidy of up to six months to encourage firms to hire and train JTPA participants (economically disadvantaged adults and youths). Some effort is made to develop job slots and to link participants with jobs.	Thirty-month follow-up results form random assignment evaluation imply substantial and sustained positive earnings impacts (10% for men and 15% for women) for adults enrolled in the service strategy emphasizing private-sector placement in subsidized OJT slots. No impacts apparent for out-of-school youths.

(*Table continues on p. 48.*)

Table 1.4 *Continued*

Program	Description	Estimated Impacts
Youth Incentive Entitlement Pilot Project (YIEPP), 1978–1981	Demonstration project that guaranteed full-time, minimum-wage summer jobs and part-time school-year jobs to disadvantaged youth aged 16–19 in selected communities provided they stayed in school. 100% wage subsidies for private-sector employers and direct job creation in the public sector.	Doubled school-year employment rates and earnings and greatly increased summer employment and earnings of youths in treatment communities. Increased private-sector employment of eligible youths by 18%. Substantial positive earnings effects persist at least one year after the program.
Homemaker-Home Health Aide (HHHA) demonstrations, 1983–1986	Provided "job-ready" AFDC recipients with four to eight weeks of training and up to twelve months of subsidized employment under close supervision with private and quasi-public nursing homes and home health agencies.	HHHA demonstrations produced significant earnings gains for participants in five of seven states. Earnings gains averaged $2,000 annually in first two years of program and gains of $500 were sustained four to five years after exit from program.

economically disadvantaged youth. The evidence from the YIEPP also suggests that a saturation job creation strategy that combines direct public job creation and private-sector subsidies with an aggressive effort to develop job slots can play an important role in improving the employment and earnings of disadvantaged youth.

Employer-side wage subsidies appear to be a potentially valuable tool as part of a broader strategy to improve the labor market earnings of less skilled workers. But the low-wage labor market does not operate like a frictionless bourse, and information/stigma problems appear to limit somewhat the effectiveness of an approach that uses targeted wage subsidies in isolation. Wage subsidies for less skilled workers are likely to be more effective when utilized in conjunction with labor market intermediaries that help provide some training, placement services, and job retention assistance.

The original version of this chapter was prepared for the Russell Sage Foundation Conference on Labor Demand Policies and Low-Skilled Workers, New York, New York, June 26–27, 1995. I am grateful to Richard Freeman and the conference participants for helpful comments, to David Lah for valuable information and data on the targeted jobs tax credit, and to Marianne Bertrand for excellent research assistance.

Notes

1. Since there is a burgeoning literature that examines the effects of employee-side earnings supplements such as the earned income tax credit in the United States (for example, Hoffman and Siedman 1990; and Eissa and Liebman 1996) and the Self-Sufficiency Project in Canada (Card and Robbins 1996), I limit my focus to employer-side wage subsidies.
2. An alternative approach is to simulate the effects of wage subsidies in more fully developed (but still highly stylized) general-equilibrium labor market models. See Mortensen (1994) for an interesting attempt to simulate the effects of a general new hire subsidy; and Davidson and Woodbury (1995) for an ambitious simulation model to analyze wage-rate subsidies for dislocated workers.
3. The most recent authorization of the TJTC expired at the end of 1994. The TJTC had expired several times in the past and then been reinstated. The work opportunity tax credit (WOTC), a modestly less generous modification of the TJTC covering a somewhat more limited group of disadvantaged individuals, was authorized by Congress for a year starting on October 1, 1996. It appears likely that the WOTC will be reauthorized by Congress for several years, have its coverage expanded, and be made substantially more generous for employers that hire long-term welfare recipients.

4. An individual qualified as "economically disadvantaged" under the TJTC if he or she had a family income in the six months prior to starting a job that on an annual basis was less than 70 percent of the Bureau of Labor Statistics' lower level standard income level (LLSIL) for his or her geographic region. The LLSIL varies by family size, by metropolitan area status, and across the four census regions. Seventy percent of the LLSIL is approximately 125 percent of the poverty line for a family of four in the average geographic area. I use the March current population surveys (CPSs) to estimate the total number of economically disadvantaged youths aged eighteen to twenty-two and twenty-three to twenty-four and their employment rates in each year from 1984 to 1992. Information on annual family income for the previous calendar year, residential location (state and metropolitan area), age, and family size available in the March CPS is used to impute whether an individual would have been classified as economically disadvantaged at the time of the survey. The employment rates are based on employment status information from the March survey reference week. Since family income varies over a calendar year, the number of individuals imputed to be eligible for the program using annual income from the March CPS is likely to be somewhat of an underestimate of those actually eligible on the basis of their family income over the previous six months. Information on the LLSIL by region and metropolitan area was kindly provided by David Lah of the Employment and Training Administration of the U.S. Department of Labor. Individuals residing in Alaska and Hawaii are excluded from the analysis because of incomplete information on the official LLSIL levels for these states.

5. Contamination effects leading to an overestimate could be present if the employment rates of nondisadvantaged twenty-three to twenty-four-year-olds were increased when they became cheaper relative to disadvantaged twenty-three- to twenty-four-year-olds; an opposite contamination bias leading to an underestimate could arise if the employment rates of disadvantaged eighteen- to twenty-two-year-olds and twenty-five- to twenty-nine-year-olds were bolstered by the policy change.

6. OECD (1982) and Schwanse (1982) describe OECD employment subsidies operating in the 1970s and summarize evidence on the impacts of these policies. OECD (1990) and Grubb (1994) describe more recent efforts.

References

Ashenfelter, Orley. 1978. "Evaluating the Effects of the Employment Tax Credit." *Conference Report on Evaluating the 1977 Economic Stimulus Package.* Washington, D.C.: U.S. Government Printing Office for U.S. Department of Labor, Office of the Assistant Secretary for Policy, Evaluation, and Research.

Bell, Stephen H., and Larry L. Orr. 1994. "Is Subsidized Employment Cost Effective for Welfare Recipients?" *Journal of Human Resources* 29 (Winter): 42–61.

Bishop, John. 1981. "Employment in Construction and Distribution Industries: The Impact of the New Jobs Tax Credit." In *Studies in Labor Markets,* edited by Sherwin Rosen. Chicago, Ill.: University of Chicago.

Bishop, John, and Mark Montgomery. 1993. "Does the Targeted Jobs Tax Credit Create Jobs at Participating Firms?" *Industrial Relations* 32 (Fall): 289–306.

Bloom, Howard S., et al. 1994. "The National JTPA Study: Overview: Impacts, Benefits, and Costs of Title II-A." Bethesda, Md.: Abt Associates (January).

Bound, John, and George Johnson. 1992. "Changes in the Structure of Wages in the 1980s: An Evaluation of Alternative Explanations." *American Economic Review* 82 (June): 371–92.

Burtless, Gary. 1985. "Are Targeted Wage Subsidies Harmful? Evidence from a Wage Voucher Experiment." *Industrial and Labor Relations Review* 39 (October): 105–14.

Card, David. 1994. "Earnings, Schooling, and Ability Revisited." Industrial Relations Section Working Paper 311. Princeton, N.J.: Princeton University (May).

Card, David, and Alan Krueger. 1995. *Myth and Measurement: The New Economics of the Minimum Wage* Princeton, N.J.: Princeton University Press.

Card, David, and Phillip K. Robbins. 1996. "Do Financial Incentives Encourage Welfare Recipients to Work? Early Findings from the Canadian Self-Sufficiency Project." Industrial Relations Section Working Paper 359. Princeton, N.J.: Princeton University (March).

Couch, Kenneth A. 1992. "New Evidence on the Long-Term Effects of Employment Training Programs." *Journal of Labor Economics* 10 (October): 380–88.

Davidson, Carl, and Stephen A. Woodbury. 1995. "Wage Subsidies for Dislocated Workers." Working Paper 95-31. Kalamazoo, Mich.: W. E. Upjohn Institute for Employment Research (January).

De Koning, Jaap. 1993. "Measuring the Placement Effects of Two Wage-Subsidy Schemes for the Long-Term Unemployed." *Empirical Economics* 18(3): 447–68.

Dubin, Jeffrey A., and Douglas Rivers. 1993. "Experimental Estimates of the Impact of Wage Subsidies." *Journal of Econometrics* 56 (March): 219–42.

Eissa, Nada, and Jeffrey B. Liebman. 1996. "Labor Supply Response to the Earned Income Tax Credit." *Quarterly Journal of Economics* 111 (May): 605–37.

Farkas, George, D. Alton Smith, Ernst Stromsdorfer, Gail Trask, and Robert Jerrett III. 1982. *Impacts from the Youth Incentive Entitlement Pilot Projects: Participation, Work, and Schooling over the Full Program Period.* New York: Manpower Demonstration Research Corporation (December).

―――. 1984. *Post-Program Impacts of the Youth Incentive Entitlement Pilot Projects.* New York: Manpower Demonstration Research Corporation (June).

Freeman, Richard B., and Lawrence F. Katz. 1994. "Rising Wage Inequality: The United States vs. Other Advanced Countries." In *Working Under Different Rules,* edited by Richard B. Freeman. New York: Russell Sage Foundation and National Bureau of Economic Research.

Gera, Surendra. 1987. "An Evaluation of the Canadian Employment Tax Credit Program." *Canadian Public Policy* 13 (June): 196–207.

Grubb, David. 1994. "Direct and Indirect Effects of Active Labor Market Policies in OECD Countries." In *The UK Labor Market,* edited by Ray Barrell. London, England: Cambridge University Press.

Gueron, Judith M., and Edward Pauly. 1991. *From Welfare to Work.* New York: Russell Sage Foundation.

Hamermesh, Daniel S. 1978. "Subsidies for Jobs in the Private Sector." In *Creating Jobs,* edited by John Palmer. Washington, D.C.: Brookings Institution.

―――.1993. *Labor Demand.* Princeton, N.J.: Princeton University Press.

Heckman, James J., Rebecca L. Roselius, and Jeffrey A. Smith. 1994. "U.S. Education and Training Policy: A Re-evaluation of the Underlying Assumptions Behind the New Consensus." In *Labor Markets, Employment Policy, and Job Creation*, edited by Alec Levenson and L. C. Solmon. Santa Monica, Calif.: Milken Institute.

Hoffman, Saul D., and Laurence Siedman. 1990. *The Earned Income Tax Credit: Antipoverty Effectiveness and Labor Market Effects*. Kalamazoo, Mich.: W. E. Upjohn Institute.

Hollenbeck, Kevin M., and Richard J. Willke. 1991. "The Employment and Earnings Impacts of the Targeted Jobs Tax Credit." Kalamazoo, Mich.: W. E. Upjohn Institute (February).

Juhn, Chinhui, Kevin M. Murphy, and Robert Topel. 1991. "Why Has the Natural Rate Increased over Time?" *Brookings Papers on Economic Activity* 2: 75–142.

Kaldor, Nicholas. 1936. "Wage Subsidies as a Remedy for Unemployment." *Journal of Political Economy* 44 (December): 721–42.

Katz, Lawrence F. 1994. "Active Labor Market Policies to Expand Employment and Opportunity." In *Reducing Unemployment: Current Issues and Policy Options*, edited by Federal Reserve Bank of Kansas City. Kansas City, Mo.: Federal Reserve Bank of Kansas City.

Katz, Lawrence F., and Kevin M. Murphy. 1992. "Changes in Relative Wages, 1963-1987: Supply and Demand Factors." *Quarterly Journal of Economics* 107 (February): 35–78.

LaLonde, Robert J. 1995. "The Promise of Public-Sector Sponsored Training Programs." *Journal of Economic Perspectives* 9 (Spring): 149–68.

Lorenz, Edward C. 1988. *The Targeted Jobs Tax Credit in Maryland and Missouri: 1982-1987*. Washington, D.C.: National Commission of Employment Policy (November).

———. 1995. "TJTC and the Promise and Reality of Redistributive Vouchering and Tax Credit Policy." *Journal of Policy Analysis and Management* 14 (Spring): 270–90.

Manning, Alan. 1995. "How Do We Know That Real Wages Are Too High?" *Quarterly Journal of Economics* 110 (November): 1111–25.

Meyer, Bruce D. 1995. "Lessons from the U.S. Unemployment Insurance Experiments." *Journal of Economic Literature* 33 (March): 91–131.

Moffitt, Robert. 1992. "Incentive Effects of the U.S. Welfare System: A Review." *Journal of Economic Literature* 30 (March): 1–61.

Mortensen, Dale T. 1994. "Reducing Supply-Side Disincentives to Job Creation." In *Reducing Unemployment: Current Issues and Policy Options*, edited by Federal Reserve Bank of Kansas City. Kansas City, Mo.: Federal Reserve Bank of Kansas City.

Organization for Economic Cooperation and Development. 1982. *Marginal Employment Subsidies*. Paris: Organization for Economic Cooperation and Development.

———. 1990. *Labor Market Policies for the 1990s*. Paris, France: Organization for Economic Cooperation and Development.

———. 1993. *Employment Outlook*. Paris, France: Organization for Economic Cooperation and Development.

O'Neill, Dave M. 1982. "Employment Tax Credit Programs: The Effects of Socioeconomic Targeting Provisions." *Journal of Human Resources* 17 (Summer): 449–59.

Perloff, Jeffrey M., and Michael Wachter. 1979. "The New Jobs Tax Credit: An Evaluation of the 1977-1978 Wage Subsidy Program." *American Economic Review* (May): 173–79.

Phelps, Edmund S. 1994a. "Low-Wage Employment Subsidies vs. the Welfare State." *American Economic Review* 84 (May): 54–58.

———. 1994b. "Wage Subsidy Programs: Alternative Designs." Unpublished paper. New York: Columbia University and Russell Sage Foundation (August).

———. 1997. *Rewarding Work.* Cambridge, Mass.: Harvard University Press.

Schwanse, Peter. 1982. "European Experience." In *Jobs for Disadvantaged Workers,* edited by Robert Haveman and John Palmer. Washington, D.C.: Brookings Institution.

Snower, Dennis J. 1994. "Converting Unemployment Benefits into Wage Subsidies." *American Economic Review* 84 (May): 65–70.

U.S. Department of Labor. Office of Inspector General. 1994. *Targeted Jobs Tax Credit: Employment Inducement or Employer Windfall?* Washington, D.C.: U.S. Government Printing Office (August).

U.S. Department of Labor. Office of the Chief Economist. 1995. *What's Working and What's Not: What We Know About Getting People New Skills and New Jobs.* Washington: U.S. Government Printing Office (January).

U.S. Departments of Labor and Treasury. 1986. *The Use of Tax Subsidies for Employment.* A Report to Congress. Washington: U.S. Government Printing Office (May).

U.S. House of Representatives. Committee on Ways and Means. 1993. *1993 Green Book.* Washington: U.S. Government Printing Office.

U.S. Office of Management and Budget. 1992. *Budget of the United States Government: Fiscal Year 1993.* Washington: U.S. Government Printing Office.

Woodbury, Stephen A., and Robert G. Spiegelman. 1987. "Bonuses to Workers and Employers to Reduce Unemployment: Randomized Trials in Illinois." *American Economic Review* 77 (September): 513–30.

Chapter 2

The Spatial Dimension: Should Worker Assistance Be Given to Poor People or Poor Places?

Edward M. Gramlich and Colleen M. Heflin

The basic trends in the 1980s job market suggest a giant mismatch—demand is growing for highly skilled workers and not growing for less skilled workers. Those workers with the requisite marketable skills then get good job offers and enjoy some combination of rapidly rising employment offers and real wage growth. Those on the other side of the skill distribution, without the requisite marketable skills, suffer the reverse fate—some combination of low employment possibilities and low real wage growth.

For a long time now social scientists have wondered about the role of spatial factors in this process. While it is hard to imagine that spatial mismatch is a main cause of shifts in the entire wage distribution, many less skilled workers do live in areas without good job growth, often in high-poverty urban neighborhoods. These spatial factors may be part of the overall job problem facing less skilled workers.

Spatial mismatch factors are unlikely to be a main cause of the wage dispersion in the 1980s because less skilled workers were already concentrated in poor areas, and good manufacturing jobs were already leaving central cities, long before the dramatic spread in the real wage distribution opened up (Wilson 1987). Only if these spatial trends had hit some threshold in the 1980s would they have been an important cause of recent movements in the wage distribution. At the policy level, however, even if spatial factors were not prominent causes of recent changes in the underlying this wage distribution, programs that improve spatial mobility or reduce job mismatch could still mitigate or offset movements in wage distribution, at least for important subgroups of workers.

In this chapter we bring together various strands in the empirical literature to discuss these issues. We focus on one basic causal (or positive) question and one basic policy (or normative) question:

- What role has spatial mismatch played in the widening dispersion of real wages for American workers, either in general or for specific groups of workers?
- What form should policy interventions take? Should assistance be given directly to poor workers or poor places, or should programs target mobility issues?

We begin on the causal side by reviewing the literature on spatial mismatch. This evidence, unfortunately, is inconclusive about the impact of spatial factors on labor incomes. Since most people worry about spatial issues particularly for high-poverty urban areas, we focus on evidence from studies of urban spatial poverty. We then turn to the program side and discuss programs that aid workers, aid poor places, and improve mobility. We conclude by describing a mixed strategy for dealing with spatial problems.

Causation: Spatial Mismatch in General

Although the spatial mismatch hypothesis was initially based on empirical observations, it does have a theoretical basis. It starts from the standard urban economics model: employers locate in the central city and individuals are free to live in the suburbs. This model leads to a rent gradient—housing prices decline according to distance from the central city—and to a selection process whereby those with a taste for more expensive housing live further out in the suburbs. If the cross-sectional income elasticity of demand for housing exceeds unity, we would expect to see high-income people concentrated in the suburbs and low-income people concentrated in central cities, much as is now the case.

But at least two important complications should be introduced to this simple model. One is the recognition that employers too can locate in the suburbs; indeed, suburban employment is growing much more rapidly than central city employment in most metropolitan areas. This complication beclouds the clear predictions of the simple urban model: now both high-and low-income people can live in both central cities and suburbs.

The second complication is that not all potential home owners are free to choose where to live. Zoning restrictions exclude low-income people from some suburbs, racial discrimination does likewise for

African Americans and other ethnic groups, and many young workers or secondary earners live where their family lives. Zoning restrictions and other forms of discrimination should crowd low-income people and blacks into the central city and lower their net real wage by increasing their commuting time to some of their preferred jobs. This net wage reduction could also show up as an employment reduction or mismatch if for some reason real wages move too sluggishly to clear labor markets.

Efforts to test these models empirically have proceeded by comparing distributions of residences and distributions of employment. The first empirical paper by John Kain (1968) found that for neighborhoods in Detroit and Chicago employment shares for black adult workers depended positively on black residential shares and negatively on commuting distances. This finding led to a prediction that black employment shares could be raised slightly if they lived nearer to their work.

Kain's initial paper generated so much literature that there are now a number of summaries of this literature; three good ones are by Kain himself (1992), Jencks and Mayer (1990b), and Holzer (1991). Using data from Standard Metropolitan Statistical Area (SMSAs) in the 1970s, Offner and Saks (1971) overturned Kain's results simply by using different functional forms in their estimating equations. Friedlander (1972), Harrison (1974), Masters (1975), and Danziger and Weinstein (1976) all found that residential segregation had little effect on black employment.

More recently, either because of more recent data or different statistical methods, the results are mixed. Based on data from the 1980s, Leonard (1987), Price and Mills (1985), Ellwood (1986), and Moss and Tilly (1991) still find that spatial factors have little or no effect on black employment and/or incomes. But Farley (1987), Ihlanfeldt (1988), Ihlanfeldt and Sjoquist (1989, 1990, 1991), Kasarda (1989), and Holzer and Vroman (1992) do find that spatial factors have an important impact on relative employment and/or incomes.

No mismatch studies based on the 1990 census have been made, but Jargowsky (1994), Hughes (1995), and Abramson, Tobin, and Vander-Goot (1995) do have some disturbing and suggestive results from that census. By 1990 the number and share of blacks living in poor urban areas had increased sharply, as had the geographical size of these poor areas. Both changes continue trends observed by comparing the 1980 census with the 1970 census. It would seem possible that spatial mismatch problems will be serious in the future, even though they may not have been in the past.

Another important aspect of these mismatch studies is the group under investigation. Most past studies have been based on the employment shares of adult workers, but David Ellwood (1986) and Keith Ihlanfeldt and David Sjoquist (1989, 1990, 1991) have focused on young male black and white workers. This more pointed focus seems particularly relevant, because employment problems are much more severe for teenagers, racial disparities are greater for this age group, and teenagers are much more likely to live in a residence chosen exogenously by their family, hence mitigating problems of simultaneity. Thus far, however, focusing only on teenagers has not significantly narrowed the uncertainty about spatial mismatch: Ellwood is on the side of the spatial doves, and Ihlanfeldt and Sjoquist on the side of the hawks. It is possible that differences will become starker in the 1990 census.

There will no doubt be further attempts to refine these results with ever more recent and fine-grained data. At the same time, these studies have a number of serious limitations. Among the most serious are:

- *Endogeneity.* Which comes first, the place of residence or employment? In the standard urban economic approach, employment determines place of residence, but many scenarios could reverse the causation. People may determine their employment from their place of residence rather than the other way around.
- *Dynamics.* Employers move around a lot, within and across cities. At any point in time, some cities are adjusting to the move in or out of some large employers; eventually places of residence will adjust, but not in the short run. While cross- sectional regressions of the sort run by most investigators may find long-run relationships and be relatively immune to these problems, adjustments may take so long that the equilibrium relationship is hard to observe.
- *Heterogeneity.* Workers differ in many respects; studies of employment and residential shares of some groups may not pertain to other groups. Cities differ, and urban models applicable to some cities may be quite inapplicable to others. And time trends differ; what is true in one area in 1970 may not still be true by 1980 or 1990. The time trend problem may explain why spatial mismatch problems appear to be getting worse over time; it may also be that mismatch problems are particularly serious in particular cities.
- *Policy Relevance.* The early spatial mismatch regressions were fitted to broad masses of workers, such as black and white adult male workers. One can almost guarantee that budgetary tightness would force any spatial labor market program to be narrowly based, selectively af-

fecting particular areas, such as urban ghettos, or particular groups of workers, such as black youths. It is not clear how relevant the entire mismatch literature is in evaluating these more focused policies.

With all these uncertainties, it may be prudent not to place too much faith in the studies that have attempted to relate employment and/or income differences to spatial characteristics in general. Many of them have never found large impacts of place of residence on employment or incomes, though some of the more recent studies are beginning to do so. Such impacts may be showing up because spatial mismatch problems are gradually worsening, because these problems have always been serious but now are easier to observe, or because the difficult problems affecting, say, urban areas or particular groups of workers are becoming more noticeable. And as noted earlier, whatever the overall verdict on the contribution of spatial mismatch to wage dispersion, spatial policies could still be an important part of the solution to the problem.

A Closer Look at Poor Urban Areas

Reading through the entire spatial mismatch literature, one is nagged by the feeling that this literature may be missing the key problem: the possible existence of dysfunctional systems in a small share of the overall labor market involving high-poverty urban areas. It thus makes sense to pay particular attention to the recent literature on these areas.

This literature starts with the observation that the share of poor people located in high-poverty urban areas is rising sharply. Reischauer (1987) and Jargowsky and Bane (1991) show the changes between the 1970 and 1980 censuses, and Jargowsky (1994) between the 1980 and 1990 censuses. Further, Kasarda (1992) has shown that the increase in poverty concentration was correlated with rises in unemployment and other measures of poor work history. Gramlich, Laren, and Sealand (1992b) have shown that medium-run (five to seven years) income gains are greater for workers who move out of poor urban areas than for workers who stay, and much less for workers who move into poor urban areas than for workers who do not move in. O'Reagan and Quigley (1993) have tied employment rates of parents and children through family networks to jobs. Finally, in perhaps the starkest evidence of all, Corcoran, Gordon, Laren, and Solon (1992) have shown that over a longer run the sons of families from poor urban areas do significantly worse than others on a range of labor market outcomes.

These labor market observations are buttressed by other examinations of inner-city conditions. Hughes (1988) shows an increase in inner-city isolation and deprivation, as measured by the number of poor black neighborhoods that do not border on integrated or nonblack neighborhoods. Wilson (1987) shows the process by which the emigration of industry and middle-class blacks combined with high black male unemployment causes the deterioration of family structures and increased crime and violence in urban areas. Jencks and Mayer (1990a) have shown that in a number of dimensions, from educational attainment to teen pregnancy, those growing up in poor urban areas are likely to be in much worse shape than those who do not. Freeman (1992) shows the alarming prevalence of crime factors in inner-city life and job markets. Akerlof and Yellen (1993) have demonstrated the weird incentives of the crime problem: not only is crime endemic, but there are pathological situations in which it is not even in the interests of ordinary members of the local community to cooperate with the police. Anderson (1990) has documented the social behaviors necessary to survive in a poor urban area and their reliance on a psychology of racial fear, class prejudice, and social distancing. Whatever the impact of spatial mismatch factors on the overall labor force, it is hard to escape the conclusion that poor urban areas are in increasingly desperate straits.

At the same time, there are grounds for questioning both the pessimistic outlook for poor urban areas and the policy implications of this outlook. Edward Gramlich, Deborah Laren, and Naomi Sealand (1992a) also find enormous rates of immigration and emigration to and from these areas. Fully one-quarter of all poor white adults leave poor urban areas within one year; one-tenth of poor black adults do so. The overwhelming majority of these emigrants do not return; others from nonpoor areas take their places in the poor urban areas. With mobility rates this high, it may not be impossible to imagine programs that change outcomes significantly by altering migration propensities only slightly.

Labor Market Programs

With this background, we now take a look at some actual programs. There are four types: programs that aid poor workers, programs that aid poor places, programs that move poor workers to jobs, and programs that move jobs to workers. We review briefly how each type of program works, discuss its advantages and disadvantages, and then summarize existing evaluation evidence.

Programs That Aid Poor Workers

One main advantage of direct assistance to low-skill workers is that the assistance can be made very general. Assistance can be made available to poor workers wherever they live, and it can be phased out in a uniform way for more highly skilled workers. This advantage leads to one other: since direct assistance can be phased out for less needy workers, it is likely to be much cheaper than other forms of job assistance.

Making worker aid independent of location may also improve the social outcomes of geographic mobility. If, for example, housing vouchers enabled low-skill workers to live anywhere they could find acceptable housing, they would be more inclined to locate where they wanted, not constrained by program availability. One might predict that many low-skill workers will leave poor urban areas, lowering the concentration of such workers there, but if that did not happen, these workers will presumably be choosing their place of residence voluntarily, not on the basis of program eligibility.

But while direct assistance to workers has these desirable aspects, it may not be sufficient to deal with all aspects of urban poverty precisely because there may be spatial factors that impose particular costs—crime, the absence of job networks, poor schooling, and so forth. It is hard to imagine a comprehensive strategy to assist low-skill workers that does not entail some direct assistance, but it is also hard to imagine that direct assistance alone will be sufficient.

U.S. labor market policies already feature significant programs of direct assistance—minimum wages, the earned income tax credit, and a whole set of training programs. Since these programs are discussed elsewhere in this volume, we will confine our attention to programs involving spatial factors.

Programs That Assist Poor Urban Areas

The advantages and disadvantages of programs that aid poor urban areas are almost exactly the reverse of programs that directly aid poor workers. Whereas direct aid can be targeted to needy workers wherever they live, place-based aid cannot be. By definition it affects the residents of the designated target area, and by definition it bypasses residents who do not live in the target area, however needy they may be. Hence, horizontal equity problems across individuals are inevitable with place-based assistance.

There are also residential distortion effects. Whereas direct assistance lets residential outcomes be determined through individual choice, place-based aid necessarily contains differential subsidies: groups locating in one area get a subsidy, and groups locating in another area do not.

Place-based aid can in principle go to either public or private bodies. Since private firms come and go, they are not tied to the area the way public governments are. (Measures to support private firms are discussed later in this chapter. This section considers measures to support public services in poor urban areas.)

A straightforward case in favor of place-based assistance can be made. If the crime problems of poor urban areas are so significant that they impede business and employment activities, what could be more important than measures to improve public services such as police protection? A similar case can be made for measures to improve the local public schools, or the local labor market. Not only can the deficiencies of public services be directly offset, but in principle they can be upgraded to combat or compensate for other deficiencies.

Migration affects local public service assistance in a number of ways. Suppose a homeless shelter with decent health and mental care facilities were established in a poor urban area. Poor people from other communities might immigrate to take advantage of this facility. This outcome eliminates one potential disadvantage of spatially targeted assistance: the benefits are spread more widely than the initial target area. At the same time, the assistance could also increase the concentration of poor people in the area, an outcome that works against long-run social integration and perhaps even nullifies the effectiveness of the program.

There are two other difficulties. One is drawn from long experience studying the fungibility problem (Gramlich 1976)—how local governments respond to federal aid of various sorts. General income assistance aid or categorical assistance aid given in small amounts relative to prior local spending is unlikely to be spent on the service in question. The federal government may pass a program called local public service assistance, but the assistance may actually be used to cut taxes or to support other functions.

The other difficulty involves the politics of the donor government. While one can set up criteria determining which areas most deserve support for local public services, these support programs must be passed by legislatures consisting of representatives of all areas. To cut their own constituents in on the benefits, these legislatures can be relied on to alter legislation in ways that are not optimal from a labor market standpoint alone. For this reason, some unnecessary expenditures may inevitably be included in programs to aid poor urban areas.

Given the intrinsic limitations of directly aiding poor workers and the difficulties in aiding poor places directly, it makes sense to analyze programs that work on mobility—trying to move either workers to jobs or jobs to workers.

Moving Workers to Jobs

Perhaps the most significant advantage of programs that try to move workers to jobs is that they can be done on a limited scale. The programs can focus on particular barriers to mobility, whether housing segregation problems or inadequate commuting networks, and they do not require a radical improvement in an area's public infrastructure. Although they may never solve all the problems facing poor workers, these programs can be highly productive in their own way.

Unfortunately, there are surprisingly few programs that have tried to move inner-city residents to areas where job prospects are better. One natural experiment that has received a great deal of attention is the Gautreaux program in Chicago. Gautreaux was created by a consent decree in the aftermath of a judicial finding of widespread discrimination in Chicago's public housing program. It gives applicants for public housing the option to apply for homes in either the city or the suburbs, with the assistance of counselors. A research team compared outcomes for those leaving the city with outcomes for those remaining; all participants were members of black female-headed households (Rosenbaum and Popkin 1991). Previously employed Gautreaux participants who moved to the suburbs were 14 percent more likely to have jobs than those remaining in the city; previously unemployed participants were 50 percent more likely to be employed. In both cases there were no significant differences in observed wages, but obviously very significant differences in wage incomes. There were also striking improvements in suburban children's high school completion, college attendance, and full-time employment (Rosenbaum 1995).

Two aspects of the Gautreaux results should be specially noted. First, all participants were women, in contrast to the earlier spatial mismatch results that focused largely on males. And second, self-selection factors could have influenced the results, since the treatment group voluntarily left the city. But the influence of self-selection on the results is an interpretation problem only if one applies these results to the entire population by, say, forcibly moving nonvolunteers to the suburbs. If only volunteers move to the suburbs, the Gautreaux results should be indicative.

Additional mobility evidence comes from Detroit and Milwaukee, where separate research groups have examined the relationship between commuting times and job outcomes when large employers moved into the suburbs away from urban workers. In Detroit, where housing segregation is known to be quite high, white employees with long commutes were found to be more likely to quit their jobs than were white employees with short commutes, presumably because these white workers had other job opportunities. In contrast, increases in commuting times for black employees had no significant impact on their propensity to quit or move; the implication is that these employees lost real income (Zax and Kain 1991a, 1991b). In Milwaukee a large employer's relocation to the suburbs greatly increased commuting times for black and Hispanic workers; these workers may not have had other job opportunities and may have suffered losses of real income (Fernandez 1991). At this point it is too early in the Milwaukee evaluation to assess the impact of commuting time changes on actual patterns of employment.

If mobility assistance seems important from a residential perspective, examining the transportation perspective makes sense as well, since it may be easier to provide transportation networks than to enable people to move. Mark Alan Hughes (1995) discusses several transportation programs. The Wisconsin Department of Transportation has developed a job-ride program that secures city residents rides to jobs or job interviews for up to six months. The Chicago Suburban Job Link program operates a fleet of buses and carpools that now transport between four hundred and six hundred residents per day to the suburbs. The Southeastern Pennsylvania Transportation Authority works with local businesses to establish subsidized public transportation to suburban business parks. Public/Private Ventures is currently engaged in a demonstration project involving ten metropolitan areas funded by public agencies and a private foundation. There have been no formal evaluations of these demonstration programs.

There are three important themes in these results. One is that suburban housing discrimination against blacks and Hispanics is still an important phenomenon for which there is plenty of confirming evidence (Massey 1990; Turner, Struyk, and Yinger 1991). Another theme is that commuting times are important to workers, and commuting cost and/or the inability to commute do seem to be barriers preventing urban black and Hispanic workers from taking advantage of suburban jobs. A third theme is that mobility programs are likely to be relatively attractive: they improve job placement but require only payments for counseling or transportation, not massive subsidies for jobs themselves. All of these themes reappear in our policy section.

Moving Jobs to Workers

Many policies fit in this category. In Timothy Bartik's (1994) review of a number of federal and state economic development initiatives, he finds that the problem with most from the standpoint of low-skill workers is that they are generally designed to encourage the economic development of at least medium- to high-technology firms; if they boost the demand for any labor, it is for highly skilled labor. They should be viewed from the standpoint of research and development policy rather than labor market policy, and in fact Bartik argues that the businesses in question generally object to pressures to hire low-skill workers. These firms, often struggling to get established, have enough to worry about without complicating constraints on their hiring and/or location decisions.

The main policy initiative affecting poor areas is the urban enterprise zone (UEZ). Generally UEZs provide tax incentives and wage subsidies to firms that locate in specified areas. Currently the federal government has a small UEZ program, and thirty-seven states and the District of Columbia have also enacted such measures.

On the theoretical side, John Quigley (1994) argues strongly against UEZ-type measures. He points to the land intensity of many forms of employment that are moving to the suburbs and shows that this movement is accompanying the long-term dispersal of the population in most central cities. If there is a social problem, it is not the spreading out but rather simply poverty and discrimination. As such, measures that help poor people or help them move or commute to good jobs are desirable, and measures that perpetuate geographic segregation and locate jobs inefficiently are undesirable. He vastly prefers efforts to combat housing discrimination directly over efforts to subsidize jobs made necessary by discrimination.

Helen Ladd (1994) works through a number of other problems with UEZ legislation. Many of the subsidies are for capital; such subsidies may encourage firms to use not only more capital but more highly skilled labor and less low-skill labor. Moreover, the many subsidies that take the form of reductions in the corporate tax rate will not help small firms, the many that take the form of property tax abatements could largely bypass firms that rent their property, and the many that take the form of inventory tax credits encourage capital-intensive operations like warehouses to locate in the zones. Other subsidies take the form of capital gains tax reductions, which may simply bring in venture capital and again bypass small firms. Those that work by changing the effective price of labor may be unimportant if production conditions or even underlying social conditions make labor demand inelastic.

As for the empirical results, in the early 1980s the United Kingdom offered property and land tax exemptions for firms that located on vacant or deteriorating industrial land (the program has since been discontinued). Ladd reports that survey evaluations found that most of the new zone jobs came from surrounding areas, so that the effective cost per new job created was very high— much higher than the cost of the mobility programs discussed earlier. If a promising way to create urban jobs is to build up surrounding areas, one might even argue that it is preferable in the long run to have unsubsidized jobs in surrounding areas than subsidized jobs in poor urban areas. These subsidies may not last forever.

In this country one of the leading UEZ states is Indiana. Leslie Papke (1993) analyzed the experience there and found that UEZ designation did increase inventory values and decrease unemployment insurance claims. The cost per newly created job remained high, and there was still evidence that jobs were stolen from surrounding areas.

Maryland had a UEZ program in small cities with high unemployment. While there was positive employment growth in the designated areas, employer surveys indicated that this growth was due not to the UEZ legislation but rather to the apparently exogenous hiring of two new employers (Grasso and Crosse 1991). The same question applies to the results for a New Jersey program.

Ladd summarizes all of these studies and computes annual costs per new job across all programs that have been evaluated. These costs, shown in table 2.1, fall in the $40,000 to $60,000 range, a very high number. Moreover, some of the jobs may be stolen from surrounding areas, and as Bartik and Ladd both warn, they may not be the types of jobs ideally suited for workers from poor areas. In contrast to the evaluative evidence on programs that try to move workers to jobs, the evidence on at least these programs that have tried to move jobs to workers is fairly negative to date. Society does not have $40,000 to $60,000 to spend for all new jobs for poor urban workers.

Table 2.1   Annual Cost per Job in UEZ Programs

Area	Direct Cost	Net Cost
England	15,000	60,000
New Jersey	13,070	13,070
Indiana	10,170	53,506
Indiana	1,633	43,579
Maryland	Infinite	Infinite

Source: Ladd (1994, 213).

Notes: The net cost numbers are Ladd's estimates of effective jobs created for UEZ residents, divided by the true cost of the program. The England results are taken from Rubin and Richards (1992). The New Jersey results are from Rubin (1990). The Indiana results are from Papke (1991) and Rubin and Wilder (1989). The Maryland results are from the U.S. General Accounting Office (1988).

A Mixed Strategy for Spatial Assistance

Until now the chapter has looked at different types of spatial assistance. But in one sense spatial assistance programs are not mutually exclusive but can be complementary as well. Suppose, for example, a broader spatial strategy featured some direct assistance to workers, some public service assistance to poor urban areas, and some mobility assistance to unskilled central city workers in finding and holding jobs in the suburbs.

The Committee for Economic Development (CED 1995) recently came out for such a plan. The CED plan contains a number of community-building initiatives, including measures to control guns and crime, some efforts to redress housing discrimination in suburban areas, and some private location subsidies.

The Clinton administration might also be considered a proponent of a mixed strategy. On the one hand, the White House oversaw a large expansion of the earned income tax credit in 1993 and of the minimum wage in 1996. The School-to-Work Opportunities Act of 1994 also provides federal seed money to combine work with learning. But many of these efforts to support low-wage workers could be harmed by welfare reform. The work requirements of the Personal Responsibility Act of 1996 could greatly increase the supply of low-skill workers while removing the mandate that programs include education and training. The provisions eliminating food stamps for the able-bodied and all aid for legal immigrants could greatly worsen labor market conditions in high-poverty areas. It is quite unclear how these labor markets will work when the welfare safety net is taken away.

As for assistance for local public services, the Violent Crime Control and Law Enforcement Act of 1994 contains grants to put up to one hundred thousand police on the street, primarily in urban areas, and to ban a number of assault weapons. Fungibility skeptics may doubt that this many additional police will be hired, and deeper skeptics may doubt the effectiveness of added police, but these are at least examples of support for local public services. Additionally, the president has established the Community Enterprise Board led by Vice President Al Gore to coordinate programs to distressed communities.

In the domain of moving workers to jobs, the administration has promoted the Moving to Opportunity (MTO) program. Modeled on the Gautreaux program and implemented using a scientific design for evaluation purposes, MTO began in five metropolitan areas—Baltimore, Boston, Chicago, Los Angeles, and New York. Congress has appropriated vouchers and money for counseling assistance in these cities to enable families living in public and assisted housing projects in high-poverty areas to move to low-poverty neighborhoods. Unlike the Gautreaux program, which was developed to speed up racial desegregation in Chicago, MTO is focused solely on moving participants from high- to low-poverty areas. The president has also shown a commitment to fair housing by issuing the first fair housing order in more than a decade and establishing the Fair Housing Council to oversee its implementation.

While UEZ programs do not fare so well in the hands of the evaluators, the Clinton administration also has a package for location subsidies for private business. The 1993 empowerment zone legislation creates six UEZs in big cities, three in rural areas, and ninety-five enterprise communities. These all combine tax incentives, public investment, and relief from state and local regulations. In total, $1 billion in social services and $2.5 billion in tax incentives is provided to selected communities.

Conclusion

While there is little evidence that spatial mismatch problems in general have contributed to the widening of the overall distribution of wages, a closer look at the urban poverty literature suggests that some spatial policies may still be important components of a broader labor market strategy. This strategy should undoubtedly feature some direct assistance to workers, and it might well feature some place-based assistance for public services in poor urban areas. It could also feature programs that help workers from poor urban areas take advantage of suburban jobs; these programs seem to be very effective without costing too much.

Far more difficult questions attend programs that subsidize private firms to locate in poor urban areas. These programs have a number of theoretical deficiencies, they have not fared so well in real world evaluations, and they seem quite costly.

References

Abramson, Alan, Mitchell Tobin, and Matthew VanderGoot. 1995. "The Changing Geography of Metropolitan Opportunity: The Segregation of the Poor in U.S. Metropolitan Areas, 1970 to 1990." *Housing Policy Debate* 6(1): 45–72.

Akerlof, George A., and Janet L. Yellen. 1994. "Gang Behavior, Law Enforcement, and Community Values." In *Values and Public Policy*, edited by Henry J. Aaron, Thomas E. Mann, and Timothy Taylor. Washington, D.C.: Brookings Institution.

Anderson, Elijah. 1990. *Streetwise: Race, Class, and Change in an Urban Community.* Chicago, Ill.: University of Chicago Press.

Bartik, Timothy J. 1994. *What Should the Federal Government Be Doing About Urban Economic Development?* Kalamazoo, Mich.: W. E. Upjohn Institute.

Committee for Economic Development. 1995. "Rebuilding Inner-City Communities: A New Approach to the Nation's Urban Crisis." Statement by the the Research and Policy Committee of the Committee for Economic Development. New York: Committee for Economic Development.

Corcoran, Mary, Roger Gordon, Deborah Laren, and Gary Solon. 1992. "The Association Between Men's Economic Status and Their Family and Community Origins." *Journal of Human Resources* 27(4): 575–601.

Danziger, Sheldon, and Mark Weinstein. 1976. "Employment Location and Wage Rates of Poverty-Area Residents." *Journal of Urban Economics* 3(2): 127–45.

Ellwood, David. 1986. "The Spatial Mismatch Hypothesis: Are There Teenage Jobs Missing in the Ghetto?" In *The Black Youth Employment Crisis*, edited by Richard B. Freeman and Harry J. Holzer. Chicago, Ill.: University of Chicago Press.

Farley, John E. 1987. "Disproportionate Black and Hispanic Unemployment in U.S. Metropolitan Areas." *American Journal of Economics and Sociology* 46(3): 129–50.

Fernandez, Robert M. 1991. "Race, Space, and Job Accessibility: Evidence from a Plant Location." Working Paper. Chicago, Ill.: Northwestern University.

Freeman, Richard B. 1992. "Crime and the Employment of Disadvantaged Youths." In *Urban Labor Markets and Job Opportunity*, edited by George E. Peterson and Wayne Vroman. Washington, D.C.: Urban Institute Press.

Friedlander, Stanley L. 1972. *Unemployment in the Urban Core*. New York: Praeger.

Gramlich, Edward M. 1976. "A Review of the Empirical Literature on Intergovernmental Grants." In *The Political Economy of Fiscal Federalism*, edited by Wallace E. Oates. Lexington, Mass.: Heath Lexington.

Gramlich, Edward, Deborah Laren, and Naomi Sealand. 1992a. "Moving into and out of Poor Urban Areas." *Journal of Policy Analysis and Management* 11(2): 273–87.

———. 1992b. "Mobility into and out of Poor Urban Neighborhoods." In *Drugs, Crime, and Social Isolation: Barriers to Urban Opportunity*, edited by Adele V. Harrell and George E. Peterson. Washington, D.C.: Urban Institute Press.

Grasso, Patrick, and Scott Crosse. 1991. "Enterprise Zones: A Maryland Case Study." In *Enterprise Zones: New Directions in Economic Development*, edited by Roy E. Green. Newbury Park, N.Y.: Sage Publications.

Harrison, Bennett. 1974. *Urban Economic Development* Washington, D.C.: Urban Institute Press.

Holzer, Harry J. 1991. "The Spatial Mismatch Hypothesis: What Has the Evidence Shown?" *Urban Studies* 28(1): 105–22.

Holzer, Harry J., and Wayne Vroman. 1992. "Mismatches and the Urban Labor Market." In *Urban Labor Markets and Job Opportunity*, edited by George E. Peterson and Wayne Vroman. Washington, D.C.: Urban Institute Press.

Hughes, Mark Alan. 1988. "The Underclass Fallacy." Working Paper. Princeton, N.J.: Princeton University.

———. 1995. "A Mobility Strategy for Improving Opportunity." *Housing Policy Debate* 6(1): 271–97.

Ihlanfeldt, Keith R. 1988. "Intrametropolitan Variation in Earnings and Labor Market Discrimination: An Economic Analysis of the Atlanta Labor Market." *Southern Economic Journal* 55: 123–40.

Ihlanfeldt, Keith R., and David L. Sjoquist. 1989. "The Impact of Job Decentralization on the Economic Welfare of Central City Blacks." *Journal of Urban Economics* 26: 110–30.

———. 1990. "Job Accessibility and Racial Differences in Youth Employment Rates." *American Economic Review* 80(1): 267–76.

———. 1991. "The Effect of Job Access on Black and White Youth Employment: A Cross-Sectional Analysis." *Urban Studies* 28(2): 255–65.

Jargowsky, Paul A. 1994. "Ghetto Poverty Among Blacks in the 1990s." *Journal of Policy Analysis and Management* 13(2): 288–310.

Jargowsky, Paul A., and Mary Jo Bane. 1991. "Ghetto Poverty in the United States, 1970-1980." In *The Urban Underclass*, edited by Christopher Jencks and Paul E. Peterson. Washington, D.C.: Brookings Institution.

Jencks, Christopher, and Susan E. Mayer. 1990a. "The Social Consequences of Growing up in a Poor Neighborhood." In *Inner City Poverty in the United States*, edited by Laurence E. Lynn Jr. and Michael G. H. McGeary. Washington, D.C.: National Academy Press.

Jencks, Christopher, and Susan E. Mayer. 1990b. "Residential Segregation, Job Proximity, and Black Job Opportunities." In *Inner City Poverty in the United States*, edited by Laurence E. Lynn Jr. and Michael G. H. McGeary. Washington, D.C.: National Academy Press.

Kain, John F. 1968. "Housing Segregation, Negro Employment, and Metropolitan Decentralization." *Quarterly Journal of Economics* 85(1): 175–97.

———. 1992. "The Spatial Mismatch Hypothesis: Three Decades Later." *Housing Policy Debate* 3(2): 371–460.

Kasarda, John D. 1989. "Urban Industrial Transition and the Underclass." *Annals of the American Academy of Political Science and Social Science* 501(1): 26–47.

———. 1992. "The Severely Distressed in Economically Transforming Cities." In *Drugs, Crime, and Social Isolation: Barriers to Urban Opportunity,* edited by Adele V. Harrell and George E. Peterson. Washington, D.C.: Urban Institute Press.

Ladd, Helen F. 1994. "Spatially Targeted Economic Development Strategies: Do They Work?" *Cityscape* 1(1): 193–218.

Lehman, Jeffrey S. 1994. "Updating Urban Policy." In *Poverty and Public Policy,* edited by Sheldon Danziger, Gary Sandefur, and Daniel Weinberg. Cambridge, Mass.: Harvard University Press.

Leonard, Jonathan. 1987. "The Interaction of Residential Segregation and Employment Discrimination." *Journal of Urban Economics* 21(3): 323–46.

Massey, Douglas S. 1990. "American Apartheid: Segregation and the Making of the Underclass." *American Journal of Sociology* 96(3): 329–57.

Masters, Stanley. 1975. *Black-White Income Differences: Empirical Studies and Policy Implications* New York: Academic Press.

Moss, Philip, and Christopher Tilly. 1991. "Why Black Men Are Doing Worse in the Labor Market: A Review of Supply Side and Demand Side Explanations." Social Science Research Council, New York. Unpublished paper.

Offner, Paul, and Daniel Saks. 1971. "A Note on John Kain's 'Housing Segregation, Negro Employment, and Metropolitan Decentralization.'" *Quarterly Journal of Economics* 85(1): 147–60.

O'Reagan, Katherine M., and John M. Quigley. 1993. "Family Networks and Youth Access to Jobs." *Journal of Urban Economics* 34(2): 230–48.

Papke, Leslie E. 1991. "Tax Policy and Urban Development: Evidence from an Enterprise Zone Program." Working Paper. Cambridge, Mass.: National Bureau of Economic Research.

———. 1993. "What Do We Know About Enterprise Zones?" National Bureau of Economic Research Reprint 1817. Cambridge, Mass.: National Bureau of Economic Research.

Price, Richard, and Edwin Mills. 1985. "Race and Residence in Earnings Determination." *Journal of Urban Economics* 17(1): 1–18.

Quigley, John M. 1994. "New Directions for Urban Policy Debate." *Housing Policy Debate* 5(1): 97–106.

Reischauer. Robert D. 1987. *The Geographic Concentration of Poverty: What Do We Know?* Washington, D.C.: Brookings Institution.

Rosenbaum, James E. 1995. "Changing the Geography of Opportunity by Expanding Residential Choice: Lessons from the Gautreaux Program." *Housing Policy Debate* 6(1): 231–69.

Rosenbaum, James E., and Susan J. Popkin. 1991. "Employment and Earnings of Low Income Blacks Who Moved to Middle Class Suburbs." In *The Urban Underclass,* edited by Christopher Jencks and Paul E. Peterson. Washington, D.C.: Brookings Institution.

Rubin, Barry M., and Craig M. Richards. 1992. "A Transatlantic Comparison of Enterprise Zone Impacts: The British and the American Experience." *Economic Development Quarterly* 6(4): 431–43.

Rubin, Barry M., and Margaret G. Wilder. 1989. "Urban Enterprise Zones: Employment Impacts and Fiscal Incentives." *APA Journal* 55(4): 418–31.

Rubin, Marilyn. 1990. "Urban Enterprise Zones: Do They Work? Evidence from New Jersey." *Public Budgeting and Finance* 10(4): 3–17.

Turner, Margery A., Raymond Struyk, and John Yinger. 1991. *Housing Discrimination Study: A Synthesis* Washington, D.C.: U.S. Department of Housing and Urban Development.

U.S. General Accounting Office. 1988. *Enterprise Zones: Lessons from the Maryland Enterprise.* Washington: U.S. Government Printing Office.

Wilson, William Julius. 1987. *The Truly Disadvantaged: The Inner City, the Underclass, and Public Policy.* Chicago, Ill.: University of Chicago Press.

Zax, Jeffrey, and John Kain. 1991a. "Commutes, Quits, and Moves." *Journal of Urban Economics* 29(409): 153–65.

———. 1991b. "The Substitution Between Moves and Quits." *Economic Journal* 101(409): 1510–21.

Chapter 3

The Impact of Changes in Public Employment on Low-Wage Labor Markets

Peter Gottschalk

With government employing roughly 15 percent of the workforce, this sector could have a substantial impact on the labor markets for less skilled workers. Government is simply too big an actor in the labor markets to be ignored. More modest in size are the highly targeted public service employment (PSE) programs that have been used to deal directly with the labor market problems of specific groups, such as welfare recipients and unemployed youth.

PSE jobs have now almost disappeared, but they were a major tool of New Deal legislation and played a prominent role in the legislation of the mid-1970s.[1] In 1934, the Civil Works Administration employed more than four million workers. At its peak in 1938 the Works Progress Administration (WPA) enrolled more than three million workers. Forty years later the peak enrollment in PSE jobs under the Comprehensive Employment and Training Act (CETA) was just under one million, with an additional one million summer jobs for youth.[2]

While the political mood of the mid-1990s makes it highly unlikely that the United States will enact PSE programs in the near future—much less programs of this size—the welfare debate has reopened the question of whether government should be the employer of last resort for people who cannot find work in the private sector.

What are the difficulties in providing such jobs? On what basis should they be evaluated? In this chapter, I review the experience in the United States and other OECD countries with PSE strategies. A recurring theme is that any assessment of the effectiveness of PSE depends largely on the evaluation criterion used.

Before turning to the evaluation literature on U.S. programs, I place PSE in a broader context by first contrasting the size of PSE programs with overall employment in the public sector and then contrasting PSE programs in the United States with programs in other OECD countries.

Employment in the Public Sector

While traditional, tightly focused public service employment programs for less advantaged workers receive disproportionate attention in this chapter, it is important to remember that even small changes in overall government hiring may have a larger impact on low-wage labor markets than even historically large changes in PSE. Together, federal, state, and local governments employ 11.7 percent of all high school dropouts and 12.6 percent of high school graduates. To put the size of the public sector into perspective, roughly the same proportion of workers with low education (a high school education or less) were employed in all nondurable manufacturing industries in 1990 as in the public sector. Put another way, as many less educated workers would lose their jobs from a 10 percent proportional reduction in government employment as from the total elimination of the textile industry.[3]

Changes in demand for less skilled workers by the public sector can therefore have a substantial impact on these labor markets. In this section, I explore the possible impact of a reduction in total employment at all levels of government and the impact of a decentralization to lower levels of government.

Changes in the Size and Level of Government

Powerful political forces are pushing for smaller and more decentralized government, but any shifts in the size and level of government are likely to have unintended distributional consequences.[4] If the public sector and each level of government (federal, state, and local) hired workers of different skill levels in the same proportions, and if all sectors paid identical wages for similar workers, then shifts between the public and private sectors or between different levels of government would have no distributional impact. On the other hand, if the private sector, which is less skill-intensive than the public sector, expanded, then reducing the size of government and increasing the private sector would increase the demand for low-skill workers. Likewise, decentralization of government would decrease the wages of less skilled workers if the federal government paid higher wages than state or local governments.

Differences in Skill Intensity by Sector

Figure 3.1 presents skill intensities by sector. Each bar represents the number of high school dropouts and high school graduates within that sector as a proportion of all persons employed in it.[5] These skill intensities, displayed separately for males and females, are shown for 1979 and 1989.

The private sector uses a higher proportion of both high school dropouts and high school graduates, male as well as female, than each of the three levels of government. The lower skill intensity of the private sector implies that shifts in employment from the public to the private sector raise the demand for less educated workers, thereby putting upward pressure on their wages. This scenario assumes, of course, across-the-board cuts in public employment matched by a corresponding increase in private employment. If public employment were cut disproportionately in areas that hire less skilled workers (for example, building maintenance) or if private employment increased in sectors that use relatively few low-educated workers (for example, legal services), then the shift would lower the demand for less educated workers.

Decentralizing government is not likely to have a large impact on the demand for less educated workers, for two reasons. First, delivery of the same services by a different level of government would not affect the type of workers demanded. If cuts in employment at the federal level were used for unrestricted block grants, then there might be a shift in the types of workers demanded. However, as figure 3.1 indicates, the differences in skill intensity across government sectors are not large. The federal government hires a somewhat greater proportion of male high school dropouts than either state or local governments do, but a smaller proportion of female high school dropouts. While the federal government hires a greater proportion of both male and female high school graduates than state and local governments do, the differences are small for females.

Differences in Wage Rates by Sector

Shifts in the size or level of government might also have a distributional impact if wages differ across sectors, even if all sectors use the same factor proportions. In other words, economic rents may differ across sectors. Even if there were no changes in market forces, wage levels would change as the rents that low-skill workers received changed with their move across sectors. Since the federal government pays a premium

Figure 3.1 High School Dropouts and High School Graduates as Proportions of Total Employees by Sector, 1979 and 1989

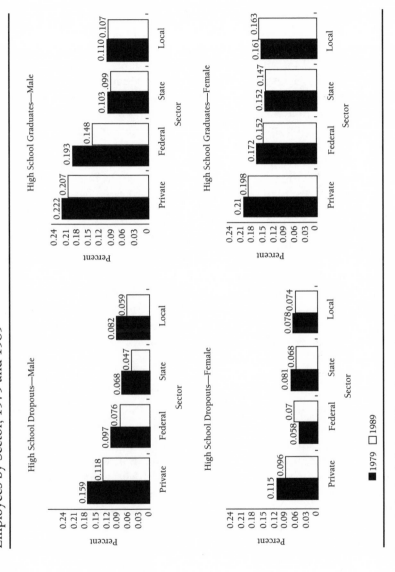

Source: Author's tabulation of Outgoing Rotation Groups.

(relative to both the private sector and state and local governments) for less skilled workers, reductions in the size of the federal government would lead to a reduction in the wages of low-skill workers.

Figure 3.2 shows the premia paid by federal, state, and local governments (relative to the private sector) for male and female high school dropouts and high school graduates in 1979 and 1989.[6] These data show that by 1989 the federal government was paying close to a 10 percent premium for all but male high school graduates (who received a 5 percent premium). Scaling down the size of the federal government and increasing the private sector is therefore likely to result in a reduction in the rents paid to less educated workers who switch sectors.

Decentralizing from the federal level of government to the state and local levels is also likely to reduce wages for less educated workers as rents are eroded. Males could be expected to experience a 10 percent decline in wages, while the decline for females could range from as little as 2 to 3 percent (for high school graduates going from federal to state jobs) to as much as 4 to 5 percent (for high school dropouts going from federal to either state or local jobs).

In summary, the data presented in this section show that the current push to downsize and decentralize government is likely to have distributional consequences. Fortunately, not all forces are pushing to depress the wages of less educated workers. While erosion of rents would put downward pressure on wages, the shift to the private sector is likely to put upward pressure on the wages of less educated workers (since they are used in greater proportion in the private sector than the public sector).

Direct Job Creation

Understanding what other countries have done with public service employment provides some perspective on the size and scope of U.S. programs. Some countries spend considerably more on PSE than the United States did even during the 1970s. However, PSE was not widely used in any country during the 1980s and 1990s. Many countries with labor market policies much more extensive and active than ours also spend little or nothing on PSE. Where the United States stands out is not in the small size of its recent programs but in its focus on less advantaged workers.

PSE in OECD Countries

Figure 3.3 shows expenditures on active labor market policies (in contrast to "passive" policies that offer income support to the unemployed)

Figure 3.2 Pay Differentials by Level of Government for High School Dropouts and High School Graduates, All Occupations

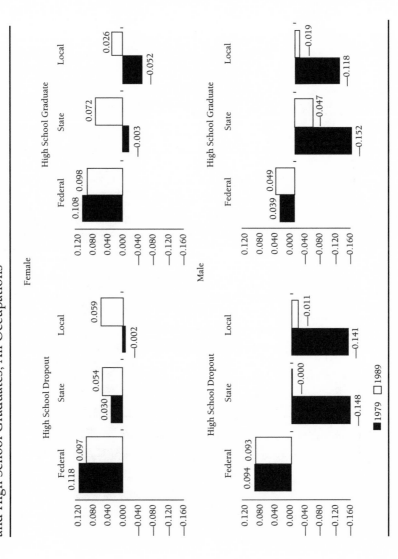

Figure 3.3 Active Labor Market Programs as a Percentage of GDP, 1990

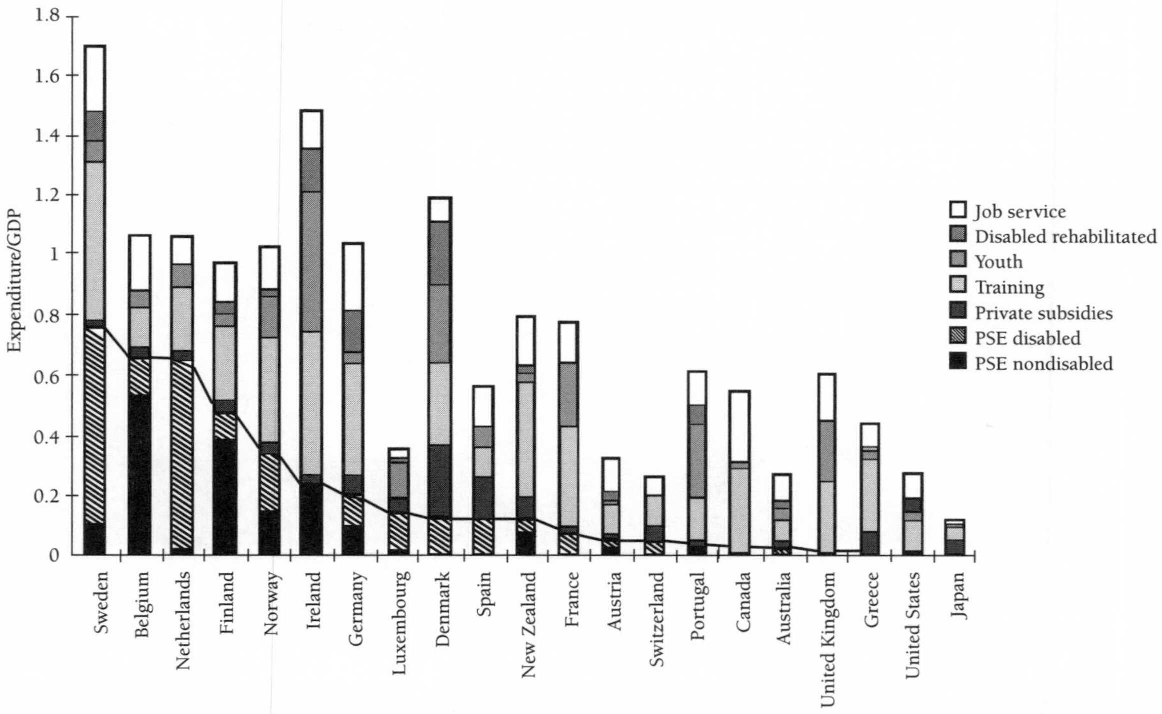
1.8
1.6
1.4
1.2
1
0.8
0.6
0.4
0.2
0
Expenditure/GDP
Sweden
Belgium
Netherlands
Finland
Norway
Ireland
Germany
Luxembourg
Denmark
Spain
New Zealand
France
Austria
Switzerland
Portugal
Canada
Australia
United Kingdom
Greece
United States
Japan
Job service
Disabled rehabilitated
Youth
Training
Private subsidies
PSE disabled
PSE nondisabled

Source: OECD (1992a).

as a percentage of gross domestic product (GDP) for a variety of Organization for Economic Cooperation and Development countries in 1990. These programs include PSE, training, employer subsidies, programs for youth, vocational rehabilitation for disabled workers, and the Employment Service. Since countries differ widely in the proportion of PSE provided to disabled workers and others, I show these separately. Countries are ranked according to expenditures on PSE (relative to GDP) in 1990.

Several patterns emerge. First, there is a clear geographic pattern. The northern European and Nordic countries were the largest users of PSE. Sweden devoted .8 percent of GDP to PSE, followed closely by Belgium (.7 percent) and the Netherlands (.7 percent). PSE workers comprised 1.8 percent of the labor force in Belgium and 1.1 percent in Finland (OECD 1990, table 11). In Sweden, PSE workers comprised up to 2 percent of the labor force during recessions (Bjorklund 1994). To reach the Swedish level, the United States would have had to have more than two million public service jobs.

Second, countries with substantial active labor market policies (as indicated by the total height of the bar) tend to have large PSE programs, though the correlation is far from perfect. Sweden spends the most on active labor market policies, as well as on PSE. At the other extreme, countries like Canada, Australia, and the United Kingdom have both small PSE expenditures and small total expenditures. However, there are many examples of disproportionately large PSE expenditures (Belgium, the Netherlands, and Luxembourg) and disproportionately small total expenditures (France, the United Kingdom, and New Zealand).

An examination of descriptions of PSE programs reveals striking differences in objectives between the United States and other OECD countries. In the United States during the 1980s, PSE was largely viewed as a tool to address the labor market problems of less skilled workers.[7] In most other OECD countries, the stated objective is either to decrease unemployment or to replace unemployment and disability insurance with work. While PSE programs in the United States in the 1970s were largely targeted at disadvantaged workers, programs in other OECD countries have been aimed almost exclusively at the unemployed and the disabled, regardless of income. The focus on the unemployed regardless of income may reflect the European tendency to offer social insurance rather than public assistance. Their view of PSE as social insurance rather than an alternative to public assistance has led many countries to pay market or union-level wages to participants rather than the minimal wages paid in U.S. programs.

The programs in the Nordic countries and Ireland all provide temporary work to the long-term unemployed. The program instituted in Norway in 1989, Arbeid for Trygd (Work in Place of Welfare), provides funds to local authorities to hire young unemployed workers or older workers who have exhausted their eighty weeks of unemployment insurance (UI) (OECD 1993b). These workers can be hired for up to ten months in local public works or social service projects (OECD 1993b). Since 1987 Finland has offered public service jobs that pay market wages to persons unemployed one year or more (three months for youth) (OECD 1992b). Jobs are provided by the central or local governments. While Sweden focuses most of its PSE funds on disabled workers, it still has one of the largest PSE programs for the nondisabled. Sweden's work relief program, Beredskapsarbete, offers work in the public sector to persons who have exhausted their sixty weeks of UI benefits. The short duration of work relief enrollment and the expansion of enrollment during recession are consistent with the program's focus on income insurance for the cyclically unemployed (Edin and Holmlund 1991, 409).

Similarly, Ireland's Social Employment Scheme, instituted in 1985, offers temporary employment to older, long-term unemployed workers (Reynolds and Healy 1990). What all these programs have in common is that they target the long-term unemployed and offer only temporary work. It is noteworthy that none of these countries offer PSE as a "job of last resort" open to all takers.

Spain provides one of the few examples of a PSE program that, while not targeted at low-skill workers per se, at least provides employment opportunities to persons who are not unemployed. The labor ministry contracts with local agencies or private enterprise to provide "works of public and social interest." As many as 50 percent of the contracted workers need not be formerly unemployed (OECD 1993c). Expanding PSE to low-wage workers makes Spain unique in the European context.

The low 1990 level of expenditure on PSE in the United States (see figure 3.3) reflects a sharp drop from the 1980s, though admittedly a drop from a low base in the international context. Did other countries also scale back their programs? The right panel of figure 3.4 shows expenditures for the six countries with falling expenditures, while the left panel shows the patterns for the five countries with rising expenditures on PSE. The remaining ten countries have experienced little change in PSE/GDP since the mid-1980s.

The decline in expenditures in Australia, New Zealand, the United Kingdom, and the Netherlands reflects legislative changes that either greatly scaled back or eliminated PSE programs for the nondisabled in

Figure 3.4   Public Service Employment as a Percentage of GDP, 1985 to 1992

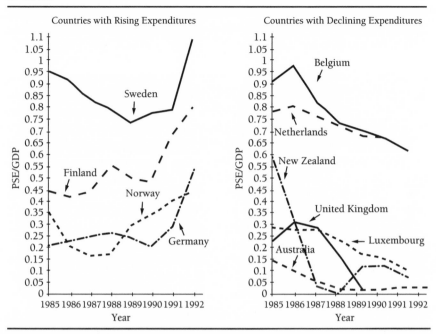

Source: OECD (1992a).

favor of increased training programs (OECD 1988). The rationale for these changes was the belief that training is more effective than PSE in helping the unemployed make the transition to the private sector. Belgium is unique in moving in the opposite direction. Temporary public service jobs were replaced by subsidies to local governments that gave long-term contracts to the unemployed (Worden and Vroman 1992; OECD 1992a; OECD 1990).

Some countries did increase expenditures on PSE, but usually as a response to increased demand for existing programs rather than as a policy decision to widen the scope of the programs. For Finland, Norway, and Sweden, these increases largely reflect increases in the rate of unemployment, which greatly expanded the population eligible for PSE.

The expansion in PSE expenditures in Germany offers one of the few cases of increased expenditures due to program expansion. Employment companies (Beschaftigungsgesellschaften) were introduced into East Germany as a response to very high unemployment. These small (typically five to six employees), quasi-public companies hired the long-term unemployed and older or disabled workers at union or market wages to upgrade and renovate industrial sites (OECD 1992c; Zimmerman 1993; Worden and Vroman 1992). Beschaftigungs-gesellschaften hired fully 5.8 percent of the workforce in the former East Germany.[8]

There are some signs of a revival of interest in PSE in Europe, driven by the same "work is better than welfare" sentiments found in the United States. A striking example is the Netherlands' Youth Work Guarantee Plan, which replaces cash grants with the right to a temporary job for unemployed youth. By 1998 all youth up to twenty-one years old (and school leavers up to twenty-seven) will be covered under this fast-growing program (OECD 1993a). Likewise after a period of sharp retrenchment, the United Kingdom enacted the Employment Action program in 1991. The benefits in this program, which offers employment in community service jobs to persons unemployed six months or longer, are marginally higher than UI benefits (OECD 1993d).

PSE in the United States

PSE programs in the United States underwent a sharp shift during the mid-1970s: instead of focusing on cyclical unemployment, as the Europeans do, the government adopted PSE programs with a clear distributional focus.

The job creation programs of the Roosevelt administration were viewed as temporary measures to address the broad-based employment problems caused by the Great Depression.[9] This broad focus on reducing unemployment or offering an alternative form of income insurance continued through the Public Employment Program (PEP), which provided 185,000 jobs at its peak in 1972, and the early stages of the Comprehensive Employment and Training Act. By 1976 nearly 300,000 PSE CETA jobs had been created as a counter-cyclical measure. These public service jobs were established in state and local government agencies or nonprofit organizations in locations where there was substantial unemployment. The work itself, which ranged from child care to police and fire protection, was intended to provide transitional employment for unemployed, underemployed, and low-income persons.

The first round of CETA jobs were targeted neither at groups with flat labor supply functions (to minimize inflationary pressure) nor at groups with the greatest need for income. In large part as a result of the autonomy given local governments in administering programs, 75 percent of the early CETA slots were filled by high school graduates, and less than half of the jobs were filled by people from low-income households. Many CETA programs "creamed" the more highly skilled workers—hiring enrollees with previous job experience because they were more productive, even if they benefited less from the program. In reaction, the 1976 amendments to CETA required that disadvantaged workers be given priority in public service employment.

The shift to hiring more disadvantaged workers was accompanied by a rapid decline in the number of CETA slots even before President Reagan, who adamantly opposed direct job creation efforts, entered the White House. Large-scale PSE programs came to an end in 1982 when the Job Training Partnership Act (JTPA) replaced CETA. The only programs to survive the transition were some small programs for the Summer Youth Employment and Training Program, which is much less expensive since it covers employment for only six weeks.

During the early 1980s, government abandoned PSE and focused its limited labor market resources on training programs. The welfare debates of the mid-1990s, however, rekindled interest in a limited type of PSE. Public sentiment swung strongly away from cash transfers, and public rhetoric strongly supported a jobs strategy to raise the incomes of poor mothers. Some arguments in favor of this shift to jobs were based on the assumption that being employed improves the life chances of welfare recipients. Policy makers argued that work provides skills that make recipients more attractive to future employers as job applicants.

This human capital or screening rational for getting welfare recipients to work was accompanied by a quite different type of argument based on taxpayer preferences. According to this normative view, welfare recipients should have to work for their incomes, just like the vast majority of taxpayers. While economists could rightly point out that following a jobs strategy was often more expensive than providing transfers directly, this fact did not dissuade those who stressed taxpayers' preferences for the way in which income was redistributed.

The notion that work should replace welfare and that transfer benefits should be of limited duration led policy makers back to PSE under a different guise. If welfare recipients were required to work, where would they find the jobs? Interestingly, the first answer was public service jobs, though no one used the term. The initial battles were fought over "workfare": requiring some welfare recipients to work in a public-sector job in return for a welfare check. Workfare was not traditional PSE, but it raised all the same issues. Would the jobs performed by welfare recipients displace other jobs? Would there be any long-term benefits to workfare participants?

The second stage in the welfare debate focused on time limitations on benefits and further rekindled interest in PSE. If welfare benefits were available only for a fixed period, recipients would have to find jobs. But there was ample reason to believe that those welfare recipients with the least skills would be those most likely to face the time limitation, and they were unlikely to find jobs in an economy that was having increasing difficulty generating jobs for low-skill workers. This dilemma led naturally back to PSE as a job of last resort for welfare recipients.

Evaluations of PSE

As we have seen, PSE has been advocated for two very different reasons. The aim of European programs and of many of the early U.S. efforts, including the WPA projects, was to reduce the aggregate unemployment rate and/or to provide an alternative form of income to the unemployed. Little distinction was made between advantaged and disadvantaged workers. Less skilled workers would benefit along with more advantaged workers through a "trickle-down effect" as less skilled workers had fewer competitors for private-sector jobs. In the second phase of PSE in the United States, attention was redirected from increasing the aggregate number of jobs to putting specific groups to work. Since these two goals suggest very different evaluation criteria, we consider them each in turn.

INCREASING AGGREGATE EMPLOYMENT Hiring a public service worker obviously increases employment, just as hiring any other worker in the public or private sector. However, if expansion of PSE results in offsetting reductions in employment in other sectors, then PSE does not meet the goal of increasing aggregate employment. At least four different forms of displacement tend to reduce the initial impact of PSE.

The first displacement mechanism, financing PSE, is well known. The cost of any government employment program must be financed either through taxation or through the sale of bonds. Taxation tends to reduce aggregate demand, while deficit financing may crowd out private investment. This form of displacement, however, is generic to all public expenditures. If PSE is rejected on these grounds, subsidies to employers, training programs, and all other policies with a budgetary cost must be rejected as well.

The second form of displacement may reduce employment by agencies that receive the PSE workers. Direct job creation in the United States and other OECD countries has largely taken the form of grants to state and local governments to hire public workers. If new jobs, financed at the central level, partially replace jobs that would have been financed at the state and local level, then the job creation program has had a reduced effect. This source of displacement, known as fiscal substitution, tends to grow over time as local governments make adjustments in their normal hiring.[10] A natural way to reduce the effects of fiscal substitution is for the federal government to provide funds only for projects that local governments would not otherwise undertake. However, determining what a government would have done in the absence of a program is not an easy task.

Two other forms of displacement occur through price adjustments. Direct job creation, raise the demand for specified types of workers, which may lead to higher wages (unless supply is perfectly elastic). The wage increase leads private employers to substitute away from the preferred groups, thus partially offsetting the increased employment in the public sector.

The final form of displacement works through the product market. If newly employed workers produce goods that are sold in the market, then those goods compete with other goods. Unless there is an increase in aggregate demand, the net result is increased production in the public sector and decreased production in the nonsubsidized sector. This form of displacement, however, also occurs when private firms are induced to hire disadvantaged workers through tax and other incentives. One way of avoiding this type of displacement is to provide public goods that are not produced in the market, such as clean parks or improved infrastructure. It should be recognized, however, that one of the reasons public service jobs are sometimes thought of as "make-work" is that the jobs are designed not to directly compete with the private sector, both for political reasons and to reduce displacement. The fact that public service workers sometimes produce goods with little or no market value may partially reflect this tension between job creation and the desire to reduce displacement.

Given these forms of displacement and the small size of PSE programs in the United States, one might not expect those programs to have large employment impacts. While there is evidence that CETA increased employment in the short run when the economy was below full employment (Sawhney, Jantzen, and Herrnstadt 1982), there is wide agreement that fiscal substitution eroded part of those gains over time, though there is substantial disagreement about the magnitude of the displacement. As state and local governments adjusted to CETA financing of public service positions, they reduced the number of workers they hired with their own funds. Early empirical studies indicate that after a period of one year the net impact of federally financed jobs under CETA was almost totally offset by reductions in state and local employment. Charles Adams, Robert Cook, and Arthur Maurice (1983) dispute these early studies and suggest that fiscal substitution may have been as low as a reduction of twenty-three cents in local spending for every dollar of federal funds for public service employment. All these estimates are based on crude nonexperimental data dating back to the late 1970s. Without better data, it is difficult to have much faith in any of them.

At one extreme, if one assumes that fiscal substitution was only 25 percent, then at its peak CETA lowered the unemployment rate by about .5 percent. In today's labor market, that would produce jobs for half a million unemployed workers—not an inconsequential figure. However, higher levels of fiscal substitution would, lower this number.[11]

REDISTRIBUTING JOBS TO THE LESS ADVANTAGED   Before examining the empirical evidence on the effectiveness of PSE in redistributing earnings opportunities to less advantaged workers, it is instructive to contrast several alternative evaluation criteria that have been applied to these programs.

First, consider the standard cost-benefit criterion, which weighs the efficiency loss against the distributional gains from instituting a PSE program. As Arthur Okun (1975) proposed in his "leaky bucket" analogy, society may be willing to accept some output loss in order to meet an equity objective. The question is not whether there are efficiency losses, but whether the cost of these losses is smaller than the value society places on the distributional gains.[12]

The efficiency costs depend crucially on the labor supply response to PSE. Suppose that disadvantaged workers are willing to work in public service jobs at the same wage being paid in the private sector (that is, labor supply is infinitely elastic at the market wage). Wage rates in the private sector would not be affected by the introduction of public service jobs. There would therefore be no efficiency loss due to private firms altering their behavior in response to changes in wages (in other words, there would be no price distortion). As long as society places value on reducing the unemployment rates of less skilled workers, PSE would provide a gain.[13]

Unfortunately, this advantage of PSE is also its limitation. If low-skill workers were willing to work in public service jobs at the same wage that similar workers are paid in the private sector, then PSE would reduce unemployment rates of less skilled workers but have no effect on the distribution of wages, since private-sector wages would not be affected by the creation of public service jobs. PSE would not be an effective strategy to offset the decline in private-sector wages for less skilled workers.

When public service workers have to be paid a higher wage to induce them to enter the labor market (labor supply is not infinitely elastic), an increase in demand from the introduction of a PSE program will bid up the wages of less skilled workers in the private sector as firms are compelled to compete with the government to attract workers.[14] If PSE is being used to offset shifts in wage distribution caused by declines in private demand—as occurred during the 1980s—then this bidding up of wages by PSE is an intended benefit with implied equity gains.

Whether these wage changes are distorting depends on the social value of the product produced by public service workers.[15] If these workers produce public goods (such as cleaner parks) with a social value that equals or exceeds the cost of providing these jobs, the wage changes are not distortionary. The fact that public service jobs bid up the wages of private-sector workers is no different than if a private employer bid up the market wage of less skilled workers. Thus, the crucial issue is the value of goods produced by public service workers.

The foregoing is a straightforward application of well-developed economic principles. What is striking about these evaluation criteria is that they do not depend on whether PSE raises the future wages of participants, the focus of most evaluations of PSE. In other words, PSE may be a socially desirable mechanism for lowering the unemployment rates or raising the current wages of less skilled workers not working in public service jobs whether or not it raises the future wages of those less skilled workers in such jobs.

The emphasis on raising the future wages of PSE participants through human capital accumulation implies a very different evaluation criterion. In the 1960s and 1970s, PSE was offered as an alternative or supplement to training.[16] It was argued that these human capital strategies could provide skills that would raise the future earnings of participants. PSE enrollees might learn everything from simple rules of the workplace to specific skills that carry over into the private sector. Under this view, PSE was a successful human capital strategy if future earnings exceeded the costs of the program.

It should be noted that this evaluation criterion is not routinely applied to employment in the private sector. In the debates about the effectiveness of welfare reform and other policies that try to place low-skill workers in private-sector jobs, a private placement is considered a success whether or not the job has any impact on the person's future wage. Thus, requiring that public service jobs do more than provide employment is placing an additional onus on these jobs.

So far we have considered the efficiency costs of PSE, but in the political arena the budgetary costs may be paramount. One might think that PSE always has a higher budgetary cost than employer subsidies (because the government must pay the full cost of public service workers but only the subsidy for private-sector workers). As Lawrence Katz shows in chapter 1 of this book, however, the budgetary cost per net job created is raised by the economic rents gained by firms that would have created the jobs even without the subsidy. When these additional budgetary costs are taken into account, it is no longer clear that public service jobs are not the cheaper strategy.

While the United States has had less experience with large-scale PSE projects than some OECD countries, the United States has undertaken many more demonstration and experimental projects. I now turn to a review of the findings from the most important of these programs.

Youth Incentive Entitlement Pilot Project   Between 1978 and 1981 the United States experimented for the first time with what comes as close as possible to a guaranteed job. The Youth Incentive Entitlement Pilot Project (YIEPP) guaranteed a part-time minimum-wage job and a full-time summer job to any person between the ages of sixteen and nineteen who stayed in school.[17] While most jobs were in the public or nonprofit sector, nearly one-quarter of the jobs were in the private sector, where wages were fully subsidized. Even with a 100 percent subsidy, only 18 percent of the eligible employers chose to participate (Gueron 1984). This figure indicates just how difficult it is to induce the private sector to offer jobs to disadvantaged youth

This saturation program, which served seventy thousand youth, was instituted in seventeen cities, four of which were chosen as evaluation sites. Outcomes in these cities and in four control cities were compared. While the control cities did not have a YIEPP saturation project, they were receiving other services under the Youth Employment and Training Programs. Therefore the evaluations contrast YIEPP with alternative programs, not with no services.

Evaluation of the program was hampered by the difficulty of controlling for differences between the experimental and control sites and by the premature termination of the experiment. Without being able to follow youth over a substantial period, it is impossible to determine whether the program had any long-term effect on post-program earnings.

The program's impact on current earnings, however, is encouraging. Earnings during the school year were estimated to be 46 to 161 percent higher in the experimental cities than in the control cities. For summer jobs, earnings were estimated to be 48 to 65 percent higher (Haveman and Hollister 1991). The fact that earnings increased indicates that displacement did not fully offset the impact of the program. Furthermore, blacks gained disproportionately from the guaranteed availability of a job. As a result, the unemployment differentials between black and white youth were largely eliminated during the existence of the program. Clearly more young people, especially blacks, were willing to work at minimum-wage jobs than were being hired in the absence of the program. If the objective of PSE is to redistribute employment in favor of specific groups, this program has to be judged a success.

Comprehensive Employment and Training Act   CETA did not use random assignment to evaluate the effectiveness of its PSE component.[18] Without a random control group, evaluations were based on the Continuous Longitudinal Manpower Survey (CLMS) data, which include Social Security earnings records for a sample of CETA participants and for a random sample drawn from the CPS who serve as a control group. Laurie Bassi and Orley Ashenfelter (1986) review much of the work based on this data and conclude that some consistent patterns emerge from disparate studies based on these data. Men's earnings and hours in the post-program period were not substantially different from the labor market experiences of men who did not participate in the program. On the other hand, women did benefit from employment programs, mostly because they increased the number of hours they worked in the post-program period.

Furthermore, the PSE component of CETA was one of the more successful strategies for raising future earnings.[19] Burt Barnow (1987) reviews both the conclusions and the methodologies of four CETA evaluations based on the CLMS data. These studies show positive impacts for women and generally little impact for men. On-the-job training and PSE were more effective than either classroom training or work experience. Barnow's more general conclusion, however, is that these studies showed considerably different results for subpopulations. He concludes that "there is simply not enough evidence to argue that one study's methods are clearly superior to another's" (p. 188) and that the only solution to many of the methodological issues is an evaluation based on an experimental design.

Recent studies of job training have shown that a more detailed analysis of nonexperimental data can greatly narrow the range of estimates and bring them closer to the experimental results.[20] The nonexperimental evaluation studies of PSE, however, have not yet been updated.

Supported Work   The mid-1970s interest in more targeted employment and training programs was reflected in the establishment of an ambitious four-year demonstration project in 1975 aimed at increasing the employability of some of the most disadvantaged workers in the United States. More than ten thousand long-term welfare mothers, ex-offenders, ex-drug addicts, and teenage high school dropouts were enrolled in the five-year National Supported Work demonstration program, which guaranteed participants work for one year. The objective of this program was not to teach specific skills but to increase employability by giving participants actual work experience and getting them accustomed to workplace environments and expectations. Jobs included painting fire hydrants, recapping tires, building furniture, and working in day-care centers. For each participant, the program gradually increased the requirements with respect to attendance, punctuality, and other worker qualities valued in the market.

Supported Work applicants were randomly assigned to experimental and control groups. Data were collected through interviews with both the controls and the participants prior to participation and in up to four additional interviews at nine-month intervals. Robinson Hollister, Peter Kemper, and Rebecca Maynard (1984) conclude that the intensive intervention provided under Supported Work significantly increased the employment and earnings of all four target groups during their participation in the program. In the post-program period, only the AFDC target group experienced earnings gains. These gains included a 5 to 10 percent increase in employment rates and increases of $50 to $80 in monthly earnings (Fraker and Maynard 1987).

Considerable effort has gone into calculating overall cost/benefit ratios for Supported Work. The cost of the program was high—$10,000 per service year, about the same cost as the Job Corps but more expensive than public service jobs under CETA. Comparing social costs and benefits (excluding stipends, since they were a transfer payment from taxpayers to participants), the program was cost-effective for welfare mothers and ex-addicts. The net benefit of more than $8,000 for welfare mothers was largely a consequence of increased post-program earnings, and the large net benefit for ex-addicts was primarily a result of reduced criminal activity (Burtless and Haveman 1984). The evaluation of future net benefits for the two other groups, however, showed less promising results. There were negative net benefits for youth, and the results for ex-offenders were inconclusive.

Employment Opportunity Pilot Program   The Employment Opportunity Pilot Program (EOPP) was a demonstration project authorized by Congress in 1978 to determine whether a voluntary guaranteed-jobs program could increase employment and reduce welfare participation. The EOPP demonstration began primarily as a test of the guaranteed-jobs concept but was modified to test new job search strategies. It was terminated prematurely, however, as a result of the Reagan administration's strong opposition to any program with a PSE component.

Although EOPP's value as a social experiment was limited by the changing objectives of the demonstration and its premature end, it does offer some general conclusions about the effectiveness of employment programs in encouraging increased workforce participation. Gary Burtless and Robert Haveman (1984) conclude that EOPP probably raised the employment rates of welfare mothers (the largest group served) by ten to twelve points. They also point out that of the 120,000 potential enrollees eligible for the full range of EOPP services, fewer than 3 percent actually obtained public service jobs.

Job Corps   The Job Corps, one of the few youth programs still in existence, is a combination PSE and training program. It is expensive, costing more than $10,000 per trainee, and it serves a limited number of the most severely disadvantaged youth between the ages of sixteen and twenty-one, in either residential centers or neighborhood programs. Glen Cain (1968) and Charles Mallar et al. (1980) conducted major evaluations of the Job Corps program. Both studies found significant employment and earnings gains for up to four years after leaving the program for all but young women with children. Weeks worked and yearly earnings were raised by three weeks and $655, respectively. Program participation was also favorably associated with reductions in welfare participation, unemployment insurance usage, criminal activity, and out-of-wedlock births, and increases in acceptance into the military and participation in further education and training.

Although the Job Corps is as expensive as Supported Work, it appears to have a positive cost/benefit ratio overall ($1.45 for every dollar of benefits) and is nearly cost-effective ($.96 for each dollar spent) in terms of government expenditures alone (Mallar et al. 1980). These benefits include in-program output, increased tax payments on post-program income, reduced transfer payments, reduced criminal activity, and reduced use of other federally provided services.

Community Work Experience Program   While the United States abandoned PSE as an antipoverty strategy in the early 1980s, the concept of providing work in the public sector reemerged as a welfare strategy. Just as CETA was being phased out in 1982, Congress passed the Community Work Experience Program (CWEP), which allowed states for the first time to require welfare recipients to work. This legislation was viewed by many as punitive "workfare" and not, at first, as a form of PSE. However, as the focus of the welfare debate moved from workfare in the early 1980s to time limitations in the 1990s, programs evolved in several states that looked more and more like standard PSE programs that offered a guaranteed job to one segment of the disadvantaged population. In fact, Clinton's initial welfare reform proposal included an explicit PSE program for welfare recipients who could not find private-sector employment after their two years of welfare eligibility had expired.

Initially CWEP offered a minimum-wage job for the number of hours it took a recipient to "work off" his or her welfare grant (Brock, Butler, and Long 1993). This provision was interpreted as unpaid work experience, but it could equally well have been interpreted as offering a minimum-wage job for a fixed number of hours. Either way, work had to be found for the enrollees and all the same displacement issues had to be faced.

Evaluations of CWEP programs were undertaken in several states. These programs offered services and jobs that were primarily entry-level clerical and maintenance work. The program in West Virginia came closest to the PSE model by offering a job of unlimited duration to a sample of AFDC recipients and to all AFDC-U (for unemployed parents) recipients. West Virginia was the only state to rely solely on a jobs strategy and to offer jobs to all eligible AFDC-U cases in selected sites. Other states mixed work experience with job search and other services and offered a limited number of jobs. Random assignment to experimental and control groups was used in all but the AFDC-U saturation sites in West Virginia.[21]

Participants agreed that requiring work for welfare was fair. However, the evaluation studies give little evidence that CWEP increased post-program wages or hours. Experimentals and controls in the West Virginia program had very similar post-program outcomes. Similar patterns among experimentals in other states indicate that even adding services to work does not lead to improved post-program outcomes.

New Hope   As a postscript, it should be noted that a new PSE project is under way in Milwaukee, Wisconsin. The New Hope project guarantees that anyone working at least thirty hours per week will have an income above the poverty line. The project offers a temporary community service job to anyone who cannot find work after eight weeks of searching. This goes well beyond any of the previous PSE experiments, which limited eligibility to welfare participants, youth, or other specified disadvantaged groups. New Hope applicants are randomly assigned to experimental and control groups. Interestingly, the evaluation focuses primarily on differences between the two groups during, rather than after, the three-year project period (Doolittle and Robling 1994).

Summary   The U.S. experiments with PSE indicate that minimum-wage jobs would be demanded if offered. Voluntary programs have consistently had little trouble in filling job slots. The experience with YIEPP is encouraging in that it showed that making an open-ended commitment to providing jobs not only raises earnings but also largely eliminates the difference between the unemployment rates of blacks and whites. PSE, however, has had only limited success as a human capital strategy. Postprogram earnings were raised in some but not all experiments; where PSE did increase earnings, the increases were in the $500 to $1000 range.

EVALUATION OF PSE PROGRAMS IN OTHER OECD COUNTRIES   The evaluation literature on PSE in other OECD countries is paltry in comparison to the literature on the much smaller programs in the United States. Policy makers in Europe seem generally less interested in evaluation studies of social programs, including PSE. This attitude may reflect differences in social outlook or differences in the infrastructure necessary to undertake large-scale evaluations. Americans' skepticism about the value of social programs may increase the demand for studies that might show their ineffectiveness. On the other hand, the availability of researchers who specialize in program evaluation both at the Manpower Demonstration Research Corporation (MDRC) and in academic institutions may make it easier to evaluate programs in the United States than in other OECD countries.

Differences in goals for PSE may also partly explain the difference in the prevalence of evaluation studies between the United States and other OECD countries. The U.S. focus on raising post-program outcomes leads immediately to questions about whether the program changed future hours, wages, or welfare participation. PSE programs in other

OECD countries are almost always viewed as an alternative form of support for persons who cannot find employment in the private sector. Viewed solely as social insurance, the programs are successful as long as they reach those for whom they were intended and do not cause more displacement than the alternative income transfer strategies.

PSE is also viewed in many countries as a way to lower unemployment. The ability of the program to meet that goal is not as clear. As discussed earlier, PSE may displace other public- or private-sector workers. One would certainly have to question whether Belgium's subsidy to local governments to hire the long-term unemployed is reducing the stock of unemployed or simply reshuffling the employed and the unemployed. Likewise, the sheer size of the employment program in East Germany has led to accusations that the quasi-public employment companies are displacing jobs in the private sector (OECD 1992c). Local entrepreneurs have successfully argued that they cannot compete with companies whose above-market wage rates are offset by federal subsidies. As a result of these conflicts, the government agreed in 1991 to allow the local chambers of commerce to veto projects that could be carried out by local entrepreneurs. While one can speculate about program effectiveness in Belgium and Germany, those speculations might not be confirmed in a serious program evaluation.

It probably comes as no surprise that there are no randomized experiments with PSE outside the United States. One would, however, expect substantial evaluation studies of the programs in several countries that employ more than 1 percent of the labor force. Swedish work relief programs have received the most attention, but little can be concluded from these studies. Suzanne Ackum (1991) finds that long-time work relief participants have lower wages. One strongly suspects, however, that unobservable characteristics of some participants both lower their wages and keep them on the program. Likewise, Anders Bjorklund (1991) reports the results of a 1988 Ministry of Labor study that finds work relief to have no impact. That study, however, also does not seem to control for key variables.

Limited information is also available from duration models that use program participation as covariates. According to a summary of these studies, participation in a public service job increased the probability of finding a private job in Finland and in Germany but not in the United Kingdom (OECD 1994). Again, however, these studies cannot sort out the impact of program participation per se from unobservables that may increase both program participation and employment in the private sector.

Conclusion

Policies that affect employment in the public sector can partially offset the impact of the decline in demand for less skilled workers that occurred during the 1980s. With 12 percent of workers with a high school education or less working for federal, state, or local governments, this sector can have a substantial impact on labor markets for less educated workers. Since less educated workers make up a larger proportion of private employment than of public employment, shifts in employment from the public sector to the private sector are likely to cause market pressures that tend to raise wages for less skilled workers. These pressures would be partially offset, however, by the elimination of rents received by less skilled workers in the federal government.

Direct job creation for low-skill individuals provides a more explicit link between public employment and labor markets for less skilled workers. The U.S. experience with public service employment has been limited compared to the history of PSE in some other OCED countries The focus of programs has also differed. Other OECD countries use PSE either to reduce unemployment or to provide an alternative form of social insurance. Since the late 1970s, the United States has focused its more limited programs on the least advantaged workers.

Wheather or not these programs have been successful depends crucially on the goal. If PSE is offered as a way of reducing aggregate unemployment, its effectiveness depends largely on the amount by which lower levels of government shift existing tasks to public service workers rather than expand employment. The available estimates of the size of this fiscal substitution are imprecise and based on old data, making it difficult to evaluate the argument for PSE based on its employment impact.

An alternative goal of PSE is to raise future earnings of participants. Here the evidence is also mixed. Welfare mothers benefited from work experience and a variety of services under the National Supported Work program but not under CWEP. The post-program earnings of youth were raised in Job Corps, but high school dropouts participating in Supported Work showed no significant changes in future labor market outcomes. While this evidence has been used to argue that PSE is not effective, it is important to recognize that private employment is not evaluated by this criterion. A private employer's offer of a job to a less skilled person is considered a success, whether or not the job experience raises that person's future wages.

A third goal of PSE is to provide work opportunities for persons who cannot find work in the private sector. This is the implicit goal of current efforts to put welfare mothers to work, even if government jobs, a form of PSE, are necessary. Many Americans believe that work is good in its own right, whether it has a lasting impact on participants or not. Do persons who do not find work in the private sector simply not want work at the minimum wage? Here the evidence is stronger. When minimum-wage public service jobs have been offered, the take-up rates have been high. Probably the most impressive experiment is the Youth Incentive Entitlement Pilot Project. Employment rates were 41 percent in sites that offered a job to any youth still in school. In the comparison sites the rate was 25 percent (Gueron 1984, table 2). Furthermore, the take-up rates for blacks were sufficiently high to eliminate the gap between black and white unemployment rates.[22]

My overall conclusion based on the literature reviewed in this chapter is that PSE is a potentially important tool for dealing with the distributional issues addressed in this book. Participants in PSE programs have shown that they are willing to take even low-wage jobs. On the donor side, taxpayers have voiced their preference for dealing with distributional issues through jobs rather than transfers. We have already seen the result of this convergence in preferences in the welfare reform arena. The question is whether we are willing to expand PSE to the larger population. If we move in this direction, it will be important to be clear about the goals we are trying to achieve with PSE. Claims that PSE will substantially lower aggregate unemployment rates may turn out to be valid, but predictions about the employment impact depend crucially on estimates of the amount of fiscal substitution, which are currently measured very imprecisely. Claims that PSE will raise future wages are easier to substantiate, but these human capital effects are limited to only some groups. If, on the other hand, PSE is evaluated on the same basis as a new job in the private sector—which only claims to provide employment, not future increases in wages—the case for PSE is much stronger.

Notes

1. The only major program to survive into the 1990s is the Summer Youth Employment and Training Program, which has served 326,000 recipients.
2. See Kesselman (1978, table 1) for enrollment and expenditures under works programs during the Roosevelt administration. Since CETA was composed of

many different programs with a varying mix of training and employment, the number of public service jobs differs according to which programs are included in the count. Vee Burke (1982) shows 596,000 enrollees under CETA's Titles II-D and VI, which cover the major countercyclical programs and programs targeted at disadvantaged workers. An additional 398,000 jobs for youth are included under Youth Employment Demonstration Programs. While the Summer Youth Employment and Training Program enrolled another 1.009 million youth, the expenditures on this program were roughly 10 percent of the expenditure on the other programs. Nathan, Cook, and Rawlins (1981) report 750,000 public service jobs under CETA.

3. Based on the 1990 Current Population Survey Outgoing Rotation Group (ORG) files.

4. Rebecca Blank (1994) also explores the distributional impact of changes in the size of government.

5. High school graduates do not include persons with any college education.

6. Figure 3.2 shows the coefficients on sector dummies from ln wage regressions using the 1980 and 1990 Public Use Microdata Sample (PUMS) files. The equations include experience, experience squared, and dummy variables for black, white, part-time, and married as covariates. Three-digit occupation-fixed effects are differenced out. Regressions were run separately for each sex and education group. To further ensure that differences across sectors do not reflect differences in occupations, we also limited the sample to occupations open to less skilled workers that were used in all four sectors. These results show very similar patterns. Katz and Krueger (1991) and Poterba and Rueben (1994) also examine sectoral differences in wages.

7. This objective is very different from that of programs used during the Great Depression, when skilled as well as less skilled workers were hired for WPA jobs.

8. Zimmerman (1993, 236) indicates that 68,000 workers were hired in West Germany and 366,000 in East Germany. Table 6.7 shows 6.3 million persons gainfully employed in East Germany and 29.4 million in West Germany.

9. The founding of the WPA in 1935 predates the introduction of unemployment insurance in 1938 (Cook et al. 1985).

10. Note that the displacement effect of financing PSE is reduced as fiscal substitution grows. In the limit, if fiscal substitution is 100 percent, there is no financing effect, since local taxes (or borrowing) can be reduced by the same amount as federal taxes are raised.

11. Bassi and Ashenfelter (1986) find that funding levels were poorly coordinated with the unemployment rate, suggesting that political factors may have limited the impact of PSE programs on net employment.

12. A subsidiary question is whether PSE offers the lowest-cost method of attaining the equity objective. The standard economist's argument that cash transfers offer the least costly way of attaining distributional objectives ignores the preferences of some donors for non-cash transfer strategies, such as PSE.

13. One potential inefficiency occurs when the value of the output produced by the public service workers is less than the value of leisure, home production, or other production while unemployed.

14. Note that if the higher wage reflects only a compensating differential that has to be paid to induce a person to work in the public sector, then private employers will not have to pay that premium and PSE will again have no efficiency effect.

15. There is no reason to go through this exercise if the increase in demand comes from the private sector rather than the public sector because, under appropriate conditions, the value of the output in the private sector is the price determined in competitive markets. Firms bid up the price of less skilled workers only if the value of the product they produce in that firm exceeds the value produced in other firms. Note that subsidies to employers also create price distortions by driving a wedge between the cost and the value to the firm of hiring another subsidized worker.

16. This link was enshrined in the titles of programs such as the Comprehensive Employment and Training Act.

17. See Gueron (1984) for a description of YIEPP as part of a larger set of programs focused on youth. See Betsey, Hollister, and Papageorgiou (1985) for a summary of these projects grouped under the Youth Employment and Demonstration Projects Act of 1977 (YEDPA).

18. Titles II and VI of the CETA legislation provided pubic service jobs.

19. Bassi (1983) focuses specifically on the costs and benefits of the PSE component of CETA and concludes that while the program increased post-program earnings by $661, the benefits of the program were less than the cost unless one placed intrinsic value on helping disadvantaged workers.

20. Burtless (1995) and Heckman and Smith (1995) discuss the relative merits of experimental versus nonexperimental evaluations.

21. These sites were compared to sites that limited participation to 40 percent of the AFDC-U caseload. Since the program was mandatory, differences between the control and saturation sites give a measure of the ability of localities to provide work, not the willingness of participants to take the offered jobs.

22. Gueron (1984, 21) estimates that the cost of implementing a similar program nationwide that guaranteed a minimum-wage job to every young person still in school would be $1.6 billion to $1.8 billion (in 1980 dollars, roughly $3 billion in 1995 dollars).

References

Ackum, Suzanne. 1991. "Youth Unemployment: Labor Market Programs and Subsequent Earnings." *Scandinavian Journal of Economics* 93(4): 531–43.

Adams, Charles F., Jr., Robert F. Cook, and Arthur J. Maurice. 1983. "A Pooled Time Series Analysis of the Job Creation Impact of Public Service Employment Grants to Large Cities." *Journal of Human Resources* 18(2): 283–94.

Barnow, Burt S. 1987. "The Impact of CETA Programs on Earnings: A Review of the Literature." *Journal of Human Resources* 22(2): 157-93.

Bassi, Laurie J. 1983. "The Effect of CETA on Participants' Post-Employment Earnings." *Journal of Human Resources* 18(4): 539–56.

Bassi, Laurie J., and Orley Ashenfelter. 1986. "The Effect of Direct Job Creation and Training Programs on Low-Skilled Workers." In *Fighting Poverty: What Works and What Doesn't*, edited by Sheldon Danziger and Daniel Weinberg. Cambridge, Mass.: Harvard University Press.

Betsey, Charles L., Robinson G. Hollister Jr., and Mary R. Papageorgiou, eds. 1985. *Youth Employment and Training Programs: The YEDPA Years*. Washington, D.C.: National Academy Press.

Bjorklund, Anders. 1994. "Evaluations of Labour Market Policy in Sweden." *International Journal of Manpower* 15 (5):16–32.

Blank, Rebecca. 1994. "Public Sector Growth and Labor Market Flexibility: The United States Versus the United Kingdom." In *Social Protection Versus Economic Flexibility: Is There a Trade-off?*, edited by Rebecca Blank. Chicago, Ill.: University of Chicago Press.

Brock, Thomas, David Butler, and David Long. 1993. "Unpaid Work Experience for Welfare Recipients: Findings and Lessons from MDRC Research." New York: Manpower Demonstration Research Corporation. Mimeo.

Burke, Vee. 1982. "Cash and Noncash Benefits for Persons with Limited Income: Eligibility Rules and Recipients, Fiscal Year 1978–1980." Report 82–113. Washington, D.C.: Congressional Research Service.

Burtless, Gary. 1995. "The Case for Randomized Field Trials in Economic and Policy Research." *Journal of Economic Perspectives* 9(2): 63–84.

Burtless, Gary, and Robert Haveman. 1984. "Policy Lessons from Three Labor Market Experiments." In *Employment and Training R & D*, edited by R. Thane Robson. Conference proceedings of the National Council on Employment Policy. Kalamazoo, Mich.: W. E. Upjohn Institute for Employment Research.

Cain, Glen. 1968. "Benefit-Cost Estimates for Job Corps." Institute for Research on Poverty Discussion Paper 9-68. Madison, Wisc.: University of Wisconsin.

Cook, Robert F., Charles F. Adams Jr., V. Lane Rawlins, and Associates. 1985. *Public Service Employment: The Experience of a Decade*. Kalamazoo, Mich.: W. E. Upjohn Institute for Employment Research.

Doolittle, Fred, and Irene Robling. 1994. *Research Design for the New Hope Demonstration*. New York: Manpower Demonstration Research Corporation.

Edin, Per-Anders, and Bertil Holmlund. 1991. "Unemployment, Vacancies, and Labour Market Programmes: Swedish Evidence." In *Mismatch and Labour Mobility*, edited by Fiorella P. Schioppa. Cambridge, England: Cambridge University Press.

Fraker, Thomas, and Rebecca Maynard. 1987. "The Adequacy of Comparison Group Designs for Evaluations for Employment-Related Programs." *Journal of Human Resources* 22(2): 194–227.

Gueron, Judith M. 1984. *Lessons from a Job Guarantee: The Youth Incentive Entitlement Pilot Projects*. New York: Manpower Demonstration Research Corporation.

Haveman, Robert, and Robinson Hollister. 1991. "Direct Job Creation: Economic Evaluation and Lessons for the United States and Western Europe." Part 1 of *Labour Market Policy and Unemployment Insurance*, edited by Anders Bjorklund, Robert Haveman, Robinson Hollister, and Bertil Holmlund. Oxford, England: Clarendon Press.

Heckman, James J., and Jeffrey A. Smith. 1995. "Assessing the Case for Social Experiments." *Journal of Economic Perspectives* 9(2): 85–110.

Hollister, Robinson G., Jr., Peter Kemper, and Rebecca Maynard. 1984. *The National Supported Work Demonstration.* Madison, Wisc.: University of Wisconsin Press.

Katz, Lawrence F., and Alan B. Krueger. 1991. "Changes in the Structure of Wages in the Public and Private Sectors." *Research in Labor Economics* 12: 137–72.

Kesselman, Jonathan R. 1978. "Work Relief Programs in the Great Depression." In *Creating Jobs,* edited by John L. Palmer. Washington, D.C.: Brookings Institution.

Mallar, Charles, et al. 1980. *The Lasting Impact of Job Corps Participation: Final Report.* Princeton, N.J.: Mathematica Policy Research.

Nathan, Richard, Robert Cook, and Lane Rollins. 1981. *Public Service Employment, a Field Evaluation.* Washington, D.C.: Brookings Institution.

Okun, Arthur M. 1975. *Equality and Efficiency: The Big Tradeoff.* Washington, D.C.: Brookings Institution.

Organization for Economic Cooperation and Development (OECD). 1988. "Profiles of Labour Market Budgets 1985–1987." In *Employment Outlook, 1988.* Paris, France: Organization for Economic Cooperation and Development Publications.

———. 1990. *Labor Market Policies for the 1990s.* Paris, France: Organization for Economic Cooperation and Development Publications.

———. 1992a. "Monitoring Labour Market Developments." In *Employment Outlook, 1992.* Paris, France: Organization for Economic Cooperation and Development Publications.

———. 1992b. *OECD Economic Surveys: Finland, 1991–1992.* Paris, France: Organization for Economic Cooperation and Development Publications.

———. 1992c. *OECD Economic Surveys: Germany, 1991–1992.* Paris, France: Organization for Economic Cooperation and Development Publications.

———. 1993a. *OECD Economic Surveys: Netherlands, 1992–1993.* Paris, France: Organization for Economic Cooperation and Development Publications.

———. 1993b. *OECD Economic Surveys: Norway, 1992–1993.* Paris, France: Organization for Economic Cooperation and Development Publications.

———. 1993c. *OECD Economic Surveys: Spain, 1993.* Paris, France: Organization for Economic Cooperation and Development Publications.

———. 1993d. *The Public Employment Service in Japan, Norway, Spain, and the United Kingdom.* Paris, France: Organization for Economic Cooperation and Development Publications.

———. 1994. "Labour Adjustments and Active Labour Market Policies." In *Jobs Study, 1994.* Paris, France: Organization for Economic Cooperation and Development Publications.

Poterba, James M., and Kim S. Rueben. 1994. "The Distribution of Public Sector Wage Premia: New Evidence Using Quantile Regression Methods." Working Paper 4734. Cambridge, Mass.: National Bureau of Economic Research.

Reynolds, Brigid, and Sean Healy, eds. 1990. *Work, Unemployment, and Job-Creation Policy.* Milltown Park, Dublin, Ireland: Justice Commission, Conference of Major Religious Superiors.

Sawhney, Pawan K., Robert H. Jantzen, and Irwin L. Herrnstadt. 1982. "The Differential Impact of CETA Training." *Industrial and Labor Relations Review* 35 (January): 173–79.

Worden, Kelleen, and Wayne Vroman. 1992. "Job Creation in Germany, Belgium and Sweden." Urban Institute. Unpublished paper.

Zimmerman, Klaus F. 1993. "Labour Responses to Taxes and Benefits in Germany." In *Welfare and Work Incentives: A Northern European Perspective,* edited by A. B. Atkinson and Gunnar V. Mogensen. Oxford, England: Clarendon Press.

Part II

Changes in Modes of Pay

Chapter 4

Profit-Sharing and the Demand for Low-Skill Workers

Douglas L. Kruse

Unemployment is a major difficulty of low-skill workers. Lower levels of education are associated with higher unemployment rates,[1] reflecting in part a higher risk of job displacement among low-educated workers (Seitchik 1991); in addition, after displacement workers with low levels of education have longer periods of joblessness than do more educated workers (Swaim and Podgursky 1991). Policies that lower unemployment and increase job security would have particular benefit for low-skill workers.

One proposed solution to the problem of high unemployment is widespread employee participation in profit-sharing. It has been theorized that profit-sharing decreases unemployment levels and the severity of recessions by increasing the demand for workers. Distinct from the long-standing interest in profit-sharing as a means to motivate employees, improve firm performance, and integrate workers into a market economy (Gilman 1899; Askwith 1926; U.S. Senate 1939), the "share economy" theory, developed primarily by Martin Weitzman (1983, 1984, 1985, 1986), holds that profit-sharing changes the incentives for employers to hire and lay off workers.

There have been more than forty studies in the past fifteen years on both the performance and employment effects of profit-sharing (summarized in Kruse 1993); none, however, has examined the extent and effects of profit-sharing among low-skill workers. Very little information on the relation between profit-sharing and skill levels has been available, since almost all data sources employed are based on firm-level data with little information on the skills and characteristics of individual employees.

Since there is no prior evidence on profit-sharing and low-skill workers, this study focuses on providing new evidence on both the extent and effects of profit-sharing among workers of different skill levels. For the six most recent years of the National Longitudinal Survey-Youth (NLSY), 1988 through 1993, each respondent has been asked whether profit-sharing (among other benefits) is made available to him or her by the principal employer. Among the variety of personal and job information available, skill level can be measured most directly by educational levels, and indirectly by the skill requirements of the jobs held by respondents.

This chapter first examines the prevalence of profit-sharing, along with other benefits and types and levels of pay, by individual and job characteristics. The relationship between profit-sharing, pay levels, and other benefits is assessed next. Finally, the potential effects of profit-sharing on demand for workers is explored by tracing the ultimate disposition of a job, focusing on the risk of layoff. If profit-sharing does have favorable effects on demand for workers, profit-sharing workers should be at lower risk of layoff when their firm's product demand declines. This relationship is examined both for workers overall and for different groups of workers based on skill levels.

Profit-Sharing Theory and Prior Evidence

The theory of the "share economy" predicts that the widespread use of profit-sharing will help inoculate the economy against instability and unemployment (Weitzman 1983, 1984, 1985, 1986). I discuss only the fundamentals of the theory here (with a more complete discussion of firm behavior in Kruse 1993, appendix D). The key element is that firms essentially ignore the profit share when making employment decisions in the short run; instead, they base their decisions only on the fixed wage that must be paid to each worker. If the profit share substitutes in some fashion for the fixed wage, the profit-sharing firm has a stronger incentive to hire and retain workers than does a comparable firm paying a higher fixed wage. A fixed-wage firm paying $10/hour, for example, would lay off workers if a decrease in demand for the firm's products caused the marginal revenue product of labor to fall to $9.50/hour.[2] A profit-sharing firm paying the same average compensation, but with a $9/hour base wage and an average $1/hour profit share, would hold on to workers in the short run since the lowered marginal revenue product of labor still exceeds the base wage paid to workers (therefore making it profitable to retain the worker, even if a portion of those profits go to workers). In a sense, a "cushion" of workers is retained by the profit-sharing firm when product demand declines.

The same incentive that impels the firm to retain workers in bad times also causes it to look hard for workers during normal times. Once the firm establishes its base wage and profit share, it endeavors to hire workers as long as their marginal revenue product exceeds the base wage.

While employers ignore the profit share in their short-run decisions, workers do not. As more workers are hired, the profit share established by the employer must be divided among a larger number of workers, decreasing its value to any one worker. Since workers base their labor supply decisions on total compensation, they are not attracted to firms where the expected compensation falls below the market average. Faced with this labor supply constraint, in the long run such profit-sharing firms adjust their base wages and profit shares so that the expected total compensation to workers equals the marginal revenue product of labor; in the short run, however, profit-sharing firms maintain an incentive to hire any worker as long as the worker's output exceeds the base wage. (As discussed later, the theory may still work if the profit-sharing base wage is no lower than the non-profit-sharing wage, provided the profit-sharing workers are more productive.)

The incentive to hire more workers is the driving force in the share economy theory. In full-employment equilibrium, the compensation and employment levels of fixed-wage and profit-sharing firms are similar (assuming they face the same product market and labor market conditions). If new workers enter the labor market, though, a profit-sharing firm is eager to hire them, while a fixed-wage firm does not want to hire them unless and until the new workers bid down wages sufficiently. An economy of profit-sharing firms, Weitzman claims, "looks very much like a labor-shortage economy. Share firms ever hungry for labor are always on the prowl—cruising around like vacuum cleaners on wheels, searching in nooks and crannies for extra workers to pull in at existing compensation parameter values" (1984, 98–99). The theory concludes that widespread use of profit-sharing not only decreases unemployment but makes an economy more resistant to recession.

The theory has engendered a substantial amount of debate, with objections focusing on resistance by current employees to new hires (Summers 1986); possible disincentives for new capital investment (Summers 1986; Estrin, Grout, and Wadhwani 1987); disincentives for new hiring if the lower average compensation lowers worker productivity (posited by some efficiency wage theories) (Levine 1987, 1989); the sensitivity of worker turnover to compensation changes (Nordhaus 1988); and the possibility that firms will set up "cosmetic" schemes without the desirable properties of "true" profit-sharing if tax incentives are granted for profit-sharing (Estrin, Grout, and Wadhwani 1987).[3]

Prior research has focused on two propositions of the share economy theory:

1. Firms do not view profit-sharing payments as part of the short-run marginal cost of labor in making employment decisions; and
2. Firms that pay part of their compensation in the form of profit shares have greater employment stability than non-profit-sharing firms, particularly with regard to negative demand shocks.

The eighteen empirical studies of these two propositions are summarized in table 4.1. The studies of the first proposition have estimated labor demand equations with separate terms for fixed wages and profit shares to test whether the coefficients are distinct for these two types of compensation.[4] The findings have been mixed: six studies (numbers 2, 3, 5, 13, 14, and 18) have results generally favorable to the share economy theory; three studies (7, 15, and 17) have unfavorable results; and one (10) has mixed results.

Eleven studies have directly measured employment stability or layoffs. It is difficult to implement a full test since there is no simple specification (such as those for standard productivity or labor demand equations) that captures the theoretically predicted employment movements. Rather, the theory predicts a nonlinear relationship that depends (among other things) on the size and direction of the demand shock, the size of the typical profit share, the degree of substitution between the profit share and fixed compensation, and whether the firm is recovering from a prior demand shock (Kruse 1993, 225–33, 245). Lacking information for a full test, most studies have employed simpler and more direct techniques, estimating linear relationships between employment changes and measures of profit-sharing (simple existence, percentage of workers covered, or size of profit share). Such simplifications can provide useful evidence but may in themselves provide disparate results owing to lack of data on the factors theorized to be important.

A number of the existing studies suggest that employment behavior is different under profit-sharing, but there is no simple and clear overall conclusion. Five studies provide generally favorable findings, indicating that greater stability is associated with profit-sharing (1, 4, 7, 9, and 11, although results are not significant in 1); four studies indicate support in some but not all samples (6, 12, 14, and 16); and two studies show little or no support for the stabilizing effects of profit-sharing (2 and 8, the for-

(*Text continues on p. 114.*)

Table 4.1 Studies of Profit-Sharing and Labor Demand

Study	Data Source	Unit of Analysis	Sample size[a]	% with PS[b]	Time Period	Profit-Sharing Measures	Main Results
Disaggregated data							
1. Beil and Neumark 1993	U.S. publicly traded firms with union contracts	Firm	204	8%	1978–1987	Dummy for PS negotiated in union contract	Weakly favorable: Adoption of PS in union contract associated with higher employment growth and lower employment variability, though effects not statistically significant
2. Bradley and Estrin 1992	Large British retail chains	Firm	5	20%	1971–1985 (balanced)	PS dummy and B/W	Mixed: PS firm had higher employment than others, and B/W positively related to employment changes, but similar employment changes over the business cycle
3. Cahuc and Dormont 1992	French manufacturing firms	Firm	565	46%	1986–1989	B/W	Mixed/favorable: B/W negatively related to employment levels if firm effects not included, but not in within-firm specifications

1) U.S. small

(*Table continues on p. 110.*)

Table 4.1 *Continued*

Study	Data Source	Unit of Analysis	Sample size[a]	% with PS[b]	Time Period	Profit-Sharing Measures	Main Results
4. Chelius and Smith 1990	businesses	Firm	2997	31%	1987	PS dummy and B/W (cash and deferred plans)	Generally favorable; PS firms have smaller employment decreases when sales decline; result is stronger for PS dummy than for B/W
	2) Quality of Employment Survey	Persons	404	26%	1977	PS dummy	Weakly favorable: Workers in PS plans less likely to be laid off, but not statistically significant
5. Estrin and Wilson 1989	British metal-working and engineering firms	Firm	52	40%	1978–1982 (balanced)	PS dummy and B/W	Generally favorable: Authors reject hypothesis that PS payments are part of the marginal cost of labor
6. Finseth 1988	U.S. publicly traded manu-facturing firms	Firm	133	54%	1971–1985 (balanced)	PS dummy and B/W (both cash and de-ferred plans)	Mixed: B/W more respon-sive than W to changes in profits; mixed results on stability (PS increases employment when prof-its per employee is used as demand measure)
	French manufac-						

Study	Sample	Unit	N	%	Years	Variables	Findings
7. Fitzroy and Vaughn-Whitehead 1989	turing firms	Firm	116	25%	1983–1985 (balanced)	PS dummy and profit share per worker	Mixed: Profit share per worker negatively related to employment, but cash PS firms maintain higher employment in downturn
8. Florkowski 1994	U.S. publicly traded firms	Firm	443	[c]	1971–1987 (balanced)	PS dummy	Mixed/unfavorable: Pre/post comparisons showed similar stability but higher average employment after adoption; small firms had lower cutbacks for negative shocks and more growth under positive shocks after adoption
9. Gerhart 1991	Exempt employees, U.S. business units	Firm	156	80%[d]	1981–1985 (unbalanced)	B/W, net of human capital and job factors	Favorable: Higher B/W associated with lower variability of exempt employment, controlling for variability of firm performance
10. Jones and Pliskin 1989	British printing, footwear, and clothing firms	Firm	127	87%	1890–1975 (unbalanced)	PS dummy and B/W	Mixed: PS dummy associated with lower employment, but B/W coefficient sensitive to whether measures of worker participation are included
	West German						

(*Table continues on p. 112.*)

Table 4.1 *Continued*

Study	Data Source	Unit of Analysis	Sample size[a]	% with PS[b]	Time Period	Profit-Sharing Measures	Main Results
11. Kraft 1991	U.S. publicly traded firms	Firm	65		1977, 1979	PS dummy	Favorable: PS firms had lower dismissal rate
12. Kruse 1991a	U.S. publicly traded firms	Firm	1383	47% 40%	1971–1985 (balanced)	PS dummy, and percent of worker covered (deferred plans)	Generally favorable: PS associated with more stability in the face of negative demand shocks in manufacturing, but not in nonmanufacturing
13. Kruse 1991b	U.S. publicly traded firms	Firm	568	32%	1980–1986 (unbalanced)	B/W	Generally favorable: PS payments, unlike wages and defined benefit payments, do not appear to be treated as part of marginal cost of labor
14. Kruse 1993	U.S. publicly traded firms	Firm	500	40%	1971–1991 (unbalanced)	PS dummy and B/W (both cash and deferred plans)	Mixed: No general evidence of lower responsiveness to negative demand shocks after adoption of PS, except when PS appeared to substitute for fixed wages/benefits
15. Wadhwani and Wall 1990	British publicly traded firms	Firm	101	21%	1972–1982 (balanced)	PS dummy and B/W	Unfavorable: Both PS measures statistically in-

Study		Time period	Sample size	Conclusion
Aggregate data				
16. Bhargava 1994	Japanese aggregate and British industry data	1955–1986	% of workers covered in UK	Mixed: Employment less variable in Japanese bonus system than in UK, but higher PS coverage within UK industries was not associated with lower variability
				significant, but magnitudes indicate B/W depresses employment more than wages do
17. Estrin, Grout, and Wadhwani 1987	Japanese aggregate data	1959–1983	B/W	Unfavorable: Wages and bonuses have slightly positive, insignificant coefficients when controlling for capital and not output (in contrast to Freeman and Weitzman, 1987)
18. Freeman and Weitzman 1987	Japanese aggregate and industry-level data	1959–1983	B/W	Favorable: Bonus appears to have profit-sharing component and, unlike wages, relates positively to employment (controlling for output changes)

PS = profit-sharing   B/W = profit-sharing bonus/wage   W = wage

[a] Sample size represents number of firms or persons in sample (not total firm-years for panel data).

[b] Percentage of firms or people with profit-sharing at any point in the period studied.

[c] The 443 profit-sharing adopters were compared to industry mean values from an unreported number of other firms.

[d] The percentage is of employees eligible for bonuses in the sample firms.

mer based on analysis of only one profit-sharing firm). As an illustration of the mixed findings, in Kruse (1993) I found no general stabilizing effect of all types of profit-sharing but did find smaller employment decreases in response to downturns among firms where the profit share seemed to substitute for fixed compensation (as assumed by the theory).

No research has focused on the effects of profit-sharing on low-skill workers, but two studies provide indirect evidence. James Chelius and Robert Smith (1990) find that workers in nonsupervisory positions (where low-skill workers are concentrated) were less likely to be laid off if profit-sharing was reported, but the result was not statistically significant (t-statistics were 1.2–1.3). Also, low-skill workers were more likely to be in production/service or technical/clerical jobs than in professional/administrative jobs; in my pre/post comparisons, I found no automatic stabilizing effects of profit-sharing adoption for any of these groups (Kruse 1993).

In sum, previous research has given several findings of support for the stabilizing effects of profit-sharing, but the results have not been uniformly favorable (as might be expected, given the simplified tests and the variety of forms of profit-sharing studied). No research has focused on the prevalence and effects of profit-sharing for low-skill workers.

Dataset and Overall Prevalence of Profit-Sharing

The National Longitudinal Survey-Youth Cohort began in 1979 with interviews of 12,686 youth between the ages of fourteen and twenty-two. This sample has been reinterviewed every year since then, with fifteen years of data available for this study (through 1993). Respondents were first asked questions about profit-sharing and other benefits in 1988 with reference to their primary employer of the preceding week or to their most recent job if not currently employed (provided the respondent usually worked at least twenty hours per week at his or her job and was not self-employed in an unincorporated business). The questions (including only the benefits asked about in each year from 1988 to 1993) were:

> Does/did your employer *make available* to you . . .
> A. medical, surgical, or hospital insurance that covers injuries or major illnesses off the job
> B. life insurance that would cover your death for reasons not connected to your job
> C. dental benefits
> D. maternity/paternity leave that will allow you to go back to your old job or one that pays the same as your old one

E. retirement plan other than Social Security
F. profit-sharing
G. training or educational opportunities including tuition reimbursement
H. company provided or subsidized childcare

An important issue for this study is how respondents interpreted the question about whether their employer "makes available" profit-sharing. The tally may undercount participants in a profit-sharing plan if some plan participants respond "no" in years when there are no employer profits, so that the employer does not "make available" a profit-sharing contribution that year. The results may overcount profit-sharing participants, however, if the employer makes available a plan in which the employee does not participate. This is highly unlikely for most cash and deferred profit-sharing plans, which do not require the employee to give up anything (leading to 100 percent participation). Profit-sharing 401(k) plans, on the other hand, do not have so high a participation rate because the employer contribution is tied to the employee's contribution as well as to firm performance. When employee contributions are required, and the employer's matching contribution is tied to profits, employees may choose not to participate but still count profit-sharing as "available." Across all 401(k) plans, available data indicate that 63 to 85 percent of eligible employees participate (Papke 1995).

How many employees are covered by profit-sharing? Close to one-third of young private-sector employees (not self-employed) report profit-sharing in a given year (32 percent in 1988, 34 percent in 1989 to 1991, and 35 percent in 1992 to 1993) (table 4.2). The proportion drops to about one-fifth (19-21 percent) if one counts only those who report profit-sharing in every year of the job. (For example, if the 1988 job was held for three of the years, profit-sharing availability is reported in each of those years.) This latter number may reflect an undercount of actual plan participants if profit-sharing plans were stopped or started over the job tenure or the participant reports that profit-sharing was not "available" when profits were low and no profit share was distributed by the employer. On the other hand, the higher number probably reflects a significant amount of measurement error, where the employee's responses vary by year with no change in the available benefits or type of pay. The number who report profit-sharing in every year of the job may be seen as an approximate lower bound to the true number who have it available (keeping in mind that "profit-sharing" may be subject to multiple interpretations).

Table 4.2 Prevalence of Reported Profit-Sharing, 1988 to 1993

	1988	1989	1990	1991	1992	1993
Young employees reporting availability of profit-sharing (NLSY)						
1. In given year	32%	34%	34%	34%	35%	35%
2. In every year for job held this year	21	20	19	19	20	21
3. Medium and large firms	28	26		26		29
4. Small firms			17		16	
Employee coverage reported by firms (BLS)						
5. Medium and large firms	18	16		16		17
6. Small private firms			15		16	
7. Profit-linked matches to 401(k) savings/thrift plans[a]	2	3		4		4
Professional/administrative employees						
Young employee reports (NLSY)[b]						
8. In given year	39	42	36	(48[c])	(34[c])	(43[c])
9. In every year for this year's job	23	24	20	(27[c])	(18[c])	(28[c])
Firm reports (BLS)						
10. Medium and large firms	20	15	16	(13[c])		(14[c])
11. Small private firms					(18[c])	

Technical/clerical employees

Young employee reports (NLSY)[b]

12. In given year	51	51	36	(50c)	(36c)	(53c)
13. In every year for this year's job	35	31	21	(29c)	(19c)	(36c)
Firm reports (BLS)						
14. Medium and large firms	21	13		(16c)		(17c)
15. Small private firms			17		(19c)	
Production employees						
Young employee reports (NLSY)[b]						
16. In given year	36	39	20	38	21	42
17. In every year for this year's job	25	24	11	22	13	27
Firm reports (BLS)						
18. Medium and large firms	15	18		18		18
19. Small private firms			13		14	

NLSY: National Longitudinal Survey-Youth Cohort.

BLS: U.S. Department of Labor, Bureau of Labor Statistics, *Survey of Employee Benefits in Medium and Large Firms* (1989, 1990, 1992, 1994) and *Survey of Employee Benefits in Small Private Firms* (1991, 1993).

[a] In the BLS surveys, savings/thrift 401(k) plans (requiring employee contributions) are distinguished from profit-sharing plans (many of which are 401(k)s that allow, but do not require, employee contributions). Some of the savings/thrift plans, though, use profit-linked matches to employee contributions; the estimates are provided in row 7 (derived from published data).

[b] To compare with BLS, the NLSY occupational data are for small firms in 1990 and 1992, and medium/large firms in other years.

[c] BLS occupational categories were changed in 1991; the "professional/administrative" number after 1990 (in parentheses) includes technical workers, while the "technical/clerical" number is for clerical/sales. The NLSY categories are changed to provide comparable estimates for these years.

These employee reports can be compared to the employee coverage reported by firms in the employee benefits surveys of the Bureau of Labor Statistics (U.S. Department of Labor, Bureau of Labor Statistics 1989 to 1994). This comparison (see table 4.2) shows that the prevalence of profit-sharing reported by young employees is higher than employer-reported coverage in medium and large firms (more than one hundred employees) but is very similar in small private firms.[5] The gap in estimates within medium and large firms may indicate either a higher prevalence of profit-sharing among young employees or a more expansive definition of profit-sharing among employees.

The substantial sample of young employees reporting profit-sharing provides a useful source for examining its incidence and effects. A limitation is that nothing is known about the form of profit-sharing—to what kind of policy or plan the employee may be referring, and the profit-sharing formula (if any) and rules for allocation of the share to employees. This information would clearly be useful for examining the effects of profit-sharing; for example, some employers maintain plans they call "profit-sharing" in which the employer contribution is simply a fixed percentage of participant pay, a formula that does not appear to change the employer's perceived marginal cost of labor or the incentives for hiring or laying off employees. This problem is not peculiar to employee-reported data, however, since most firm-based datasets have not included data on profit-sharing formulas and allocation rules; most empirical tests have consequently relied on the presence or absence of profit-sharing as reported by the firm. Unlike the firm-based datasets, the National Longitudinal Survey provides a wealth of information on the personal and job characteristics of profit-sharing and non-profit-sharing employees, to which we now turn.

Pay Levels and Types, and Personal and Job Characteristics

What is the skill level of individuals in this dataset, and how are they paid? Table 4.3 provides a breakdown of the 6,720 private-sector employees in 1989 (representing an estimated 18.5 million employees); this year was chosen owing to the additional questions in 1989 about the schooling and training required of respondents to get their jobs. The table provides the average hourly pay and the incidence of profit-sharing, performance-linked pay, and benefits, broken down by education levels and skill requirements for jobs.

(Text continues on p. 125.)

Table 4.3 Education Levels, Skill Requirements for Current Jobs, and Pay Levels and Types for Private-Sector Employees, 1989

| | Sample Size | | | | Pay Levels (Mean) and Performance-Linked Pay (% Covered) | | | | | | | |
	Un-weighted (1)	Weighted (Millions) (2)	Weighted (%) (3)	Average Hourly Pay (4)	Profit-Sharing 1989 (Every Year)[a] (5)		Bonuses (6)	Commis-sions (7)	Piece Rates (8)	Stock Options (9)	Tips (10)	Any Perfor-mance-Linked (11)
Overall	6,720	18.5	100.0%	$ 9.68	34.0%	(20.2)	14.8%	7.5%	2.6%	1.4%	3.6%	48.9%
Education level												
<12 years	1,082	1.9	10.3	7.16	19.7	(12.0)	8.3	2.6	4.8	0.7	4.6	34.4
12 years	3,073	8.6	46.5	8.57	32.1	(19.5)	11.7	5.7	3.6	1.0	3.7	45.6
13–15 years	1,396	3.9	21.4	9.95	36.4	(20.1)	16.6	10.4	1.5	1.7	5.1	54.4
16 years	820	2.9	15.9	13.06	43.8	(27.1)	23.2	12.7	0.7	1.6	1.5	60.4
>16 years	304	1.1	6.0	14.11	39.6	(21.7)	22.9	6.6	0.0	3.7	2.4	54.5
Schooling req. to get job												
None	774	1.5	8.4	7.24	15.3	(9.2)	9.2	4.9	7.1	0.7	8.0	36.5
Grade school (1–8 grades)	264	0.5	2.8	6.69	28.5	(17.5)	8.0	1.0	6.8	0.0	6.2	41.5
Some high school (9–11 grades)	884	1.9	10.6	7.18	25.7	(15.0)	8.6	3.1	3.6	0.6	7.6	39.4
High school (12 grades)	2,860	8.1	44.2	8.97	35.9	(21.2)	12.5	7.3	2.7	1.4	3.7	49.7

(Table continues on p. 120.)

Table 4.3 *Continued*

| | Sample Size | | | Pay Levels (Mean) and Performance-Linked Pay (% Covered) | | | | | | | |
	Un-weighted (1)	Weighted (Millions) (2)	Weighted (%) (3)	Average Hourly Pay (4)	Profit-Sharing 1989 (Every Year)[a] (5)	Bonuses (6)	Commissions (7)	Piece Rates (8)	Stock Options (9)	Tips (10)	Any Performance-Linked (11)
Some college/ associate degree	1,050	3.2	17.5	10.63	39.2 (20.7)	18.7	10.1	0.7	1.1	1.4	54.0
College degree	690	2.6	14.0	14.20	43.3 (28.8)	25.6	11.1	0.0	2.7	0.4	58.1
Graduate/prof. degree	123	0.5	2.5	16.36	33.3 (18.0)	23.2	5.6	2.2	3.5	1.1	48.8
Work exp. or training req. to get job											
Yes	3,919	11.3	61.2	10.44	34.3 (20.2)	16.4	8.7	1.8	1.6	3.2	50.2
No	2,795	7.2	38.8	8.54	33.5 (20.1)	12.3	5.7	3.9	1.0	4.3	46.8
No, and no college req.	2,317	0.1	30.3	7.44	31.2 (18.2)	9.4	4.6	4.7	0.9	5.3	44.9
Type of exp./training req.											
Trade, voc., bus., tech. school	1,001	2.9	15.9	10.49	32.2 (19.3)	15.6	8.7	1.8	1.7	2.7	48.4

Apprenticeship	300	1.0	5.3	11.98	30.7 (15.7)	16.7	9.6	3.3	1.4	1.5	47.0
Formal co. training program	606	1.7	9.2	11.18	44.1 (22.9)	23.6	14.0	1.2	3.9	2.6	61.1
On-the-job training/exp.											
With cur. employer	2,092	6.2	33.3	10.49	36.7 (21.9)	17.3	7.8	1.8	2.4	2.7	52.0
With prev. employer	2,089	6.2	33.7	10.52	35.5 (21.0)	19.0	8.5	1.6	1.6	3.2	52.0
Armed forces training program	69	0.2	1.1	12.44	44.0 (27.4)	14.6	8.0	0.0	0.0	3.3	53.2
Other	188	0.6	3.2	11.65	31.3 (15.6)	21.6	16.6	0.2	0.5	2.5	51.0
Months of training req. to become fully qualified to do job											
≤1 month	2,239	5.0	27.2	7.17	25.8 (15.8)	9.1	5.1	3.7	0.7	8.1	42.8
2–6 months	1,796	4.8	26.3	9.15	37.7 (22.4)	13.0	8.4	2.6	0.9	2.1	50.9
7–12 months	951	2.9	15.7	10.06	37.0 (21.5)	16.1	8.6	1.7	1.4	2.4	50.3
>12 months	1,688	5.7	30.8	12.40	36.7 (21.7)	21.0	8.5	2.0	2.3	1.6	52.5

(Table continues on p. 122.)

Table 4.3 Continued

| | Benefits Available | | | | | | | | | |
	Total Number (Mean) (12)	Health Insurance (% Covered)[a] (13)	Life Insurance (% Covered)[a] (14)	Dental Insurance (% Covered)[a] (15)	Paid Vacation (% Covered)[a] (16)	Paid Sick Leave (% Covered)[a] (17)	Maternity/ Paternity Leave (% Covered)[a] (18)	Retirement Plan (% Covered)[a] (19)	Child Care (% Covered)[a] (20)	Training/ Educational Opportunities (% Covered)[a] (21)
Overall	4.9	78.0% (69.8)	65.9% (53.6)	51.7% (42.1)	80.2% (71.7)	60.6% (44.6)	62.8% (37.0)	53.9% (41.4)	5.0% (1.6)	47.5% (32.7)
Education Level										
<12 years	3.1	60.6 (52.2)	44.7 (34.2)	33.0 (24.2)	68.4 (59.6)	36.0 (24.9)	46.6 (26.2)	32.2 (20.56)	2.3 (0.7)	23.3 (12.6)
12 years	4.7	76.3 (68.0)	63.2 (50.4)	48.6 (39.0)	79.2 (70.6)	53.6 (38.9)	61.9 (36.0)	51.6 (39.2)	3.7 (1.4)	41.3 (27.6)
13–15 years	5.3	81.6 (72.1)	69.9 (56.1)	56.9 (46.2)	82.0 (72.1)	66.5 (50.6)	67.5 (42.7)	57.8 (43.0)	5.5 (1.7)	53.3 (36.6)
16 years	6	87.4 (81.6)	79.5 (69.6)	63.2 (54.8)	88.3 (81.5)	83.0 (62.5)	71.8 (42.4)	65.4 (55.9)	8.2 (2.8)	68.2 (52.8)
>16 years	5.8	87.8 (79.5)	77.8 (66.2)	62.5 (52.7)	85.0 (76.2)	83.5 (60.0)	61.2 (31.2)	68.6 (55.5)	10.7 (1.8)	66.4 (46.2)
Schooling req. to get job										
None	2.7	52.3 (43.9)	38.9 (29.7)	25.6 (18.8)	58.0 (49.6)	29.8 (21.0)	40.0 (22.4)	26.4 (17.2)	2.7 (1.7)	17.8 (11.2)
Grade school	3	57.6 (53.4)	43.4 (35.6)	29.9 (25.6)	60.1 (55.8)	27.5 (17.5)	45.0 (25.5)	35.2 (25.8)	2.1 0.0	21.2 (14.6)
Some high school	3.3	62.4 (53.5)	45.3 (35.3)	33.6 (26.0)	70.7 (60.0)	35.6 (25.4)	46.5 (27.0)	36.5 (24.2)	2.1 (1.1)	24.2 (12.8)
High school	4.9	80.0 (71.2)	67.2 (53.6)	52.7 (42.3)	81.4 (72.8)	57.8 (42.6)	64.5 (37.1)	54.5 (40.5)	3.8 (1.3)	44.1 (28.1)
Some college/ associate degree	6	86.1 (78.4)	76.1 (62.3)	62.7 (51.4)	88.9 (79.9)	79.3 (58.8)	75.4 (49.3)	63.7 (52.0)	8.2 (2.4)	65.0 (47.3)
College degree	6.6	94.2 (88.4)	87.3 (77.9)	70.6 (63.0)	92.5 (85.4)	90.7 (69.1)	74.6 (43.7)	75.2 (64.9)	8.9 (2.4)	78.2 (63.2)

Graduate/prof. degree	5.7	88.6 (80.5)	75.5 (61.2)	58.9 (47.0)	87.9 (79.1)	86.1 (62.7)	61.0 (32.9)	61.1 (50.5)	11.9 (2.1)	66.1 (45.6)
Work exp. or training req. to get job										
Yes	5.2	81.1 (73.3)	69.3 (56.9)	54.8 (45.1)	82.5 (74.4)	65.5 (49.0)	65.4 (38.3)	55.6 (43.2)	5.4 (1.9)	53.0 (37.6)
No	4.5	73.2 (64.5)	60.5 (48.5)	46.9 (37.4)	76.7 (67.6)	53.1 (38.0)	58.9 (35.1)	51.1 (38.8)	4.5 (1.3)	39.0 (25.3)
No, and no college req.	4	69.9 (59.9)	54.9 (43.3)	42.0 (33.0)	73.7 (64.8)	45.0 (32.2)	56.1 (33.3)	46.3 (33.6)	2.9 (1.1)	30.8 (18.1)
Type of exp./training req.										
Trade, voc., bus., tech. school	5.2	81.4 (72.9)	68.0 (54.3)	55.4 (44.8)	82.2 (74.2)	63.6 (48.4)	64.3 (38.4)	55.2 (43.6)	4.7 (1.8)	57.4 (42.8)
Apprenticeship	4.3	77.9 (66.9)	63.6 (45.2)	47.7 (35.3)	69.4 (60.6)	53.8 (40.2)	49.2 (21.2)	50.0 (31.5)	2.9 (1.1)	48.2 (30.3)
Formal co. program	6.3	90.0 (82.8)	83.6 (72.7)	67.9 (59.5)	90.1 (82.7)	78.1 (58.3)	75.9 (44.7)	71.5 (59.5)	10.5 (3.4)	69.7 (54.9)
On-the-job training/exp.										
With cur. employer	5.5	83.1 (76.1)	72.1 (60.3)	57.9 (48.0)	85.7 (77.3)	68.5 (50.2)	69.1 (39.6)	60.1 (47.7)	5.6 (1.5)	56.6 (40.9)
With prev. employer	5.2	80.9 (73.7)	69.5 (57.6)	53.8 (43.9)	83.7 (76.3)	67.9 (51.6)	65.7 (38.9)	53.5 (40.7)	5.6 (2.0)	52.0 (36.7)

(*Table continues on p. 124.*)

Table 4.3 *Continued*

| | | Benefits Available | | | | | | | | |
	Total Number (Mean) (12)	Health Insurance (% Covered)[a] (13)	Life Insurance (% Covered)[a] (14)	Dental Insurance (% Covered)[a] (15)	Paid Vacation (% Covered)[a] (16)	Paid Sick Leave (% Covered)[a] (17)	Maternity/Paternity Leave (% Covered)[a] (18)	Retirement Plan (% Covered)[a] (19)	Child Care (% Covered)[a] (20)	Training/Educational Opportunities (% Covered)[a] (21)
Armed forces training program	6.3	97.1 (90.9)	79.0 (67.4)	81.4 (73.5)	89.6 (80.9)	74.8 (54.4)	57.2 (25.9)	70.0 (53.2)	6.9 (0.3)	67.0 (52.4)
Other	5.4	82.4 (73.9)	77.1 (60.9)	53.3 (44.4)	81.8 (71.5)	69.7 (57.9)	69.7 (39.2)	52.9 (42.6)	9.9 (4.4)	54.8 (37.2)
Months of training req. to be fully qualified to do job										
≤1 month	3.7	65.0 (56.4)	50.3 (39.6)	40.2 (32.3)	69.6 (61.1)	44.1 (32.7)	55.4 (33.6)	40.2 (28.6)	3.6 (1.1)	28.9 (17.1)
2–6 months	5.3	81.4 (73.7)	69.9 (57.1)	56.0 (46.1)	83.5 (75.1)	63.8 (48.3)	69.6 (43.9)	59.0 (45.2)	5.6 (1.9)	50.6 (34.9)
7–12 months	5.5	84.5 (76.9)	73.2 (60.6)	57.5 (48.4)	86.3 (77.9)	71.0 (52.2)	67.5 (40.0)	58.2 (46.5)	5.7 (1.9)	55.0 (39.3)
>12 months	5.4	84.2 (76.2)	73.4 (60.6)	55.8 (44.8)	84.3 (75.8)	67.9 (49.0)	61.2 (32.7)	59.8 (48.0)	5.6 (1.8)	58.3 (41.7)

[a] First number is percentage reporting benefit in 1989, while number in parentheses is percentage reporting it in every year for job held in 1989.

Education levels are strongly associated not only with pay levels but with types of pay. Profit-sharing is less common for those who have not completed high school: only 20 percent report it in 1989, and only 12 percent report it in each year of the 1989 job, a prevalence that is half that of those with four or more years of college (column 5). Performance-based bonuses, commissions, and stock options are also much more common among those with more education, while piece rates and tips are more common for those with less education.[6] Overall, more than half of those who have attended college report some form of performance-linked pay in 1989 (profit-sharing or one of the individual incentives), compared to only one-third (34 percent) of those who have not completed high school (column 11). Education is also strongly associated with the availability of employee benefits: those who have not attended any college are less likely to receive each of the nine benefits listed in table 4.3 (columns 12 to 20), with the biggest gaps for retirement plans, paid sick leave, and opportunities for training or more education.[7]

Required schooling, experience, and/or training are potential measures of the job-relevant skills and experience of young employees. The jobs with higher schooling requirements follow (not surprisingly) the pattern associated with higher levels of attained education: higher pay and benefit levels; higher likelihood of profit-sharing, bonuses, commissions, and stock options; and lower likelihood of piece rates or tips. This same pattern prevails for jobs that require "work experience or special training" (on top of regular schooling), except in the case of profit-sharing, for which there is only a small and nonsignificant difference in the prevalence. The prevalence of profit-sharing does not differ notably by the type of experience or training required.

The reported length of time it takes an average new person to become fully trained and qualified to do his or her job (on top of regular schooling) is also strongly related to pay levels, bonuses, and stock options; for other pay types and benefits, however, the relationship is discontinuous, with few differences among jobs requiring more than one month of training. For example, for jobs requiring one month or less of training, only 26 percent of employees report profit-sharing, while the prevalence is close to 37 percent for each category representing more than one month of training.

Table 4.4 focuses on profit-sharing, examining its prevalence according to a variety of additional demographic and job characteristics. A clear conclusion is that profit-sharing is not randomly distributed, being less common among those who are black or Hispanic, separated

(*Text continues on p. 130.*)

Table 4.4 Prevalence of Profit-Sharing, by Demographic and Job Characteristics, for Private-Sector Employees, 1989

| | Sample Size | | % Reporting Profit-Sharing (Weighted) | |
	Unweighted (1)	Weighted (Millions) (2)	In 1989 (3)	In Every Year for Job Held in 1989 (4)
Overall	6,720	18.5	34.0%	20.2
Gender				
Male	3,662	10.4	34.7	20.5
Female	3,058	8.1	33.2	19.7
Race				
Black	1,628	1.9	29.5	18.6
Hispanic	1,124	0.8	32.7	19.4
Other	3,968	15.8	34.7	20.4
Marital status				
Married, sp. present	3,319	9.9	35.9	21.7
Separated/divorced	957	2.4	28.6	17.6
Single	2,444	6.2	33.2	18.7
Family poverty status				
In poverty last year	656	1.3	18.4	10.3
Not in poverty last year	4,913	14.5	36.5	21.8

Location				
Northeast	1,209	3.7	34.6	20.2
North Central	1,583	5.5	35.7	21.8
South	2,601	6.1	33.5	19.2
West	1,277	3.2	32.1	19.8
Rural	1,369	3.7	31.1	18.2
Urban	5,201	14.7	34.9	20.8
Tenure with employer				
6 months or less	1,454	3.7	22.7	15.1
6 months to 1 year	916	2.3	30.6	20.7
1 to 2 years	1,176	3.1	33.2	17.1
2 to 5 years	1,763	5.0	38.6	22.3
More than 5 years	1,346	4.1	40.5	23.9
Establishment size				
10 employees or fewer	1,655	4.8	21.9	11.2
11–50 employees	1,912	5.3	29.4	18.0
51–100 employees	715	1.8	39.9	26.8
101–500 employees	1,328	3.5	45.7	28.1
More than 500	933	2.7	46.9	27.0
Employer has other locations				
No	2,261	6.3	20.4	10.1
Yes	4,438	12.2	41.2	25.0

(*Table continues on p. 128.*)

Table 4.4 *Continued*

| | Sample Size | | % Reporting Profit-Sharing (Weighted) | |
	Unweighted (1)	Weighted (Millions) (2)	In 1989 (3)	In Every Year for Job Held in 1989 (4)
Occupation				
White-collar	3,329	10.1	41.7	24.9
Managerial	625	2.0	43.8	24.6
Professional	503	1.7	43.9	19.6
Technical	263	0.9	40.3	22.0
Sales	777	2.4	42.2	26.7
Clerical	1,160	3.1	43.9	27.2
Blue-collar	3,385	8.3	24.7	14.4
Service	917	2.1	16.8	9.3
Farming	122	0.3	19.8	8.2
Precision production/crafts	815	2.4	26.0	16.3
Operators, fabricators	769	1.7	33.6	20.2
Transportation, moving	371	0.9	31.2	18.3
Laborers	388	0.9	17.5	8.2
Industry				
Agriculture	108	0.3	30.1	11.9
Mining	43	0.2	29.2	19.8

Construction	502	1.5	16.3	9.7
Durable manufacturing	742	1.9	42.4	25.6
Nondurable manufacturing	919	2.7	45.9	28.9
Transportation	259	0.7	39.3	18.0
Communications	111	0.3	43.1	29.5
Utilities	86	0.3	40.2	30.9
Wholesale trade	292	0.8	42.2	26.8
Retail trade	1,263	3.3	32.3	18.8
Finance, insurance, real estate	519	1.6	49.0	30.8
Services				
Business	385	1.0	36.6	21.7
Health	598	1.6	21.1	8.6
Other	884	2.5	21.0	12.1
Union contract coverage				
Covered	965	2.4	32.6	17.5
Not covered	5,653	15.9	34.4	20.6

Notes: The year 1989 was chosen owing to availability of data on education/training requirements for current job (see table 4.1). Patterns are very similar for other years. The differences within each category are all statistically significant at $p < .05$, except for the union/nonunion difference in column 7 ($p = .098$).

or divorced, from a poverty household, or from small or single-estab-lishment companies. White-collar workers are more likely than blue-collar workers to report that profit-sharing is available, particularly in managerial, sales, and clerical occupations. Also, the prevalence differs notably by industry, with the highest prevalence in the manufacturing, communications, utilities, and finance industries. Perhaps surprisingly, given that unions have often resisted profit-sharing plans, there is not a strong difference according to whether one is covered by a union contract.[8]

In sum, profit-sharing appears to be more common among highly skilled workers (those with higher education, tenure, and months of training required to become fully qualified for their jobs). This may re-flect either supply or demand factors. On the supply side, workers with high incomes tend to be less risk-averse and more willing to accept vari-ability in a portion of their pay.[9] On the demand side, highly skilled workers may be more likely to occupy jobs that depend on employee dis-cretion, jobs for which it is in the employer's interest to motivate higher performance (additional effort, cooperation, care, and so on) by tying pay to organizational outcomes. While profit-sharing is less common among low-skill workers, it may nonetheless have favorable effects on the employment of low-skill workers (for example, by increasing or sta-bilizing the employment of such workers).

Relationship of Profit-Sharing to Pay and Other Benefits

The theory that profit-sharing increases demand for workers assumes that the profit share substitutes, at least to some extent, for fixed wages and benefits, thereby lowering the firm's perceived short-run marginal cost of labor (see chapter 5). Measuring whether such substitution does take place is not a simple matter. Several past studies of the relationship of pay to profit-sharing have found that workers who share profits also receive a higher fixed wage, so that the profit share appears to be pure "gravy" on top of the wage (Mitchell, Lewin, and Lawler 1990; Hart and Hubler 1991; Hubler 1993; Carstensen, Gerlach, and Hubler 1992).[10] It is possible, however, that profit-sharing workers would command even higher wages and benefits if profit-sharing were not present, as sug-gested by similar findings for other benefits. For example, the frequent finding that workers receiving pensions also receive equivalent or higher wages has generally not been taken as a refutation of the theory of com-pensating differentials but as an indication of data problems in measuring worker ability or job characteristics (Smith and Ehrenberg 1983; Mitchell and Pozzebon 1986; Gustman and Steinmeier 1993, 1995; Even and MacPherson 1990).

The profit share may also partially substitute for a fixed wage, without the fixed wage being lower than among non-profit-sharing workers, if the profit share rewards higher average work effort and productivity in profit-sharing companies. If, for example, average productivity goes up by 4 to 5 percent when profit-sharing is implemented (as suggested by past research, summarized in Kruse 1993), the extra worker effort, information-sharing, and so on, may be rewarded through the profit share; consequently, the (unchanged) fixed wage has declined in relation to the effort expended, and the profit share has substituted for the fixed wage in rewarding total effort. In this case the profit share may still provide a cushion to absorb demand shocks without worker layoffs.

What are the pay and benefit levels of profit-sharers compared to non-profit-sharers? Table 4.5 provides an overview for this sample. Those with profit-sharing have access, on average, to more benefits (other than profit-sharing) than those who do not (columns 1 and 2). This relationship exists not just in the overall sample but within each of the breakdowns presented (by education, job requirements, and broad occupation). Similarly, the mean hourly pay of profit-sharers is consistently higher across each of the breakdowns (columns 3 and 4).

The differences in pay and benefits may represent different personal or job characteristics—in particular, as seen in table 4.4, profit-sharing is more common in white-collar occupations, which also tend to have higher pay and benefits. Columns 5 to 8 of table 4.5 present the relationship of profit-sharing to pay, controlling for these other characteristics.[11] Cross-sectional results are provided in column 5, showing that profit-sharers have, on average, 5.5 percent higher pay than non-profit-sharers.[12] To control for potentially higher ability not captured in the observable characteristics, job changers were tracked to examine the change in pay associated with joining or dropping out of profit-sharing.[13] The profit-sharing estimate is still positive, indicating average pay gains for those joining a profit-sharing firm and pay losses for those leaving such a firm.[14] These estimates vary by educational level, job requirements, and occupation, but almost all are positive.

These estimates show that profit-sharing is typically associated with higher pay; as noted, however, those who receive higher benefits often receive higher pay as well. In addition, the higher pay may reflect other types of incentives. The relationship of pay to profit-sharing after controlling for pay's relationship to other benefits and individual incentives

Table 4.5 Pay Levels for Profit Sharers and Non-Profit-Sharers, by Education/Training and Job Characteristics, 1989

| | Total Number of Benefits Available | | Mean Hourly Pay | | Pay Difference Associated with Profit-Sharing | | | |
| | | | | | Controlling for Standard Determinants | | Also Controlling for Other Pay Types, Benefits | |
	No Profit-Sharing in 1989 (1)	Profit-Sharing in 1989 (2)	No Profit Sharing in 1989 (3)	Profit-Sharing in 1989 (4)	1989 Cross-Section (5)	Job Changers (6)	1989 Cross-Section (7)	Job Changers (8)
Overall	3.9[a]	6.7	$8.60[a]	$10.07	5.5%[a]	3.6%[a]	−0.3%	−0.5%
Education								
Less than 12 years	2.5[a]	5.7	6.87[a]	7.55	1.8	7.2[a]	−4.5	2.6
12 years	3.7[a]	6.6	7.71[a]	9.06	8.7[a]	1.7	2.0	−2.6
13–15 years	4.4[a]	6.9	9.25	9.70	1.5	4.5[a]	−4.3[a]	0.6
16 years	5.4[a]	7.1	12.85	13.80	4.9	2.2	0.3	−0.8
More than 16 years	5.3[a]	7.0	14.07	15.28	9.1	11.0[a]	7.8	7.2
Schooling required for job								
Less than high school	2.4[a]	5.7	6.59[a]	7.59	6.1[a]	0.4	−0.7	−1.2
High school degree	4.0[a]	6.7	8.32[a]	9.06	3.4[a]	3.1	−2.6	0.8
At least some college	5.7[a]	7.2	11.89	12.14	3.4	4.8	−0.5	1.6
Experience/training required for job								
Yes	4.2[a]	6.8	9.58[a]	10.62	2.1	1.4	−2.9[a]	−2.8

No	3.4[a]	6.5	7.29[a]	9.23	10.0[a]	5.9	3.0[a]	1.4
No college required	3.0[a]	6.3	6.57[a]	8.22	10.2[a]	6.3[a]	2.6	1.7
Months of training to be fully qualified for job								
One month or less	2.8[a]	6.4	6.47[a]	8.02	6.2[a]	−12.2[a]	0.4	−16.0[a]
2–6 months	4.4[a]	6.8	8.24[a]	9.32	6.4[a]	3.8	−0.2	0.1
7–12 months	4.5[a]	6.9	9.52	9.97	0.8	5.0	−4.9[a]	0.4
More than 12 months	4.5[a]	6.8	11.79	12.83	2.1	5.1	−1.5	0.5
Occupation								
White-collar	4.9[a]	7.0	9.92[a]	10.75	4.4[a]	2.3	−1.0	−1.4
Managerial/professional	5.5[a]	7.0	12.45	13.10	4.1	2.4	−0.2	−0.5
Technical/sales/clerical	4.5[a]	6.9	8.55[a]	9.64	4.6[a]	2.3	−1.5	−1.9
Blue-collar	3.1[a]	6.2	7.60[a]	8.94	7.6[a]	4.9[a]	0.7	0.6
Service	2.6[a]	6.2	6.26[a]	7.71	8.2[a]	2.0	1.2	−2.2
Precision production/ crafts	3.1[a]	6.1	9.79[a]	10.69	−3.5	5.7	−0.8	1.2
Other blue-collar	3.3[a]	6.2	7.32[a]	8.52	8.8[a]	5.8[a]	1.3	1.5

Notes: Columns 5 and 7 represent percentage difference in pay of profit-sharers from non-profit-sharers. In both columns, controls are present for education, sex, race, tenure, and experience and their squares, union coverage, establishment size, and thirty-five occupation and fifteen industry dummies. In column 7, additional controls comprise five individual incentive systems and nine other benefits. Columns 6 and 8 represent percentage difference in pay associated with change in profit-sharing for those who changed jobs in the period. Column 6 includes controls for firing or layoff from previous job and changes in union coverage, establishment size, tenure and its square and averge occupation and industry earnings, while column 8 also includes controls for changes in the nine other benefits.

[a] Difference associated with profit-sharing is significant at $p < .05$.

is explored in columns 7 and 8. There it can be seen that, both in the cross-sectional and longitudinal estimates, profit-sharers are estimated to have no higher pay than non-profit-sharers with equivalent benefits who are paid in other ways.[15] The estimates again vary by educational level, job requirements, and occupation; there is no clear pattern, however, indicating that the relationship of pay to profit-sharing varies systematically with education or skill requirements.

Therefore profit-sharers appear to have higher average pay, and more access to other benefits, than comparable workers who do not have profit-sharing. If one compares, however, profit-sharing workers to comparable workers with similar pay types and access to benefits, the positive relationship disappears, making it appear that profit-sharing workers cost no more or less (on average) than other workers with similar pay types and benefits. Neither comparison supports the idea that profit-sharing is typically a substitution for fixed pay or benefits (as assumed by the share economy theory).

This conclusion should not close the door, however, on attempts to examine the demand effects of profit-sharing. First, as noted earlier, data problems prevent the researcher from knowing what the pay or benefit levels would be in the absence of profit-sharing; while this study controlled for fixed individual effects by examining job changers, it is very possible that other characteristics of the job, or of the match between the employee and the old and new jobs, are contaminating the estimates. Second, it is worth noting that employers are very unlikely to simply give away profits, expecting nothing in return. The employer may be seeking to economize on other wages and benefits or "buying" from the employees increased attachment, willingness to share ideas, efforts to work hard or cooperate with others, and so forth. In the latter case, if profit-sharing is successful, the workers are more valuable to the company and the profit share becomes a part of compensation that substitutes for fixed wages/benefits in rewarding this higher value. Finally, even if profit-sharing does not, on average, substitute for fixed wages and benefits, it is nonetheless possible to examine situations where it may substitute and the theoretical predictions apply.

Disposition of Jobs

If profit-sharing does increase demand for workers, one would see both increased incentives to hire workers and decreased incentives to lay them off. This study focuses on the latter, since there is no straightforward way to compare the hiring probabilities and profit-sharing status of jobs that have not yet been filled; in contrast, the profit-sharing status of filled jobs is known whether or not a layoff is subsequently made.

Two methods are used here to analyze layoff probabilities. The first is to examine the ultimate disposition of all jobs held in 1989 (the year when questions were asked about schooling and training requirements for jobs), measuring the determinants of layoffs, quits, firings, and job retention until the end of the period. The second method is to use survival analysis to examine the layoff hazard across the life of a job, using only new jobs. Layoff probabilities are clearly affected by the firm's product market, and it is possible that the firms offering profit-sharing may be particularly stable or unstable. These comparisons control for several employer characteristics along with occupation and industry effects, but there is no means of assessing the employer's demand shocks, or stability, in the absence of profit-sharing.[16]

Tabulations of the disposition of the 1989 jobs are displayed in table 4.6, with breakdowns according to education, job requirements, broad occupation, and tenure. Close to one-tenth (10.5 percent) of the workers were laid off in the subsequent five years, while four times as many quit (41.1 percent); a small portion were fired (3.6 percent), and about one-third retained the job through 1993 (35.7 percent).[17] There were significant differences by profit-sharing status: profit-sharers were only two-thirds as likely as non-profit-sharers to be laid off (9 percent compared to 13.1 percent, in columns 5 and 6) and much more likely to maintain the job (36.8 percent compared to 24.5 percent, in columns 11 and 12).

Higher levels of education appear to decrease the chance of layoff (column 1). Profit-sharing is associated with significantly lower layoff rates for those who have not completed four years of college, but not for college graduates (columns 5 and 6). The breakdowns by job requirements, however, do not permit easy generalizations. Profit-sharers are less likely than non-profit-sharers to be laid off whether or not the job requires special experience or training, but the breakdown by months of training required shows a significant difference only for jobs requiring more than one month of training to be fully qualified. The profit-sharing difference in layoff rates is greatest for blue-collar workers and nonexistent for managers/professionals. While those who have been with their employer less than one year as of 1989 are at greater risk of layoff, both high-tenure and low-tenure profit-sharing workers are significantly less likely to be laid off.

Table 4.6 Disposition of 1989 Job over Five-Year Period, by Skill Level and Job Characteristics

| | Full Sample | | | | Comparison of Non-Profit Sharers (NPS) to Profit-Sharers (PS)[b] | | | | | | | |
| | | | | | Laid Off | | Fired | | Quit | | Kept Job | |
	Laid Off (1)	Fired (2)	Quit (3)	Kept Job (4)	NPS (5)	PS (6)	NPS (7)	PS (8)	NPS (9)	PS (10)	NPS (11)	PS (12)
Overall												
Number	760	292	2,692	1,909	542	118	204	58	1,787	517	702	402
Percentage (weighted)	10.5%	3.6%	41.1%	35.7%	13.1%[a]	9.0%	4.6%[a]	3.5%	47.3%[a]	42.4%	24.5%[a]	36.8%
Education												
Less than 12 years	15.5	5.7	44.7	23.3	17.1[a]	11.0	6.3	7.9	48.0	48.7	17.4[a]	23.3
12 years	12.0	4.2	38.4	36.3	14.4[a]	10.3	5.4[a]	3.1	44.2[a]	40.8	25.5[a]	35.9
13–15 years	9.9	3.3	42.3	35.6	12.6[a]	8.9	4.1	3.4	48.5	47.5	24.8[a]	33.1
16 years	6.8	1.6	43.8	40.5	8.9	7.1	1.3[a]	3.7	53.5[a]	42.2	26.7[a]	41.7
More than 16 years	2.8	1.4	43.6	41.1	4.3	3.8	1.9	2.1	54.7[a]	32.1	26.1[a]	50.0
Schooling required for job												
Less than high school	15.3	5.2	46.6	23.1	16.5	14.8	6.1	4.4	52.6[a]	42.5	14.6[a]	26.4
High school degree	11.2	4.2	38.3	37.3	13.9[a]	8.4	5.1	4.3	43.3	42.7	27.2[a]	35.6
At least some college	6.3	1.8	41.0	42.2	8.5	7.5	2.2	2.3	47.9[a]	42.3	30.2[a]	41.5
Experience/training required for job												
Yes	9.7	3.5	40.8	37.1	12.5[a]	8.1	4.1	4.0	46.2	44.5	27.0[a]	35.0
No	11.7	3.8	41.4	33.7	14.1[a]	10.4	5.3[a]	2.6	48.8[a]	39.0	20.8[a]	33.5
No college required	13.2	4.6	40.2	32.8	14.9	12.5	6.2[a]	3.0	47.9[a]	38.7	21.0[a]	35.9

Months of training to be fully qualified for job											
One month or less	11.9	5.3	45.8	28.1	12.7	13.0	6.4[a]	4.3	53.8[a]	38.5	17.2[a]	34.3
2–6 months	11.2	3.3	42.1	35.0	14.0	8.9	4.0	3.0	48.6	44.4	25.5[a]	33.5
7–12 months	10.2	2.4	38.7	38.5	13.5	7.6	3.1	3.5	42.7	41.7	28.1[a]	40.3
More than 12 months	8.8	2.9	37.6	41.7	12.7	7.0	3.7	3.3	42.7	43.1	29.9[a]	39.9
Occupation											
White-collar	7.4	2.8	43.0	38.3	9.3[a]	7.3	3.8	3.5	49.3[a]	45.0	27.1[a]	37.3
Managerial/professional	5.8	2.4	42.3	40.0	6.7	8.4	3.4	3.4	50.1[a]	40.1	27.7[a]	42.6
Technical/sales/clerical	8.4	3.1	43.4	37.3	10.9[a]	6.7	4.1	3.5	48.8	47.4	26.7[a]	34.6
Blue-collar	14.3	4.5	38.7	32.6	16.5[a]	12.6	5.2[a]	3.4	45.5[a]	36.8	22.4[a]	35.7
Service	6.6	5.2	54.8	25.0	7.1	3.7	6.2[a]	2.1	59.7	44.5	18.3[a]	35.6
Precision production/ crafts	18.0	2.5	34.3	35.6	21.9[a]	12.9	2.8	1.2	41.3	36.5	24.0[a]	39.8
Other blue-collar	16.2	5.4	33.0	34.7	19.1[a]	15.2	6.1	5.2	39.1[a]	34.6	23.9[a]	33.0
Tenure in 1989											
12 months or fewer	13.6	5.7	53.4	17.5	15.3[a]	12.8	6.8[a]	4.0	56.9[a]	53.4	10.1[a]	21.3
More than 12 months	9.1	2.6	35.3	44.3	11.8[a]	7.7	3.0	3.3	40.9	38.3	34.2[a]	42.2

Notes: Numbers represent (weighted) percentage of 1989 jobs that ended in given way by 1993 or were kept through 1993. Remaining jobs (differences between 100 percent and sum of four outcomes) could not be tracked (6.5 percent dropped out of sample, and 2.5 percent had missing information).

[a] Difference between profit-sharers and non-profit-sharers is significant at $p < .05$.

[b] Profit-sharers are those who reported its availability in every year for job held in 1989. Those reporting it only in some years are included in columns 1–4 but omitted in columns 5–12

The disposition of the job is predicted with a multinomial logit technique, to account for the potential influences of personal and job characteristics (particularly education and occupation, as shown in the tabulations of table 4.6). Unlike previous analyses that look at only one method of ending a job (for example, looking only at quits), this method estimates how these characteristics relate to several ways in which a job can end (layoff, quit, or firing).[18] The results for layoff and quit probabilities are reported in table 4.7 (with job retention as the base category, and coefficients for other outcomes not reported but available). The reported estimates represent the relative risk ratio associated with a one-unit change in the dependent variable. As shown in column 1, for example, the layoff risk for women is only 72.7 percent of the risk for men. Race also appears important, as blacks and Hispanics face significantly higher risks of layoff than do non-Hispanic whites. Education is a powerful predictor: those with a high school degree have only 67 percent the layoff risk, and those with a graduate degree only 11 percent the layoff risk, faced by those who have not completed high school. Among job characteristics, the only two significant predictors are firm size (with lower layoff risks among larger firms) and employer tenure in 1989 (with layoff risks declining with tenure).[19]

The key variable of interest is whether the employer makes profit-sharing available to the employee. If so, the employee's risk of being laid off is only 52 percent of the risk facing a similar worker without profit-sharing (consistent with the simple comparisons presented in table 4.6). The estimates in the quit column indicate that profit-sharing employees are also significantly less likely to quit (consistent with the results of Wilson and Peel 1991), as are females, older employees, and those with more education. While higher pay and union coverage do not predict higher risks of layoff, they do predict lower quit rates.[20]

These results may reflect different layoff and quit rates by occupation and industry; in addition, the profit-sharing estimate may reflect the influence of other benefits (as appears to be the case in predicting pay levels). The second specification presented in table 4.7 controls for occupation and industry (with ten and eleven dummies, respectively) and other benefits.[21] With these controls, there is no longer a significant difference in quits associated with profit-sharing, but there remains a significant difference in the risk of layoff, with profit-sharers only 61 percent as likely as non-profit-sharers to be laid off.

Not only profit-sharing but also employer-provided educational/training opportunities and paid vacation are associated with significantly lower layoff risks. Educational/training opportunities are more likely to be offered to employees whom the employer wants to retain, while the

Table 4.7 Predicting Disposition of 1989 Job

| | Multinomial Logits on Ultimate Disposition of All 1989 Jobs[b] | | | | Weibull Survival Model on New Jobs[c] | | |
| | (1) | | (2) | | (3) | (4) | (5)[d] |
	Layoff	Quit	Layoff	Quit	Layoff	Layoff	Layoff
Demographic characteristics							
Female	0.727[a] (3.12)	1.243[a] (3.05)	1.116 (0.81)	1.465 (0.81)	0.507[a] (4.92)	0.778 (1.30)	0.687[a] (2.30)
Age	1.044[a] (1.97)	0.964[a] (2.36)	1.041 (1.62)	0.955 (1.62)	1.036 (1.33)	1.039 (1.17)	1.022 (0.82)
Black	1.449[a] (3.25)	1.010 (0.11)	1.548[a] (3.32)	1.012[a] (3.32)	1.170 (1.10)	1.252 (1.33)	1.142 (0.91)
Hispanic	1.471[a] (3.03)	1.124 (1.23)	1.642[a] (3.40)	1.127[a] (3.40)	1.176 (1.00)	1.319 (1.44)	1.228 (1.24)
Education (less than high school omitted)							
High school	0.671[a] (2.91)	0.700[a] (3.19)	0.840 (1.10)	0.760[a] (2.14)	0.803 (1.50)	0.905 (0.56)	0.873 (0.91)
Some college	0.481[a] (4.48)	0.746[a] (2.35)	0.620[a] (2.47)	0.788 (1.63)	0.606[a] (2.54)	0.742 (1.24)	0.659[a] (2.02)
Bachelor's degree	0.392[a] (4.50)	0.822 (1.36)	0.632 (1.80)	0.828 (1.09)	0.480[a] (2.70)	0.640 (1.27)	0.665[a] (1.37)
Graduate degree	0.108[a] (4.96)	0.849 (0.86)	0.215[a] (3.01)	0.825 (0.85)	0.099[a] (3.18)	0.296 (1.61)	0.146[a] (2.58)
Benefits							
Profit-sharing	0.516[a] (5.97)	0.727[a] (4.31)	0.611[a] (3.53)	0.956 (0.50)	0.552[a] (3.55)	0.738 (1.31)	0.642[a] (2.30)
Health insurance			0.983 (0.09)	1.079 (0.50)		1.171 (0.72)	0.999 (0.00)
Life insurance			0.862 (0.89)	0.779[a] (2.04)		0.909 (0.43)	1.099 (0.50)
Dental insurance			0.883 (0.88)	0.969 (0.32)		0.649[a] (2.05)	0.760 (1.57)
Paid sick leave			1.109 (0.73)	0.987 (0.13)		1.132 (0.61)	1.329 (1.69)
Maternity/paternity leave			1.041[a] (0.28)	0.727[a] (3.08)		1.014 (0.07)	1.030 (0.17)
Paid vacation			0.623[a] (2.52)	0.652[a] (2.88)		0.618[a] (2.22)	0.470[a] (3.94)
Retirement plan			0.751 (1.90)	0.772[a] (2.44)		0.947 (0.25)	0.985 (0.08)

(*Table continues on p. 140.*)

Table 4.7 Continued

	Multinomial Logits on Ultimate Disposition of All 1989 Jobs[b]				Weibull Survival Model on New Jobs[c]		
	(1)		(2)		(3)	(4)	(5)[d]
	Layoff	Quit	Layoff	Quit	Layoff	Layoff	Layoff
Child care support			1.026 (0.11)	0.829 (1.15)		1.430 (0.98)	1.352 (0.90)
Education/training opportunities			0.751[a] (2.08)	1.017 (0.18)		0.524[a] (2.92)	0.558[a] (3.26)
Job characteristics							
Union coverage	1.088 (0.68)	0.563[a] (5.56)	1.119 (0.77)	0.583[a] (4.49)	1.574[a] (2.75)	1.756[a] (2.77)	1.570[a] (2.56)
Ln (firm size)	0.943[a] (2.32)	0.883[a] (6.85)	1.003 (0.09)	0.943[a] (2.55)	0.985 (0.46)	1.059 (1.27)	1.057 (1.41)
Multiestablishment firm	0.817 (1.92)	0.954 (0.60)	0.930 (0.58)	1.079 (0.83)	0.731[a] (2.50)	0.802 (1.43)	0.760[a] (2.08)
Ln (1989 hourly pay)	0.899 (0.91)	0.613[a] (5.69)	0.821 (1.33)	0.738[a] (2.92)	1.056 (0.36)	0.870 (0.70)	0.833 (1.08)
Tenure (1989)	0.675[a] (7.66)	0.670[a] (10.87)	0.705[a] (5.99)	0.701[a] (8.52)			
Tenure squared	1.019[a] (3.91)	1.020[a] (5.64)	1.017[a] (3.07)	1.017[a] (4.35)			
Occupation/industry controls	No		Yes		No	Yes	Yes
Sample size	5,966		4,870		1,983	1,507	2,055
Log-likelihood	−7652.2245		−6000.796		−952.449	−670.012	−921.344
Sigma					0.986 (0.03)	0.896 (0.03)	0.917 (0.03)

[a] $p < .05$ (null hypothesis is relative risk ratio of 1)(T-statistics in parentheses).

[b] The multinomial logits have five possible outcomes: layoff, firing, quit, retention, or unknown status. Estimates for being fired, or having unknown status, are not reported but available (job retention is base category).

[c] The Weibull survival model predicts the hazard of layoff in the current week, given that one has not been laid off yet. Jobs not ending in layoff are treated as censored.

[d] To test for sensitivity to restricted sample from missing benefits data, column 5 includes dummy variables for each benefit's missing values.

incentive to retain employees may be particularly strong if training investments have been made.[22] There is no obvious reason for an association between paid vacations and lower layoffs.[23] This result appears to reflect the fact that, as paid vacation is the most common benefit, it signals that a basic benefits package is available to the employee.[24] Additional tests found that paid vacation does not have a significant effect after controlling for benefits intensity; in fact, profit-sharing is the only benefit to have a significant effect in this case.[25]

The profit-sharing variable may reflect substantial measurement error, as discussed earlier. The estimates were also made using a variable representing those who reported profit-sharing in each year of the job, with very similar qualitative and quantitative results.[26]

Layoff risks over the life of a job are also assessed using new jobs in 1989.[27] While the multinomial logit model looks only at the ultimate disposition of a job, taking no account of the length of time until that disposition, the survival model uses information on the length of a job and the timing of layoffs to predict the likelihood of layoff across the life of the job. The estimates here use the Weibull specification, assuming a monotonic baseline hazard and time-invariant predictors.

Employees in new jobs with profit-sharing are at significantly lower risk of layoff, as shown in column 3. The estimated magnitude of the layoff risk in any given period (55 percent) is comparable to the risk that a job will ultimately end in layoff (51 percent, in column 1). This estimate is sensitive, however, to the inclusion of other benefits as predictors.[28] When other benefits and occupation and industry controls are included in column 4, the layoff risk for profit-sharers is still lower but no longer statistically significant. This result appears to be partly due to the restriction of the sample to those with valid data on every benefit; to increase the sample, column 5 reports estimates where the missing values for each benefit are represented by dummy variables (so that missing benefits data are also used to predict the hazard of layoff). When this is done, profit-sharers are again predicted to be at lower risk of layoff than non-profit-sharers with similar benefits and other observable characteristics. When benefits intensity is controlled, however, the lower layoff risk for profit-sharers is no longer significant.[29]

Does the layoff risk for profit-sharers, and those with other benefits, vary by skill level? Table 4.8 examines the effects by skill level, presenting results when the specifications are run using subsamples based on education levels or job requirements. While the tabulations of table 4.6 showed that there were significant differences in layoffs and job retention between profit-sharers and non-profit-sharers with low levels of ed-

Table 4.8 Benefits and Layoff Risk, by Skill Level

	Profit-Sharing (1)	Paid Vacation (2)	Education/Training Opportunities (3)	Retirement Plan (4)
Multinomial logit models				
Education				
Less than 12 years	1.097 (0.23)	0.857 (0.35)	0.787 (0.62)	0.561 (1.46)
12 years	0.702 (1.84)	0.610 (1.93)	0.769 (1.42)	0.990 (0.05)
More than 12 years	0.508[a] (2.77)	0.576 (1.46)	0.712 (1.40)	0.520[a] (2.41)
Schooling required for job				
High school or less	0.677[a] (2.39)	0.602[a] (2.49)	0.850 (1.06)	0.848 (0.95)
Less than high school	0.576 (1.89)	0.602 (1.69)	0.797 (0.78)	0.820 (0.68)
High school degree	0.693 (1.82)	0.585 (1.85)	0.908 (0.51)	0.832 (0.82)
At least some college	0.587 (1.87)	0.744 (0.58)	0.529[a] (2.15)	0.569 (1.75)
Training required for job				
Yes	0.684[a] (2.04)	0.639 (1.73)	0.823 (1.08)	0.877 (0.65)
No	0.563[a] (2.76)	0.636 (1.65)	0.694 (1.77)	0.586[a] (2.37)
No college work required	0.654 (1.83)	0.662 (1.44)	0.717 (1.47)	0.666 (1.63)
Months of training to be fully qualified for job				
One month or less	0.533[a] (2.46)	0.567 (1.87)	0.848 (0.68)	0.859 (0.56)
More than one month	0.689[a] (2.24)	0.563[a] (2.37)	0.716[a] (2.05)	0.655[a] (2.32)

Weibull survival models

	(1)	(2)	(3)	(4)
Education				
Less than 12 years	0.457 (1.52)	0.403ᵃ (2.26)	0.840 (0.45)	1.302 (0.63)
12 years	0.906 (0.37)	0.482ᵃ (2.77)	0.564ᵃ (2.27)	1.027 (0.11)
More than 12 years	0.531 (1.66)	0.543 (1.38)	0.353ᵃ (2.95)	0.647 (1.07)
Schooling required for job				
High school or less	0.711 (1.57)	0.429ᵃ (4.13)	0.611ᵃ (2.49)	1.154 (0.72)
Less than high school	0.414ᵃ (2.29)	0.476ᵃ (2.57)	0.557 (1.73)	1.609 (1.58)
High school degree	1.035 (0.12)	0.400ᵃ (2.85)	0.674 (1.53)	0.831 (0.67)
At least some college	0.594 (1.07)	1.123 (0.19)	0.275ᵃ (3.00)	0.561 (1.22)
Training required for job				
Yes	0.687 (1.59)	0.529ᵃ (2.55)	0.447ᵃ (3.63)	0.887 (0.54)
No	0.775 (0.73)	0.335ᵃ (3.52)	0.744 (0.95)	1.096 (0.28)
No, and no college required	0.634 (1.16)	0.320ᵃ (3.62)	0.780 (0.74)	1.284 (0.72)
Months of training to be fully qualified for job				
One month or less	0.497ᵃ (1.96)	0.430ᵃ (3.07)	0.637 (1.47)	1.447 (1.33)
More than one month	0.799 (0.94)	0.473ᵃ (2.73)	0.459ᵃ (3.41)	0.708 (1.41)

Notes: Drawn from specifications done separately for each group listed at left (based on models 2 and 5 of table 4.7). Numbers represent risk of layoff for those with the benefit, relative to those without it (no difference = 1). All variables from table 4.7, specifications 2 and 5, were included, but only those that attract a significant coefficient in any subsample are presented here.

ᵃ $p < .05$ (null hypothesis is that relative risk ratio equals one).

ucation, significant differences do not show up for these workers once other characteristics and benefits are held constant. The only significant profit-sharing coefficient in the education breakdowns is for those with more than twelve years of schooling, who are estimated to have only half the layoff chance of similar non-profit-sharers.

The lower risk of layoff for profit-sharers relative to non-profit-sharers does not appear to vary much by the schooling or training requirements of the job. Most of the estimates indicate that profit-sharers are 50 to 70 percent as likely as non-profit-sharers to be laid off, with the differences generally significant ($p < .05$) in the multinomial logits but not in the survival models for new jobs.

This table also presents the breakdown of layoff risks associated with paid vacations and employer-provided educational opportunities, since they attract significant coefficients in the overall sample (although paid vacation in particular may reflect the presence of a basic benefits package, and neither were significant when controlling for benefits intensity). These are only occasionally significant in the multinomial logits on the ultimate disposition of a job, but frequently significant in the models predicting survival of new jobs. As was true with profit-sharing, the estimated effects do not vary greatly by education or job requirements.

Finally, does the role of profit-sharing in layoffs vary by wage level? The share economy theory predicts favorable demand effects for profit-sharing when it substitutes in some fashion for fixed compensation. While such substitution cannot be directly measured, one can measure the pay of an individual profit-sharer and compare it to that of a non-profit-sharing employee with the same personal and job characteristics, in the same occupation and industry. The lower pay of a profit-sharer in this case may represent some substitution of profit-sharing for pay. On the other hand, it may simply reflect otherwise unmeasured ability, tastes, and circumstances. To examine the potential role of substitution, profit-sharers were divided into those with pay above and below what would be predicted for a non-profit-sharer with similar characteristics.[30] The coefficients for the two groups of profit-sharers are very close, but there is a lower (but not statistically significant) relative layoff risk for the low-paid profit-sharers (61 percent) than for the high-paid profit-sharers (67 percent).

Summary and Conclusion

What role does profit-sharing play in the employment of low-skill workers? This analysis of longitudinal data from young employees has examined the prevalence of profit-sharing, its relationship to pay and other benefits, and its association with layoffs and other dispositions of jobs. The major findings are as follows.

First, about one-third of young private-sector employees report the availability of profit-sharing in any one year, but only one-fifth report it in every year of their job. The difference reflects either measurement error, the starting and stopping of plans, or the lack of profit-sharing contributions in some years.

Second, when examined by skill level, profit-sharing is more common among workers with higher education levels and higher schooling requirements for jobs, although the prevalence does not differ greatly by training requirements for jobs. Those with higher education levels and job requirements also have a greater number of benefits, are more likely to be paid by bonuses, commissions, or stock options, and are less likely to be paid by piece rates or tips.

Third, profit sharing does not generally appear to substitute directly for wages or other benefits. Average pay levels and the prevalence of other benefits are significantly higher for profit-sharers than for non-profit-sharers. This is true not only in cross-sectional comparisons of otherwise comparable workers but in longitudinal comparisons of those who gain or forgo profit-sharing when they change jobs. When controlling for the presence of other benefits, however, the relationship of pay to profit-sharing is close to zero.

Fourth, the estimated layoff risk for profit-sharers is about 60 percent of the risk faced by non-profit-sharers, across all employees and for new employees. Two of the other nine benefits examined—employer-provided educational/training opportunities and paid vacation—were also found to be associated with lower risks of layoff. These two benefits may simply reflect better benefits packages; when accounting for benefits intensity, profit-sharing was the only benefit predicting significantly lower layoff risks among all employees (although the profit-sharing estimate was no longer significant for new employees).

Fifth, the estimates of lower layoff risks for profit-sharers do not vary substantially by education and job requirements, indicating that if profit-sharing does affect labor demand, it appears to do so equally across skill levels.

The lower layoff rates for profit-sharers support the idea that profit-sharing can increase the demand for workers. An important caveat, however, is that the theory predicting favorable demand effects assumes substitution between the profit share and fixed pay, and there is little indication that profit-sharing typically substitutes directly for fixed pay. As discussed earlier, it is possible that profit-sharing substitutes indirectly for fixed pay, either by encouraging employee loyalty and retention (taking the place of additional fixed benefits in doing so) or by rewarding higher employee performance through the profit share rather than through higher fixed pay. It is nonetheless also possible, given that an assumption of the theory has apparently not been met, that the lower layoff risks of profit-sharers are not due to favorable demand effects. Profit-sharing may be a component of a "good job" that helps benefit and protect those who can obtain the job but does not create more jobs. The idea that employee benefits signal "good jobs" is supported by the finding that layoffs are generally lower as a greater number of benefits are made available to workers. Additional benefits may be extended to workers whom the employer plans to retain, so that the lower layoffs result from a selection effect. Profit-sharing seems to reduce layoffs more than other benefits do, but this could also result from a selection effect rather than a change in labor demand.[31] Future research may usefully be directed to the issues of substitution between profit-sharing and fixed pay, and of what types of workers are offered various benefits.

The question of whether profit-sharing increases demand for workers cannot be answered with a simple yes or no. There are intriguing indications that profit-sharing enhances demand for workers, manifested by lower layoffs, but the apparent lack of substitution for fixed pay raises the question of whether profit-sharing in fact results in decreased layoffs, as predicted by theory.

Three broad types of government action that have been used to encourage profit-sharing are legislative and constitutional mandates, tax incentives, and advisory institutions (reviewed in Kruse 1993, 167–69). Weitzman makes the case that the social benefits of lower unemployment and greater economic stability justify the use of tax incentives to encourage the spread of profit-sharing. Accumulated empirical evidence does not yet make a strong case for such incentives (although, as noted by Mitchell [1993], empirical research is inconclusive on even so basic an issue of economic theory as the employment effects of the minimum wage).[32] There are, however, many indications in this and other studies of differences in employment behavior when profit-sharing is present, making a strong case for increased attention and research on the employment-enhancing potential of profit-sharing.

Richard Freeman, David Levine, Erica Groshen, David Wray, and seminar participants at the Russell Sage Foundation, Rutgers University, and the Federal Reserve Bank of Dallas provided useful ideas and comments. Substantial help in accessing the NLS data was received from Barbara Rau.

Notes

1. Over the past twenty years, the unemployment rates for workers with less than four years of high school have consistently been about four times higher than the rates of workers with four or more years of college, while the unemployment rates of workers with only high school degrees have been about twice the rates of workers with four or more years of college (U.S. Department of Commerce, Bureau of the Census 1994, 418).

2. This abstracts from concerns introduced by firm-specific skills and turnover costs, which do not change the logic of the model.

3. For responses to several of these objections, see Weitzman (1986, 1988).

4. Several studies take account of the endogeneity of the profit-sharing variable, since it is likely to be directly affected by the factors determining labor demand.

5. The BLS employee benefits survey covered medium and large firms in 1988, 1989, 1991, and 1993, and small private firms in 1990 and 1992. The employer coverage figures exclude 401(k) plans; when profit-linked matches to 401(k) plans are included, the coverage increases slightly (by 2 percent) and slightly more (perhaps 1 percent) when considering the availability of such plans to nonparticipants (based on participation estimates from Papke [1995]). Nonetheless, the employer-reported coverage remains lower than the coverage reported by young employees. The occupational breakdowns show that this gap is highest for technical/clerical employees, and lowest for professional/ administrative employees.

6. For individual performance-based pay, respondents were asked the following: "The earnings on some jobs are based all or in part on how a person performs the job. On this card are some examples of earnings that are based on job performance. Please tell me if any of the earnings on your job are based on any of these types of compensation. Please do not include profit sharing or employee stock purchase plans." The options were: piece rate, commissions, bonuses (based on job performance), stock options, tips, or other. This question was asked only in the 1988 to 1990 surveys.

7. Ideally one would know the dollar value or percentage of pay represented by these benefits. Employer survey data for those employers providing a specific benefit were used to assign mean employer costs to each of these benefits (based on Chamber of Commerce 1990, table 14); the average cost of these benefits is estimated to be 17.8 percent of payroll for this sample. While the use of the average benefit cost data may be valid in looking at overall sample averages, it would be misleading to do this calculation for the subsamples in table 4.3 because of the strong pay differences and the fact that the values of many benefits are a function of pay (for example, pensions).

8. For a description and analysis of profit-sharing in U.S. union contracts in the 1980s, see Bell and Neumark (1993). In Kruse (1993), I found that profit-sharing was more common in nonunion public companies, but that (consistent with Bell and Neumark) union presence was positively associated with the adoption of a cash profit-sharing plan in the 1976 to 1991 period.

9. For example, asked to choose between individual incentives, companywide incentives, and a straight wage salary, low-income workers were more likely than

high-income workers to prefer a straight wage salary (Bureau of National Affairs 1988).

10. Profit-sharing did, however, appear to directly substitute for wages or benefits in many concessionary union contracts in the 1980s (Bell and Neumark 1993). In addition, subsequent wage growth was lower in those companies.

11. Similar estimates (not presented) show that profit-sharing is a strong positive predictor of the availability of each of the benefits, using a probit specification with the same controls employed for columns 5 and 6 of table 4.5.

12. This closely matches the result that Ewing (1996) finds for performance-based pay, using 1990 data from the NLSY.

13. The additional controls are listed at the bottom of table 4.5. The cross-sectional estimates are based on a dummy variable representing profit-sharing, while the longitudinal estimates are based on a variable taking the value 1 for those joining profit-sharing, -1 for those leaving profit-sharing, and 0 for all other job changers. The occupational and industry earnings controls are the difference between the average pay in the old occupation/industry and the pay for new workers (less than twelve months' tenure) in the new occupation/industry. (Similar results were obtained with a set of broad occupation and industry dummies for old and new jobs.) The breakdowns of job requirements refer to the characteristics of the new job.

14. When separate estimates are made for profit-sharing joiners versus leavers, the coefficients tend to be of equal magnitudes and opposite signs.

15. The benefits attracting significant positive coefficients, both in the cross-sectional and longitudinal estimates, are health insurance, dental insurance, retirement plan, and educational/training opportunities; sick leave also attracts significant positive coefficients in the cross-sectional estimates. In addition, piece rates, commissions, and bonuses attract significant positive coefficients. No benefits or pay types attract significant negative coefficients. The strong correlation between profit-sharing and these other benefits and pay types accounts for the significant positive profit-sharing coefficients when these are excluded in columns 5 and 6.

16. While firm-level datasets can often measure demand shocks through sales changes, these measures are problematic for testing the theory (Kruse 1993, 126-27). Another problem with firm-level datasets is that stability in the absence of profit-sharing cannot be assessed (although three datasets approximate this with pre/post comparisons).

17. Of the remaining 9 percent, 6.5 percent dropped out of the sample, and 2.5 percent had missing information on how the job ended.

18. For previous analyses with individual data of the determinants of displacement, see Hamermesh (1990); for comparable analyses of quits, see Meitzen (1986), Zax (1989), and Wolpin (1992).

19. Nonlinear relationships were also tested using dummies for firm size categories (1 to 10, 11 to 50, 51 to 100, 101 to 500, and 501+) and tenure categories (less than six months, six months to one year, one to two years, two to five years, and more than five years). Results conformed with the relationship presented in table 4.7, with little change in the coefficients of interest.

20. The union results are consistent with Freeman (1980). Concerning the pay level, ideally one would have measures both of fixed compensation in the absence of profit-sharing and of the degree to which profit-sharing is substituting for fixed compensation, but these data are not available.

21. Also, the different types of individual incentives were used in predicting job disposition, but none produced a significant effect on any outcome. (The closest was tips, which predicted a higher likelihood of quitting at $p < 10$.)

22. Employers do not want to lay off workers in whom the firm has made training investments and expects to recoup some of those investments through higher worker performance. Human capital theory predicts that employers will share in the costs and rewards only of firm-specific training, since employees bear the full costs and reap the full rewards of investments in general training. This measure provides no indication of the generality of the skills from the employer-provided educational/training opportunities.

23. One possibility is that, for employers able to schedule mandatory vacations, the vacations may partially substitute for layoffs as an employer technique for managing short-term fluctuations in demand.

24. Not only is paid vacation the most common benefit overall, but it is most likely to be the first benefit offered to employees (44 percent of employees with only one benefit report paid vacation, compared to no more than 17 percent for any other benefit). Paid vacation is available in 95 percent of the cases in which four or more benefits are offered. (The comparable figure for profit-sharing is 42 percent.)

25. Benefits intensity was measured as the sum of all benefits, and to avoid collinearity, each benefit was entered singly in separate specifications to measure the effect of that particular benefit apart from simply adding to the benefits package. Alternative measures of benefits intensity were also used, such as dummy variables for any benefits and for given levels of benefits, as well as the squared sum of benefits. The results indicated that a greater number of benefits was linearly related to lower layoff probabilities, with an average 17 percent lower probability for each new benefit. When profit-sharing is tested, the relative risk ratio from adding any new benefit is .86, and the relative risk ratio associated with profit-sharing is .72 ($t = 2.22$), so that the overall effect from adding profit-sharing is .72*.86 =.62. No other benefit attracted a T-statistic at the 95 percent, or even the 90 percent, level.

26. This required specifying separate variables indicating whether profit-sharing and each of the other benefits was reported in some years but not others.

27. "New jobs" were defined as those begun within the past year. Ideally one can trace all jobs from the beginning; this sample does not include some jobs that were begun but did not survive long enough to become the primary job (the "CPS job," for which the benefits questions were asked). The sample was restricted to those with tenures of less than six months and less than three months at the 1989 interview, but results did not differ notably.

    Specifications were also run on all new jobs started within the 1988 to 1992 period; results are reported for the 1989 new jobs because of the job requirements questions.

28. As in the multinomial logits, the individual incentives made little difference in layoff probabilities, and their inclusion did not change the coefficients of interest.

29. Benefits intensity was constructed in the same way as reported earlier for the multinomial logits. The profit-sharing estimate indicated a similar magnitude, but the T-statistic was only 1.2. As noted in table 4.4, workers who are new to jobs are less likely to receive profit-sharing; the power of the estimates is thus limited (only 21 percent reported profit-sharing in the sample analyzed in table 4.7).

30. Pay was predicted with the model used for table 4.5, column 5, but without the profit-sharing variable. The mean pay residual for non-profit-sharers was calculated, and profit-sharers were split, according to whether the individual's pay residual was above or below this mean. In other estimates, to allow for possibly different roles of profit-sharing at different skill levels, the non-profit-sharing mean residual was calculated separately by educational level before the profit-sharers were divided.

31. Experiments were made to account for the selection effect using instrumental variables in the multinomial logits. The estimates were dispersed and limited by difficulty in finding predictors of profit-sharing other than those already used to predict job disposition.

32. Mitchell goes on to say, "If we cannot settle that issue empirically, what hope is there for convincingly and definitively demonstrating (or refuting) the macro effects of particular pay systems?" (1993, 22). Elsewhere he argues that profit-sharing is a candidate for subsidy based on the strong theory and the paucity of alternatives for attacking the problems of unemployment and instability (1994).

References

Askwith, M. E. 1926. *Profit-Sharing: An Aid to Trade Revival.* London, England: Duncan Scott.

Bell, Linda, and David Neumark. 1993. "Lump Sum Payments and Profit-Sharing Plans in the Union Sector of the United States Economy." *Economic Journal* 103 (May): 602–19.

Bhargava, Sandeep. 1994. "The Macroeconomic Implications of Profit Sharing: Another Look at the Evidence from Japan and U.K.," Department of Economics and Related Studies, University of York. Unpublished paper (May).

Bradley, Keith, and Saul Estrin. 1992. "Profit Sharing in the British Retail Trade Sector: The Relative Performance of the John Lewis Partnership." *Journal of Industrial Economics* 40(3): 291–304.

Bureau of National Affairs. 1988. *Changing Pay Practices: New Developments in Employee Compensation.* Washington, D.C.: Bureau of National Affairs.

Cahuc, Pierre, and Brigitte Dormont. 1992. "Profit-Sharing: Does It Increase Productivity and Employment? A Theoretical Model and Evidence on French Microdata." Working Paper 92.4. Paris, France: Cahiers Ecomath, University of Paris.

Carstensen, Vivian, Knut Gerlach, and Olaf Hubler. 1992. "Profit Sharing in German Firms: Institutional Framework, Participation, and Microeconomic Effects." Working Paper. Berlin, Germany: Institut fur Quantitative Wirtschafts-forchung, Hannover University.

Chamber of Commerce. 1990. *Employee Benefits.* Washington, D.C.: Economic Policy Division, Chamber of Commerce of the United States.

Chelius, James, and Robert Smith. 1990. "Profit Sharing and Employment Stability." *Industrial and Labor Relations Review* 43(3): 256S–73S.

Estrin, Saul, Paul Grout, and Sushil Wadhwani. 1987. "Profit Sharing and Employee Share Ownership." *Economic Policy* (April): 13–62.

Estrin, Saul, and Nicholas Wilson. 1989. "Profit Sharing the Marginal Cost of Labour and Employmnet Variability," Draft. London, England: Center for Labor Economics, London School of Economics.

Even, William, and David MacPherson. 1990. "The Gender Gap in Pensions and Wages." *Review of Economics and Statistics* 71 (May): 259–65.

Ewing, Bradley T. 1996. "Wages and Performance-Based Pay: Evidence from the NLSY." *Economic Letters* 51(2): 241–46.

Finseth, Eric. 1988. "The Employment Behavior of Profit-Sharing Firms: An Empirical Test of the Weitzman Theory." Senior thesis, Department of Economics, Harvard University..

Fitzroy, Felix, and Daniel Vaughan-Whitehead. 1989. "Employment, Efficiency Wages, and Profit Sharing in French Firms." London School of Economics. Unpublished paper (May).

Florkowski, Gary. 1994. "Employment Growth and Stability Under Profit Sharing: A Longitudinal Study." *British Journal of Industrial Relations* 32(3): 303–18.

Freeman, Richard. 1980. "The Exit-Voice Trade-Off in the Labor Market: Unionism, Job Tenure, Quits and Separations." *Quarterly Journal of Economics* 94 (June): 643–73.

Freeman, Richard, and Martin Weitzman. 1987. "Bonuses and Employment in Japan." *Journal of the Japanese and International Economies.* 1 (June): 168–94.

Gerhart, Barry. 1991. "Employment Stability Under Different Managerial Compensation Systems." Working Paper 91-02. Center for Advanced Human Resource Studies, Cornell University.

Gilman, Nicholas Paine. 1899. *A Dividend to Labor: A Study of Employers' Welfare Institutions.* Boston, Mass.: Houghton Mifflin.

Gustman, Alan, and Thomas Steinmeier. 1993. "Pension Portability and Labor Mobility." *Journal of Public Economics* 50(3): 299–323.

———. 1995. *Pension Incentives and Job Mobility.* Kalamazoo, Mich.: W. E. Upjohn Institute for Employment Research.

Hamermesh, Daniel. 1990. "Wage Concessions, Plant Shutdowns, and the Demand for Labor." In *Job Displacement: Consequences and Implications for Policy,* edited by John Addison. Detroit, Mich.: Wayne State University Press.

Hart, R. A., and Olaf Hubler. 1991. "Are Profit Shares and Wages Substitute of Complementary Forms of Compensation?" *Kyklos* 44(2): 221–31.

Hubler, Olaf. 1993. "Productivity, Earnings, and Profit Sharing: An Econometric Analysis of Alternative Models." *Empirical Economics* 18(2): 357–80.

Jones, Derek, and Jeffrey Pliskin. 1989. "British Evidence on the Employment Effects of Profit Sharing." *Industrial Relations* 28 (Spring): 276–98.

Kraft, Kornelius. 1991. "The Incentive Effects of Dismissals, Efficiency Wages, Piece-Rates, and Profit-Sharing." *Review of Economics and Statistics* 73(3): 451–59.

Kruse, Douglas L. 1991a. "Profit Sharing and Employment Variability: Microeconomic Evidence on the Weitzman Theory." *Industrial and Labor Relations Review* 44(3): 437–53.

———. 1991b. "Profit Sharing in the 1980s: Disguised Wages or a Fundamentally Different Form of Compensation?" In *Structural Changes in U.S. Labor Markets: Causes and Consequences*, edited by Randall Eberts and Erica Groshen. Armonk, N.Y.: M. E. Sharpe.

———. 1993. *Profit Sharing: Does It Make a Difference?* Kalamazoo, Mich.: W. E. Upjohn Institute for Employment Research.

Levine, David. 1987. "Efficiency Wages in Weitzman's Share Economy." *Economics Letters* 23(3): 245–49.

———. 1989. "Efficiency Wages in Weitzman's Share Economy." *Industrial Relations* 23(3): 321–34.

Meitzen, Mark E. 1986. "Differences in Male and Female Job-Quitting Behavior." *Journal of Labor Economics* 4(2): 151–67.

Mitchell, Daniel J. B. 1993. "Profit Sharing and Employee Ownership: Policy Implications." Working Paper Series 251. Institute of Industrial Relations, University of California-Los Angeles.

———. 1994. "Profit Sharing and Gain Sharing for Improved Job Security and Macroeconomic Performance." Testimony before House Committee on Small Business, Subcommittee on Regulation, Business Opportunities, and Technology (July 15).

Mitchell, Daniel J. B., David Lewin, and Edward E. Lawler III. 1990. "Alternative Pay Systems, Firm Performance, and Productivity." In *Paying for Productivity: A Look at the Evidence*, edited by Alan S. Blinder. Washington, D.C.: Brookings Institution.

Mitchell, Olivia, and Silvana Pozzebon. 1986. "Wages, Pensions, and Wage Pensions Tradeoffs." In *Explaining Patterns in Old-Age Pensions*, edited by Olivia Mitchell. Washington, D.C.: National Institute on Aging.

Nordhaus, William. 1988. "Can the Share Economy Conquer Stagflation?" *Quarterly Journal of Economics* 103(1): 201–17.

Papke, Leslie. 1995. "Participation in and Contributions to 401(k) Pension Plans." *Journal of Human Resources* 30(2): 311–25.

Seitchik, Adam. 1991. "Who Are Displaced Workers?" In *Job Displacement: Consequences and Implications for Policy*, edited by John Addison. Detroit, Mich.: Wayne State University Press.

Smith, Robert, and Ronald Ehrenberg. 1983. "Estimating Wage-Fringe Tradeoffs: Some Data Problems." In *Measurement of Labor Cost*, edited by Jack E. Triplett. Chicago, Ill.: University of Chicago Press.

Summers, Lawrence. 1986. "On the Share Economy." *Challenge* (November-December): 47–50.

Swaim, Paul L., and Michael J. Podgursky. 1991. "Displacement and Unemployment." In *Job Displacement: Consequences and Implications for Policy,* edited by John Addison. Detroit, Mich.: Wayne State University Press.

U.S. Department of Commerce, Bureau of the Census. 1994. *Statistical Abstract of the United States.* Washington: U.S. Government Printing Office.

U.S. Department of Labor, Bureau of Labor Statistics. 1989. *Survey of Employee Benefits in Medium and Large Firms.* Washington: U.S. Government Printing Office.

———.1990. *Survey of Employee Benefits in Medium and Large Firms.* Washington: U.S. Government Printing Office.

———.1992. *Survey of Employee Benefits in Medium and Large Firms.* Washington: U.S. Government Printing Office.

———. 1994. *Survey of Employee Benefits in Medium and Large Firms.* Washington: U.S. Government Printing Office.

———. 1991. *Survey of Employee Benefits in Small Private Firms.* Washington: U.S. Government Printing Office.

———. 1993. *Survey of Employee Benefits in Small Private Firms.* Washington: U.S. Government Printing Office.

U.S. Senate, Subcommittee of the Committee on Finance. 1939. *Survey of Experiences in Profit Sharing and Possibilities of Incentive Taxation.* Washington: U.S. Government Printing Office.

Wadhwani, Sushil, and Martin Wall. 1990. "The Effects of Profit Sharing on Employment, Wages, Stock Returns, and Productivity: Evidence from UK Microdata." *Economic Journal* 100 (March): 1–17.

Weitzman, Martin L. 1983. "Some Macroeconomic Implications of Alternative Compensation Systems." *Economic Journal* 93(372): 763–83.

———. 1984. *The Share Economy.* Cambridge, Mass.: Harvard University Press.

———. 1985. "The Simple Macroeconomics of Profit-Sharing." *American Economic Review* 75 (5): 937–53.

———. 1986. "Macroeconomic Implications of Profit-Sharing." *National Bureau of Economic Research Macroeconomics Annual 1986.* Cambridge, Mass.: MIT Press.

———. 1988. "Comment on 'Can the Share Economy Conquer Stagflation?'" *Quarterly Journal of Economics* 103(1): 219–23.

Wilson, Nicholas, and Michael J. Peel. 1991. "The Impact on Absenteeism and Quits of Profit-Sharing and Other Forms of Employee Participation." *Industrial and Labor Relations Review* 44(3): 454–68.

Wolpin, Kenneth. 1992. "The Determinants of Black-White Differences in Early Employment Careers: Search, Layoffs, Quits, and Endogenous Wage Growth." *Journal of Political Economy* 100(3): 535–60.

Zax, Jeffrey S. 1989. "Quits and Race." *Journal of Human Resources* 24(3): 469–93.

Chapter 5

The Effects of Employer Mandates

Susan N. Houseman

The wages and benefits of less educated workers have fallen both in absolute terms and relative to the wages and benefits of more educated workers over the last fifteen years. At the same time, there has been a large trend increase in the unemployment rate and a large trend decline in the labor force participation rate of less educated men. The decline in the real wages and benefits of less educated men and women and the decline in the rate of employment among less educated men have been accompanied by a dramatic increase in income inequality and poverty in the United States.

Employer mandates are perhaps the simplest and most direct policy response to the problem of poor wages, benefits, and working conditions. In response to falling real wages among low-wage workers, the government can raise the minimum wage. To address the dramatic fall in the incidence of health insurance among low-wage workers, the government can mandate that employers provide it to their workers. The government also can try to increase the job stability and lower the unemployment spells of workers by tightening advance notice requirements and introducing other restrictions on dismissals. Employer mandates are primarily designed to improve the wages, benefits, and employment conditions of low-wage workers, who have little clout in the labor market.

But are employer mandates an effective tool for redistributing income in society? The simple answer given by the theory of competitive labor markets is no. If labor markets are perfectly competitive, much of the cost of the employer mandate is likely to be borne by workers in the form of lower wages and benefits or higher product prices. To the extent that firms bear any of its cost, the employer mandate will probably reduce employment, thus harming some of the workers it is designed to assist. However, the assumptions underlying the model of perfect competition may not be an accurate description of the labor market. For instance, if it is costly to adjust capital in response to price changes, if workers have imperfect information about their job opportunities, if it is costly to monitor the performance of workers, or if it is difficult to measure workers' value added to products or services they help produce, the theoretical prediction of the effects of an employer mandate may change.

Whether employer mandates are an effective tool for improving the wages, benefits, and working conditions of low-wage workers is ultimately an empirical question. The primary purpose of this chapter is to review a large body of evidence from studies in the United States and other industrialized countries on the costs and benefits of various employer mandates.

Background on Employer Mandates

In the United States the federal and state governments require that employers provide a wide range of benefits to workers. For example, forty-eight states require that employers purchase workers' compensation insurance for employees in the event of workplace injury. Workers' compensation insurance in the United States pays medical bills for the injured worker as well as an indemnity benefit for lost work time. Unemployment insurance (UI) programs, like workers' compensation, effectively require employers to provide insurance to workers. Although unemployment insurance, unlike workers' compensation, is administered by the government and financed through a payroll tax, the theoretical analysis of the effects of unemployment insurance is similar to that of workers' compensation or other mandated benefits.[1] In the United States, unemployment insurance is financed by a payroll tax on employers. Although exact formulas vary from state to state, the tax rates partly depend on a company's past layoff history. Each state also sets minimum earnings and work-hours thresholds for benefits eligibility. Benefits are payable to workers who are laid off, but generally not to those who have quit or been fired for cause. Benefits, which are usually available for up to twenty-six weeks, are a function of past earnings, although minimum and maximum benefit levels are specified. Employers pay a tax on individual workers' earnings up to a ceiling. Because the ceiling is set quite low, the UI payroll tax usually constitutes a fixed cost of employment.

UI benefits tend to be less generous in the United States than in other industrialized countries. According to a cross-country comparison of UI benefits among Organization for Economic Cooperation and Development countries (OECD 1994), the benefit entitlements in the United States and Japan have been set at relatively low levels in terms of average replacement rate and duration of benefit for the last thirty years. In contrast, Australia, New Zealand, and most European Union countries began with much more generous benefit entitlements in the 1960s compared to the United States, and most of these countries have subsequently raised entitlements. Countries such as Spain, Portugal, Greece, Finland, Norway, and Sweden had relatively low benefit entitlements in the 1960s but now generally offer more generous UI benefits than does the United States.

Although U.S. employers are not required to provide health insurance to workers, federal and state laws mandate that employers provide a number of health-related benefits to their workers. The Pregnancy Discrimination Act of 1978, for example, requires that firms offering their employees health insurance benefits include comprehensive maternity benefits in the package. Jonathan Gruber (1994a) notes that there are more than one thousand state-mandated health insurance benefits, such as the requirement that health insurance policies cover alcoholism. The Family and Medical Leave Act passed in February 1993 requires that companies that employ fifty or more people provide their employees with at least twelve weeks of unpaid leave per year so that they may care for a child following birth or adoption, care for a seriously ill member of the family, or deal with other family emergencies. The law stipulates that employers continue the health insurance, if provided, of an employee taking this leave. In addition to the federal statute, many states have additional regulations governing parental leave.[2]

Unlike the United States, most industrialized countries have some form of mandatory health insurance for their citizens. In France, Germany, Japan, Belgium, and the Netherlands, employers are subject to a payroll tax that finances the health insurance coverage of their employees. Parental leave legislation dates back to the late nineteenth and early twentieth centuries in some European countries. This early legislation was largely designed to keep women out of the workforce during the prenatal and postnatal period. Beginning in the late 1960s, laws in many countries were reformed to allow parents time off to care for newborns and young children and at the same time to protect workers' incomes and jobs during this leave. In contrast to the situation in the United States, income support is provided for workers on parental leave in almost all industrialized countries. The wage replacement rate in other countries is almost always above 50 percent, and often above 80 percent.

Typically, the government makes the payments to those on parental leave, although Belgium, Germany, Italy, and the United Kingdom require that employers provide the income support. The duration of mandatory leave is also considerably longer in most other industrialized countries than in the United States.[3]

The requirement that employers provide workers with notice prior to dismissal is another form of employer mandate. Prior to federal legislation passed in 1988, only three states (Maine, Wisconsin, and Hawaii) mandated advance notice of plant closings or mass layoffs.[4] The 1988 Worker Adjustment and Retraining Notification Act requires that employers give workers and state and local governments sixty days' notice prior to a mass layoff or plant closure. A mass layoff is generally defined as the layoff of at least one-third of the workforce at a single site over a thirty-day period, or a situation in which at least one-third of the employees have their hours reduced by at least 50 percent over a six-month period. Because a minimum of fifty workers must be affected for the advance notice requirements to apply, the statute effectively exempts small establishments.[5] The law also exempts companies from providing sixty days' notice in a number of other circumstances, including when the company could not reasonably foresee the layoff.

Advance notice laws date back to the late nineteenth and early twentieth centuries in some European countries. Whereas U.S. law requires only that advance notice be given in the event of a mass layoff, the laws of virtually all other industrialized countries require employers to provide workers with notice prior to all layoffs.[6] The amount of mandatory notice typically varies with the laid-off worker's tenure with the company and, in some countries, according to whether that person is a blue- or white-collar worker.

In addition to mandatory advance notice, most countries require that dismissals be socially or economically justified; that employers provide workers with compensation under certain circumstances; and that additional steps be taken in the event of a mass layoff. All European Union countries require that employers notify labor authorities and inform and consult with employee representatives if contemplating a mass layoff. In cases of mass layoffs, many countries require an additional waiting period between the time the employer notifies the government and the time layoffs may occur. In some countries, including Germany and Belgium, the government may extend that waiting period, if deemed socially desirable.[7]

Both federal and state laws govern minimum wages in the United States. The first federal statute concerning minimum wages, the Fair

Labor Standards Act, was passed in 1938. Initially, federal minimum wage standards applied only to workers involved in interstate commerce. Although the coverage of workers under the federal law has expanded greatly since then, there remain some exemptions. In particular, employees in small firms are not covered by minimum-wage laws. According to a recent Department of Labor report, about 12 percent of nonsupervisory workers are not covered by federal minimum wage laws (U.S. Department of Labor 1993, table 7). Many states also have minimum-wage laws. These state laws primarily stipulate minimum wages for workers not covered by federal law. Some states, including New Jersey and California, occasionally have set minimum wages for all workers that exceeded the federal minimum.

Like the United States, most other industrialized countries have some mechanism for setting minimum wages. In Canada, France, the Netherlands, and Spain, minimum wages are fixed by statute at the federal or regional level, as in the United States. In Belgium, Germany, Italy, and Sweden, minimum wages are set through legally binding national or sectoral agreements. Comparing countries with statutory minimum wages, the OECD (1994, 47–48) reports that the ratio of the minimum wage to the average wage is low in the United States, Canada, and Spain relative to that in the Netherlands and France.

In sum, compared with other countries, employer mandates and related programs in the United States are weak. Unemployment insurance benefits and minimum wages tend to be low relative to those in other advanced industrialized countries. Moreover, mandated benefits, such as parental leave, advance notice, and other types of protection against dismissal, have either not been introduced in the United States or been introduced only recently in a comparatively weak form.

Theories of the Effects of Employer Mandates

Justifications for the imposition of employer mandates fall into two broad categories: arguments that mandates improve the efficient operation of the labor market and arguments that mandates improve equity. Economists tend to focus on the former, identifying various market failures that might warrant the imposition of specific employer mandates in order to improve economic efficiency.[8] Problems related to asymmetric information and adverse selection have been cited to justify mandates such as workers' compensation and parental leave. If only some firms offer insurance against workplace injury or parental leave, workers who are more prone to injury or expect to take parental leave will sort themselves into the firms that offer these benefits, thus raising the costs of providing the benefits and contributing to an underprovision of these benefits relative to what is socially desirable. Mandatory advance notice and requirements that firms inform and consult with worker representatives prior to layoffs are also justified on efficiency grounds if firms have better information than workers about the probability of layoff and if firms have an incentive to withhold that information from workers.

Various externalities have also been used to justify employer mandates. For example, the fact that layoffs may have societal costs that are not taken into account by firms and workers has been used to justify experience-rated unemployment insurance taxes, advance notice requirements, and other restrictions on dismissal. The widespread absence of parental leave policies in firms may impose costs on society, for example, in the form of a greater need for publicly financed remedial education. Sick people who lack health insurance are less likely to be treated and thus more likely to pass on contagious diseases to others. In addition, uninsured individuals who receive treatment often cannot pay for it and the cost of their health care is absorbed by doctors and hospitals in the form of lower profits and by other patients in the form of higher charges and insurance premiums. Such externalities have been cited by proponents of employer mandated health insurance.

Although economists tend to focus on efficiency arguments for employer mandates, achieving equity is arguably the more important political motivation for legislating employer mandates. Employer mandates are viewed as a mechanism for increasing labor's bargaining power vis-à-vis employers, and thus as a way to improve the compensation and working conditions of less advantaged workers. Indeed, the motivation underlying this chapter is to evaluate the effectiveness of employer mandates in raising earnings and labor standards among those in the bottom half of the earnings distribution, whose wages and benefits have fallen in recent years.

Whether employer mandates are effective tools to raise the compensation and improve the working conditions of low-wage workers depends on the structure of the labor market. I turn now to the effects of various employer mandates under alternative assumptions of competitive and imperfectly competitive labor markets.

The Effects of Employer Mandates with Competitive Labor Markets

Most analyses of employer mandates explicitly or implicitly assume that labor markets may be adequately characterized by models of perfect

competition. Under the assumption of perfect competition, the imposition of a mandated benefit, which may be thought of as having a cost per
unit of labor, like a payroll tax, shifts the market labor demand curve
leftward. As shown in figure 5.1, under this scenario, employment falls
from L_0 to L_1, and the wage rate falls from W_0 to W_1. This scenario over-
states the disemployment effect of the mandated benefit, however, if
workers value the mandated benefit and are willing to take wage cuts in
return for the benefit. If workers value the mandated benefit, the labor
supply curve shifts rightward, and in the diagram, wages fall further to
W_2; employment at L_2 is greater than it is when workers do not value the
benefit. The change in the wage rate with the imposition of an employer
mandate may be expressed as follows:

(5.1)
$$\frac{-(\eta^D - \alpha\eta^S)}{(\eta^D - \eta^S)}$$

where η^D is the elasticity of labor demand, η^S is the elasticity of labor
supply, and α is the fraction of the mandated benefit valued by the employee. If α equals 1, then the cost of the benefit is fully absorbed by

Figure 5.1   The Effects of a Mandated Benefit on Wages
and Employment

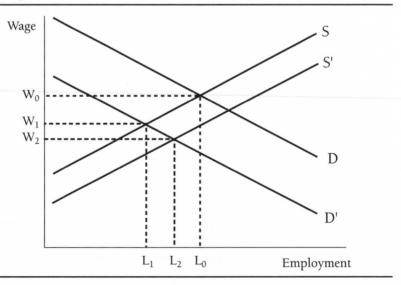

workers through lower wages and the level of employment is unaffected. Conversely, if α equals 0, workers do not value the benefit, the labor supply curve does not shift rightward, and the equilibrium outcomes are L_1 and W_1 in figure 5.1.[9] In addition, the cost of the mandated benefit is not shifted onto wages if there is a binding minimum wage.

If the mandated benefit or payroll tax represents a fixed cost of employment, then it is likely to distort the choice between hours and employment. Mandates or taxes with a large fixed-cost component are likely to result in longer hours worked per employee and lower employment levels. For this reason, economists generally have favored mandates that are a variable cost of employment. Similarly, if certain groups of workers, such as part-time and temporary workers, are exempted from coverage, imposition of the mandate leads to a substitution of exempted workers for covered workers. Patricia Anderson and Bruce Meyer (1995) point out that if a mandate or tax applies only to certain firms, those firms are less likely to be able to pass the costs of the mandate or tax on to workers, because the supply of labor to an individual firm is more elastic than to the market as a whole. In addition, the limited imposition of the mandate is likely to shift some resources in the economy away from firms in the covered sector toward firms in the uncovered sector. The imposition of employer mandates may have other distorting effects on behavior. One of the most studied examples is the effect of unemployment insurance on job search behavior.

The effect of an imposition of a binding minimum wage in a competitive labor market is analogous to that of a mandated benefit or payroll tax. In figure 5.1, labor demand and supply curves are drawn in wage and employment space, holding constant the cost per unit-labor of benefits or taxes. One could redraw the diagram in benefit per unit-labor and employment space, holding wages constant (assuming that workers receive some benefits). An increase in the minimum wage then shifts labor demand leftward and labor supply rightward. In the absence of distorting tax effects (for example, if benefits are not subject to income tax but wages are), we would expect the rightward shift in labor supply to offset fully the leftward shift in labor demand; the rise in wages is thus fully absorbed by a fall in benefits. Figure 5.2 shows the same analysis in the more familiar wage-employment space. A minimum wage set above the equilibrium wage reduces employment and, in the figure, employment falls from L_0 to L_1. However, if workers accept lower benefits in return for higher wages, demand shifts rightward, mitigating the adverse effects on employment.

Figure 5.2   The Effect of a Minimum Wage on Employment
in a Competitive Market

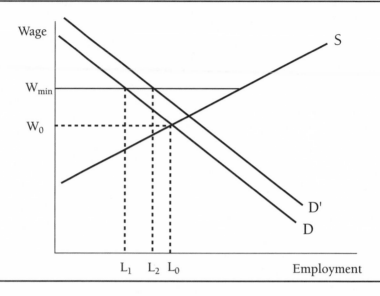

This analysis has focused on the effects of various types of employer mandates on the labor market. To the extent that the costs of the mandate are absorbed by firms, these costs may be passed on to consumers—and hence in large part back to workers—in the form of higher prices. If one assumes that product markets are competitive, and thus that excess profits are rare, profits ultimately absorb very little of the cost of an employer mandate.[10] Under the assumption that labor and product markets are perfectly competitive, workers bear most of the cost of an employer mandate through lower wages and/or other benefits, through unemployment, and through higher product prices. If one believes, therefore, that perfect competition adequately characterizes markets, there is little justification for trying to improve equity through employer mandates.

The Effects of Employer Mandates with Imperfectly Competitive Labor Markets

Relatively little theoretical work has been done on the effects of employer mandates when labor markets are imperfectly competitive. A notable exception in recent years is some of the literature on the impact of the minimum wage.[11] Various models have been developed in which firms have monopsonistic power in the labor market. Although the models typically examine the impact of the minimum wage, their conclusions generally apply to other types of mandated benefits.

In the standard monopsony model (depicted in figure 5.3), the individual firm faces an upward-sloping labor supply curve. The profit-maximizing firm sets the marginal cost of labor equal to the value marginal product of labor. The resulting equilibrium wage and employment levels, W_0 and L_0, are both below the levels that prevail in perfectly competitive markets. In the case of a monopsony, the imposition of the minimum wage could increase employment, and hence improve efficiency. A minimum wage, shown in figure 5.3, raises the equilibrium employment level to L_{min}. A minimum wage set between W_0 and W_1 increases employment, whereas a minimum wage set above W_1 decreases employment levels, as in the competitive model. Although this result has been long known, it was generally regarded as a theoretical curiosity because of the belief that, apart from one-company towns, the monopsony model was not a good description of labor markets.

However, a couple of variations on the standard monopsony model developed in recent years demonstrate the possible existence of monopsony power in labor markets under plausible circumstances. In one vari-

Figure 5.3   The Effects of a Minimum Wage on Employment
in a Monopsony Market

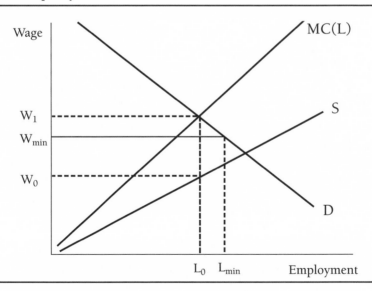

ant, workers possess imperfect information about the set of job opportunities available, firms face hiring costs and have unfilled vacancies, and equilibrium employment in a firm is determined by its quit rate and hiring rate, which, in turn, are functions of the wage the firm offers. Thus, firms effectively face an upward-sloping labor supply curve and, by implication, wages increase with firm size. In these models, a small increase in the minimum wage may increase employment, particularly in small, low-paying firms.[12]

Another source of monopsony power arises when firms face costs in monitoring employees' work. If workers are caught shirking, they are fired, and the cost to the workers of being fired is related to the difference in the wage they are paid on the job and their alternative wage. In these models, it is assumed that workers' effort depends on the size of that gap, and hence firms may induce a greater work effort from their employees by increasing wages. James Rebitzer and Lowell Taylor (1995) assume that the probability of being caught shirking is a decreasing function of firm size, and thus that the no-shirking wage is an increasing function of employment. As in the standard monopsony model, a small increase in the minimum wage increases employment in firms affected by the increase.

A further reason employment may not fall following an increase in the minimum wage or imposition of another employer mandate is that the cost of adjusting capital is high in the short run. In the extreme "putty-clay" model of capital, once capital is installed, its use cannot be changed and it requires a fixed amount of labor. No adjustment of labor occurs in the short run, and capital absorbs all the costs of the employer mandate.

More generally, both labor and capital may face costs of adjustment that arise, for example, from mobility costs and from firm-specific human and physical capital such that labor's and capital's alternative wage or rent is below their marginal product in their current use. In the presence of such adjustment costs, the incidence of the cost of an employer mandate between labor and capital is indeterminate. In a rent-sharing or bargaining model, the imposition of a minimum wage or other mandated benefit may change the division of rents between labor and capital—or, with heterogeneous labor, between different groups of workers—without affecting resource allocation, at least in the short run.

Another potential source of indeterminacy is the joint production of many goods and services: it may be difficult, if not impossible, to isolate the marginal contribution of any individual worker or piece of physical capital. Again, this source of indeterminacy suggests that the imposition of a minimum wage or other employer mandate may change the division of rents by affecting what is considered a fair division of rents or otherwise influencing labor's bargaining power in an economy.

Finally, some have argued that managers do not maximize profits strictly and thus that there is considerable slack in the economy.[13] By raising labor costs, the imposition of employer mandates may increase the efficient use of labor. Moreover, an increase in the price of labor may encourage firms to invest more in training their workers to increase their marginal product. With such dynamics, labor standards, including the sorts of employer mandates discussed in this chapter, may bump an economy out of an equilibrium of low-paying, low-skill, high-turnover jobs into an equilibrium of high-paying, high-skill, low-turnover jobs.

Empirical Evidence on the Effects of Employer Mandates

Evidence on the effects of employer mandates generally falls into three broad areas: (1) the costs, in terms of lower employment or other distortions to resource allocation; (2) the incidence, that is, who, between workers, firms, and consumers, bears the costs of employer mandates; and (3) the benefits, such as smoothing consumption (unemployment insurance), reducing unemployment durations (advance notice), and lowering poverty (minimum wages). Although most of the evidence reviewed here comes from time-series or cross-section, time-series studies of specific employer mandates in the United States, I also present selected evidence from studies of employer mandates in other countries and from cross-country comparisons of the effects of specific mandates. Arguably, the effect of one policy cannot be isolated but rather depends on the set of other policies that are in place. To conclude the section, I review evidence from several studies that have endeavored to examine the joint effect of two or more policies.

Unemployment Insurance and Workers' Compensation

Unemployment insurance may increase unemployment and/or reduce employment for two reasons: (1) the incidence of the UI tax may fall largely on employers, which in turn reduce employment levels because of the higher labor costs, and (2) the existence of unemployment insurance may lengthen unemployment spells, either because workers search less intensively for employment or because they do not drop out of the labor force as soon as they otherwise would. Most studies of unemployment insurance have focused on measuring the latter. Numerous studies using U.S. data have examined the effects of benefit entitlements and duration of benefit entitlements on unemployment duration. Estimates from these studies of the effects of a ten-percentage-point increase in the UI replacement rate—defined as the ratio of weekly UI benefits to the average weekly wage—on the duration of unemployment range from about 0 to 1.5 weeks. Estimates of the effects of a 1-week increase in the potential duration of UI benefits on the duration of unemployment vary from 0.05 to 0.5 weeks.[14]

Interestingly, despite common perceptions that more generous UI benefits have raised the unemployment rate in Europe, cross-country comparisons show no positive correlation between the generosity of unemployment benefits and aggregate unemployment rates. A recent OECD study (1994) examines the hypothesis that increases in unemployment following a macroeconomic shock persist because of generous unemployment benefits; thus, the unemployment insurance system affects unemployment levels with a long lag. Support for this hypothesis is found only in some specifications and when small countries (which are "outliers" in the initial analysis) are excluded. In view of its own findings and those of previous studies, however, the OECD concludes that changes in the unemployment insurance system in Europe are unlikely to result in major reductions in European unemployment.

It should be emphasized that the studies cited thus far focus on the relationship between UI benefits and unemployment. It is widely assumed that increased unemployment comes at the expense of employment, but it could also reflect greater labor force participation: many workers may choose not to drop out of the labor force until they have exhausted their UI benefits. The source of the increased unemployment has important implications for resource allocation in the economy.

While many studies have examined the effects of UI on unemployment, little work has been done on the incidence of the unemployment insurance tax. Patricia Anderson and Bruce Meyer (1995) note that a firm's UI tax rate may change because the UI tax rate schedule in the state in which it is located shifts or because its position on that schedule changes owing to experience rating. They theorize that an increase in a state's tax schedule, which affects all firms in the market, is more likely to be borne by workers than is an increase that is specific to the firm. They predict, in turn, that a firm-specific tax increase will have greater effects on employment than a tax increase affecting all firms in the market, and they use administrative data from eight states to test this hypothesis. Although their results are somewhat sensitive to specification, they generally find that statewide tax hikes are borne largely by workers, whereas firm-specific tax hikes are born largely by firms and result in employment declines.

Additional evidence of costs being shifted onto workers' wages in social insurance programs comes from Jonathan Gruber and Alan Krueger's (1991) study of workers' compensation. They use variation in insurance rates by state and occupation to study the incidence of workers' compensation. With data on individuals from the CPS outgoing rotation groups, they estimate that 87 percent of the insurance cost is shifted onto workers in the form of lower wages. Using the BLS's ES-202 establishment data, they estimate that between 56 and 86 percent of the insurance cost is shifted onto wages, while they find small negative, but statistically insignificant, effects of workers' compensation on employment levels.

The primary intent of unemployment insurance and workers' compensation is to smooth income and consumption of those affected by spells of unemployment or work-related disability. Such smoothing is probably most important for low-income workers, who are likely to have little savings on which to draw and few assets against which to borrow during periods of unemployment, injury, or illness.[15] Gruber (1994b) reports evidence of such consumption smoothing from unemployment insurance.[16]

Maternity Benefits and Parental Leave

Few studies have been conducted on the effects of mandatory provision of maternity benefits in health insurance coverage and of parental leave for the care of new and sick children and other family members. Several states mandated that employers providing health insurance include maternity benefits as part of the insurance package prior to the introduction of such a mandate at the federal level in 1978. Gruber (1994c) looks at the effects on wages, hours, and employment of mandated maternity benefits in health insurance in states that required such coverage relative to states not requiring such coverage prior to 1978. He also looks at similar effects in states that had not passed such legislation relative to those that had after 1978. He finds that the added cost of the maternity benefits is largely shifted onto the wages of married women of child-bearing age and, to a lesser extent, single women of child-bearing age. Curiously for his theory, he does not find substantial cost shifting onto the wages of married men of child-bearing age, whose wives are likely to be covered under their health insurance. Although the finding from this study—that beneficiaries of the maternity benefits largely bear the cost of providing them—implies that mandated maternity benefits should have few adverse employment effects, it also implies that such a mandate does not help to redistribute resources toward low-income workers.

Christopher Ruhm and Jackqueline Teague (1993) pool time-series data over the 1960 to 1989 period for seventeen countries to examine the relationship between the duration of total and paid parental leave, on the one hand, and per capita GDP and the rate of change in per capita GDP on the other. The number of countries mandating job-protected family leave and the duration of that leave grew over the period. In their cross-country comparison, they find no evidence that parental leave is associated with weak economic growth. Rather, their evidence implies a small beneficial effect on growth. They do not examine whether their findings result, in part, from a shifting of the costs of parental leave onto workers' wages or from other factors.

Although no statistical analyses have been made of the effects of the 1993 U.S. Family and Medical Leave Act, a couple of surveys conducted shortly after the law took effect find widespread noncompliance.[17] The findings from these surveys raise the important issue of enforcement, which is rarely addressed in economic studies of the effects of mandates. A law that appears to impose a significant employer mandate may have few effects—positive or negative—if there is no adequate mechanism for enforcing it and compliance is low.

Advance Notice and Other Employment Protection Laws

During the late 1960s and 1970s, many European countries strengthened their laws protecting workers against dismissal. Some blame the rise in unemployment in many European countries in the 1980s on these dismissal regulations. While employment protection laws were relaxed in several European countries during the 1980s, the United States passed its first federal requirement that companies give workers and government officials advance notice prior to mass layoffs. Higher European unemployment and changes in employment protection laws on both sides of the Atlantic spurred many to study the effects of these requirements on employment and unemployment.

Several different methodologies have been utilized to examine these effects. In one group of studies, annual cross-country, time-series data are used and an index of the stringency of employment protection laws is constructed for each country-year observation. Using this approach, Edward Lazear (1990) finds a positive relation between the level of mandatory severance pay and the level of mandatory advance notice, on the one hand, and a country's unemployment rate on the other. John Addison and Jean-Luc Grosso (1996) redo Lazear's analysis, correcting for some problems with his data. While their analysis confirms Lazear's finding that severance pay increases unemployment, they find that advance notice decreases unemployment. Giuseppe Bertola (1990) and the OECD (1993) look at the relationship between the stringency of employment protection laws and both aggregate unemployment and the persistence of unemployment. Bertola finds a weak relationship between the stringency of employment protection laws and the unemployment rate, but a strong relationship between the stringency of those laws and long-term unemployment. The OECD (1993) also finds some positive relationship between the stringency of employment protection laws and long-term unemployment but notes that the regression residuals for some countries in its study are very high, suggesting that other factors are important determinants of long-term unemployment.

One limitation of all of these cross-country studies is the crudeness of the indexes constructed to measure the stringency of employment protection laws across time and countries. The de facto stringency of a regulation often depends on nuances in the law that are difficult to capture in simple classification schemes. To illustrate this point, consider that in Germany there is no mandatory severance pay. However, the law requires that the employer negotiate with the works councils to determine compensation for workers affected by collective dismissals. In the event that the parties cannot reach agreement, the case goes to binding arbitration. Indexes that set severance pay in Germany equal to zero fail to capture the effects of an important requirement in German employment protection law. Perhaps not surprisingly, the ordering of countries in terms of the stringency of their laws varies considerably across studies, with important effects on findings.[18]

Several studies compare employment and hours adjustment patterns across countries to draw inferences about the effects of employment protection laws, and possibly other labor market institutions, on adjustment behavior. Because employment protection laws presumably raise the costs of reducing employment levels, one would expect that the adjustment of employment to changes in demand is slower in countries with strong employment protection laws than in countries with weak employment protection laws, all else being the same. However, employers in countries with strong employment protection laws may compensate by adjusting hours per employee more quickly. Researchers have viewed a slower adjustment, particularly of total labor hours, as an indication of the costs of employment protection laws. Collectively, these studies show that employment adjustment is slowest in Japan, followed by Europe, and fastest in the United States and Canada.[19] Findings are more mixed, however, from studies comparing the adjustment of total labor input to demand changes. For example, Marc Van Audenrode (1994) finds that total labor adjustment is as rapid in certain European countries with stringent employment protection laws as in the United States.[20] While Katharine Abraham and Susan Houseman (1994) find that the adjustment of total production hours in aggregate manufacturing is slower in Germany and Belgium than in the United States, the results for aggregate manufacturing are driven by sluggish adjustment in selected German and Belgian industries. Other studies (for example, Köhler and Sengenberger 1983; Houseman 1988; Abraham and Houseman 1993; and Houseman and Abraham 1995) show that cross-country comparisons of labor adjustment can be sensitive to the industry studied.

Some studies attempt to assess the effects of employment protection laws by looking at the impact of significant changes in these laws on employment and hours adjustment patterns within countries. Stephen Nickell (1979) examines the impact of the strengthening of employment protection laws in the United Kingdom. He finds that the responsiveness of employment to output slowed following the change and that the responsiveness of average hours to output increased over time, as expected. Another study (Abraham and Houseman 1994) finds little evidence of any effect of the relaxation of employment protection laws in the mid-1980s on adjustment behavior in Germany and Belgium but finds some evidence that the relaxation of such laws increased the speed of employment adjustment in France.

The passage of the first federal legislation in the United States requiring that employers give advance notice prior to a mass layoff prompted several studies of the potential benefits of advance notice. Most of these studies use data from the periodic CPS supplement on worker dislocation, which contains information on whether a worker received notice (or in earlier studies whether the worker knew of the layoff) prior to being laid off. All of these studies find that advance notice reduces the duration of expected unemployment. Estimates of the average reduction in the duration of joblessness vary from about four weeks (Addison and Portugal 1987) to just three to five days (Ruhm 1992). The reduction in the duration of joblessness associated with advance notice largely comes from workers who are able to find jobs prior to the layoff and thus avoid a spell of unemployment. Researchers generally find that the benefits of advance notice vary across groups of workers. For example, John Addison and McKinley Blackburn (1995) find that notice reduces the duration of joblessness for white-collar men and women and for blue-collar women, but not for blue-collar men. Christopher Ruhm (1992) finds particularly beneficial effects of written notice for household heads, females, nonwhites, and residents of areas with high unemployment. Ruhm (1994) also finds that workers receiving advance notice earn 10 percent more than workers receiving no notice three to five years following displacement.[21] Thus, the empirical evidence that advance notice reduces joblessness and increases income is quite strong.

No studies, to my knowledge, attempt to assess directly the effects of the advance notice requirement on employment or employer costs in the United States. However, a recent study by the U.S. General Accounting Office (1993) suggests that any effects—positive or negative—are likely to be minimal. That study examines a sample of companies that appeared to meet the criteria requiring advance notice and finds that three-quarters either failed to provide any notice or provided less than the sixty days' notice mandated by law. The implication of the study is that many companies are using one of the law's exemptions to avoid providing notice or are simply not complying with the law. This case underscores the importance of understanding the fine points of a legal mandate and the problems of enforcing a mandate when assessing its impact.

Minimum Wages

Few topics have been as widely researched by economists as the minimum wage. Recent increases in the minimum wage at the state and federal levels prompted a number of new studies on their effects. Most minimum-wage studies focus on measuring the effects of an increase in the minimum wage on employment. Estimates from earlier time-series studies in the United States typically showed that a 10 percent increase in the minimum wage resulted in a 1 to 2 percent fall in teenage employment. Brown, Gilroy, and Kohen (1982) review those studies; here I focus primarily on studies conducted in the last few years.

Several recent studies, using a variety of data sets and methodologies, find no effect or even a positive effect of the minimum wage on employment, contrary to standard theory. Using data from a survey of fast-food restaurants in New Jersey and Pennsylvania taken before and after the 1992 hike in New Jersey's minimum wage, David Card and Alan Krueger (1994) look at the effects of the New Jersey minimum-wage increase by comparing changes in employment in the sample of fast-food restaurants in New Jersey to changes in employment in the sample of Pennsylvania fast-food restaurants. Their analysis suggests that the minimum-wage increase had a positive effect on employment. Lawrence Katz and Alan Krueger (1992) use a longitudinal survey of fast-food restaurants in Texas in December 1990 and in July and August 1991 to study the effect of the April 1991 increase in the federal minimum wage from $3.80 per hour to $4.25 per hour. To measure the employment effects of the increase, they calculate the proportional increase required in the starting wage for a firm to comply with the new minimum. Their minimum-wage gap measure is positively correlated with employment—again, contrary to standard theory. They also find some evidence that full-time workers are substituted for part-time workers with an increase in the minimum wage, and little evidence of widespread use by employers of the youth subminimum. Stephen Machin and Alan Manning (1994) study the effects of minimum wages on employment in Britain. Prior to being abolished by the Conservative government in 1993, wage councils, composed of industry and labor representatives, set industry-level minimum wages in Britain. Machin and Manning find that a reduction in the minimum wage relative to the average wage was associated with no effect or even a negative effect on employment.

In two separate studies, Card (1992a, 1992b) finds little effect of minimum-wage increases on employment. Card (1992a) looks at the effect of the rise in California's minimum wage from $3.35 to $4.25 in July 1988 on teenage employment and employment in the retail trade sector. Comparing changes in teenage employment and employment in the retail trade sector in California with employment changes in comparison groups in other states, he finds no evidence that the rise affected either teenage employment or California retail employment. Card (1992b) also looks at the effect of the federal 1990 minimum-wage hike on employment and school enrollment rates of teenagers by exploiting regional variation in the minimum wage arising in large part because several states had already raised their minimum wage prior to 1990. One would expect, all else being the same, that the minimum-wage hike has a less adverse impact in states where a lower fraction of workers were initially earning less than the new minimum. Card generally finds no significant effect of the minimum-wage hike on teenage employment or on school enrollment.

Other recent studies find significant negative impacts of a rise in the minimum wage on employment. David Neumark and William Wascher (1992) construct a state panel data set on minimum wages over the 1973 to 1989 period and use cross-state variation in the minimum wage to estimate its effects on the employment of teenagers and young adults. They find that allowing for lagged effects of a rise in the minimum wage is important. In certain specifications they find a negative employment elasticity of between −.1 and −.2.[22] In another study, Neumark and Wascher (1997) try to replicate the findings of the Card and Krueger (1994) study of employment in the fast-food industry in New Jersey and Pennsylvania using data from another industry survey. They claim that the data used by Card and Krueger are implausibly noisy, a fact that they attribute to the way those data were collected. In contrast to the findings reported by Card and Krueger, their data show that an increase in the minimum wage in New Jersey was associated with a decrease in employment, as would be predicted by standard theory.[23]

Janet Currie and Bruce Fallick (1992) use the NLS survey of youth to examine the employment experiences of low-wage youth following the 1980 and 1981 federal minimum-wage increases. They find a significant negative impact of a minimum-wage increase on the probability of employment among youth directly affected by the increase.

Donald Deere, Kevin Murphy, and Finis Welch (1995) use state-level data to look at employment trends by sex, race, age, and education group following the minimum-wage hikes in 1990 and 1991. In regressions that control for the employment-to-population ratio of working-age men, they find that demographic groups with high concentrations of low-wage workers experienced lower employment growth relative to other demographic groups following the minimum-wage hikes. Their results, however, may be a product of the recession that coincided with the minimum-wage hikes. Historically, low-wage workers have experienced relatively greater employment losses than have high-wage workers during recessions.

In sum, some recent minimum-wage studies find positive effects of the minimum wage on employment, others find no effect, and still others detect negative effects. Before examining the reasons behind the different findings in these studies, one might question whether in fact the findings from all of these studies differ that much. Ronald Ehrenberg (1992), among others, argues that even in studies that show negative employment effects, as predicted by standard theory, the estimated elasticities, which typically fall between −.1 and −.2 for teenagers, are small. Others argue that, on the contrary, these elasticities greatly understate the impacts on workers directly affected by the minimum-wage increase. For example, most teenagers earn more than the minimum wage. The elasticity of employment with respect to the minimum wage for teenagers earning the minimum wage presumably is much higher.

Neumark and Wascher (1996) note that while the net effects of minimum-wage increases on teenage employment may be small, the gross flows effects may be large. Using data on individuals matched across CPS surveys, they find evidence that working teenagers are displaced by more highly skilled teenagers entering the labor force when minimum wages are raised.

Apart from criticisms of the data or methodologies used in specific studies, several hypotheses have been put forward to explain why a number of recent studies have found no effect, or even a statistically positive effect, of the minimum wage on employment. Because of the costs of adjusting labor and capital, firms may spread out any adjustment of labor and capital to the higher minimum wage over time, and thus the full effect of a minimum-wage hike may be observed only after a considerable lag. Measuring the impact of a minimum-wage increase just a few months following its implementation, as is done in several studies that find positive or no effects of minimum-wage increases on employment, may be too soon to detect effect; at least one study finds the inclusion of lagged effects important (Neumark and Wascher, 1992). The implications for policy greatly depend on how long any lagged effects are. Another possible explanation for some studies' findings of positive or no employment effects of minimum-wage hikes is that the increase may not be an exogenous event. For example, states raising their minimum wages are more likely to do so when their economies are strong and the disemployment effects are minimal. In countries where minimum wages are negotiated on an industry basis (as in the United Kingdom, studied in Machin and Manning [1994]), negotiated increases again are likely to occur when their disemployment effects are small. Under the theory of competitive labor markets, an increase in the minimum wage may not reduce employment if employers reduce fringe benefits to compensate for the increase in wages. However, there is little evidence that such an offset occurs.[24]

The effect of a specific percentage increase in the minimum wage is also likely to be related to the starting point. The higher the initial minimum wage, the greater the number of people who are affected by the increase, and the greater the expected elasticity estimate. Arguably, because the minimum wage has been set at a low level in the United States, particularly in recent years, the estimated elasticities will be low. Moreover, any employment impacts from an increase in the minimum wage are likely to be swamped by other economic forces, thus making these effects difficult to measure. Alida Castillo-Freeman and Richard Freeman (1992) examine the case of Puerto Rico, where the minimum wage was increased rapidly to align it with the U.S. mainland minimum and where the ratio of the minimum wage to the average wage is high. They argue that if a minimum-wage increase reduces employment, it should be readily apparent in the Puerto Rican data. In their aggregate time-series analysis, the estimated elasticity of the employment-to-population ratio with respect to the minimum wage is between −.11 and −.15. Although they note that the magnitude of this elasticity estimate is small, the implied disemployment effects are nevertheless large given the large increase in the minimum wage in Puerto Rico. In estimates that exploit cross-industry differences in the minimum wage, they estimate considerably larger negative employment elasticities.[25]

Finally, a minimum-wage increase may be observed to have no effect, or even a positive effect, if the wage-setting process described in the competitive model of labor markets does not apply. As noted earlier, firms may have monopsony power in the labor market such that small increases in the minimum wage have little effect or even a positive effect on employment levels. Other factors, including adjustment costs for labor and capital and the difficulty of determining individuals' marginal products when goods and services are jointly produced, may also affect wage-setting processes and the impact of a minimum-wage increase.

While a tremendous amount of research has been devoted to studying the potentially adverse efficiency effects of a minimum wage, relatively little attention has been paid to the potential equity benefits of minimum wages. Several recent studies examine the effects of minimum-wage increases on earnings and income distribution. David Card and Alan Krueger (1995) examine the effects of the 1990 to 1991 minimum-wage increase on earnings inequality. Lawrence Mishel, Jared Bernstein, and Edith Rasell (1995) simulate the effects of the Clinton administration's proposed increase to $5.15 per hour (which took effect in September 1997) and of a more generous increase that would restore the real value of the minimum wage to its 1979 level on earnings inequality. Because the minimum wage directly affects the earnings of those in the lowest percentiles, it is not surprising that both studies find that minimum-wage hikes have significant impacts on earnings distributions. For example, Card and Krueger estimate that about 30 percent of the increase in the earnings differential between the ninetieth and tenth percentiles over the 1979 to 1989 period was eliminated by the 1990 to 1991 minimum-wage increases. Mishel, Bernstein, and Rasell show that virtually all of the increase in the wage differential from 1979 to 1993 between the ninetieth and tenth percentiles for both men and women could be attributed to the falling value in real terms of the minimum wage.

The effects of a minimum-wage increase on family income distribution are more attenuated, however, because many minimum-wage workers live in high-earnings families. Recent studies have come to different conclusions about the effectiveness of minimum-wage increases in reducing income inequality. Michael Horrigan and Ronald Mincy (1993) simulate what would have happened to income inequality during the 1980s if the minimum wage had kept pace with inflation. Curiously, they find no effect on the distribution of income across quintiles and conclude that the benefits of the minimum wage accrue fairly evenly to workers at all income levels. Card and Krueger (1995) point out that this finding may be largely due to Horrigan and Mincy's inclusion of only hourly workers in their study; the distribution of income across these workers is much narrower than in the population at large. Both Card and Krueger (1995) and Mishel, Bernstein, and Rasell (1995) find that minimum-wage increases significantly reduce income inequality.

Arguably, the main political justification for increasing the minimum wage is not to reduce earnings or income inequality per se but rather to increase the incomes of poor families. Card and Krueger (1995) use state variation in the impact of the 1990 to 1991 minimum-wage increase to estimate the effects of the increase on state poverty rates. Although their estimated effect is negative, it is not statistically significant. Given that about two-thirds of adults in poverty do not work, it is perhaps not surprising that Card and Krueger are not able to measure the effects of minimum-wage increases on aggregate poverty rates with any precision. Mincy (1990) simulates the effects of an increase in the minimum wage from $3.35 to $4.25 on family poverty using 1987 CPS data. He incorporates disemployment effects into the simulation but finds that they have little effect because teenagers, who are the most likely to become disemployed by a minimum-wage hike, contribute the least to family income. Mincy estimates that a minimum wage increase from $3.35 to $4.25 in 1987 would have reduced the number of families in poverty with at least one wage earner by about 6 percent.

I have simulated the effects of the recent increase in the minimum wage from $4.25 per hour to $5.15 per hour on the poverty rates of hourly and salaried workers, using data from the March 1994 CPS.[26] For hourly workers I used the reported hourly wage; for salaried workers I divided reported weekly earnings by weekly hours worked.[27] The March CPS also reports a cutoff poverty income level for each family that depends, in part, on family size and composition and the cost of living in the region. While the wage data are for March 1994, the family income and poverty statistics refer to the previous calendar year. To minimize the problem of individuals in the sample being in different jobs in 1993 and 1994, I excluded all workers who reported working in a different industry or occupation in the two years.[28]

Table 5.1 reports the distribution of hourly and salaried workers by three wage categories—subminimum, between $4.25 and $5.14 (low-wage), and $5.15 and over—and three poverty statuses—family income below the poverty level, family income between 100 and 150 percent of the poverty level (near poverty), and family income over 150 percent of the poverty level. The table illustrates the well-known fact that most subminimum and low-wage workers are not in poverty. Only about 27 percent of workers earning subminimum wages live in poverty or near poverty, and only about 32 percent of low-wage workers live in poverty or near poverty. Nevertheless, workers in poverty or near poverty are much more likely than other workers to earn subminimum or very low wages. Among workers in poverty, about 9 percent earn subminimum wages and 37 percent earn low wages; among workers with family incomes near poverty levels, about 7 percent earn subminimum wages and 23 percent earn low wages; but among workers with family incomes

Table 5.1 Poverty Status by Wage Level for Hourly and Salaried Workers (Percentage of All Wage and Salaried Workers)

| Hourly Wage | Below Poverty | Poverty Status | | Total |
		100–150% Poverty Level	150% + Poverty Level	
<$4.25	0.45 (14.27) [9.10]	0.41 (13.07) [6.62]	2.29 (72.66) [2.58]	3.15
$4.25–5.15	1.83 (18.06) [37.10]	1.42 (14.02) [22.08]	6.89 (67.92) [7.76]	10.15
$5.15+	2.66 (3.06) [53.79]`	4.38 (5.06) [70.50]	79.66 (91.88) [89.67]	86.70
Total	4.94	6.22	88.84	100.00

Notes: Workers not reporting the same industry and occupation in the current period as in the previous year and workers reporting hourly earnings below $1 were excluded from the sample. The numbers in parentheses represent row percentages. The numbers in brackets represent column percentages.

above 150 percent of the poverty level, the percentages earning subminimum and low wages are just 3 percent and 8 percent, respectively.

Table 5.2 shows various simulations of the effect of raising the minimum wage on the percentage of workers living in poverty or near poverty. The simulations assume that no employment displacement occurs as a result of the minimum-wage increase. Even with this assumption, the simulations suggest that the increase will have very modest effects on poverty rates among the working poor. The first simulation assumes that only workers earning between the old minimum ($4.25) and the new minimum ($5.15) are affected by the increase, and the second simulation assumes that the wages of both subminimum and minimum-wage workers rise to the new minimum. In the first simulation, poverty rates among the working poor fall by just 1.5 percent, and in the second simulation they fall by just 3.2 percent.

One might ask whether the minimum-wage increase considered here is so ineffective in pulling the working poor out of poverty because the hike is too small or because the working poor, in fact, work very few hours, and thus the simulated minimum-wage hike has little effect on annual incomes. Table 5.3, which shows mean annual hours worked by poverty status, gives some support to the latter hypothesis. Mean annual hours increase with the ratio of family income to poverty-level income. The third simulation in table 5.2 shows what would happen to poverty levels if all working poor and near poor worked full-time, year-round jobs, with no increase in the minimum wage. In that simulation, all workers in poverty or near poverty were assigned two thousand annual hours if their actual annual hours fell below that level. An increase in hours by itself would have a quite significant impact on poverty rates among the working poor. In particular, almost one-quarter of the working poor would leave poverty if they worked full-time and year-round at their current wage.

The fourth and fifth simulations in table 5.2 show the combined effects of increasing working hours and increasing the minimum wage on the percentage of workers in poverty or near poverty, assuming that the minimum-wage hike affects only those earning between the old and new minimums and assuming that it affects all workers earning below the new minimum, respectively. In general, the marginal effects of an increase in the minimum wage on poverty are larger when workers work longer hours, as expected. They are nevertheless small, demonstrating that most of the working poor must not only work longer hours but also earn substantially more than $5.15 per hour to pull themselves and their families out of poverty.

Table 5.2 Simulated Poverty Status of Hourly and Salaried Workers with Minimum-Wage Increase and/or Annual Hours Increases

	Below Poverty Level		100–150% Poverty Level	
	Percent	Percent Reduction from Actual	Percent	Percent Reduction from Actual
Actual	4.94	—	6.22	—
1. Minimum wage = $5.15; only minimum-wage workers affected	4.86	−1.5	6.15	−1.2
2. Minimum wage = $5.15; minimum- and subminimum-wage workers affected	4.79	−3.2	6.08	−2.2
3. Annual hours increase; no minimum-wage increase	3.80	−23.0	5.97	−4.1
4. Annual hours increase; minimum wage =$5.15; only minimum-wage workers affected	3.75	−24.1	5.82	−6.4
5. Annual hours increase; minimum wage = $5.15; minimum- and subminimum-wage workers affected	3.44	−30.4	5.68	−8.6

Table 5.3   Mean Annual Hours of Hourly and Salaried Workers
by Poverty Status

	Below Poverty Level	100–150% Poverty Level	150% + Poverty Level
Mean	1,198	1,595	1,841

The Interaction of Government Programs

Most of the studies cited earlier try to isolate the marginal effects of changes in a particular mandate on a particular economic variable, such as employment and unemployment. Apart from the difficulty of measuring these effects in the data, the exercise may have a more fundamental conceptual problem. The economic effects of an employer mandate may depend on its interaction with other government policies and labor market institutions.

For example, any adverse employment effects from minimum wages may be mitigated by policies that help disadvantaged workers—who are the most likely to become disemployed by a minimum-wage increase—find employment. Most industrialized countries have job training programs designed to improve the skills of these workers and hence make them employable at a higher wage. Many countries also have programs that subsidize the wages of the long-term unemployed and other disadvantaged workers. In the United States the on-the-job training component of the Job Training Partnership Act (JTPA) provides a kind of temporary wage subsidy for disadvantaged workers.

The minimum wage may also affect the incidence of other employer mandates. Several studies have found that the costs of certain employer mandates are passed on to workers in the form of lower wages. The existence of a minimum wage prevents such cost shifting for low-wage workers. In a similar fashion, the minimum wage may affect the outcomes of other antipoverty measures such as the earned income tax credit (EITC). The EITC is a tax credit on an individual's income tax. To qualify, a household must have at least one dependent child, positive labor earnings, and total income less than a specified ceiling. If the credit exceeds the tax the household owes, the government pays the difference. Thus, over certain ranges, the EITC creates a negative income tax. The EITC, like the minimum wage, is designed to help the working poor. However, employers may capture some of the EITC through lower wages. In figure 5.4, the EITC would be expected to shift down labor

Figure 5.4   The Incidence of the EITC with a Minimum Wage

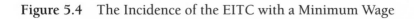

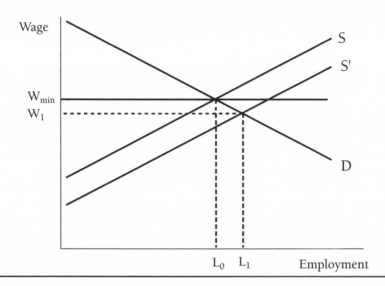

supply by the amount of the tax credit, causing wages to fall and employment to increase. As with a mandated benefit, the incidence of the EITC depends on the elasticity of labor demand and labor supply. The imposition of a minimum wage could help offset the downward shift in labor supply. In the diagram, if the minimum wage were set at W_{min}, all of the EITC benefits would accrue to workers.

The importance of the interaction of mandates with other policies in determining one mandate's effect is also nicely illustrated by employment protection laws. The employment impact of laws that place restrictions on the dismissal of workers clearly depends on the existence of laws governing fixed-term contracts. Some countries, such as Spain and Japan, have fairly stringent restrictions on the dismissal of workers but few restrictions on the use of fixed-term contracts. Consequently, much of the effect of dismissal laws in these countries is manifested in a shift from regular employment to temporary employment.

The effect of employment protection laws, which raise the costs of dismissing workers, also depends on the existence of other government policies that subsidize the costs of using alternatives to layoffs. For example, many countries with stringent employment protection laws also have unemployment insurance for short-time work and subsidies for

early retirement to encourage the use of hours reductions and retirement in lieu of layoffs. Several studies illustrate the importance of
short-time work to labor adjustment in countries with stringent employment protection laws (Abraham and Houseman 1993, 1994; Van
Audenrode 1994).

Some countries that have stringent employment protection laws,
such as Germany and Japan, also have labor market institutions that fos-
ter workplace training. Companies are less likely to lay off workers with
high levels of human capital, particularly firm-specific human capital,
during temporary downturns. Therefore, the effects of a given employment protection law on employment are likely to be less adverse in a
country with relatively high amounts of workplace training than in a
country with relatively low amounts of workplace training.

More generally, some countries with stringent employment protection laws have other policies and institutions in place that alleviate any
adverse effects of these mandates. Taken as a whole, the set of policies
and institutions results in a system that functions relatively smoothly. A
recent study by the European Commission finds a strong positive correlation between the stringency of employment protection laws and public expenditures to support employment adjustment among the four
largest member-states—France, Germany, Italy, and the United Kingdom
(Commission of the European Communities 1993). However, the commission also argues that in some cases, notably in some southern
European countries where social safety nets are not as well developed,
governments have tried to force companies to provide that safety net
by passing stringent employment protection laws. Under these circumstances, employment protection laws are likely to increase unemployment or the use of casual forms of employment not covered by the
legislation.

The broader point is that the interaction of employer mandates with
other policies and labor market institutions matters. Too few studies of
the effects of employer mandates have tried to take these interactions
into account.

Conclusion

I began this chapter by asking whether employer mandates are an effective mechanism to improve workers' wages, benefits, and other working
conditions. The answer to that question depends on (1) the extent to
which the mandates reduce employment or otherwise adversely affect

resource allocation, and (2) the extent to which workers realize substantial benefits from the mandates.

Most research on employer mandates focuses on the first set of factors. Studies generally show that employer mandates do not have large adverse effects on efficiency. Studies of mandated maternity benefits in the United States and parental leave laws in other countries show no adverse effects on employment or output. Although the availability of unemployment insurance lengthens unemployment spells, this effect primarily comes from the adverse incentives that unemployment insurance has on job search, not from the imposition of a payroll tax on employers. Some studies of the effects of employment protection laws, based on cross-country, time-series data, suggest that these laws may increase unemployment, particularly long-term unemployment. Other evidence suggests that the effects of these laws vary from country to country and depend greatly on their interaction with other government policies and labor institutions. Recent studies have reached no consensus on the employment effects of a minimum-wage increase: some studies show negative effects, some show no effect, and others show positive effects. Arguably, even if the evidence showing negative employment effects from an increase in the minimum wage is correct, the estimated elasticities are small. Of course, what constitutes small is somewhat subjective, and the view that the employment effects of a minimum-wage increase are small has many dissenters.

Research on the benefits of employer mandates is more limited. The literature on advance notice unambiguously shows that advance notice reduces the duration of joblessness, primarily because, with notice, many workers are able to line up jobs before they are laid off. One study also shows that advance notice is associated with higher wages following reemployment. The debate over the benefits of raising the minimum wage largely revolves around the extent to which minimum wage helps workers in low-income families. An increase in the minimum wage primarily benefits workers in families with below-average incomes. However, because a significant minority of minimum-wage workers are in families with above-average incomes, the minimum wage is generally regarded as a "blunt" instrument for helping low-income families. A minimum-wage increase is likely to be particularly ineffective in helping the working poor out of poverty. The simulations presented in this chapter suggest that only a very large minimum-wage increase—much larger than the one recently enacted—coupled with a large labor supply response or programs to increase hours worked among the working poor would significantly reduce poverty levels.

The benefits of mandates to workers depend in large part on who bears their cost. One reason most studies have found little or no disemployment effect from the imposition of employer mandates may be that the cost of the mandate is shifted onto workers. However, if the purpose of the mandate is to redistribute income, cost shifting onto workers is undesirable. The limited evidence on this subject is mixed. Recent studies of the incidence of workers' compensation and mandated maternity benefits suggest that much of a mandate's cost is shifted onto workers in the form of lower wages. A study of unemployment insurance finds that tax increases affecting all firms in the market are shifted onto workers, whereas firm-specific tax increases are absorbed by firms.[29] Minimum-wage hikes do not appear to result in cuts in other forms of employee compensation.

In sum, the empirical evidence suggests that the disemployment effects of employer mandates have, at most, been small. Whether employer mandates should be used as a tool to redistribute income to low-wage workers, however, depends critically on why these effects are small empirically. The strongest case in favor of the use of employer mandates to redistribute income can be made if labor markets are characterized by inelastic labor demand or if labor markets are not perfectly competitive. Then disemployment effects are likely to be small and workers are likely to receive most of the benefits from the employer mandate. The position that even low-wage labor markets may be characterized by market imperfections, that workers capture most of the benefits from employer mandates, and that employer mandates result in little disemployment has been articulated most forcefully by Card and Krueger (1995) in their recent work on minimum wages.

The case for employer mandates as a redistributive tool is weaker if the disemployment effects are small, largely because workers pay for the mandate through lower wages or benefits. However, even in this case employer mandates may benefit the low-wage worker if they are carefully coordinated with other policies. Clearly, such cost shifting could be limited for low-wage workers with the simultaneous introduction of or increase in mandated benefits and minimum wages; a floor on the entire compensation package would thus be set. Programs targeting the most disadvantaged workers—such as training or wage subsidy programs—could be used in combination with mandates to reduce any disemployment effects.

Employer mandates are no panacea for the decline in real wages and benefits among low-wage workers. Nevertheless, taken together, the evidence suggests that the employer mandates discussed here generally have small adverse effects on employment and unemployment, while they produce at least modest benefits for workers, particularly low-wage workers.

Richard Freeman, Peter Gottschalk, Philip Harvey, and Stephen Nickell provided helpful comments on an earlier version of this chapter. I am indebted to Carolyn Zinn for excellent research assistance and to Claire Black for assistance in preparing the document.

Notes

1. For a discussion of the theoretical similarities of programs financed through payroll taxes and mandated benefits, see Gruber (1994a). Summers (1989) points out some theoretical differences between programs run by the government and financed through payroll taxes and employer mandates that may affect the desirability of using one option over another.
2. For a comprehensive discussion of such state laws, see Irvin and Silberman (1993).
3. The background on parental leave in other countries presented here draws heavily on descriptions in Ruhm and Teague (1993).
4. Leigh (1989, 83–84) discusses these state laws.
5. The law also requires that advance notice be provided if five hundred or more workers are laid off, even if that number constitutes less than one-third of the workforce.
6. Exceptions to the advance notice requirements apply when individuals are dismissed for cause.
7. I discuss employment protection laws in the United States and other countries in more detail in Houseman (1990, 1994).
8. See, for example, Ruhm and Teague (1993) for a discussion of parental leave, Gruber and Krueger (1991) on workers' compensation, and Mitchell (1990) for a critique of employer mandates.
9. Gruber (1994a) notes that whether or not workers are willing to sacrifice wages in return for a mandated benefit depends not only on their valuation of that benefit but also on whether receipt of the benefit is conditional on employment. For example, if the government were to mandate health insurance benefits financed through a payroll tax but also made the benefit available to the nonemployed, we would not expect workers to be willing to accept pay reductions in return for the benefit.
10. Hamermesh (1977) takes this position. He theorizes that about half of the incidence of a payroll tax is absorbed by consumers and about half by workers.
11. See, in particular, Card and Krueger (1995, ch. 11) and the literature reviewed therein.
12. Burdett and Mortensen (1989), Mortensen and Vishwanath (1993), Chalkley (1991), Lang and Dickens (1993), Burdett and Wright (1994), and Manning (1994) present models that describe the equilibrium wage-setting process by which firms choose a wage and thereby set their quit and hiring rates. Card and Krueger (1995) present a partial-equilibrium version of this basic model and

summarize some of the equilibrium wage models. Green, Machin, and Manning (1996) and Manning (1996) provide some empirical support for the existence of monopsony power in labor markets.

13. This argument is articulated by Leibenstein (1966) in his theory of X-efficiency.

14. For a summary of this literature, see Davidson and Woodbury (1996).

15. In addition, benefits formulas in the United States are designed to provide a higher replacement rate for low-income than for high-income workers.

16. Economists have also speculated that unemployment insurance would result in better job matches. Studies have found little empirical support, however, for better matches (Meyer 1989; Woodbury and Spiegelman 1987).

17. For reports on those surveys, see Dauer (1994) and Scharlach, Sansom, and Stanger (1995).

18. See OECD (1994, 69–80) for a discussion of different indexes of the stringency of employment protection laws that researchers have constructed.

19. Studies comparing employment adjustment in the United States and various European countries include Köhler and Sengenberger (1983), Mairesse and Dormont (1985), Houseman (1988), Abraham and Houseman (1993, 1994), and Houseman and Abraham (1995). Studies comparing employment adjustment between the United States and Japan include Hashimoto and Raisian (1988), Abraham and Houseman (1989), and Hashimoto (1990). Hotz-Hart (1987, and reproduced in Sengenberger 1992) compares employment adjustment in the United States, Canada, France, Germany, the United Kingdom, and Japan.

20. Van Audenrode argues that generous short-time compensation programs account for the rapid total hours adjustment in these European countries.

21. It should be noted that a worker may receive formal notice even if such notice is not required by law. Ruhm (1992) observes that the relationship between notice and earnings may not be causal. He speculates that firms that provide workers with formal notice may also be more inclined to provide workers with job search assistance, for example.

22. Their results are quite sensitive to the inclusion of a school enrollment variable. For a criticism of this variable and other aspects of the article, see Card, Katz, and Krueger (1994), and for a reply to that critique, see Neumark and Wascher (1994).

23. Neumark and Wascher note that the noise in the Card and Krueger (1994) data would not in itself be expected to impart a bias in the results. Thus, they do not explain the completely opposite findings in the two studies. Neumark and Wascher simply argue that their results are more believable because they have better data.

24. For example, in their study of the impact of the New Jersey minimum-wage hike on employment in the fast-food industry, Card and Krueger (1994) find no evidence that employers cut benefits, which come primarily in the form of free or reduced-price meals.

25. Krueger (1994) argues that the estimates in the aggregate time-series analysis in the Castillo-Freeman and Freeman (1992) study are negatively biased because of the large effect of the minimum wage on average wages, an effect that

appears in the denominator of the Kaitz index used in the regression. He also finds that the cross-section, time-series results are quite sensitive to weighting. When they are weighted, the point estimates for the employment elasticity become positive and insignificantly different from zero.

26. The minimum wage was raised to $4.75 per hour in October 1996 and to $5.15 per hour in September 1997. Because the analysis, conducted prior to the increase, uses 1994 data, and because wages and the cost of living have increased in the interim, the results should represent upper-bound estimates of the effect of the increase on poverty.

27. There are likely to be more errors in the salaried workers' computed hourly wage than in the hourly workers' reported hourly wage. I have also done the analysis for hourly workers only, and the results are very similar to those reported here.

28. This exclusion reduced my sample by about 18 percent. Low-income workers were only slightly more likely to be excluded than high-income workers. This procedure was used in the Horrigan and Mincy (1993) analysis of the effect of minimum wages on income distribution. Mincy (1990)makes no attempt to exclude job changers in his analysis of the effects of minimum-wage increases on family poverty.

29. Even if the cost of the employer mandate is fully shifted onto workers, workers may still benefit from the mandate. Because of adverse selection, private markets may underprovide these insurance benefits. Therefore, workers may benefit from the mandate, even if they effectively have to pay for the insurance, because they might not be able to purchase the insurance, or might be able to purchase it only at higher cost, without the mandate.

References

Abraham, Katharine G., and Susan N. Houseman. 1989. "Job Security and Work Force Adjustment: How Different Are U.S. and Japanese Practices?" *Journal of the Japanese and International Economies* 3: 500–21.

———. 1993. *Job Security in America: Lessons from Germany*. Washington, D.C.: Brookings Institution.

———. 1994. "Does Employment Protection Inhibit Labor Market Flexibility? Lessons from Germany, France, and Belgium." In *Social Protection Versus Economic Flexibility: Is There a Trade-off?*, edited by Rebecca M. Blank. Chicago, Ill.: University of Chicago Press.

Addison, John T., and McKinley Blackburn. 1995. "Advance Notice and Job Search: More on the Value of an Early Start." *Industrial Relations* 34(2): 242–62.

Addison, John T., and Jean-Luc Grosso. 1996. "Job Security Provisions and Employment: Revised Estimates." *Industrial Relations* 35(4): 585–603.

Addison, John T., and Pedro Portugal. 1987. "The Effect of Advance Notification of Plant Closings on Unemployment." *Industrial and Labor Relations Review* 41(1): 3–16.

Anderson, Patricia M., and Bruce D. Meyer. 1995. "The Incidence of a Firm-Varying Payroll Tax: The Case of Unemployment Insurance." Working Paper 5201. Cambridge, Mass.: National Bureau of Economic Research (August).

Bertola, Giuseppe. 1990. "Job Security, Employment and Wages." *European Economic Review* 34(4): 851–86.

Brown, Charles, Curtis Gilroy, and Andrew Kohen. 1982. "The Effect of the Minimum Wage on Employment and Unemployment." *Journal of Economic Literature* 20 (June): 487–528.

Burdett, Kenneth, and Dale T. Mortensen. 1989. "Equilibrium Wage Differentials and Employer Size." Discussion Paper 860. Evanston, Ill.: Northwestern University Center for Mathematical Studies in Economics and Management Science.

Burdett, Kenneth, and Randall Wright. 1994. "Two-Sided Search." Staff Report 169. Minneapolis, Minn.: Federal Reserve Bank of Minneapolis, Research Department.

Card, David. 1992a. "Do Minimum Wages Reduce Employment? A Case Study of California, 1987-1989." *Industrial and Labor Relations Review* 46(1): 38–54.

———. 1992b. "Using Regional Variation in Wages to Measure the Effects of the Federal Minimum Wage." *Industrial and Labor Relations Review* 46(1): 22–37.

Card, David, Lawrence F. Katz, and Alan B. Krueger. 1994. "Comment on David Neumark and William Wascher; 'Employment Effects of Minimum and Subminimum Wages: Panel Data on State Minimum Wage Laws.'" *Industrial and Labor Relations Review* 47(3): 487–512.

Card, David, and Alan Krueger. 1994. "Minimum Wages and Employment: A Case Study of the Fast-Food Industry in New Jersey and Pennsylvania." *American Economic Review* 84(4): 772–93.

———. 1995. *Myth and Measurement: The New Economics of the Minimum Wage.* Princeton, N.J.: Princeton University Press.

Castillo-Freeman, Alida, and Richard Freeman. 1992. "Minimum Wages in Puerto Rico: Textbook Case of a Wage Floor?" *Industrial Relations Research Association Forty-third Annual Proceedings.*: 243–53.

Chalkley, Martin. 1991. "Monopsony Wage Determination and Multiple Unemployment Equilibria in a Non-Linear Search Model." *Review of Economic Studies* 58(1): 181–93.

Commission of the European Communities. 1993. *Employment in Europe 1993.* COM (93) 314, Brussels, Belgium.

Currie, Janet, and Bruce C. Fallick. 1992. "A Note on the New Minimum Wage Research." University of California-Los Angeles. Unpublished paper (November).

Dauer, Christopher. 1994. "Study: Many Firms Don't Follow Family Leave Act." *National Underwriter* (September 5): 49.

Davidson, Carl, and Stephen A. Woodbury. 1996. "Unemployment Insurance and Unemployment: Implications of the Reemployment Bonus Experiments." In *Advisory Council on Unemployment Compensation, Background Papers* 3 (January): KK1-37.

Deere, Donald, Kevin M. Murphy, and Finis Welch. 1995. "Employment and the 1990–1991 Minimum Wage Hike." *American Economic Review* 85(2): 232–37.

Ehrenberg, Ronald G. 1992. "New Minimum Wage Research: Symposium Introduction." *Industrial and Labor Relations Review* 46(1): 3–5.

Green, Francis, Stephen Machin, and Alan Manning. 1996. "The Employer Size-Wage Effect: Can Dynamic Monopsony Provide an Explanation?" *Oxford Economic Papers* 48(3): 433–55.

Gruber, Jonathan. 1994a. "Payroll Taxation, Employer Mandates, and the Labor Market: Theory, Evidence, and Unanswered Questions." Paper prepared for the W. E. Upjohn Institute Conference on Employee Benefits, Labor Costs and Labor Markets in Canada and the United States. Kalamazoo, Mich. (November 3–5, 1994).

———. 1994b. "The Consumption Smoothing Benefits of Unemployment Insurance." Working Paper 4750. Cambridge, Mass.: National Bureau of Economic Research (May).

———. 1994c. "The Incidence of Mandated Maternity Benefits." *American Economic Review* 84(3): 622–41.

Gruber, Jonathan, and Alan B. Krueger. 1991. "The Incidence of Mandated Employer-Provided Insurance: Lessons from Workers' Compensation Insurance." In *Tax Policy and the Economy,* edited by David Bradford. Cambridge, Mass.: MIT Press.

Hamermesh, Daniel S. 1977. *Jobless Pay and the Economy.* Baltimore, Md.: Johns Hopkins University Press.

Hashimoto, Masanori. 1990. *The Japanese Labor Market in a Comparative Perspective with the United States.* Kalamazoo, Mich.: W. E. Upjohn Institute for Employment Research.

Hashimoto, Masanori, and John Raisian. 1988. "The Structure and Short-run Adaptability of Labor Markets in Japan and the United States." In *Employment, Unemployment, and Labor Utilization,* edited by Robert A. Hart. London, England: Unwin Hyman.

Horrigan, Michael W., and Ronald B. Mincy. 1993. "The Minimum Wage and Earnings and Income Inequality." In *Uneven Tides: Rising Inequality in America,* edited by Sheldon Danziger and Peter Gottschalk. New York: Russell Sage Foundation.

Hotz-Hart, Beat. 1987. *Modernisierung von Unternehmen und Industrien bei unterschiedlichen industriellen Beziehungen.* Bern and Stuttgart.

Houseman, Susan N. 1988. "Shorter Working Time and Job Security: Labor Adjustment in the Steel Industry." In *Employment, Unemployment, and Labor Utilization,* edited by Robert A. Hart. London, England: Unwin Hyman.

———. 1990. "The Equity and Efficiency of Job Security: Contrasting Perspectives in Collective Dismissal Laws in Western Europe." In *New Developments in the Labor Market: Toward a New Institutional Paradigm,* edited by Katherine Abraham and Robert McKersie. Cambridge, Mass.: MIT Press.

———. 1994. "Labor Market Adjustment in Europe, Japan, and the United States." Paper prepared for the Organization for Economic Cooperation and Development workshop on Labor Market Adjustment. Paris, France (October 3–4, 1994).

Houseman, Susan N., and Katharine G. Abraham. 1995. "Labor Adjustment Under Different Institutional Structures: A Case Study of Germany and the United States." In *Institutions and Labor Market Performance: Comparative Views on the U.S. and German Economies,* edited by Friedrich Buttler et al. London, England: Routledge.

Irvin, Helen D., and Ralph M. Silberman. 1993. *Family and Medical Leaves: The New Federal Statute and State Laws.* Boston, Mass.: Warren, Gorham, Lamont.

Katz, Lawrence F., and Alan B. Krueger. 1992. "The Effect of the Minimum Wage on the Fast-Food Industry." *Industrial and Labor Relations Review* 46(1): 6–21.

Köhler, Christoph, and Werner Sengenberger. 1983. *Konjunktur und Personalanpassung: Betriebliche Beschäfingungspolitik in der deutschen und amerikanischen Automobilindustrie.* Frankfurt, Germany: Campus Verlag.

Krueger, Alan B. 1994. "The Effect of the Minimum Wage When It Really Bites: A Reexamination of the Evidence from Puerto Rico." Working Paper 4757. Cambridge, Mass.: National Bureau of Economic Research (June).

Lang, Kevin, and William T. Dickens. 1993. "Bilateral Search as an Explanation for Labor Market Segmentation and Other Anomalies." Working Paper 4461. Cambridge, Mass.: National Bureau of Economic Research. (September).

Lazear, Edward P. 1990. "Job Security Provisions and Employment." *Quarterly Journal of Economics* 105(3): 699–726.

Leibenstein, Harvey. 1966. "Allocative Efficiency vs. X-Efficiency." *American Economic Review* 56(June): 392–415.

Leigh, Duane E. 1989. *Assisting Displaced Workers: Do the States Have a Better Idea?* Kalamazoo, Mich.: W. E. Upjohn Institute for Employment Research.

Machin, Stephen, and Alan Manning. 1994. "The Effects of Minimum Wages on Wage Dispersion and Employment: Evidence from the U.K. Wage Councils." *Industrial and Labor Relations Review* 47(2): 319–29.

Mairesse, Jacques, and Brigitte Dormont. 1985. "Labor and Investment Demand at the Firm Level: A Comparison of French, German, and U.S. Manufacturing, 1970–1979." *European Economic Review* 28(1–2): 201–31 (June–July).

Manning, Alan. 1994. "Labour Markets with Company Wage Policies." Working Paper. Centre for Economic Performance, London School of Economics (December).

———. 1996. "The Equal Pay Act as an Experiment to Test Theories of the Labour Market." *Economica* 63(May): 191–212.

Meyer, Bruce D. 1989. "A Quasi-Experimental Approach to the Effects of Unemployment Insurance." Working Paper 3159. Cambridge, Mass.: National Bureau of Economic Research (November).

Mincy, Ronald B. 1990. "Raising the Minimum Wage: Effects on Family Poverty." *Monthly Labor Review* 113(July): 18–25.

Mishel, Lawrence, Jared Bernstein, and Edith Rasell. 1995. "Who Wins with a Higher Minimum Wage." Briefing Paper 53. Washington, D.C.: Economic Policy Institute.

Mitchell, Olivia S. 1990. "The Effects of Mandating Benefits Packages." *Research in Labor Economics* 11: 297–320.

Mortensen, Dale T., and Tara Vishwanath. 1993. "Information Sources and Equilibrium Wage Outcomes." In *Panel Data and Labour Market Dynamics,* edited by Henning Bunzel et al. Amsterdam, Holland: North Holland.

Neumark, David, and William Wascher. 1992. "Employment Effects of Minimum and Subminimum Wages: Panel Data on State Minimum Wage Laws." *Industrial and Labor Relations Review* 46(1): 55–81.

————. 1994. "Employment Effects of Minimum and Subminimum Wages: Reply to Card, Katz, and Krueger." *Industrial and Labor Relations Review* 47(3): 497–512.

————. 1996. "The Effects of Minimum Wages on Teenage Employment and Enrollment: Evidence from Matched CPS Surveys." *Research in Labor Economics* 15: 25–64.

————. 1997. "The New Jersey–Pennsylvania Minimum Wage Experiment: A Re-Evaluation Using Payroll Records." Unpublished paper (January).

Nickell, Stephen. 1979. "Unemployment and the Structure of Labor Costs." *Carnegie-Rochester Conference Series on Public Policy* 11: 87–122.

Organization for Economic Cooperation and Development (OECD). 1993. *Employment Outlook* (July).

————. 1994. *The OECD Jobs Study: Evidence and Explanations, Part II: The Adjustment Potential of the Labour Market.* Paris, France: Organization for Economic Cooperation and Development.

Rebitzer, James B., and Lowell J. Taylor. 1995. "The Consequences of Minimum Wage Laws: Some New Theoretical Ideas." *Journal of Public Economics* 56(2): 245–55.

Ruhm, Christopher. 1992. "Advance Notice and Postdisplacement Joblessness." *Journal of Labor Economics* 10(1): 1–32.

————. 1994. "Advance Notice, Job Search, and Postdisplacement Earnings." *Journal of Labor Economics* 12(1): 1–28.

Ruhm, Christopher J., and Jackqueline L. Teague. 1993. "Parental Leave Policies in Europe and North America." Working Paper. Center for Applied Research, University of North Carolina at Greensboro.

Scharlach, Andrew E., Stephanie L. Sansom, and Janice Stanger. 1995. "The Family and Medical Leave Act of 1993: How Fully Is Business Complying?" *California Management Review* 37(2): 66–79.

Sengenberger, Werner. 1992. "Revisiting the Legal and Institutional Framework for Employment Security: An International Comparative Perspective." In *Employment Security and Labor Market Flexibility: An International Perspective*, edited by Kazutoshi Koshiro. Detroit, Mich.: Wayne State University.

Summers, Lawrence H. 1989. "Some Simple Economics of Mandated Benefits." *American Economic Review* 79(2): 177–83.

U.S. Department of Labor. 1993. *Minimum Wage and Maximum Hours Standard Under the Fair Labor Standards Act.* Washington, D.C.: U.S. Government Printing Office.

U.S. General Accounting Office. 1993. *Dislocated Workers: Worker Adjustment and Retraining Notification Act Not Meeting Its Goals.* Report to Congressional Committees. GAO/HRD-93-18 (February).

Van Audenrode, Marc A. 1994. "Short-Time Compensation, Job Security, and Employment Contracts: Evidence from Selected OECD Countries." *Journal of Political Economy* 102(1): 76–102.

Woodbury, Stephen, and Robert Spiegelman. 1987. "Bonuses to Workers and Employers to Reduce Unemployment: Randomized Trials in Illinois." *American Economic Review* 77(4): 513–30.

Part III

Employment Regulations

Chapter 6

Work-Sharing to Full Employment: Serious Option or Populist Fallacy?

Richard B. Freeman

> The many constraints and conditions which need to be met in order to achieve a positive and lasting employment outcome preclude any across-the-board measure such as legislated or centrally agreed working-time reductions (OECD 1994, 100).

> There are . . . economic and political trends that are making work-sharing a more practical proposition. . . . There is no reason why it should not have some small positive impact on employment over the medium-term. (*Financial Times* 1994).

> Two hours of reduction of working time will permit the creation of around 400,000 employees. This will double the rate of job creation in 1996 and 1997 (OFCE, reported in *Tribune* 1995).

Work-sharing, the practice of reducing hours worked to increase employment, is controversial. Many economists and policy analysts reject work-sharing as ineffective owing to its potential adverse effects on labor costs. But other analysts favor work-sharing, stressing the benefits of distributing joblessness more evenly. In periods of high unemployment, governments often look favorably on the practice. In the 1980s, several European countries tried work-sharing schemes, and Canada and sixteen states in this country extended unemployment insurance to short-time workers to reduce layoffs. In the 1930s, President Hoover encouraged firms to reduce hours, and the Roosevelt administration enacted the time-and-a-half overtime provision in the Fair Labor Standards Act. In fact, from 1929 through 1933, and from 1937 to 1939, hours worked fell in response to declines in output.[1]

So who is right? Under what conditions and in what forms, if any, might work-sharing increase employment? How far does extant evi-

195

dence take us toward deciding whether work-sharing is a serious option or a populist fallacy?

In this chapter, I address these questions. My major conclusion is that, while work-sharing can increase employment, most government-sponsored efforts to spread work have had limited efficacy. I argue that the main reason for this is the difference in skills between the jobless and the employed and the unwillingness of most employees to accept reduced worktime. I speculate that "capital-sharing" through increased shift work combined with work-sharing and flexibility in working hours might do more to increase employment than work-sharing by itself.

The Distribution of Work

To begin, it is important to recognize that the distribution of work by hours varies greatly across countries, among workers within a country, and over time. These differences suggest that work-sharing policies operate in a context of considerable "natural variation" in the allocation of person-hours worked.

Column 1 of table 6.1 shows the percentage of fifteen- to sixty-four-year-olds[2] employed around the world. Column 2 gives the average hours worked over the year for employees. Column 3 shows the proportion of employees who are part-time workers. Column 4 records the number of vacation days granted to employees. The figures show that Americans work more hours than the workers of all other countries, save Japan. Americans work nearly eighteen hundred hours per year, compared to between fourteen hundred and sixteen hundred hours for Western Europeans. The Swedes, Germans, Dutch, French, and British take longer vacations than Americans do. In contrast to most advanced countries, the United States has no legislated vacation time.

Other sources of variation in the distribution of work include the use of part-time work (generally more common in Europe than in the United States), student work (more common in the United States than in Europe), early retirement (found among men in many countries), and withdrawal from the labor force because of disability (more common in Europe than in the United States).

The distribution of work also varies secularly and over the business cycle. The number of hours worked has gone down in the twentieth century, while the increased labor participation of women has raised the share of the population engaged in market activities. Overtime hours

Table 6.1   The Distribution of Person-Hours Worked, 1992

	% of 15- to 64-Year-Olds Employed (1)	Annual Hours Worked (2)	% Part-time (3)	Vacation/ Holiday Weeks (4)
United States	70.4%	1,768	17.5%	4.6
United Kingdom	67.6	—	23.5	6.6
Canada	66.8	1,715	16.8	—
France	59.5	1,666	12.7	7.0
Germany	67.3	1,618	14.1	8.5
Italy	54.9	(1,764)	5.9	8.1
Japan	73.9	1,965	20.5	4.4[a]
Australia	66.3	—	24.5	5.8[a]
Austria	65.9	—	9.1	7.8
Belgium	58.5	—	12.4	6.2
Denmark	73.8	—	22.5	7.0
Finland	64.3	1,741	7.9	9.8
Netherlands	63.5	1,415	32.8	8.3
New Zealand	65.1	—	21.6	5.8[a]
Norway	72.6	1,415	26.9	6.4
Spain	47.0	1,911	5.9	7.5
Sweden	76.9	1,485	24.3	7.6

Sources: Column 1 calculated by multiplying 1-standardized unemployment rate (normal rate if no standardized rate) by labor participation rate in OECD, *Employment Outlook* (December 1993). Column 2: OECD, *Employment Outlook* (1994, table B), using total employment except for the Netherlands and Italy for 1983. Column 3: OECD, *Employment Outlook* (1994, table D, 198). Column 4: Bell and Freeman (1995, table 2), for full-time manufacturing workers.

[a] Based on minimum legal annual leave from OECD (1994, table 6.12).

typically vary cyclically but have gone up in the United States (see figure 6.1). In 1993 U.S. manufacturing firms used 4.1 hours of overtime, an extremely high figure by historical standards. Hours are changed in response to cyclic swings in output more frequently in Europe than in the United States, which relies more on employment adjustments (Abraham and Houseman 1993). The fluctuations in registered short-time in Germany exceed fluctuations in unemployment (Best 1988, table 1.1).

Figure 6.1 Overtime Hours in U.S. Manufacturing, 1959 to 1993

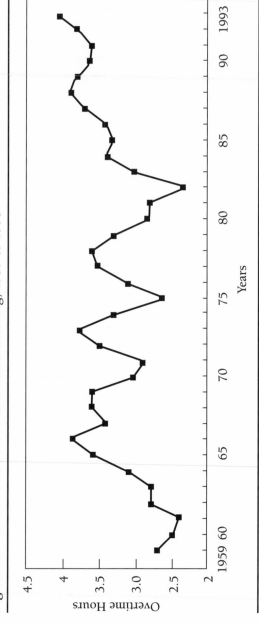

Source: Council of Economic Advisors, Economic Report of the president, 1994, table B45, p 320.

In the United States, worktime varies greatly among employees (see table 6.2). Some Americans hold second jobs. Some hold part-time jobs. Some work more than sixty hours a week. Some work less than twenty hours. Measured by the ln variance, time worked varies nearly as much among employees as hourly earnings.[3] The notion that we all work a forty-hour week year-round is simply not true. In advanced countries, "nonstandard" work has become normal.

Table 6.2   Variation in Time Worked in the United States, 1985

	%
Usual hours worked	
per week	
1–24	12%
25–29	2
30–34	4
35–39	7
40	54
41–48	8
49 or more	12
Usual days worked	
per week	
1–3	8
4	6
5	74
6	10
7	2
Shift workers	16
Evening	6
Night	3
Rotating	4
Split	1
Other	2
Multiple jobholders	5
Weekend work	44
Overtime work	12

Sources: Shirley Smith, "The Growing Diversity of Work Schedules"; Earl Mellor, "Shiftwork and Flexitime: How Prevalent Are They?"; John F. Stinson, "Moonlighting by Women Jumped to Record Highs"; Daniel Carr, "Overtime Work: An Expanded View"; all in U.S. Department of Labor, *Monthly Labor Review* (November 1986), special section on time spent

Given this variable distribution of work, it is natural to ask whether in periods of high joblessness, the state, or unions and employers, can shift the distribution through work-sharing.[4] The efficacy of work-sharing policies depends on three factors: the responses of employers to reduced hours worked; the responses of workers to reduced hours; and market/macro-economic responses that arise through the interaction of firms and individuals.

Demand-Side Responses: Theory

Under specified conditions, reductions in hours worked lead profit-maximizing firms to substitute employees for hours. The strongest case for work-sharing—the "ideal work-sharing model"—posits a production function $f(hN)$, where h = average hours and N = employment, so that hours and numbers employed are perfectly substitutable; hourly wages (w) are constant; and there are no fixed costs of employment. In this case, the firm maximizes $f(hN) - whN$, with an equilibrium condition, $f_N = w$. Assuming that hours are an exogenous control variable, the elasticity of employment to hours worked is unitary. Total person-hours and aggregate output are thus constant, so that work-sharing affects only the distribution of worktime and is supportable in the product market with no accompanying macro policies.

This model can be criticized in several ways.

The assumption that hours and employment are perfect substitutes is unrealistic. Two employees working five hours do different things than one employee working ten hours, making it more sensible to view the production relation as $f(h, N)$ than as $f(hN)$. In this case, the effect of changes in hours on employment depends on f_{Nh}, the cross-derivative of hours and employment, whose sign is indeterminant in the maximizing calculus. Decreases in hours raise employment when $f_{Nh} < f_N$—a condition that holds for standard production functions.

The assumption that the fixed costs of employment are negligible is also unrealistic. From one-third to one-half of labor costs consist of fringe benefits, many of which vary with employees but not with hours worked, and there are hiring and training costs for new employees. It is more sensible to write the cost of labor as $whN + fN$, where f is the fixed cost of labor, or as $whN(1 + \lambda)$, where λ is the ratio of fixed costs to earnings. With fixed costs, reductions in hours raise the average hourly cost of labor ($w + f/h$), since the fixed cost is spread over fewer hours.

The assumption that the firm can increase hours indefinitely without affecting pay must also be modified. By law or negotiation, employees who work more than the normal workweek (H) for the same employer are usually paid an overtime premium. With an overtime premium of p percent (so workers earn $w(1 + p)$ per hour for $h - H$ hours of overtime), labor cost is wh ($1 + \lambda + po$) N, where o is the proportion of worktime that consists of overtime hours ($= (h - H)/h$). If the firm is at the margin of overtime, $h = H$, the marginal cost of an additional employee is wH ($1 + \lambda$). By contrast, the marginal cost of getting the equivalent work (H hours) by overtime is ($1 + p$) w ($H/N)N$.[5] The relative cost of a new employee-hour versus comparable overtime is ($1 + \lambda)/(1 + p$).

It is also unrealistic to assume that work-sharing policies effectively determine hours worked. Policies can reduce the standard workweek but cannot control actual hours worked, given overtime and the possibility that workers will seek a second job. If employees work overtime, reducing the normal workweek raises the costs of hiring a worker and may not necessarily affect hours worked; as a result, employment is reduced rather than increased.[6]

Imperfect substitution between hours and bodies, fixed costs of employment, and overtime weaken the prediction of the ideal work-sharing model that reductions in hours will increase employment. Almost any model beyond the work-sharing ideal predicts that employment will rise or fall depending on the size of various parameters. For instance, the greater the effect of a change of hours on output relative to the effect of a change in employment on output, the more likely it is that employment will increase when hours fall. The substitution effect in response to reduced hours increases employment, whereas the scale effect tends to decrease employment. Moreover, in these cases, aggregate production is likely to change, possibly requiring changes in macroeconomic policies.

In sum, demand theory does not answer unequivocally the question of whether work-sharing is a serious option or populist fallacy. It shows that, with hourly wages fixed, work-sharing *could* increase employment through substitution of bodies for hours. But it could also reduce employment by raising the cost of labor. To determine whether work-sharing works, it is necessary to consider evidence on the substitutability between hours and employment, to look at the results of actual work-sharing policies, and to assess wage responses to work-sharing.

Hours-Employment Substitution in Market-Generated Data

Empirical studies have examined the link between hours and employment (1) with time-series data on the relation between employment and average hours worked; (2) time series data on the relation between output and average hours worked; (3) with data on the responses of employment to overtime premium; and (4) through simulations of the effect of worktime reductions on employment in macroeconomic models. The relation between vacations given to employees and the timing and size of staff also provides insight into the substitutability between time worked per employee and employment.

Employment-Hours and Output-Hours Elasticities

Several studies regress employment on average hours worked and other postulated determinants of employment in time-series or pooled time-series, cross-industry data, often instrumenting hours on other variables.[7] The sign of the coefficient on hours must be negative for work-sharing to succeed. What do these studies show?

In a 1993 survey of European studies, Houpis reports that all the researchers find that reductions in hours are associated with increased employment with elasticities less than one (line 1 of table 6.3). As an example, consider John Pencavel and Bertil Holmlund's 1988 analysis of Swedish manufacturing employment from 1950 to 1983. The key equation in this study is a regression of manufacturing employment on cost factors (wages, payroll taxes, user cost of capital, price of raw materials) and on product market factors (disposable income and producers' prices) under various specifications. The elasticity of employment to hours is large when hours are taken as exogenous (−0.67 in the short run, and about −1.00 in the long run) but smaller when hours are endogenous (around −0.20 to −0.30). Pencavel and Holmlund also find, however, a high elasticity of employment to wages (−0.7); that finding suggests that if work-sharing raises the hourly cost of labor, it could induce an offsetting or dominating fall in employment.[8]

Other time-series studies tell a similar story. In their analyses of the effects of the 1977–78 new jobs tax credit, John Bishop and Robert Haveman (1979) and Bishop and Mark Montgomery (1986) find that the credit raised employment but reduced hours in retail and construction, consistent with an hours-employment trade-off (Eisner 1978). As noted, Katharine Abraham and Susan Houseman (1993) show consid-

Table 6.3 Summary of Studies That Use Market-Generated Evidence to Assess the Effects of Hours Reductions on Employment

Studies	Percent Change Per 1% Change in Independent Factor
1. Studies of employment responses to hours	
Six estimated elasticities using time-series data:	−0.1 to −1.7
2. Studies of output responses to hours worked	
Six estimated elasticities using time-series data:	0.8 to 2.5
3. Studies of hours responses to overtime pay	
Four studies, cross-section, estimated percentage change[a] in employment from raising premium from 50 to 100 percent	1.6 to 2.0
One study, automobile time-series, employment effect of one week from raising overtime	
4. Macroeconomic studies, simulated effects of work-sharing	
United Kingdom, average of five macroeconomic models	−0.3 to −0.6
Treasury model	−.05 to −0.3
Belgium, two models	−.02 to −0.4
France, two models	−0.3 to −0.6
Germany, one model	−0.7 to −0.8
Netherlands, two models	0.2 to −0.1

Sources: Lines 1 and 2, studies summarized in Houpis (1993); line 3, Ehrenberg and Smith (1982, table 5.3); Smyth and Karlson (1991); Nussbaum and Wise (1978); line 4, Houpis (1993); Owen (1989, table 9.1); van Ginneken (1984).

[a] I averaged the Solnick and Swimmer high and low estimates (as reported in table 5.3 of Ehrenberg and Smith 1982)

erable substitution between hours and employment over the business cycle. Marc Van Audenrode (1994) reports country differences in the cyclical adjustment of labor between employment and hours (though he also notes problems with measures of hours worked versus hours paid for) and smaller changes in overall person-hours in countries whose policies favor hours adjustments.

A number of studies regress output on average hours worked and employment. With production function $h^b N^c$, the elasticity of employment to hours is approximately $(1 − b)(1 − c)$ absent overtime, so that if $b < 1$, a reduction in hours increases employment. Houpis's review

(1993) shows a range of output-hours elasticities: the most recent estimates are less than one, but the 1967 estimate by Martin Feldstein exceeds one (table 6.3, line 2). If overtime is important, however, the overtime premium requires higher marginal productivity to hours, possibly producing $b > 1$ without gainsaying a possible hours-employment trade-off. Sherwin Rosen (1978) interprets Feldstein's high output elasticities of hours relative to output elasticities of employment as a reflection of overtime premium.

All told, the bulk of time-series demand and production function analyses suggest that hours reductions generated by market forces do indeed create additional jobs.

Responses to Overtime Premium/Fringe Benefits

Overtime premia raise the relative costs of an additional hour of work versus hiring an additional worker. To focus on the cost side, consider a firm with production function $f(hN)$ operating at the standard workweek H. The firm's sole concern in choosing between overtime hours and employment is with the relative costs of hiring an additional worker versus the comparable amount of overtime. The cost of adding an employee *relative* to adding H/N hours of overtime per existing employee is $(1 + \lambda)/(1 + p)$. Increases in fixed costs make hiring more expensive while increases in overtime premium make hours more expensive. A longer normal workweek $H' > H$ reduces p to 0 for $H' - H$ hours, whereas a decrease in H to H'' raises p for the incremental hours. Moreover, changes in p, H, or λ, since they affect the hourly cost of labor, can also change total person-hours and output.

In 1956 H. Gregg Lewis examined the effects of the 1938 Fair Labor Standards Act's overtime premium on hours worked and concluded that the overtime law contributed modestly to the downward trend on hours—a prerequisite for it to raise employment. Ensuing studies of the employment-hours trade-off use variation in fringes across firms or sectors over time to infer possible responses of employment to higher overtime and lower standard workweeks. These estimates show relatively modest responsiveness of employment and hours to fringe cost (line 3 of table 6.3).

Macro-Simulations

Macroeconomic models that separate hours and employment in production or demand equations provide additional information on the possible employment effect of changes in hours. Line 4 of table 6.3 summarizes the findings of macro-model simulations of work-sharing in European economies. Some simulations assume a constant wage; others assume some increase in hourly pay in response to reduced hours. All but one predict that employment will respond positively to reductions in hours, with an elasticity below unity. In part, these results reflect the negative correlation between hours and employment in time-series data. They also partly reflect, however, the fact that most macro-models postulate a Keynesian-style economy. In models in which wage pressures rise when unemployment exceeds "the natural rate" and reductions in hours do not affect wages, work-sharing has no effect on employment (Layard, Nickell, and Jackman 1991, 503). Models that distinguish Keynesian from classical unemployment allow work-sharing to increase or decrease employment, depending on the cause of unemployment and the pattern of overtime and compensation.[9] The one macro-model that predicts that reducing hours will reduce employment has a neoclassical structure.

I have sufficient doubts about the validity of the macro-models that I would not put great stress on these results.[10]

Vacation Time and Summer Work

Weeks worked by employees vary depending on how much vacation time they take. If firms respond to loss of labor services due to vacations by hiring replacements or maintaining a larger workforce over the year than they otherwise would, the case for work-sharing is strengthened.

In the United States, employment of young workers in nonagricultural work increases during the peak summer vacation period, raising the possibility of a significant trade-off between weeks worked and employment. To examine this relation, figure 6.2 contrasts the number of employees with a job but not working because of vacation with the seasonal employment factor for nonagricultural workers aged sixteen to nineteen and twenty to twenty-four in 1985 to 1994. The number of employees on vacation jumps in June, July, and August. In June, 2.6 times as many workers are on vacation as in May; in July, 4.9 times as many are on vacation as in May; and in August, 4.7 times as many take time off. In 1985 to 1994, 23 million workers had a job but were not at work owing to vacation during one of the three summer months. This substantial reduction in worktime might be expected to create demand for temporary replacement workers. The figure shows a moderate increase in the number of young workers employed in the period: employment of sixteen- to nineteen-year-olds rises by 30 percent from May to July,

Figure 6.2 Number of Young Workers on Vacation and Number of Young Workers, by Month, 1985 to 1994

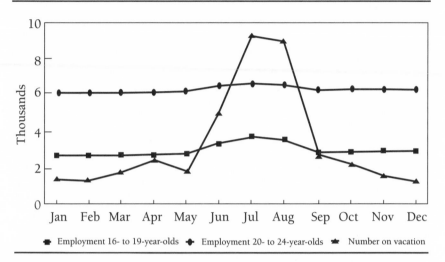

Source: Bureau of Labor Statistics.

and employment of twenty- to twenty-four-year-olds by 6 percent. Treating the seasonal fluctuations of vacation time as an exogenous decline in work by regular employees, and the seasonal fluctuation in the number of young workers as the accompanying substitution, I calculate an elasticity of employment to vacation time of .04 (twenty- to twenty-four-year-olds) to 0.16 (sixteen- to nineteen-year-olds).

Summary

The bulk of the nonexperimental evidence suggests that work-sharing *can* raise employment through the substitution of bodies for hours. However, most of this evidence is generated by employer and employee interactions, not by governmental interventions in markets. Employers and employees may respond differently to state-imposed hours reductions, or to reductions in hours negotiated by union and management, than to changes that arise from their own initiative. In addition, most of the studies do not explore the possible effects of work-sharing on hourly pay, effects that can be crucial to its impact on employment.

To assess the potential for work-sharing *interventions* to raise employment, I turn next to the results of actual public and private experiments in work-sharing.

Experiments in Work-Sharing

As noted at the outset, governments and collective-bargaining partners have tried a number of work-sharing schemes. In this section, I examine work-sharing programs in Europe and the United States and Canadian short-term compensation programs.

European Government Programs

Analyses of European programs to share work and reduce unemployment are limited. I know of no controlled experiment evaluations, nor of any econometric effort to mimic an experimental design. Rather, most European evaluations consist of surveys of firms before and after work-sharing policies have been introduced. The OECD (1994) judiciously refers to these assessments as "reported impacts."

Table 6.4 summarizes information on European work-sharing programs.[11] Perhaps the most prominent effort to shift worktime toward employment was the 1981 French Socialist policy to reduce hours worked from forty to thirty-five per week and increase vacation time, with full wage compensation. The program lasted one year, then was halted as a failure. From 1981 to 1982, it reduced hours from forty to thirty-nine and added one week of vacation time—changes that, if effective, cut worktime by roughly 5 percent (consistent with OECD data [*Employment Outlook*] on annual hours worked in France from 1979 to 1983). According to Jean-Pierre Jallade, "the macroeconomic model of the INSEE [found that] about 110,000 jobs were said to have been created or maintained ... but [this was] more than offset by the damage caused to firms' competitiveness by the resulting increase in wage costs" (1991, 72). The OECD summary of "reported impacts" shows a range of 14,000 to 70,000 jobs created, which is on the order of 0.1 to 0.4 percent of the 17 million employees in France in this period— giving an implicit elasticity of jobs to hours of 0.02 to 0.08.

In 1983 to 1986 Belgium tried a more "market-friendly" way to induce firms to share work, trading wage restraint for reduction in worktime and increased employment through its 3–5–3 plan (3 percent wage reduction, 5 percent reduction in worktime, 3 percent increase in employment). The number of jobs reportedly created was small—23,000 out of roughly 2.9 million employees, or 0.8 percent of employment, giving an elasticity of jobs to hours of 0.4 percent (ignoring the wage incentive to increase employment).[12]

In 1980 to 1982 the Netherlands offered firms a subsidy to create part-time jobs and instituted a policy to encourage collective bargainers

Table 6.4   European Work-Sharing Schemes, 1972 to 1986

Reducing Hours per Week

1982—France: Statutory reduction of workweek from forty to thirty-nine hours; increase in paid leave from four to five weeks; and restriction on overtime, with full compensation for workers. The initial plan was to reduce hours worked to thirty-five between 1981 and 1985, but the estimated employment effect of sixteen thousand to seventy thousand was so low that the government abandoned the program.

1983 to 1986—Belgium: The 3-5-3 plan. Firms paid a 3 percent lower increase in wages and were supposed to reduce worktime by 5 percent and increase employment by 3 percent. Those that failed to increase employment had to pay the 3 percent wage reduction into an employment fund. The claimed employment effect was twenty-three thousand jobs.

France: Contrats de Solidarité induces firms to hire to offset reductions in worktime.

Part-Time Job Sharing

1982—United Kingdom: Job-splitting scheme. Individual retired early on half-time basis and was replaced by half-time unemployed person. Program judged a failure in terms of take-up rate.

1983—France: Job-splitting scheme. Failed.

1984—Benelux countries: Public servants hired for four days of work. Uncertain outcome.

Early-Retirement Schemes

1972—Netherlands: Early-retirement scheme pays 70 percent of wages if workers retire at age sixty but no mandatory replacement. Judged not successful.

1977—Belgium: Early retirement with requirement that retiree be replaced with unemployed person aged less than thirty.

1976 to 1977—United Kingdom: Job release scheme. Gives workers weekly allowance for retiring early, provided employer replaces them. Judged successful.

1977—Netherlands: Solidarity contracts. Workers aged 55 to 59 can retire with 70 percent of gross wages if replaced by 1-1.

1981—France: Contrats de Solidarité. Similar scheme. Judged successful, but abandoned in 1983 for program of early retirement without mandatory replacement.

Sources: Dreze (1991); Hinrichs, Roche, and Sirianni (1991); OECD (1994, 1995).

to reduce worktime from forty to thirty-eight hours per week. According to a follow-up survey, the results were minimal. One estimate is that employment was 1.5 percent higher in the affected sectors, giving an elasticity of employment to hours of 0.3. In 1985 the government put civil servants on a thirty-eight hour workweek, in the hope of sharing government employment. Chris de Neuborg's review of these and other Dutch efforts to alter the distribution of worktime to increase employment concluded that "working time policy did not create a growth in employment that can be assumed to lower overt unemployment considerably" (1991, 141).

The only government programs for which credible analysts claim substantial positive results are early-retirement schemes that are conditioned on firms replacing early retirees (Dreze 1991). For instance, the Netherlands introduced a program that offers early retirement for firms that agree to employ young workers for thirty-two hours a week for each retiree. The French have a similar scheme: "solidarity contracts" between the government and firms whereby firms offer early retirement to employees at 70 percent of gross wages provided that new workers replace them. Belgium has introduced various early-retirement schemes since the late 1970s. Dreze views these and related programs as having successfully substituted younger for older workers with no adverse labor cost effects and concludes that "work-sharing [is] easier to implement through early withdrawal from the labor force than through the 35-hour week" (1991, 74). Given the financial difficulties of social security programs, however, I am dubious about the virtues of early-retirement schemes. They may create long-term problems greater than the benefits of opening up jobs for the young.

Private-sector programs, in the form of collectively bargained reductions in working hours, may have had some success. The leader in reducing working hours to maintain employment has been IG Metall, the German metalworkers union. Work-sharing aside, the success of the German unions in reducing worktime since the 1950s is impressive. In 1950 Germans working full-time worked 2,420 hours a year (including overtime)—far more than Americans. In 1990 Germans worked 1,800 hours, including overtime—less than Americans. The workweek in Germany fell from forty-eight hours in the early 1950s to forty-five in 1956 to forty in 1967. In 1984, IG Metall struck to reduce the workweek and gained a drop to thirty-eight and a half hours in 1985, thirty-seven and a half hours in 1988, thirty-seven hours in 1989, thirty-six hours in 1993, and thirty-five hours in 1995 in exchange for giving employers authority to allocate hours more flexibly.[13] Estimates of the employment effects of the 1984 to 1985 one-and-a-half-hour reduction in hours range from 24,000 to 102,000 in the engineering sector of the workforce (Seifert 1991; Bosch 1990; OECD 1995).

Finally, in 1991, British engineering unions negotiated a reduction in the standard workweek from forty hours to thirty-seven and a half. Because the United Kingdom is a country with high overtime levels, the prediction of the standard demand model was that employment would fall. The absolute number employed did not fall, but productivity increased substantially (Richardson and Rubin 1993), a result that could be interpreted as consistent with the basic work-sharing analysis. This response could also be interpreted, however, as a movement of firms that were initially "within" their production frontier toward that frontier. To the extent that reduction in hours worked leads to higher productivity but to no sizable increase in output, it is self-defeating in terms of employment creation.

Overall, European governments have not succeeded much in raising employment through work-sharing.[14] The countries that tried work-sharing had already made extensive use of short-time work and had low levels of normal worktime; thus, their margins on which to work were not very large. Work-sharing might arguably be more successful in economies in which employees work many hours, such as in Spain, Japan, the United States, or Canada.

Work-Sharing Through Unemployment Benefits

The unemployment insurance (UI) systems of the United States and Canada have traditionally provided benefits for laid-off workers but not for short-time workers. This policy biases reductions in person-hours toward layoffs. (The earnings disregard in the U.S. program is a minor element, allowing at most one day of work.) By contrast, most European unemployment insurance programs pay benefits to workers on short-time (Van Audenrode 1994, appendix).

In 1978, motivated by fears that Proposition 13 would produce mass public-sector layoffs, California introduced a short-term compensation (STC) UI benefits program for workers who suffered hours reductions rather than layoffs. Other states followed suit, and by 1992 sixteen states offered STC (Vroman 1992). In 1977 Canada amended its unemployment insurance act to permit short-time compensation, and it implemented twenty-four pilot projects in 1979 to 1980. In 1980 it rejected work-sharing, only to reintroduce it in the 1981 recession; STC has been maintained in Canada ever since (Meltz and Reid 1983).

Table 6.5 summarizes evaluations of the U.S. and Canadian programs. The early 1980s evaluation of the California experience focused on the administrative workability of the program and on the attitudes of employers and unions toward it. Because the study had insufficient funds to survey firms that did not use the program,[15] it lacked an ade-

Table 6.5   U.S. and Canadian Short-Term Compensation Programs

---

U.S. Program

Allows UI eligibles short-time compensation when their employer reduces days worked; sometimes there is an extra charge to employers; reduction in regular UI if laid off.[a]

1982 California Evaluation

1. Program costs more in UI system; reduced federal and state taxes.
2. Assumed number on STC saved proportionate number of jobs.

1986 U.S. Evaluation

1. Program costs more in UI charges and in employer costs.
2. Employers used STC and layoffs rather than substituting STC for layoffs completely.
3. Employees in firms using STC receive regular UI for 1 to 2 percent fewer hours; in STC firms, 11 to 12 percent were unemployed compared to 14 percent in control group.
4. Hours on UI and STC greater in STC firms than UI hours in control group, implying some increased reduction in person-hours in STC firms.
5. Most employers were satisfied with STC because it retains valued employees.
6. No noticeable productivity effects.

Canadian Program

Allows UI eligibles to gain twenty-six to thirty-eight weeks of short-time compensation; no reduction in regular UI; more stringent requirements on firms than in the United States; higher replacement rate than in the United States.

1982 Canadian Evaluation

1. Program cost more in UI charges, but not in employer costs.
2. One-quarter use STC and layoffs; many (43 percent) laid off after program.

(*Table continues on p. 212.*)

Table 6.5 *Continued*

---

3. Three-fourths of layoffs averted (by asking employers/looking at post-program layoffs).
4. Estimated 5.7 to 1.0 benefit/cost ratio.

1993 Canadian Evaluation

---

1. Work-sharing cost 33 percent more in UI charges per layoff (no waiting period).
2. Program averted 62,800 layoffs in 1991. 29 percent of those on work-sharing were laid off later, so that the program averted 43,200 in 1991.[b]
3. Participants had fewer weeks laid off/work-sharing than comparison employees.
4. Work-sharing workers reported higher job satisfaction and were more likely to be employed one to two years later.
5. Firms returned to full production sooner but did not adjust; provided less training.

---

[a] States with short-time compensation laws are California, Arizona, Oregon, Florida, Washington, Illinois, Maryland, Hawaii, and Pennsylvania.

[b] The 29 percent refers to a population of 67,500. The study finds 67,500 jobs saved but notes that 7 percent of the comparison firms that considered layoffs did not do so, suggesting that only 63,000 jobs were saved. The 43,200 is based on a calculation that deducts 29 percent of 67,500 and 7 percent of 67,500.

quate control group and thus could neither determine "whether use of work sharing encourages firms to increase or decrease loss of work among participating employees" (Best 1988, 77) nor provide good estimates of the number of jobs saved. At best, it could calculate, by assuming that total person-hours was fixed (or changed by some fixed amount), how many layoffs were averted.

In 1982 Congress directed the Department of Labor to examine the American experience with short-time compensation; DOL contracted with Mathematica to undertake the work. The DOL-Mathematica study compared STC employers in California, Oregon, and Arizona with matched employers, in the same states, that did not use the program. Because of possible unobserved differences between firms that chose STC and those that did not, this is not an ideal research design— an alternative would have been to survey matched employers in states without STC as well—but it is the best assessment available on the U.S. experience. The study found that work-sharing had relatively modest effects on employment. Many firms that used work-sharing also used layoffs: in work-sharing firms the proportion of hours unemployed was 11 to 12 percent, compared to 14 percent of hours in the control group. Firms that used STC also reduced total working hours more than did those in the control group. In the aggregate, moreover, U.S. STC programs have had minimal effect on unemployment because utilization of STC has been uniformly low (Vroman 1992). STC claims averaged 0.27 percent of regular UI weeks claimed in the United States, compared to 13.1 percent in Belgium and 5 percent in Germany over the comparable 1982 to 1991 period (calculated from Vroman 1992, tables 2 and 5).

In 1993 the Canadian government funded an extensive evaluation of work-sharing in which 620 firms that used STC were compared to 460 firms that did not, and 1,000 employees who experienced work-sharing were compared to 1,000 who were laid off (Employment and Immigration Canada 1993). The Canadian evaluation is more favorable than the U.S. evaluation. For starters, STC is more widely used in Canada than in the United States: in 1991, 196,500 Canadians participated in the work-sharing program (17 percent of the 1.4 million unemployed that year). In addition, work-sharing did not seem to lead to reduced person-hours worked in Canada: firms that used STC had smaller work-hours reductions than those that did not use it. The study estimated that the program cut layoffs by 43,200 to 62,800 in 1991, compared to 11 million employees—or about 0.4 to 0.6 percent. Employees who experienced work-sharing rather than layoffs were more likely to be employed one to two years later and had better health and job satisfaction.

The Canadian assessment looked at a wider spectrum of outcomes than the U.S. study did. It compared the health and job satisfaction of work-sharing employees and laid-off employees. The estimated benefit-cost ratio for the program was 2.6 to 1. The only negative findings was that firms that chose STC trained workers less and seemed to restructure their operations less than those that used layoffs. In 1987, Noah Meltz and Frank Reid calculated a larger benefit-cost ratio of 5.7 to 1 for the Canadian program, so it is possible that the program has become less effective over time. Still, for whatever reason, Canada's experience with work-sharing through unemployment benefits seems to have been more successful than the American experience.

Wage and Supply Responses to Work-Sharing

The reduction of working time without loss of wages remains a fundamental demand in a period of unemployment when work-sharing is
imperative (European Trade Union Confederation 1994).

A key issue in discussions of work-sharing is what adjustment in pay, if
any, accompanies reductions in hours worked. At one point, unions and
some governments favored work-sharing with full compensation, by
which is meant an increase in hourly pay that maintains monthly or
yearly income. Such an increase adds to labor costs and thus limits the
success of any work-sharing scheme. At the enterprise level, if we allow
for a response of hourly pay with respect to hours, the employment
effect of work-sharing includes a term that depends on the elasticity of
demand for labor. If employees gain full compensation for the reduction
in hours, the hours-employment substitution effect has to exceed the
elasticity of demand for labor. If employees gain partial compensation
of say r percent, the increase in employment induced by the hours-
employment trade-off must exceed r times the elasticity of demand for
labor. Unfortunately, we lack reliable estimates of elasticities of demand,
or of responses of wages to hours, to enable us to determine with any
surety the net of these effects.

But as experience with work-sharing has developed, union attitudes
have changed; many now recognize that work-sharing requires some
earnings sharing if it is to have a chance at increasing employment.
European analysts have examined how unions concerned with both
employment and wages might respond to work-sharing imposed by the
state (Calmfors 1985; Hoel 1987). Given that leisure has some positive
value, these models predict that unions will seek not full compensation
but rather some wage increase to ameliorate the fall in annual earnings.
In most models, the increase in earnings does not overwhelm the work-
sharing substitution effect. Much depends, however, on whether or not
employees work their desired level of hours when work-sharing is initiated. Meltz and Reid (1983) argue that if workers are at their equilibrium, they are likely to prefer work-sharing (which saves their jobs)
to risking layoffs. If employees are working more hours than they would
like, their demand for compensation will be small, increasing the effectiveness of work-sharing (Houpis 1993). But if employees are working
fewer hours than they want to (say, working no normal overtime)—
a likely scenario in a recession, when work-sharing programs are most
likely to be initiated—demands for compensating wage increases may be
higher.

In the United States, where many employees hold second jobs, the issue is not so much what unions representing groups of employees want, but what individual employees want. A work-sharing scheme that cuts the hours of employees who do not want to lower their worktime could generate additional moonlighting, thus limiting the effectiveness of work-sharing in the aggregate. Studies of moonlighting find that persons take second jobs because they are constrained by the hours available on their first job (see Conway and Kimmel 1992, and the literature cited therein). Thus, a work-sharing program that constrains at least some employees may lead to additional labor supply. The result could be a rise in total person-hours worked and output, but it would not be sustainable absent changes in macroeconomic policy.

Why Has Work-Sharing Not Fulfilled Its Promise?

One possible explanation why work-sharing has not fulfilled its promise is that the substitution elasticity between hours and employment for comparable workers is too small to permit any substantial expansion of jobs. I do not think technological substitutability is the reason for the minimal effect of work-sharing. With an elasticity of employment to hours of, say, 0.4, which is in the range of existing estimates, employment would increase by 4 percent for a reduction in hours of 10 percent—enough to cut unemployment rates massively. The optimistic simulations of what work-sharing might do are, in fact, predicated on just such substitution parameters.

A second possibility is that work-sharing founders on the macroeconomic wage adjustments just discussed. Short hours either induce additional wage demands or fail to ameliorate those that result when unemployment falls. I do not think that wage demands are the reason for the minimal effect of work-sharing. Too many unions have been willing to accept wage cuts for promised employment expansion, and most unions recognize that full compensation makes work-sharing potentially too costly and counterproductive. In at least some countries with collectively bargained wages (such as Belgium, which has been a hotbed for work-sharing), wage restraint is generally viewed as a necessary component of any work-sharing arrangement (vide the 3–5–3 plan).

A third explanation for the ineffectiveness of work-sharing is that generally it is poorly targeted, given the substantial difference in skills between those who are jobless and the employed. The simple work-sharing models posit a trade-off between hours worked and employment of a homogenous population of substitutes. But there is a sharp difference between the skills of the employed and the unemployed. A work-sharing scheme that requires skilled complements to work less could reduce the demand for the less skilled workers who make up the bulk of the unemployed. Work-sharing schemes that are poorly targeted and reduce the hours that capital or human capital is used may backfire. To avoid such problems, German unions and employers have negotiated greater flexibility in setting hours worked, exempting a proportion of the workforce from reductions in the standard workweek, and in some instances reorganizing work to increase plant utilization—for instance, by adding shifts. I believe that the difference in skills between the jobless and the bulk of the employed helps account for the weak aggregate employment effects of work-sharing. If the workforce is homogeneous, a 5 percent reduction in the hours of all workers could, with a 0.4 substitution elasticity, induce 2 percent greater employment. But if the jobless are all unskilled, and the unskilled make up one quarter of the employed workforce, the 5 percent reduction in total hours would increase total employment by just 0.5 percent, even assuming that reducing the hours of skilled workers does not adversely affect demand for the less-skilled. In this model, it would take a 20 percent reduction in the hours of unskilled workers to raise employment by 2 percent.

A fourth explanation for the modest gains from work-sharing, implicit in the earlier discussion of labor supply, is that most employed workers are no more willing to cut hours and monthly earnings to provide jobs for others than they are to reduce hourly pay to create additional employment. Work-sharing cannot succeed if workers do not accept it. The May 1985 CPS contained detailed questions on work scheduling and preferences for hours worked among U.S. workers, including the following question:

> If you had a choice would you prefer to work: (1) the same number of hours and earn the same money; (2) fewer hours at the same rate of pay and earn less money; (3) more hours at the same rate of pay and earn more money?

Just 8 percent of wage and salary workers said that they preferred fewer hours and less money; 65 percent wanted the same hours and money, and 28 percent more hours and more money.

A 1989 EEC survey of worktime preferences asked a question that relates directly to work-sharing:

> If the choice were offered in the next wage round between an increase in pay for the same hours of work and shorter working time for the same pay you get now, which would you prefer?

Fifty-six percent of Europeans preferred an increase in pay, compared to 34 percent who said they preferred shorter worktime. Moreover, the proportion of European workers who reject shorter worktime seems to have increased. In 1982 to 1985 surveys of Dutch employees, 40 percent favored a work-sharing option, whereas in the 1989 EEC survey just 29 percent favored that option. And while the EEC survey shows Germans about evenly split between the options, other surveys of German workers show that between 1977 and 1985 the proportion who preferred higher wages to reduced hours rose from 35 percent to 56 percent (Hinrichs, Roche, and Sirianni 1991, 43). With real wages stagnant or falling for large segments of the American workforce and increasing less rapidly in Europe in the 1990s than in the 1980s, the willingness to engage in work-sharing society-wide seems limited.

Conclusion

This review of experiences with work-sharing has three messages:

1. Work-sharing is not inhibited by labor demand behavior. As far as we can tell from time-series data, hours reductions generated by market forces induce substitution of bodies for hours. Employers and employees are sufficiently flexible to adjust labor services to changes in hours.
2. The efforts of European governments, however, to create jobs through mandated cuts in hours have been, at best, marginally successful. Short-time compensation in Canada contributed modestly to reducing layoffs, while those in the United States have had only negligible effects.
3. Labor supply factors, including divergencies between the skills of the jobless and those of the employed, and workers' limited willingness to accept the income reductions that accompany hours reductions, do inhibit work-sharing.

These conclusions raise the question of whether the goal of creating employment solely through reduced hours is misplaced. Employment involves use of capital, so perhaps work-sharing would be more effective if it involved the sharing of capital as well—say, through weekend work, multiple shifts, or elimination of store closing hours to increase operating hours. The movement toward flexible hours and nonstandard work and the differences in shift work across economies (Commission of the European Community 1991) and firms (OECD 1995) present the opportunity to combine work-sharing and capital-sharing. It would be interesting to see whether the unemployed accept jobs at the going wage rate for late shift work subsidized, say, by unemployment benefits. Additional shift work might also partly reduce the practical difficulties in determining marginal employment in employment subsidy schemes. While I doubt that any form of labor market "flexibility" can make a major dent in unemployment, my guess is that some combination of work-sharing and capital-sharing would do more than extant work-sharing programs have done in creating employment for the jobless.

Notes

1. Upwards of 56 percent of employees in large firms were part-time in 1932, usually through reduction in days worked per week (cited in MaCoy and Morand 1984, p. 17). Hours fell from 44.2 hours per week in 1929 to 38.3 in 1932, and with the NRA, to 34.6 in 1934 (see U.S. Dept. Commerce, Series D-803). The 1938 recession saw a drop in hours from 42.1 to 33.1 according to MaCoy and Morand (p 43).

2. I use this age group as the base because the OECD reports comparable statistics for this base group.

3. Among U.S. men in the 1990 census of population, the variance of ln hours over the year in 1989 was .47 compared to a variance in ln of hourly earnings of .48.

4. I do not give the normative case for work-sharing here. Any plausible social maximand that posits declining material utility from employment would rate an even distribution of joblessness higher than an uneven distribution.

5. By getting H/N overtime hours from N workers, the firm gets the same H hours it would get from a single new hire.

6. Differentiate the cost of an additional employee with respect to H. This yields $-pH$, which implies that decreases in the standard workweek raise the cost of an additional employee. This operates to lower employment.

7. There are no "natural experimental" instruments, so many of these analyses use lagged values of different variables as instruments.

8. In this summary, I use results in Pencavel and Holmlund (1988), table 1, columns iv and ii, and in table 3, line h, column ii.

9. Shorter standard hours increase employment absent overtime and compensation with either Keynesian or classical unemployment but have different effects in the presence of overtime and compensation: in the Keynesian case, employment effects are positive in the presence of overtime and enhanced by wage gains, whereas in the classical case, shorter hours reduce employment and the employment response (Toedter 1988).

10. The forecasts of employment gains from work-sharing in the 1980s in INSEE's macro-model for France exceeded the most optimistic assessment of those gains after introduction of the program.
11. Table 6.4 is not a compendium of European programs to create/save jobs by trading hours for employment. I have left out some efforts that I know about (such as the 1983 German government extension of short-time compensation benefits from two to three years to reduce unemployment), and there are surely others about which I do not know.
12. Belgium had already reduced hours considerably, from 42.7 hours per week for blue-collar workers in 1970 to 35.7 in 1985.
13. The degree of added flexibility is considerable. As of 1994, firms can alter work-time without paying premium—as long as worktime averages out over one year to the agreed-upon amount—and they can have from 13 to 18 percent of workers employed up to forty hours, on average.
14. This is the consensus view, held by those who initially expected work-sharing to work as well as by those who did not expect it to succeed. Dreze writes: "Those who have looked for evidence of the new hirings [resulting from hours reductions] have not found it (p. 170).
15. Best (1988) reports that funds were cut midway in the evaluation.

Bibliography

Abraham, Katharine G. and Susan N. Houseman. 1993. *Job Security in America: Lessons from Germany.* Washington, D.C.: Brookings Institution.

Bell, Linda, and Richard B. Freeman. 1995. "Why Do Americans and Germans Work Different Hours?" In *Institutional Frameworks and Labor Market Performance: Comparative Views on the U.S. and German Economies,* edited by Friedrich Butler, Wolfgang Franz, Ronald Schettkat, and David Soskice. New York: Routledge.

Best, Fred. 1988. *Reducing Workweeks to Prevent Layoffs.* Philadelphia, Penn.: Temple University Press.

Bishop, John H., and Robert Haveman. 1979. "Selective Employment Subsidies: Can Okun's Law Be Repealed?" *American Economic Review.* 69(2): 124–30.

Bishop, John H., and Mark Montgomery. 1986. "Evidence on Firm Participation in Employment Subsidy Programs." *Industrial Relations* 25(1): 56–64.

Bosch, Gerhard. 1986. "The Dispute over the Reduction of the Working Week in West Germany" *Cambridge Journal of Economics* 10(3): 271–90.

———. 1990. "From 40 to 35 hours: Reduction and Flexibilisation of the Working Week in the Federal Republic of Germany." *International Labour Review* 129(5): 611–27.

Calmfors, Lars. 1985. "Work Sharing, Employment, and Wages." *European Economic Review* 27(3): 293–309.

Commission of the European Community. 1991. *European Economy* (March).

Conway, Roger K., and Jean Kimmel. 1992. "Moonlighting Behavior: Theory and Evidence." Working Paper (May). Kalamazoo, Mich.: W.E. Upjohn Institute for Employment Research.

Council of Economic Advisors. 1994. *Economic Report of the President*. Washington: United States Government Printing Office. (February).

Dreze, Jacques. 1991. "Work-Sharing: Some Theory and Recent European Experience." *Economic Policy* 3: 562–619.

Ehrenberg, Ronald G. 1971. *Fringe Benefits and Overtime Behavior.* Lexington, Mass.: Lexington Books.

Ehrenberg, Ronald G., and Robert S. Smith. 1982. *Modern Labor Economics: Theory and Public Policy.* Glenview, Ill.: Scott, Foresman and Co.

Employment and Immigration Canada, Strategic Policy and Planning. 1993. *Program Evaluation Report: Work-Sharing Evaluation* (March). Ottawa, Canada: Employment and Immigration Canada, Strategic Policy and Planning.

Eisner, Robert. 1978. "Employment Taxes and Subsidies." In *Work Time and Employment,* Special Report 28 (October). Washington, D.C.: National Commission for Manpower Policy.

European Trade Union Confederation. 1994. *A Time for Working/A Time for Living* (December). Brussels, Belgium: Trade Union Division of the Directorate.

Feldstein, Martin. 1967. "Specification of the Labour Input in the Aggregate Production Function." *Review of Economic Studies* 34: 375–86.

Financial Times. 1994. (editorial) (fall).

Hart, Robert A. 1988. *Working Time and Employment.* London, England: Allen and Unwin.

Hinrichs, Karl, William Roche, and Carmen Sirianni. 1991. *Working Time in Transition.* Philadelphia, Penn.: Temple University Press.

Hoel, Michael. 1987. "Can Shorter Working Time Reduce Unemployment." In *Unemployment in Europe: Analysis and Policy Issues,* edited by C.H. Siven. Stockholm, Sweden: Timbro.

Hoel, Michael and Bent Vale. 1986. "Effects on Unemployment of Reduced Working Time in an Economy Where Firms Set Wages." *European Economic Review* 30(5): 1097–1104.

Houpis, George. 1993. "The Effects of Lower Hours of Work on Wages and Employment." Discussion Paper 131 (March). London, England: London School of Economics Centre for Economic Performance.

Houseman, Susan. 1988. "Shorter Working Time and Job Security: Labor Adjustment in the Steel Industry." In *Employment, Unemployment, and Labor Utilization* edited by Robert A. Hart. London, England: Unwin Hyman.

Jallade, Jean-Pierre. 1991. "Working Time Policies in France." In *Working Time in Transition,* edited by Karl Hinrichs, William Roche, and Carmen Sirianni. Philadelphia, Penn.: Temple University Press.

Lammers, John, and Timothy Lockwood. 1984. "Short-Time Compensation: At Home and Abroad: The California Experiment." In *Short-Time Compensation: Formula for Worksharing,* edited by Ramelle MaCoy and Martin J. Morand. New York: Pergamon Press.

Layard, Richard, Stephen Nickell, and Richard Jackman. 1991. *Unemployment.* New York: Oxford University Press.

Lewis, H. Gregg. 1956. "Hours of Work and Hours of Leisure." Industrial Relations Research Association. Proceedings of the Ninth Annual Meeting (December).

MaCoy, Ramelle, and Martin Morand. 1984. *Short-Time Compensation*. New York: Pergamon Press.

Mayshar, Joram, and Yoram Halevy. 1997. "Shiftwork." *Journal of Labor Economics* (January): 198–222.

Meltz, Noah, and Frank Reid. 1983. "Reducing the Impact of Unemployment Through Work-Sharing: Some Industrial Relations Considerations." *Journal of Industrial Relations*, 25(3): 153–61.

Meltz, Noah, Frank Reid, and Gerald Shwartz. 1981. *Sharing the Work: An Analysis of the Issues of Work-Sharing and Job Sharing*. Toronto, Canada: University of Toronto Press.

de Neuborg, Chris. 1991. "Where Have All the Hours Gone? Working-Time Reduction Policies in the Netherlands." In *Working Time in Transition: The Political Economy of Working Hours in Industrial Nations*, edited by Karl Hinrichs, William Roche, and Carmen Sirianni. Philadelphia, Penn.: Temple University Press.

Nussbaum, Joyce M., and Donald Wise. 1978. "The Overtime Pay Premium and Employment" in *Work Time and Employment* Special Report 28 (October). Washington, D.C.: National Commission for Manpower Policy.

Organization for Economic Cooperation and Development. 1994. *Jobs Study*. Paris, France: Organization for Economic Cooperation and Development.

———. 1995. *Flexible Working Time*. Paris, France: Organization for Economic Cooperation and Development.

———. Various editions. *Employment Outlook*. Paris, France: Organization for Economic Cooperation and Development.

Owen, John D. 1989. *Reduced Working Hours: Cure for Unemployment or Economic Burden?* Baltimore, Md.: Johns Hopkins University Press.

Pencavel, John, and Bertil Holmlund. 1988. "The Determination of Wages, Employment, and Work Hours in an Economy with Centralised Wage-Setting: Sweden, 1950–1983." *Economic Journal* 98(393): 1105–26.

Plasmans, Joseph and Annemie Vanroelen. 1988. "Reducing Working Time for Reducing Unemployment?: A macroeconomic stimulation study for the Belgian Economy." In *Economic Modelling in the OECD Countries,* edited by Homa Motamen, International Studies in Economic Modelling Series. London, England: Routledge.

Reid, Frank, and Noah Meltz. 1984. "Canada's STC: A Comparison with the California Version." In *Short-Time Compensations,* edited by Ramelle MaCoy and Martin Morand. New York: Pergamon Press.

Richardson, Ray, and Marcus Rubin. 1993. "The Shorter Working Week in Engineering: Surrender Without Sacrifice." Discussion Paper 113. London, England: London School of Economics, Centre for Economic Performance.

Rosen, Sherwin. 1978. "The Supply of Work Schedules and Employment" in *Work Time and Employment,* Special Report 28 (October). Washington, D.C.: National Commission for Manpower Policy.

Seifert, Hartmut. 1991. "Employment Effects of Working Time Reductions in the Former Federal Republic of Germany." *International Labour Review,* 130(4): 495–510.

Smyth, David J. and Stephen H. Karlson. 1991. "The Effect of Fringe Benefits on Employment Fluctuations in U.S. Automobile Manufacturing." *Review of Economics and Statistics* 73(1): 40–49.

Toedter, Karl-Heinz. 1988. "Effects of Shorter Hours on Employment in Disequilibrium Models." *European Economic Review* 32(6): 1319–33.

Tribune, Desfosses, La. 1995. editorial. (March 29, 1995).

United States Department of Commerce. 1975. *Historical Statistics of the United States: Colonial Times to 1970: Part 1.* Washington, D.C.: U.S. Bureau of the Census.

United States Department of Labor. 1982. "An Evaluation of Short-Time Compensation Programs." Unemployment Insurance Service Occasional Paper 86-4. Washington: U.S. Government Printing Office.

————. 1986. *Monthly Labor Review.* (November 1986). Washington : U.S. Government Printing Office.

Van Audenrode, Marc. 1994. "Short Time Compensation, Job Security, and Employment Contracts: Evidence from Selected OECD Countries." *Journal of Political Economy,* 102(11): 76–102.

van Ginneken, Wouter. 1984. "Employment and the Reduction of the Workweek: A Comparison of Seven European Macro-Economic Models." *International Labor Review,* 123(1): 35–52 (Jan/Feb).

Vroman, Wayne, 1992. "Short Time Compensation in the U.S., Germany, and Belgium." Working Paper (June). Washington, D.C.: The Urban Institute.

Chapter 7

Employer Hiring Decisions and Antidiscrimination Policy

Harry J. Holzer

I n the past few decades, the employment and earnings of young blacks have deteriorated significantly, especially among the less educated. This deterioration has occurred in spite of efforts to protect and enhance their employment status through a variety of governmental antidiscrimination efforts, such as federal equal employment opportunity (EEO) laws and affirmative action programs for government contractors. Furthermore, the employment and earnings of females have improved during the same period, and even less educated females have made gains relative to less educated males.

A fairly large body of research suggests that various changes on the demand side of the labor market, such as employers' growing skill needs and their changing geographic locations, have contributed heavily to these developments. But little direct evidence has been available on these issues to date, since so little data have been available from the demand side of the labor market.

In this chapter, I provide some new evidence on employer skill needs, hiring behavior, and the effects of these factors on employment for minorities and women, using data from a new survey of more than three thousand two hundred employers in four large metropolitan areas.

I begin by reviewing the literature on government antidiscrimination policies and on the recent deterioration in labor market outcomes for blacks. I then present empirical evidence on employer hiring of minorities and women. I conclude with a discussion of implications for antidiscrimination policies and for government efforts more generally aimed at the demand side of the labor market facing minorities and women.

Discrimination, Government Policy, and
Minority/Female Employment: The Literature

Federal antidiscrimination efforts in the past thirty years have largely consisted of two types of policies: (1) legislation (beginning with the Civil Rights Act of 1964) that makes it illegal for employers to discriminate against minorities and women in hiring, pay, and promotion; and (2) executive orders (first issued in the Kennedy and Johnson administrations) requiring that employers with federal contracts undertake "affirmative action" to improve the relative employment and earnings of these "protected groups."[1]

Have these policies been successful in reducing labor market discrimination against minorities and women, thereby increasing their employment and earnings? This question has been the subject of a great deal of research over the last few decades. The rapid improvement in the relative occupational status and earnings of blacks during the late 1960s and early 1970s, particularly in the South, has been attributed by some (Freeman 1973, 1981; Heckman and Payner 1989; Donahue and Heckman 1991) to a reduction in labor market discrimination associated with the passage of the Civil Rights Act in 1964. Others have stressed south-to-north migration and improvements in the relative quantity and quality of education attained by blacks over longer time periods as major determinants of their economic progress (Smith and Welch 1989; Margo 1990; Card and Krueger 1992).[2] But federal antidiscrimination activities, especially through court rulings on school desegregation (such as *Brown v. Board of Education* in 1954), appear to be at least partly responsible for the relative educational improvements as well (Boozer, Krueger, and Wolkon 1992).

Some improvements in the relative earnings and occupational status of women have also been attributed to EEO policies, though these effects were somewhat harder to discern until the 1970s. Apparently the increased labor force participation of less experienced women in the 1960s and 1970s at least partly offset the impact of EEO policies on the relative earnings of females during those decades.[3]

The impact of affirmative action requirements of government contractors on the employment and earnings of minorities and women has been analyzed most extensively by Jonathan Leonard.[4] He has found clear evidence that during the 1970s affirmative action programs helped raise the employment, earnings, and occupational status of minorities and women in contractor establishments relative to those of white males. Leonard argues that affirmative action programs achieved these results without the use of rigid "quotas" and without generating reduced productivity in heavily targeted areas and industries (Leonard 1984a).

Furthermore, the costs imposed on white males through these policies have not been enormous, even while generating significant improvements for minorities (and somewhat smaller ones for white females).[5] The benefits to minorities and women (and apparently the costs to white males) in contractor establishments can also be found across the entire range of occupations and skill categories, though the magnitudes of the changes appear to be somewhat larger among white-collar than blue-collar occupations.[6] These findings parallel those from earlier work on the distributional effects of EEO policies, which showed greater relative gains for more educated young blacks than for others.[7]

But the apparent success of EEO laws and affirmative action in improving labor market outcomes for minorities and women during the 1960s and 1970s raises some additional questions. For one thing, does discrimination against these groups in the labor market persist, despite these governmental efforts to eliminate it? It is well known that gaps in earnings and employment by race or gender, even after controlling for *observable* differences in personal characteristics or jobs, cannot necessarily be attributed to labor market discrimination. Unobserved differences in preferences or skills across various groups of workers may instead account for any such remaining statistical gaps.[8]

But more direct evidence on the existence of discrimination in hiring against minorities has recently appeared in a few different contexts. One is the use of labor market *audit* studies in which pairs of white and minority job applicants with comparable education and work experience are matched and sent to seek job offers. These studies, reviewed and critiqued recently in a volume of papers edited by Michael Fix and Raymond Struyk (1994), have found evidence of lower probabilities of receiving job offers among both black and Hispanic job applicants compared to whites, thereby refuting the notion that "reverse discrimination" against white males is more prevalent today than is discrimination against traditionally disadvantaged groups.[9]

More qualitative evidence, based on interviews with employers, has been presented by Joleen Kirschenman and Katherine Neckerman (1991) and by Philip Moss and Chris Tilly (1995). These studies generally document very negative employer perceptions of blacks, especially young black males, in terms of skills, work performance, and attitudes toward work, and it is presumed that these stereotypic perceptions reduce employer hiring out of these groups. Whether such discriminatory behavior would be "pure" or "statistical" in nature is, of course, harder to discern from these studies.[10]

The apparent persistence of labor market discrimination against minorities also raises some questions about the overall effectiveness of governmental antidiscrimination efforts, despite the successes described earlier. For instance, John Donohue and Peter Siegelman (1991) argue that rising federal enforcement activities and expenses during the 1970s generated greatly diminished returns as EEO activity became increasingly concentrated in individual *discharge* cases rather than in the more effective class-action hiring or promotion cases.[11] Indeed, they argue (as does Bloch 1994) that employer fears of lawsuits from potential hires could actually have led to *greater* discrimination at the hiring stage (though no clear evidence of this has ever been provided).

While rising employment discrimination cannot possibly be attributed to affirmative action programs (which have led to both rising employment levels and rising wages for minorities and women at contractor firms), the weakening of federal enforcement of affirmative action during the 1980s apparently led to some reversals of the gains enjoyed by these groups during the previous decade (Leonard 1990).

Though we have no direct evidence, it is also possible that the degree of labor market discrimination against some of these groups has actually risen in the past decade or so. For instance, the employer fears of young, less educated black males that are documented by Kirschenman (1991) may have grown worse over time as the participation of young black males in crime has increased (Freeman 1994) and as the available supply of less educated immigrants (who may be preferred by some employers) has grown.[12]

Of course, these forces are part of a much broader set of labor market developments that have affected the labor market outcomes of blacks, women, and other groups in recent years. By the mid-1970s, employment levels of blacks (especially among the young) had been declining for at least three decades, while their relative earnings were improving.[13] But in the past fifteen to twenty years, both the real earnings and employment levels of blacks and less educated males more generally have sharply deteriorated. In contrast, those of women have risen in relative terms. Indeed, the real earnings and employment of college-educated young women have grown substantially, while those with a high school education or less have not deteriorated nearly so much as have those of less educated males.[14]

The literature on the growing employment problems of less educated black males during this period attributes them to a variety of other labor market forces besides discrimination, including: (1) employers' growing skill needs, which have reduced the employment and earnings of less skilled males, among whom blacks happen to be overrepresented (Juhn, Murphy, and Pierce 1993); (2) declining employment in blue-collar jobs and/or manufacturing (Bound and Freeman 1992; Bound and Holzer 1993; Kasarda 1995); (3) the movement of employers away from inner-city areas, while the mobility of minorities remains impeded by residential segregation and/or transportation problems (Ihlanfeldt and Sjoquist 1990; Holzer 1991; Kain 1992); and (4) declining labor force activity in response to declining market wages and/or rising returns to illegal activities (Juhn 1992; Freeman 1994).

All of these factors (including, at least partly, the last) directly originate in changes that have apparently occurred on the *demand* side of the labor market for less skilled and minority workers, and to which adjustments by these groups on the *supply* side have lagged behind. The resulting "mismatches" in the labor market (Wilson 1987) result in lower wages and/or employment for these groups, at least in the short run.[15]

Despite the central role played by labor demand shifts in these hypotheses, we have had very little direct evidence on these forces from the demand side of the labor market. Much of the evidence has instead come from traditional supply-side data sources, such as the current population survey or the census of population, to which more aggregated industry- or area-level data are sometimes appended.[16]

In addition to generating cleaner tests of the various demand-side micro-level hypotheses already cited, demand-side data (especially on the hiring behavior of employers and on the characteristics of jobs they are filling) should enable us to answer some questions that are critical for the formation of appropriate policy responses to these problems. For instance, exactly where in the economy are the jobs for less skilled workers, and where are they located geographically? What skills do employers seek, and how do they recruit and screen applicants with these skills? What kinds of applicants do they receive in terms of race and/or gender? Who ultimately gets hired in different kinds of jobs, and does affirmative action have any independent effects on these outcomes?

Answers to these questions would surely give us greater insight into the relative roles of discrimination and other demand-side forces in limiting the employment options of minorities as well as women. They might also enable us to modify existing antidiscrimination efforts by identifying areas and sectors where such policy currently appears to be less effective.

To date, the paucity of available demand-side data on labor markets has limited our understanding of these issues. We therefore turn to results from a new survey of employers.

Employer Data and Results

As part of a project entitled the Multi-City Study of Urban Inequality (funded by the Ford and Russell Sage Foundations), I recently administered a phone survey of roughly eight hundred employers in each of four metropolitan areas: Atlanta, Boston, Detroit, and Los Angeles. The survey was administered from May 1992 through May 1994. The characteristics of the survey instrument and the sample of firms are described in greater detail in the appendix to this chapter.

Summary Data

Table 7.1 presents the employment outcomes at these firms by race and gender for all employees and for the last employee hired at each firm. These outcomes are presented for all recently filled jobs as well as for subsets of firms and jobs based on educational requirements (college diploma required/not required);[17] for location within the metropolitan area (primary central city/suburbs/other locations, the last category including other central cities in the metropolitan area and other municipalities with at least 30 percent black populations);[18] and for whether or not the respondent reported that affirmative action was used by the firm in filling jobs.[19] The results by location and by use of affirmative action are presented only for positions that do not require college degrees. All results are sample-weighted.

The results show that blacks account for under 20 percent of employees and recent hires in these metropolitan areas, while Hispanics account for an additional 12 to 14 percent and Asians for 4 to 5 percent.[20] Furthermore, females account for more than half of newly hired workers. This is not a surprise considering the distribution of occupations represented in this sample—more than half of these employees are in white-collar jobs, with clericals alone accounting for 30 percent.[21] Depending on location, the median starting wages on the noncollege jobs in the sample are in the range of $7 to $8 an hour, with 70 to 80 percent providing health care coverage for the employee and about half providing employer contributions to pensions (Holzer 1996).[22]

I find that the representation of blacks and especially Hispanics rises higher in jobs that do not require college degrees, and that the

Table 7.1 Employment Outcomes by Race and Gender: Means (and Standard Deviations)

	All Jobs	Jobs Require College		Noncollege Jobs			Affirmative Action[a]	
		Yes	No	Primary Central Cities	Suburbs	Other Areas	Yes	No
Percentage of employees								
White males	—	—	.335	.243	.370	.361	.311	.366
White females	—	—	.353	.265	.375	.334	.360	.344
Black males	—	—	.092	.149	.064	.123	.099	.082
Black females	—	—	.092	.166	.054	.103	.101	.079
Hispanics	—	—	.124	.145	.128	.097	.130	.117
Asians	—	—	.043	.056	.040	.025	.051	.034
Last hired worker								
White males	.286	.373	.260	.167	.301	.263	.217	.314
White females	.350	.384	.341	.293	.370	.310	.358	.318
Black males	.083	.049	.096	.149	.063	.126	.098	.093
Black females	.088	.055	.102	.170	.070	.109	.112	.090
Hispanic males	.081	.045	.089	.092	.086	.094	.092	.085
Hispanic females	.060	.034	.067	.067	.067	.065	.074	.058
Asian males	.026	.034	.023	.038	.019	.011	.027	.017
Asian females	.020	.022	.017	.012	.021	.012	.016	.019

Notes: All means are sample-weighted.

[a]Both columns refer only to jobs that do not require a college degree.

proportion of jobs filled by blacks is two to three times higher in primary central cities than in the suburbs. Likewise, the proportion of minorities and females among employees and new hires is consistently higher for firms that use affirmative action, while the proportion of white males is lower by several percentage points. Thus, the preliminary results at least suggest that the skill needs, spatial locations, and antidiscrimination efforts of employers all affect their tendencies to hire minority workers.

In table 7.2, I present summary data on several other characteristics of these jobs, for the same sample and subsamples used in the previous table. These include whether each of a particular set of social and cognitive tasks (such as directly dealing with customers, reading or writing paragraphs, performing arithmetic, or using computers) is generally performed on a daily basis and whether each of a set of credentials (having a high school diploma, general or specific work experience, references, or vocational training) is absolutely necessary or strongly preferred for getting hired. The percentages of jobs requiring *none* of these tasks or none of the credentials are also presented.

The results of table 7.2 show that for the vast majority of new jobs social and cognitive tasks must be performed daily and major credentials are required. While the level of task performance and required credentials are clearly higher for jobs that require college degrees than for those that do not, even among the latter they are substantial.[23] Thus, each of the tasks is performed daily in 50 to 70 percent of all newly filled noncollege jobs, and all of the credentials are required or preferred in 40 to 70 percent. Furthermore, *the percentage of noncollege jobs in which either none of the cognitive tasks or none of the hiring credentials are required is very small*—just 6 percent and 4 percent of the total, respectively, in the central city, and a bit higher in the suburbs.[24]

Though we do not have exactly comparable data from the supply side of the market on the characteristics of potential workers, the data we do have suggest that the number of such workers in the central cities is likely to be greater than the number of available jobs, and that this imbalance is likely to be aggravated by welfare reform legislation, which will soon require many more less educated people to enter the labor force in these areas.[25]

Furthermore, while these labor markets may adjust somewhat over time to shifts in local labor supplies, downward wage rigidities may well limit the magnitudes of any potential adjustments. Thus, the skill requirements for new jobs suggest a very limited availability of employment to the least skilled workers in urban areas, even at very low wages.

Table 7.2 Means on Characteristics of Firms and Jobs

	All Jobs	Jobs Require College		Noncollege Jobs			Affirmative Action[a]	
		Yes	No	Primary Central Cities	Suburbs	Other Areas	Yes	No
Daily task performance								
Customers	.716	.825	.702	.768	.678	.683	.711	.690
Reading/writing	.647	.898	.613	.659	.613	.543	.643	.575
Arithmetic	.664	.775	.650	.650	.649	.651	.623	.684
Computers	.537	.735	.511	.571	.495	.469	.561	.446
None of above	.070	.001	.079	.056	.084	.100	.074	.086
Hiring requirements[b]								
High school diploma	.748	1.000	.715	.761	.704	.684	.780	.632
General experience	.694	.766	.684	.722	.670	.672	.705	.656
Specific experience	.627	.740	.612	.667	.596	.582	.652	.561
References	.742	.863	.726	.735	.721	.728	.752	.691
Previous training	.400	.530	.383	.417	.388	.310	.399	.362
None of above	.051	.020	.055	.041	.061	.054	.038	.077

[a]Both columns refer only to jobs that do not require a college degree.

[b]A given factor is counted as a hiring requirement if a firm considers that factor either absolutely necessary or strongly preferred in order to be hired.

In table 7.3, we consider one additional characteristic of firms: the percentage of job applicants as well as employees or new hires who are black males, black females, Hispanics, or Asians. The applicant variables measure the quantity of labor *supply* that firms face from each of these demographic groups, while the ratio of employees or new hires to applicants measures the relative labor *demand* for the applicants of each group.[26] Ratios greater than one indicate a relative inclination of employers to hire from a particular group of applicants, while those less than one indicate a disinclination.[27] Both the applicant measures and the ratios appear in table 7.3, for the entire sample of firms and for each of the subsets used in tables 7.1 and 7.2.

The results show several important findings. Blacks and Hispanics are more likely to apply for jobs that do not require college degrees, that are located in primary central cities, and that practice affirmative action in hiring. The last of these findings holds for Asians as well.

The gap in black application rates between firms located in central cities versus those in the suburbs is striking. Indeed, the magnitude of this locational gap in applicants parallels that in employment for blacks between these two areas. This large racial gap in applicant locations suggests that it may be access to jobs, rather than skill gaps or the racial attitudes of employers, that limits the employment of blacks in suburban areas. Thus, this evidence is very consistent with the idea of *spatial mismatch:* blacks whose residences are concentrated in the central city (owing to housing market segregation and discrimination) having difficulty obtaining suburban jobs because of transportation costs, limited information, or other problems (Holzer 1991; Kain 1992).[28]

On the other hand, there is some evidence here that applicants *self-select* into firms by applying where they are most likely to be hired. For instance, the higher applicant rates of minorities (especially black females) at firms that use affirmative action suggest some responsiveness of labor supply to differences in the demand for these groups, thus making it more difficult to infer exogenous determinants of outcomes from either side of the market using these data.

As for the ratios of employees and new hires to applicants, I find that:

- these ratios are generally closest to one for Hispanics, somewhat lower for Asians, and lowest for blacks;
- they are lower for black males than for females, and lower in the suburbs than in the central cities;

Table 7.3 Applicants and Hires by Race and Gender

	All Jobs	Jobs Require College		Noncollege Jobs			Affirmative Action[a]	
		Yes	No	Primary Central Cities	Suburbs	Other Areas	Yes	No
Percentage of applicants who are								
Black males	.146	.082	.168	.242	.125	.205	.170	.165
Black females	.124	.111	.128	.190	.095	.145	.149	.103
Hispanics	.137	.109	.145	.155	.144	.135	.149	.141
Asians	.058	.068	.055	.055	.058	.045	.067	.041
Ratio[b] of new hires to applicants								
Black males	.568	.598	.571	.616	.504	.615	.576	.564
Black females	.710	.495	.797	.895	.737	.752	.752	.874
Hispanics	1.029	.725	1.076	1.026	1.063	1.178	1.114	1.014
Asians	.793	.824	.727	.909	.690	.511	.642	.878
Ratio of employees to applicants								
Black males	—	—	.630	.616	.512	.600	.588	.497
Black females	—	—	.742	.874	.568	.710	.678	.767
Hispanics	—	—	.905	.935	.889	.719	.872	.830
Asians	—	—	.741	1.018	.690	.556	.761	.829

[a] Both columns refer only to jobs that do not require a college degree.

[b] "Ratios" refer to ratios of means rather than vice versa.

- for black males and Hispanics, they are higher in jobs where affirmative action is used (though the opposite appears to be true for black females and Asians);[29]
- for all minority groups except Asians, the ratios are comparable or higher in jobs that do not require college degrees.

Of course, without controlling for the *quality* of applicants (in terms of skills, attitudes, and so on) relative to skill needs on jobs, it is hard to make inferences about discrimination from these relative preferences of employers. Differences across groups in the average qualities of applicants whom employers face may arise because of either population-wide differences or the self-selection process by which applicants choose where to apply for work. For instance, it is at least possible that whites and Hispanics are more likely than blacks to apply for jobs at which their chances of receiving an offer are higher.[30]

On the other hand, population-wide education levels and test scores are generally higher among blacks than Hispanics. Furthermore, the gaps between education levels of whites and blacks are generally higher among central-city residents and employees than among suburban ones, and as noted earlier, task and credentials requirements are generally higher in the central city as well.[31]

These factors suggest that the biases caused by omitted measures of applicant quality probably go in the opposite direction from the results presented earlier. Therefore, the findings here strongly imply that *employer discrimination in hiring is relatively more severe against blacks than Hispanics, and relatively more severe among suburban than central-city employers.*

In table 7.3, we see that the relative employer preference for Hispanics over blacks is especially pronounced among noncollege jobs. This is also true for jobs in which cognitive and social task requirements are relatively low, such as blue-collar and manufacturing jobs (Holzer 1996). Indeed, the percentages of Hispanics employed in these jobs and industries are well above those observed for whites, while for black males the opposite is now true in these areas.[32]

The hiring patterns noted here are also consistent with more qualitative evidence in which employers generally express their preferences for immigrants over native-born blacks in jobs that require few skills, and for black females over black males (Kirschenman 1991; also Kirschenman and Neckerman 1991). These preferences seem to reflect widespread employer perceptions that immigrants have better attitudes and a better "work ethic" than do native-born blacks, as well as employers' relatively greater fears of behavioral problems and crime from young black males.

The relatively low preference of suburban employers for black applicants is also consistent with the notion that employers are not randomly distributed within metropolitan areas; indeed, those with discriminatory tastes are more likely to choose to locate in suburban areas (Kain 1992). Thus, at least part of the difference in employment locations across geographic areas may be due to *race* rather than *space* (Ellwood 1986).

Furthermore, these differences are relatively more pronounced in some occupations and industries than in others. In Holzer (1996), I present hiring ratios in suburbs and central cities for blacks by one-digit occupation and industry. In general, I find particularly low ratios of employees to hires for black males at retail trade and service firms and in clerical and sales jobs located in the suburbs. These findings suggest hiring behavior that may be related to the tastes of customers, as in Becker's seminal model (1971). I explore this possibility more systematically later in this chapter.[33]

Regression Estimates

The data presented in the previous section suggest that the geographic location, group preferences, and use of affirmative action of employers all affect their tendencies to hire minorities and women. Other factors, such as their task performance needs and required credentials, may affect these tendencies as well. But employers located in the central city are also more likely to use affirmative action in hiring. Firms in both categories not only are more likely to receive black applicants than are others but are also generally larger and more likely to receive black customers.[34] Since all of these factors may be associated with the hiring of blacks, we need multivariate regression analysis to separate out their effects to the greatest extent possible.

Table 7.4 presents the results of an estimated equation for the probabilities that firms hire individuals from various race/gender groups. The dependent variable is categorical, based on the race and gender of the last worker hired.[35] The sample is limited to workers hired into jobs that do not require college degrees. The equation has been estimated through multinomial logit, with white males as the omitted group.

The independent variables consist of both firmwide and job-specific measures in the latter. The firmwide measures include industry dummies, dummies for central city/suburban/other location as well as for

Table 7.4 Effects on Race/Gender of Most Recent Hire: Multinomial Logit Estimates

	White Female	Black Male	Black Female	Hispanic Male	Hispanic Female	Asian Male	Asian Female
Geographic location							
Primary central city	.074	.846	.902	.808	.624	1.290	-.092
	(.150)	(.204)	(.205)	(.243)	(.249)	(.375)	(.463)
Other areas	-.050	.459	.458	.355	-.070	.248	.034
	(.162)	(.232)	(.236)	(.274)	(.318)	(.509)	(.529)
Establishment size							
1–20	-.180	-1.270	-1.523	-.611	-.394	-1.077	-1.664
	(.228)	(.308)	(.301)	(.407)	(.407)	(.584)	(.616)
21–50	.056	-.811	-.769	-.051	.001	-.795	-1.828
	(.239)	(.320)	(.310)	(.421)	(.424)	(.588)	(.777)
51–100	.078	-.488	-.508	-.206	.228	-.864	-.052
	(.255)	(.332)	(.329)	(.431)	(.430)	(.631)	(.602)
101–500	.177	-.297	-.327	-.129	.072	-.540	-.608
	(.229)	(.286)	(.283)	(.385)	(.386)	(.512)	(.540)
Percentage of applicants who are in group[a]	—	.030	.051	.024	.028	.048	.054
		(.004)	(.006)	(.004)	(.005)	(.011)	(.012)
Percentage of customers who are in group[b]	—	.019	.025	.016	.017	.017	.007
		(.005)	(.005)	(.007)	(.007)	(.010)	(.011)

Daily tasks							
Customers	.970	.068	.973	−.221	.166	−.902	.118
	(.148)	(.203)	(.232)	(.240)	(.264)	(.385)	(.438)
Reading/writing	−.279	−.292	−.305	.210	.049	−.012	−.150
	(.131)	(.184)	(.188)	(.217)	(.232)	(.392)	(.424)
Arithmetic	−.046	−.751	−.392	−.337	.002	.073	−.066
	(.129)	(.181)	(.182)	(.209)	(.224)	(.359)	(.409)
Computers	1.000	.116	.825	−.424	.697	.510	.166
	(.128)	(.193)	(.189)	(.233)	(.233)	(.387)	(.424)
Hiring requirements							
High school diploma	.332	−.030	.112	−.653	.007	−.580	.084
	(.155)	(.207)	(.220)	(.229)	(.266)	(.408)	(.526)
Specific experience	−.083	−.231	−.329	−.314	−.287	.130	.245
	(.132)	(.192)	(.190)	(.228)	(.238)	(.393)	(.450)
Vocational training	−.273	−.252	−.233	.007	−.205	−.720	−.159
	(.126)	(.192)	(.188)	(.226)	(.328)	(.367)	(.387)
Affirmative action	.164	.264	−.163	.402	.338	.283	−.066
	(.122)	(.183)	(.182)	(.210)	(.224)	(.362)	(.403)
Log L	−3204.5	−3204.5	−3204.5	−3204.5	−3204.5	−3204.5	−3204.5

Notes: White males are the omitted category for the multinomial logit equations. Other controls include dummy variables for MSA, industry, and collective bargaining at the firm, as well as the age and education of the last worker hired.

[a]Identified by race for all groups except whites and by gender for blacks only.

[b]Identified by race for all groups except whites.

Metropolitan Statistical Area (MSA), percentage of employees covered by collective bargaining, establishment size dummies, use of affirmative action, and the race/gender compositions of customers and applicants. The job-specific measures include dummies for daily task performance and credentials needed for the job, as well as the age and education of the worker hired. Thus, despite the fact that the data come from just a single cross-section of employers, I control for a very wide range of employer skill needs and determinants of racial preferences, as well as some personal human capital characteristics of workers.

Though not presented here, a variety of specifications of this equation have been estimated. For instance, the racial composition of customers and applicants across firms may well be endogenous to the use of affirmative action and to minority employment more generally. Including these variables reduces the estimated effects of others, such as affirmative action and central-city location, on the hiring of minorities and may generate downward biases in these estimates. On the other hand, controlling for the supply of minority applicants to firms gives us at least some confidence that most other estimated effects truly reflect the choices of employers, conditional on the characteristics of the applicant pool.

Turning to the results presented in table 7.4, we generally find that affirmative action raises the employment of at least some minority and female groups relative to white males. The effect on the employment of Hispanic males is largest and most significant, while the effects for white and Hispanic females as well as black and Asian males are at least marginally significant as well.

How much redistribution of employment from less educated white males to those in "protected groups" do these estimates imply? Estimates from equations in which the dependent variables reflect the hiring of white males suggest that the presence of affirmative action reduces their employment shares by roughly three and a half percentage points, or 10 percent.[36]

These estimates are larger than Leonard's and may well reflect further unobserved heterogeneity across firms, though the range of control variables for skill needs and employer preferences is quite extensive.[37] It is also unclear whether the increases in minority and female employment simply offset the declines in male employment or actually exceed them among noncollege jobs (the latter result would imply some net substitution of noncollege for college jobs).[38]

Overall, the results suggest that affirmative action continues to improve the employment prospects of less skilled females and minorities.

Of course, many important questions remain: for instance, are the minorities or women hired under affirmative action less qualified and/or less productive than the white males they are replacing? If so, the charges that these programs generate "reverse discrimination" against white males would gain somewhat greater credence.

Elsewhere I use these data to present new evidence on this issue (Holzer and Neumark 1996). The results show that minorities hired under affirmative action are, in fact, relatively more likely to lag behind white males in educational attainment than they are in nonaffirmative action establishments. But, using a variety of measures of job performance, we find little evidence of weaker job performance for most groups of minorities and women in these establishments.[39]

The data therefore suggest that affirmative action largely accomplishes what it was intended to: giving minorities and women with relatively weaker formal credentials on paper the opportunity to prove themselves in actual job performance. Though this result may seem highly unfair to white males with stronger credentials, the policy does seem to equalize opportunity for those who continue to be hampered by poorer family backgrounds, school quality, and so on, as well as by labor market discrimination. But to dispel any doubts about this result, more research on this controversial issue is warranted.

We find a variety of results in table 7.4 regarding issues other than affirmative action:

- Establishment size has powerful effects on the hiring of minorities, with larger firms hiring more blacks (but smaller firms hiring somewhat more Hispanics).
- The race/gender compositions of customers as well as of applicants also have large effects on who gets hired.
- Firms located in primary central cities generally hire more minorities.
- Firms with high task performance needs and hiring criteria generally hire fewer minorities.

The estimated effects of skill needs on hiring are jointly significant, and many of the individual effects are at least marginally significant as well. In general, there are gender as well as race effects; for instance, females are more likely than males of each racial group to be hired into jobs requiring customer contact or computer use.

But within each gender, these tasks and credentials have important effects on hiring patterns by race. In particular, black and Hispanic males are the most negatively affected by cognitive skill requirements and hiring credentials. Black males are particularly hurt by the need for arithmetic and reading/writing skills on jobs, as well as requirements of previous vocational training and specific experience. Hispanic males are hurt by some of these same requirements (arithmetic, specific experience, and computer use), and especially by the requirements of high school diplomas. The last effect appears to reflect the continuing high dropout rate of Hispanics (Hauser and Phang 1993).

The employment of black and Hispanic females is also reduced, *especially relative to white females*, by many of these same job characteristics. Furthermore, the magnitudes of these effects are not necessarily small when converted into partial derivatives (evaluated at sample means), relative to the means for group-specific employment that appear in table 7.1.[40]

These findings suggest that minorities are hurt in the hiring process by employer perceptions of their weaknesses in cognitive skills and observable credentials. To some extent, these perceptions are no doubt accurate; despite recent gains, blacks and Hispanics continue to score lower than whites on tests measuring cognitive abilities (Grissmer et al. 1994). Other studies have found that these gaps explain major parts of black-white earnings and employment differences (see, for instance, O'Neill 1990; Rivera-Batiz 1992; Ferguson 1993; and Neal and Johnson 1996). Differences in education levels and in early labor market experience also contribute to the lower credentials that employers perceive for these groups.[41]

But employer perceptions of these weaknesses among minority job candidates may be overstated, especially with regard to credentials that they do not observe at the time of hiring; the extent to which these weaknesses predict future job performance remains unclear as well.[42] Thus, the estimated effects of skill needs and hiring requirements may well reflect some degree of employer discrimination (whether pure or "statistical") as well as legitimate skill needs.

A few other points deserve some mention. First, most of these hiring requirements have significant effects on wages as well as on who gets hired.[43] These wage effects indicate that, on average, these requirements represent meaningful skills in the eyes of employers. They also suggest that, in conjunction with their effects on who gets hired, the skill requirements may contribute somewhat to observed wage differentials between race and gender (as well as educational) groups. Indeed, the various hiring requirements account for a substantial fraction (roughly 30 percent) of the residual wage differences between black and white males (after controlling for other observable characteristics of individuals, jobs, and firms) in this sample (Holzer 1995b).

These hiring requirements and skills account for virtually none of the gender differences in wages, as is clear from the fact that women are employed in jobs that contain relatively more of them. Remaining gender differences in *starting* wages (that is, when no job tenure has been accumulated) after controlling for educational attainment of individuals, skill requirements of jobs, and other firm characteristics may reflect factors such as occupational choice, expected future job tenure, or discrimination (Gunderson 1989). On the other hand, the apparent growth in the demand for many of these tasks (such as computer use) may well have contributed to the improved relative wages of less educated women in the past decade and to the deteriorating relative wages of less educated (and especially minority) males (Holzer 1995b).

Customer composition, establishment size, and central-city location have strong effects as determinants of hiring even after controlling for the racial composition of the applicant pool and for a wide range of employer skill needs. As before, it is possible that these effects reflect unobserved differences in skill needs or in applicant quality by race across firms. But once again, it seems more likely that these biases run in the opposite direction from the results presented here.[44]

Therefore, the observed effects of these variables on employment by race probably reflect various demand-side factors, such as employer preferences.[45] The effects of customer composition suggest that employers cater to their perceptions of their customers' tastes. Large employers and/or those located in central cities may feel particular pressure to hire minorities and women, owing to their greater visibility and proximity to these groups, or they may actually prefer these employees to a relatively greater extent than do their smaller and suburban counterparts.[46]

Whatever the exact interpretation, these results suggest that hiring behavior tends to be relatively more discriminatory among small and suburban employers, thus limiting the employment prospects of minorities at these firms. On the other hand, differences in task performance and credential requirements can account for more of the observed differences in earnings between whites and blacks than had previously been noted, and they may help account for the relatively strong performance of less educated females in the last one or two decades.

Conclusion

In this chapter, I have reviewed the literature on the effectiveness of antidiscrimination activities by the federal government and on the persistence of discrimination against minorities and women in the labor market more generally. I have also presented some new evidence on the determinants of hiring wages for members of different race/gender groups, primarily in jobs that do not require college degrees. The evidence is based on a new survey of employers in four large metropolitan areas that I recently administered.

This review of the literature showed that both antidiscrimination laws and affirmative action programs caused significant improvement in the relative earnings of blacks and females during the 1960s and 1970s. While both caused greater relative improvement among more highly educated groups, the benefits of these programs could be seen across the educational and occupational spectrum. Employment has clearly been redistributed away from white males in firms that practice affirmative action (and presumably they have experienced downward pressure on their wages in other firms), but the level of redistribution does not appear to be too severe in magnitude.

On the other hand, the more recent evidence on these programs has been somewhat more discouraging. EEO activities are increasingly focused on individual discharge cases rather than on class-action suits against hiring and promotion practices; the latter are likely to generate legal precedents and have larger effects on relative labor market status. There has been speculation (though no real evidence) that these legal activities may contribute to employer reluctance to hire minorities in the first place. Enforcement of affirmative action regulations also deteriorated during the 1980s, as did their relative effects on the employment of minorities at contractor establishments.

Both quantitative and qualitative evidence suggest that blacks continue to be discriminated against in employment. Furthermore, their relative labor market status has clearly declined in the past ten to twenty years as labor demand has apparently shifted away from less educated workers in general and away from less educated blacks in particular. On the other hand, the relative earnings of women clearly improved in this period.

The empirical results presented in this chapter imply that discrimination continues to limit the employment prospects of less educated blacks. The data suggest that hiring discrimination is relatively more severe against blacks than Hispanics, against black males than black females, and in smaller and/or suburban establishments, especially in jobs that involve contact with predominantly white customers.

Other factors, such as lower access to suburban firms and the various skill requirements of employers, also seem to have important effects on where central-city blacks are employed. Increases in those skill needs may play major roles in accounting for differing trends over time in the relative earnings of blacks and females among the less educated.

What do these results imply about policies—especially those targeted to the demand side of the labor market—to improve the employment and earnings prospects of less educated minorities and females?

It seems unlikely that any major expansion of affirmative action programs can be realistically considered at this time. Given the strong political opposition that these programs seem to face, the major question for the short term is whether they will survive at all. Aside from political constraints, we still have too little evidence on whether these programs are efficient, or whether they generate any net new employment for less educated workers. Thus, arguing for a major expansion of affirmative action seems premature, though more rigorous enforcement of existing guidelines may well be in order.

But these results do suggest some possibilities for strengthening government antidiscrimination efforts. In particular, we need to improve our monitoring of employment practices in smaller and/or suburban firms and to increase social and legal pressure on these firms to improve their hiring of minorities. Such activities would effectively extend the scope of current antidiscrimination activity and therefore might avoid the "diminishing returns" that appear to be plaguing these efforts.

But exactly how to bring greater pressure to bear on such establishments is not clear. Legal proof of employment discrimination at any establishment often depends on the racial composition of its employees relative to the composition of the local population (Bloch 1994). Since at least some of the suburban firms deliberately located far away from minority populations, the basis for claiming employment discrimination in many such cases may be lacking.

An alternative legal strategy might rely on the racial composition of *job applicants* at firms as well as the local population in computing the relevant base with which to compare the racial composition of employment. Indeed, the use of audits by applicants to generate legal proceedings against firms, one version of such a strategy, has recently been debated in policy circles and in the courts.

We might more generally be interested in using the composition of job applicants to measure the minority labor supply faced by firms; numbers of job applicants might be especially useful in suburban areas. But many firms do not keep records of rejected applicants and may not record race even when they do. Other ways of monitoring the racial composition of applicant flows at individual firms would have to be developed for such an approach to work.

More important is the larger question of how to generate more minority job applicants in suburban areas in the first place. Indeed, we might view various *mobility* strategies, designed to raise the supply of minority labor in suburban areas, as complementary with (and even preconditions for) effective antidiscrimination efforts targeted at the demand side of the labor market in these areas.

Proponents of residential mobility strategies for increasing black representation in the suburbs (such as Kain) argue for stricter enforcement of antidiscrimination laws in housing and for housing vouchers for low-income residents; others (Hughes and Sternberg 1992, for instance) place more emphasis on transportation and job placement approaches for those who will continue to be residents of central cities. Over the long term the former approach has greater appeal, though the latter appears to be more cost-effective and politically popular.[47]

In addition to these issues, we must also confront the problem of real deficiencies in skills and credentials among minority applicants. The need for improved education and job training for these applicants is quite obvious. While a full discussion of these issues is clearly beyond the scope of this chapter, one potential policy targeted at firms deserves some mention here. Since there is evidence that minorities are given less formal on-the-job training than white employees are (see, for example, Lynch 1992), lowering the cost of such training to employers (through subsidies for private-sector training, and so on) might increase their willingness to provide it to minority employees and might even make them willing to lower the preemployment screens that clearly limit minority employment in many cases.[48]

Providing meaningful private-sector work experience to inner-city minorities early in their working careers (through improved job placement, apprenticeships, and other programs that speed the "school-to-work transition") might also improve their ability to pass through these screens at the hiring stage.

Finally, there are only a very small number of new jobs, especially in central-city areas, that require no major credentials at the hiring stage or no major task performance after hiring. Given the large number of inner-city youth who have experienced long periods of nonemployment and who have poor cognitive skills, and given the current popularity of proposals to push more long-term AFDC recipients into the labor force, there seems to be a clear need for more job creation for very low-skilled workers. Whether this is accomplished through some type of wage subsidy to employers or through direct public-sector employment, the need to create more such jobs seems quite clear.[49]

Appendix: Characteristics of Employer Survey

The data presented in this chapter are from a survey of thirty-two hundred employers in Atlanta, Boston, Detroit, and Los Angeles that was administered over the phone between May 1992 and May 1994.

Survey questions focused on employment characteristics of the overall establishment, such as numbers of recent hires, turnover, current job vacancies;, the last worker hired into the firm, and the job filled by that person. These questions included frequency of performance of certain tasks, recruiting and screening methods, other hiring requirements, and some demographics of the worker hired (such as race, gender, age, and education level). The race and/or gender composition of the firm's applicants, customers, and current employers were all noted as well.

The sample was drawn from two sources: (1) employers identified by respondents in household surveys that were being administered concurrently in each city (as part of the Multi-City Study of Urban Inequality); and (2) listings of firms and phone numbers from Survey Sampling Inc. (SSI) that are primarily generated from phone directories. About one thousand employers were generated by the first source, and the remainder were generated by the second.

For the SSI sample, I focused on the last worker hired into jobs that did not require workers with four-year college degrees; for the household-generated sample, I focused on workers hired into the same job categories as were listed by household respondents. In either case, firms had to have hired someone in the relevant category within the past three years in order to pass the screening and be included in the survey.

The SSI sample was drawn as a stratified random sample that oversampled large employers in order to generate a sample of firms distributed across size categories in roughly the same way as are current employees.[50] The household-based sample is implicitly weighted by employees already. Therefore, both samples are essentially employee-weighted and can be pooled.[51] Furthermore, the sample of recently filled jobs in these firms represents an employee-weighted sample of new jobs and workers that reasonably well represents the appropriate universe in each case.[52]

Response rates for firms that passed the screening averaged about 67 percent. Given that I had some data on all firms generated by SSI, including those that did not respond to the survey, I could check for significant differences in response rates across certain variables—industry, location, firm size—that would suggest the presence of sample selection bias. Overall I found little evidence of major differences in response rates across these variables, indicating little selection bias across these observable categories.[53]

Comparisons of the industrial and size distributions of these firms with those listed for the relevant metropolitan areas in the *County Business Patterns* also indicated the employer samples are quite representative.

I thank the Russell Sage and Rockefeller Foundations for financial support, and conference participants for helpful comments.

Notes

1. The various laws, court rulings, and enforcement activities by federal agencies of this period are described elsewhere in great detail. See, for instance, Donohue and Siegelman (1991) or Bloch (1994). I do not discuss the various activities that have been undertaken at the state and local levels of government, such as "comparable worth" policies to equalize pay across predominantly male versus female occupations. For discussions of these issues, see Killingsworth (1990) and Sorensen (1994).

2. The studies focusing on the impacts of migration and improved education among blacks generally use data from several decennial censuses to document long-run effects. In contrast, the papers by Freeman and by Heckman and his coauthors show large discrete improvements (in both short-run outcomes and trends over time) in relative earnings or employment starting in 1965, with striking changes occurring fairly quickly in the South. While some authors (for example, Butler and Heckman 1977) had earlier contended that these changes might reflect a rising tendency of low-wage blacks to drop out of the labor force, it now appears that dropouts cannot account for more than a small fraction of the relative wage improvements of blacks in this period (Brown 1984; Donohue and Heckman 1991).

3. Though the unadjusted ratio of female to male earnings in the United States did not improve until the 1980s, the adjusted differential (that is, after accounting for differences in experience and other personal characteristics) did fall by about four percentage points during the 1970s (Blau and Beller 1988). For more discussion of these issues, see Gunderson (1989).

4. Leonard's 1990 review paper summarizes a lengthy body of his own work on this topic. See also Brown (1982) for a review of earlier research on the effects of EEO and affirmative action.

5. Leonard's data (as reported in his 1990 paper) indicate that the share of employment accounted for by white males in establishments (which constitute about 60 percent of all the contractor establishments in his sample) declined by just one and a half percentage points (or 2.7 percent) more than in noncontractor establishments between 1974 and 1980 (the period during which the monitoring and enforcement of affirmative action policies was significantly increased). Assuming inelastic labor supply among white males and the standard range of estimates of labor-demand elasticities (Hamermesh 1993), the wages of white males (and perhaps other workers as well) in the noncontractor sector would have declined by roughly 1 to 2 percent. On the other hand, the increases in shares of employment accounted for by black males and females in the contractor sector were half a percentage point and three-tenths of a percentage point, respectively, constituting increases of 7.8 percent and 7.1 percent; while for white females it was six-tenths of a percentage point (or 2.1 percent). The relative earnings and occupational status of blacks and females also improved within the contractor sector in addition to these employment shifts.

6. Leonard (1984b) finds that employment shares for black males in contractor establishments rose in each occupational category except for laborers and white-collar trainees, while for black females they increased in each category except for technical, craft, and white-collar trainees. On the other hand, increases for black males in the white-collar and craft occupations exceeded those in the operative, laborer, and service categories.

7. Freeman (1973) showed that black-white earnings gaps had traditionally been largest among the most highly educated workers, implying that educated blacks had suffered the worst discrimination (and lower rates of return to education than comparable whites). But these patterns disappeared in the 1970s, and young blacks enjoyed rates of return to education in that decade that were as high or higher than those of their white counterparts.

8. For women, the issues of occupational preferences and gaps in labor market experience or job tenure associated with periods of withdrawal from the labor force have long been associated with reduced earnings; see, for example, Gunderson (1989) or Killingsworth (1990). For blacks, unobserved skill differences (as explanations of recent changes in relative wages) are emphasized in Juhn, Murphy, and Pierce (1993).

9. For instance, a study of black and white auditors in Chicago and Washington, D.C., finds that 29 percent of white auditors received job offers compared to 19 percent for blacks; thus, the offer arrival rate was more than half as large for white applicants within the relevant time period. For audit evidence on gender differences in hiring, see Neumark, Bank, and Van Nort (1996).

10. "Statistical" discrimination (Cain 1986) would imply that negative employer perceptions of blacks are correct at the mean, although variance in productivity among blacks cannot be discerned by these employers. On the other hand, the perceived gaps in prospective productivity may be exaggerated by employers, partly out of their own preferences for white employees. While the audit studies suggest "pure" discrimination, since they control for observable personal characteristics such as education and experience, employer perceptions

of average racial differences in *unobservables* (which may or may not be accurate) probably influence their hiring behavior here.

11. Donohue and his coauthors argue that the effectiveness of EEO laws during the 1960s was primarily due to the targeting of the South, where discriminatory employer behavior was so blatant; they question the ability of these laws to generate major improvements where forms of discrimination are more subtle. Leonard (1990) also stresses the relative effectiveness of the class-action hiring and promotion suits that generated major legal precedents, such as the "disparate impact" ruling in the *Griggs v. Duke Power* case of 1971.

12. Kirschenman and Neckerman (1991) report that employers frequently express a preference for immigrants over native-born blacks for low-skill work. Borjas, Freeman, and Katz (1992) and Topel (1994) relate declining wages for less educated workers to rising immigrant populations, though Jaeger (1995) shows that these effects are substantial only in those geographic areas (such as the Pacific coast region) where immigrants settle in substantial numbers.

13. Cogan (1982) attributes much of the employment decline of blacks in the earlier part of this period to the disappearance of low-wage jobs in southern agriculture associated with mechanization. The papers in Freeman and Holzer (1986) provide evidence that a variety of demand- and supply-side factors limited the employment of blacks in the 1970 to 1980 period.

14. For a good review of the overall trends in earnings, see Levy and Murnane (1992). Bound and Freeman (1992) and Moss and Tilly (1992) provide reviews of the labor market changes affecting blacks, while Blau and Kahn (1994) provide evidence on the changing relative fortunes of less educated males and females.

15. "Mismatch" does not necessarily imply the existence of disequilibrium or high unemployment in the labor market; but as long as labor supply elasticities among the relevant groups are positive, the shifts in labor demand away from the less skilled should generate both lower employment levels and lower wages until offsetting labor supply shifts occur (through higher educational attainment, migration, and so on). Wage rigidities and disequilibria would exacerbate the effects of demand shifts on employment and unemployment while reducing them on wages.

16. Inferences about the roles of demand shifts in these data have come from positive correlations between wage and employment changes across groups (Katz and Murphy 1992); from data on changes in the industry or occupational composition of employment that are sometimes interpreted as exogenous labor demand shifts (as with declining manufacturing employment); from industry-level data on R&D expenditures (Berman, Bound, and Griliches 1994) or import penetration (Sachs and Shatz 1994); or from area-level data on average commute times (Ihlanfeldt and Sjoquist 1990).

17. Overall employment levels of firms by race are gauged in the survey only for positions that do not require college degrees.

18. The Census Bureau categorizes municipalities as "central cities" based on their population size, the ratios of employees to residents, and the proportion of workers who also live there. Other central cities (besides the primary ones, which are the largest in each metropolitan area) are Marietta in the Atlanta area; Brockton, Cambridge, Framingham, Gloucester, Haverhill, Lawrence, Lowell,

Lynn, Salem, and Waltham in the Boston area; Dearborn and Pontiac in the Detroit area; and Long Beach, Pasadena, and Pomona in the Los Angeles area.

19. The survey gauged whether or not respondents had used affirmative action during either the recruiting or the screening process of filling the most recent job; a "yes" answer to either question is interpreted as use of affirmative action. Though the questions were asked only about the most recent hire, any use of affirmative action probably reflects government contractor status by the establishment and therefore can be applied to the larger measure of its employees as well.

20. Blacks are concentrated in Atlanta and Detroit, while Hispanics and Asians are concentrated in Los Angeles (and to a lesser extent in Boston). Dummies for metropolitan area are included in all estimated regression equations presented later in this chapter.

21. This sample overrepresents high-turnover jobs *within* firms and also jobs experiencing net employment growth. But the distributions of all employees and of new hires across occupations do not look very different from one another.

22. Wages are generally higher in Boston and Los Angeles than in Atlanta and Detroit, and they are consistently higher for jobs located in primary central cities than in other areas. Even in jobs that do not require college, starting wages for white males are 8.5 percent higher than for white females, and 20 to 30 percent higher than those for blacks and Hispanics (though at least part of the racial difference reflects the relatively greater concentration of whites in Boston and Los Angeles).

23. Standard errors on these dichotomous variables can be calculated as the square root of $(P*(1-P)/N)$, where P is the mean and N is the sample size. Standard errors on *differences* across nonintersecting categories can be calculated as the square root of the sum of the squared individual standard errors. Differences in means that are discussed in the text are generally those that are significant at the conventional levels.

24. If we allow for somewhat less restrictive definitions of very low-skill jobs—for example, those that require only a high school diploma or only interactions with customers on a daily basis—these percentages rise to 10 percent and 7 percent, respectively, in the central city.

25. I make this inference from the percentage of working-age and nonenrolled residents of the central cities who have no high school diploma or recent work experience. For example, medium- and long-term AFDC recipients (those who have been on the rolls for more than two years) alone account for 10 to 15 percent of household heads in these cities; the majority of these women have no high school diplomas, no recent work experience, poor reading/writing abilities (as measured by test scores), and little history of job search in suburban areas. See Holzer (1996, ch. 3).

26. The applicant questions in the survey were not specific to the last filled job, suggesting that comparison with the establishment-wide employee measures may be more appropriate. On the other hand, the most recently filled jobs reflect recent hiring behavior; the wider employee measures may not. Furthermore, the most recently filled jobs in firms should (on average) be more heavily represented in their overall employees as well, thus making comparisons

between the applicant measure and either measure of hiring fairly reasonable in large samples.

27. Appropriately weighted averages of these ratios across all groups, including whites, should sum to one. However, I did not gauge these measures for whites in the survey.

28. Since these data tell us *where* rather than *whether* different groups of people work, we cannot directly infer "mismatch" from these results. Indeed, if employers and jobs were distributed in direct proportion to where people live, or if commuting over local distances were relatively costless, the location of employment for different groups would tell us nothing about their relative employment or wage rates. However, the relatively lower ratios of vacancies to unemployed workers and lower wages in jobs located near minority residences (see, for example, Holzer 1996; Ihlanfeldt 1995; Holzer and Ihlanfeldt 1996) suggest that labor markets for less educated workers are tighter in the suburban areas, implying some disadvantage for those who have limited access to these markets.

29. For black females and Asians, employment rises in jobs and firms that use affirmative action, but applicants rise by even greater proportions.

30. This might be true if, for example, some groups had lower reservation wages than others and were therefore more likely to apply for low-wage jobs or for jobs where they have some personal contacts. For evidence of black-white differences in search behaviors among young males, see Holzer (1986, 1987).

31. See Hauser and Phang (1993) for evidence on education levels, and Grissmer et al. (1994) for data on test scores across racial and ethnic groups. In Holzer (1995a), I show that whites who work in the city of Detroit have higher education levels than those working in the suburbs, while the opposite is true for blacks.

32. For instance, 45 percent of recent Hispanic male hires were in manufacturing, relative to 29 percent and 20 percent for white and black males, respectively. For blue-collar jobs, comparable fractions are 56 percent, 43 percent, and 40 percent, respectively. The relative underrepresentation of black males in manufacturing constitutes a major reversal from twenty years earlier in the industrial Midwest, where blacks were heavily overrepresented in this type of work. See Bound and Holzer (1993).

33. Becker's model also implies that employers' discrimination is based on their own preferences as well as those of their employees. I have no direct evidence on the former, since a few survey questions that tried to gauge such preferences yielded little variance and few believable results. The same was true of a question that tried to gauge employer perceptions of employee preferences for those of their own race or ethnic group. While I did gauge the race/gender of the respondent (who was responsible for hiring), these measures are quite highly correlated with race/gender of new hires, and I could not sort out causal effects of the former on the latter from their being jointly determined by the same set of other factors.

34. Blacks account for 26 percent of customers at firms in the primary central cities, but only 15 percent at suburban firms. Also, establishments with one hundred or more employees account for 40 percent and 34 percent of those in each lo-

cation, while they constitute 45 percent of establishments practicing affirmative action but only 23 percent of those that do not.

35. Males and females appear separately in the logits, as they were separately gauged in the question for last-hired worker, though independent variables for race of applicant and customers generally do not distinguish gender within racial groups.

36. This estimate is derived (1) from a tobit equation with the same firmwide variables as the equation in table 7.4, except that the dependent variable is the percentage of noncollege employees at each firm who are white males, and (2) from a binomial logit with exactly the same specification as in table 7.4, in which the dependent variable is a dummy for whether or not the last-hired noncollege worker is a white male.

37. Leonard used federal contractor status rather than self-reported use of affirmative action as his primary measure of that activity. Firms that practice affirmative action in response to various state-level requirements, or because they choose to do so, are included in the affirmative action sector in my results but not in Leonard's. Also, Leonard uses *changes* between 1974 and 1980 rather than levels of employment as his dependent variables, and his controls generally differ from those included here.

38. It is possible that employment gains induced by affirmative action for minorities and women exceed the losses of white males among the *less* educated, while the opposite is true among the more educated. The program could also cause a shift in employment *between* the educational categories as well as within them. But within this single cross-section of firms we find a strong *positive* correlation between education levels of hires and affirmative action, implying a shift toward more educated groups that is very likely upward-biased and that would cause the within-group estimates to be biased in the opposite direction.

39. We measure job performance through the skills needed on the job into which the worker is hired, the worker's wage, whether or not he or she has been promoted, and a subjective employer rating of his or her performance (on a scale of 0 to 100). Only among Hispanic males did we generally find evidence of relatively weaker job performance in establishments that use affirmative action. In some equations, we used establishment size categories as instruments for affirmative action at the establishment to generate a more exogenous measure than the self-reported measure; the results are qualitatively unchanged in these specifications.

40. Partial derivatives on all of the tasks and hiring requirements for black males (including customer contact and computer use) are all negative and in the range of one to eight percentage points (Holzer 1995b). The customer and computer partials are negative for white males as well as black males, thus explaining the lack of negative coefficients on these attributes in table 7.4.

41. The estimated experience effects differ somewhat from those estimated by Ellwood (1982), Meyer and Wise (1982), and others, who found negative effects of early unemployment on later wages but not on later employment. Those results were based on data from the early 1970s; whether or not they would hold up today is unclear. Indeed, some recent work by Rich (1994) suggests long-term effects on employment of early unemployment among youth.

42. One interpretation of the audit studies described earlier, in which blacks and whites with identical *observable* characteristics are paired, is that employers believe that whites dominate blacks in terms of *unobservables* (work attitudes, for instance); whether they are correct is unclear. The question of the extent to which hiring criteria actually predict job performance is at the center of the legal issues of disparate impact and the validation of these criteria that began with the Supreme Court ruling in *Griggs v. Duke Power* (1971) and was addressed more recently in the Civil Rights Act of 1991.

43. Indeed, all have significant positive effects on wages except for customer contact and the requirement that workers have references. See Holzer (1995b).

44. For instance, all of the observed measures of skill needs are higher in larger establishments, making it likely that unobserved skill needs are higher there as well; these establishments should thus have a greater tendency to hire whites. There is no reason to believe that the relative quality of black applicants at larger establishments is higher than at smaller ones. As noted earlier, firms that are located in the central cities and have many black customers probably attract black applicants with lower average qualities than those attracted by suburban employers.

45. If the minority applicant measures are endogenous with respect to race and gender hiring patterns more generally, the estimated coefficients on other determinants of minority hiring will likely be biased toward zero.

46. Larger employers generally have personnel departments that use more formal recruitment and screening methods, which may be relatively beneficial for blacks (Holzer 1987), and their relative proximity to the black population in central cities may tend to reduce the spread of stereotypical notions among their employees about the characteristics and behavior of blacks (Bobo and Klugel 1991). It seems unlikely that the greater tendency of large and/or inner-city firms to hire more minorities can be attributed to their receiving a higher *quality* of minority applicants there relative to whites, as noted earlier.

47. The potential benefits of residential mobility programs in raising employment among minority and low-income people were most clearly demonstrated in the evaluation of the Gautreaux housing experiments (Rosenbaum and Popkin 1991). Though no transportation program has yet been rigorously evaluated, Hughes and Sternberg (1992) provide some descriptions and casual data on various local programs that seem promising.

48. See Holzer et al. (1993) for evidence on a state-level training subsidy to firms that appeared to increase the incidence of training and improve the quality of worker output in small manufacturing companies. The possible beneficial effects of such subsidies on minority hiring presuppose that screens for employee quality at the hiring stage and training for those who are hired are complements rather than substitutes.

49. For discussions of the advantages and disadvantages of various types of targeted wage subsidies for less skilled workers, see Burtless (1985), Haveman (1988), and Lehman (1994). Also see the chapters in this volume by Lawrence Katz and Peter Gottschalk for the relative merits of such subsidies and direct public service employment.

50. Firms were sampled across size categories as follows: 25 percent from firms with between one and nineteen employees; 50 percent from firms with twenty to ninety-nine employees; and 25 percent from firms with one hundred employees or more. This distribution is relatively comparable to that observed in the *County Business Patterns* for the relevant metropolitan areas.

51. Sample weights for household respondents were used to weight the firms generated by the household surveys. Additional weights were used to adjust for the undersampling of college graduates in the SSI sample.

52. A sample of jobs weighted by current employment at an establishment underweights establishments with many hires due to turnover or net employment growth. At least the first of these is desirable, since high turnover generates no additional net employment. Furthermore, turnover accounts for most of the variance across firms in gross hire rates (Holzer 1996). Focusing on the last hire in firms also leads to an oversampling of high-turnover jobs within these firms and of those experiencing net employment growth. But the occupational distributions of the new hires do not look very different from the distribution of overall employment in these firms or from distributions across occupational categories within the census.

53. Response rates in construction and in the public sector were significantly lower and higher, respectively, than were those in other sectors, while no other industry measures were significant. Response rates were also a bit higher in larger firms. See Holzer (1996) for more details on the selection tests.

References

Becker, Gary. 1971. *The Economics of Discrimination*. Chicago: University of Chicago Press.

Berman, Eli, John Bound, and Zvi Griliches. 1994. "Changes in the Demand for Skilled Labor Within U.S. Manufacturing: Evidence from the Annual Survey of Manufactures." *Quarterly Journal of Economics* (May): 367–97.

Blau, Francine, and Andrea Beller. 1988. "Trends in Earnings Differentials by Gender, 1971–1981." *Industrial and Labor Relations Review* (July): 513–29 .

Blau, Francine, and Lawrence Kahn. 1994. "Rising Wage Inequality and the U.S. Gender Gap." *American Economic Review* (May): 23–38.

Bloch, Farrell. 1994. *Antidiscrimination Law and Minority Employment*. Chicago, Ill.: University of Chicago Press.

Bobo, Lawrence, and James Klugel. 1991. "Modern American Prejudices: Stereotypes, Social Distance, and Perceptions of Discrimination Toward Blacks, Hispanics and Asians." Unpublished paper.

Boozer, Michael, Alan Krueger, and Shari Wolkon. 1992. "Race and School Quality Since *Brown v. Board of Education*." *Brookings Papers on Economic Activity: Microeconomics*.

Borjas, George, Richard Freeman, and Lawrence Katz. 1992. "On the Labor Market Effects of Immigration and Trade." In *Immigration and the Workforce: Economic Consequences for the United States and Source Areas*, edited by George Borjas and Richard Freeman. Chicago, Ill.: University of Chicago Press.

Bound, John, and Richard Freeman. 1992. "What Went Wrong? The Erosion of Relative Earnings and Employment Among Young Black Men in the 1980s." *Quarterly Journal of Economics* (February): 210–32.

Bound, John, and Harry J. Holzer. 1993. "Industrial Shifts, Skill Levels, and the Labor Market for White and Black Males." *Review of Economics and Statistics* (August): 387–96.

Brown, Charles. 1982. "Federal Antidiscrimination Law: The Mouse That Roared?" In *Research in Labor Economics,* edited by Ronald Ehrenberg, vol. 6. Greenwich, Conn.: JAI Press

———. 1984. "Black/White Earnings Ratios Since the Civil Rights Act of 1964: The Importance of Labor Market Dropouts." *Quarterly Journal of Economics* (February): 31–44.

Burtless, Gary. 1985. "Are Targeted Wage Subsidies Harmful? Evidence from a Wage Voucher Experiment." *Industrial and Labor Relations Review* (October): 105–14.

Butler, Richard, and James Heckman. 1977. "The Government's Impact on the Labor Market Status of Black Americans: A Critical Review." In *Equal Rights and Industrial Relations,* edited by Farrell Bloch, Leonard Hausman, Orley Ashenfelter, Bayard Rustin, Richard Schubert, and Donald Slaiman. Madison, Wisc.: Industrial Relations Research Association.

Cain, Glen. 1986. "The Economics of Discrimination: A Survey." In *Handbook of Labor Economics,* edited by Orley Ashenfelter and Richard Layard. Amsterdam, Holland: North-Holland.

Card, David, and Alan Krueger. 1992. "School Quality and Black-White Relative Earnings: A Direct Assessment." *Quarterly Journal of Economics* (February): 151–200.

Cogan, John. 1982. "The Decline in Black Teenage Employment, 1950–1970." *American Economic Review* 72 (September): 621–38.

Donohue, John, and James Heckman. 1991. "Continuous Versus Episodic Change: The Impact of Civil Rights Policy on the Economic Status of Blacks." *Journal of Economic Literature* (December): 1603–43.

Donohue, John, and Peter Siegelman. 1991. "The Changing Nature of Employment Discrimination Litigation." *Stanford Law Review* 43 (May): 983–1033.

Ellwood, David. 1982. "Teenage Unemployment: Permanent Scars or Temporary Blemishes?" In *The Youth Labor Market Problem: Trends, Causes and Consequences,* edited by Richard Freeman and David Wise. Chicago, Ill.: University of Chicago Press.

———. 1986. "The Spatial Mismatch Hypothesis: Are Jobs Missing in the Ghetto?" In *The Black Youth Employment Crisis,* edited by Richard Freeman and Harry J. Holzer. Chicago, Ill.: University of Chicago Press.

Ferguson, Ronald. 1993. "New Evidence on the Growing Value of Skill and Consequences for Racial Disparity and Returns to Schooling." John F. Kennedy School of Government, Harvard University. Unpublished paper.

Fix, Michael, and Raymond Struyk. 1994. *Clear and Convincing Evidence.* Washington, D.C.: Urban Institute Press.

Freeman, Richard. 1973. "Changes in the Labor Market Status of Blacks, 1948–1972." *Brookings Papers on Economic Activity* 1: 67–131.

―――. 1981. "Black Economic Progress Since 1964: Who Has Gained and Why?" In *Studies in Labor Markets,* edited by Sherwin Rosen. Chicago, Ill.: University of Chicago Press.

―――. 1994. "Crime and the Job Market." Working Paper. Cambridge, Mass.: National Bureau of Economic Research.

Freeman, Richard, and Harry Holzer. 1986. *The Black Youth Employment Crisis.* Chicago, Ill.: University of Chicago Press.

Grissmer, David, Sheila Kirby, Mark Berends, and Stephanie Williamson. 1994. "Student Achievement and the Changing American Family." Los Angeles, Calif.: RAND Corporation.

Gunderson, Morley. 1989. "Male-Female Wage Differentials and Policy Responses." *Journal of Economic Literature* (March): 46–72.

Hamermesh, Daniel. 1993. *Labor Demand.* Princeton, N.J.: Princeton University Press.

Hauser, Robert, and Hanam Samuel Phang. 1993. "Trends in High School Dropout Rates Among White, Black, and Hispanic Youth: 1973–1989." Discussion Paper. Madison, Wisc.: Institute for Research on Poverty.

Haveman, Robert. 1988. *Starting Even.* New York: Twentieth-Century Fund.

Heckman, James, and Brook Payner. 1989. "Determining the Impact of Federal Antidiscrimination Policy on the Economic Status of Blacks." *American Economic Review* (March): 138–77.

Holzer, Harry. 1986. "Reservation Wages and Their Labor Market Effects for White and Black Youth." *Journal of Human Resources* (Spring): 157–77.

―――. 1987. "Informal Job Search and Black Youth Unemployment." *American Economic Review* (June): 446–52.

―――. 1991. "The Spatial Mismatch Hypothesis: What Has the Evidence Shown?" *Urban Studies* 28: 105–22.

―――. 1995a. "The Detroit Labor Market: A View from the Household Side." Unpublished paper.

―――. 1995b. "Employer Skill Needs and Labor Market Outcomes Across Groups." Working Paper. New York: Russell Sage Foundation.

―――. 1996. *What Employers Want: Job Prospects for the Less Educated.* New York: Russell Sage Foundation.

Holzer, Harry, Richard Block, Marcus Cheatham, and Jack Knott. 1993. "Are Training Subsidies for Firms Effective? The Michigan Experience." *Industrial and Labor Relations Review* (July): 625–36.

Holzer, Harry, and Keith Ihlanfeldt. 1996. "Spatial Factors and the Employment of Blacks at the Firm Level." *New England Economic Review* (May/June): 65–82.

Holzer, Harry, and David Neumark. 1996. "Are Affirmative Action Hires Less Qualified? Evidence from Employer-Employee Data on New Hires." Working Paper. Cambridge, Mass.: National Bureau of Economic Research.

Hughes, Mark, and Julie Sternberg. 1992. *The New Metropolitan Reality: Where the Rubber Meets the Road in Antipoverty Policy.* Washington, D.C.: Urban Institute.

Ihlanfeldt, Keith. 1995. "Information on the Spatial Distribution of Employment Opportunities Within the Metropolitan Area." Georgia State University. Unpublished paper.

Ihlanfeldt, Keith, and David Sjoquist. 1990. "Job Accessibility and Racial Differences in Youth Employment." *American Economic Review* (March): 267–76.

Jaeger, David. 1995. "Skill Differences and the Effects of Immigrants on the Wages of Natives." Unpublished paper.

Juhn, Chinhui. 1992. "Decline of Male Labor Market Participation: The Role of Declining Market Opportunities." *Quarterly Journal of Economics* (February): 79–122.

Juhn, Chinhui, Kevin Murphy, and Brook Pierce. 1993. "Wage Inequality and the Rise in the Returns to Skill." *Journal of Political Economy* (June): 410–22.

Kain, John. 1992. "The Spatial Mismatch Hypothesis Three Decades Later." *Housing Policy Debate* 3: 371–462.

Kasarda, John. 1995. "Industrial Restructuring and the Consequences of Changing Job Locations." In *State of the Union,* edited by Reynolds Farley. New York: Russell Sage Foundation.

Katz, Lawrence, and Kevin Murphy. 1992. "Changes in Relative Wages, 1963-1987: Supply and Demand Factors." *Quarterly Journal of Economics* (February): 35–78.

Killingsworth, Mark. *The Economics of Comparable Worth.* Kalamazoo, Mich.: W. E. Upjohn Institute for Employment Research.

Kirschenman, Joleen. 1991. "Gender Within Race in the Labor Market." University of Chicago. Unpublished paper.

Kirschenman, Joleen, and Katherine Neckerman. 1991. "We'd Love to Hire Them But. . . ." In *The Urban Underclass,* edited by Christopher Jencks and Paul Peterson. Washington, D.C.: Brookings Institution.

Lehman, Jeffrey. 1994. "Updating Urban Policy." In *Confronting Poverty,* edited by Sheldon Danziger, Gary Sandefur, and Daniel Weinberg. Cambridge, Mass.: Harvard University Press.

Leonard, Jonathan. 1984a. "Anti-Discrimination or Reverse Discrimination: The Impact of Changing Demographics, Title VII, and Affirmative Action on Productivity." *Journal of Human Resources* (Spring): 145–74.

———. 1984b. "Employment and Occupational Advance Under Affirmative Action." *Review of Economics and Statistics* (August): 377–85.

———. 1990. "The Impact of Affirmative Action Regulation and Equal Opportunity Law on Black Employment." *Journal of Economic Perspectives* (Fall): 47–63.

Levy, Frank, and Richard Murnane. 1992. "U.S. Earnings Level and Earnings Inequality: A Review of Recent Trends and Proposed Explanations." *Journal of Economic Literature* (September): 1332–81.

Lynch, Lisa. 1992. "Private Sector Training and the Earnings of Young Workers." *American Economic Review* (March): 299–312.

Margo, Robert. 1990. *Race and Schooling in the South, 1880-1950: An Economic History.* Chicago, Ill.: University of Chicago Press.

Meyer, Robert, and David Wise. 1982. "High School Preparation and Early Labor Force Experience." In *The Youth Labor Market Problem: Trends, Causes and Consequences,* edited by Richard Freeman and David Wise. Chicago, Ill.: University of Chicago Press.

Moss, Philip, and Chris Tilly. 1992. "Why Black Men Are Doing Worse in the Labor Market: A Review of Supply-Side and Demand-Side Explanations." New York: Social Science Research Council.

————. 1995. "Soft Skills and Race." Working Paper. New York: Russell Sage Foundation.

Neal, Derek, and William Johnson. 1996. "The Role of Pre-Market Factors in Black-White Wage Differences." *Journal of Political Economy* (October): 869–95.

Neumark, David, Roy Bank, and Kyle Van Nort. 1996. "Sex Discrimination in Restaurant Hiring: An Audit Study." *Quarterly Journal of Economics* (August): 915–42.

O'Neill, June. 1990. "The Role of Human Capital in Earnings Differences Between White and Black Men." *Journal of Economic Perspectives* (Fall): 25–46.

Rich, Lauren. 1994. "The Long-Run Impact of Early Nonemployment: A Reexamination." University of Michigan. Unpublished paper.

Rivera-Batiz, Francisco. 1992. "Quantitative Literacy and the Likelihood of Employment Among Young Adults in the U.S." *Journal of Human Resources* (Spring): 318–28.

Rosenbaum, James, and Susan Popkin. 1991. "Employment and Earnings of Low-Income Blacks Who Move to Middle-Class Suburbs." In *The Urban Underclass,* edited by Christopher Jencks and Paul Peterson. Washington, D.C.: Brookings Institution.

Sachs, Jeffrey, and Howard Shatz. 1994. "Trade and Jobs in U.S. Manufacturing." *Brookings Papers on Economic Activity* 1: 1–84.

Smith, James, and Finis Welch. 1989. "Black Economic Progress After Myrdal." *Journal of Economic Literature* (June): 519–64.

Sorensen, Elaine. 1994. *Comparable Worth: Is It a Worthy Policy?* Princeton, N.J.: Princeton University Press.

Topel, Robert. 1994. "Regional Labor Markets and the Determinants of Wage Inequality." *American Economic Review* (May): 17–22.

Wilson, William. 1987. *The Truly Disadvantaged.* Chicago, Ill.: University of Chicago Press.

Chapter 8

Contingent Work in a
Changing Labor Market

Rebecca M. Blank

T he recent structural changes in the U.S. labor market have generated growing concern about the increasing use of nonstandard employer-employee contracts, often referred to as "contingent work."
In this chapter, I use the term "contingent work" to refer to all jobs that
involve nonstandard employer-employee contracts where a standard contract is assumed to be a full-time, permanent employment relationship.
Contingent work typically includes part-time work, work performed by
independent contractors and on-call workers, and work done by temporary workers, hired either directly for limited-duration projects or through
temporary help firms. Various authors have claimed that employers are increasingly dividing their workforce into a set of core permanent jobs, with
high wages, good benefits, and long-term, implicit employment contracts,
and a set of peripheral or contingent jobs, with low wages, few benefits,
and no permanent connection between employer and employee.

Others have defined contingent work more narrowly. For instance,
the Bureau of Labor Statistics (BLS) added a special supplement to the
current population survey in February 1995 in order to collect additional information on contingent work, defining it as "any job in which
an individual does not have an explicit or implicit contract for long-term
employment" (Polivka 1996a, 4).[1] While this definition obviously includes temporary workers, it excludes many part-time or contract workers. I use a more inclusive definition in part because much of the public
discussion of contingent work assumes a broader definition, and in part
because I want to consider the full range of issues raised by the use of
nonstandard contracts.

The growing evidence of serious wage deterioration among less
skilled workers raises the question of whether the increasing use of con-

tingent work contracts is one reason behind falling real wages among the less skilled. This chapter discusses the changing use of contingent work in the U.S. labor market over time, and the extent to which contingent jobs are "bad jobs" that create problems for the workers who hold them. Particular attention is paid to the overlap of this phenomenon with changes in labor market opportunities for less skilled workers. The final part of the chapter discusses policy issues related to the use of contingent work and outlines some key unanswered research questions.

Why Are Nonstandard Employment Contracts Used?

There are both demand- and supply-side reasons behind the use of nonstandard employment contracts. Understanding these reasons provides a better sense of the role that contingent work plays in the labor market.

Demand-Side Reasons

There are at least four demand-side reasons why employers utilize nonstandard employment contracts. Most commonly, nonstandard contracts are used when employers face a product market with variable demand or demand spread over nonstandard hours of the day. For instance, as discussed later, the vast majority of employers who offer part-time jobs claim that they use these workers to solve scheduling problems that require them to meet client demands outside of normal business hours. Thus, sales and service jobs are often filled by part-timers who work in the evening or on weekends. Similarly, employers who face seasonal work peaks may use temporary workers during these times. Temporary assistance for tax preparation or for the completion of a big project is not uncommon.

Second, employers may use nonstandard contracts as a way to lower labor costs. Those costs are lowered not only by paying lower wages or benefits to these workers but by saving on fixed hiring, training, or monitoring costs. There is evidence of substantial variability in wages across employers: some tend to be "high-wage" across all jobs, and others are "low-wage" across all jobs.[2] High-wage employers who want to limit labor costs for certain worker categories may find it easier to contract out these services than to create and maintain a low-wage tier in the midst of a high-wage firm. Other employers may simply be looking for ways to cut their cost margins. If an employer can hire four part-time workers to do the same work as two full-time workers, and give them lower wages and no fringe benefits, profits will be higher. Of course, this assumes that four part-time workers can do as effective a job as two full-time workers. If there are fixed costs in starting and ending work over the day, or if clients demand to see only one employee during standard work hours, or if there are production advantages to having one worker perform a continuous sequence of tasks, then the employer does not necessarily save money with part-time workers, but faces lower productivity along with lower labor costs.

Third, the use of contingent workers may increase employers' flexibility in hiring and firing labor quickly in a changing macro-economic environment. Greater use of temporary workers or contracted services gives firms the opportunity to increase employment in the short term without making any permanent commitment to the workers, and to decrease employment without creating the internal morale problems that often arise when a share of the permanent workforce must be laid off.

Fourth, employers use nonstandard contracts as a way to screen workers for full-time permanent positions. Many employers who use temporary workers permanently hire those they think are particularly good employees. If it is hard to determine whether a worker is motivated or fits well into a work culture from a written job application, then observing that person on a limited-term contract may provide much better information about his or her potential as a good employee.

Supply-Side Reasons

Just as there are demand-side reasons why employers offer nonstandard work contracts, there are also supply-side reasons why some workers explicitly seek these contracts. First, many workers appreciate the more limited work hours or the greater flexibility in scheduling that nonstandard employment offers. Mothers of young children often do not want full-time work. Full- or part-time students often want supplementary income but are available only at limited times during the week.

Second, some workers like the greater independence and variety of nonstandard work contracts. Experiencing multiple workplaces as a temporary worker or working on various projects as an independent consultant provides a diversity of experience that gives pleasure to some workers. In addition, not being attached to a particular company often gives a worker the freedom to ignore some of the "office politics" and jealousies of the workplace.

Third, some workers use nonstandard jobs as a way to search for full-time employment. Many employees of temporary help firms see this work as a way to "test out" employers, and they accept a permanent job offer when they find a place they like. A closely related reason some take part-time and temporary jobs is to gain experience and build a résumé that will get them a permanent full-time job.

With these multiple reasons for nonstandard work contracts, it should be clear that contingent jobs cannot be automatically categorized as "good jobs" or "bad jobs." A worker who seeks full-time permanent employment but can find only part-time work or temporary work with fewer hours and lower earnings than desired, would clearly feel constrained and harmed by being forced into such employment. Other workers actively seek such jobs and are happy to accept them. One survey of temporary workers finds that 38 percent turned down full-time permanent job offers, preferring to continue to work for a temporary help firm (National Association of Temporary Services 1994)

When Are Contingent Jobs "Bad Jobs"?

Imbedded in much of the discussion about contingent work is an assumption that such jobs are bad for workers (for instance, see Appelbaum 1989 or Callaghan and Hartmann 1991). Indeed, even the term "contingent work" suggests a problem. Who would choose to be contingent rather than permanent? One of the primary conclusions of this chapter is that contingent work cannot be automatically classified as problematic. This section, however, describes the attributes that might lead an observer to classify some contingent jobs as "bad jobs." In general, four negative attributes are often ascribed to contingent work (for further discussion, see Nardone and Polivka 1989 or Polivka 1996b).

Uncertainty in Employment and Earnings

A common criticism of contingent work is that it creates substantial risk or uncertainty among workers about employment and employment hours. For instance, an employee with a temporary help firm may not know whether he or she will be placed on a job or how many hours of work will be available in any week. Similarly, independent contractors for business services may face financial insecurity because of the uncertainty about whether another client will be available when the current contract ends. There may also be uncertainty with regard to earnings. Obviously, if hours of work are uncertain, earnings are uncertain. Across different short-term jobs, earning rates themselves may also vary. Workers with uneven and uncertain streams of employment and income may have problems paying regular monthly household bills and experience serious stress regarding their ability to provide steadily for themselves and their families.

Low Returns to Human Capital

Contingent work is problematic if it provides lower payments to workers of equivalent education or experience. For instance, as discussed later, substantial evidence indicates that many part-timers are paid a lower wage than full-time workers with equivalent skills. It is often claimed (with less evidence, as we shall see) that temporary work has similar low returns to human capital.

There are three theories about why contingent work pays less: employers invest less in contingent workers' training or in capital equipment to enhance contingent workers' productivity; contingent workers are less career-oriented or less motivated; and in a more radical political interpretation of the labor market, firms pay wages below their competitive level because they have greater market power over contingent workers. This last theory could apply if "good jobs" were rationed in an economy and if employers were able to exercise monopoly control over the wages of contingent workers.

Limited Access to Nonwage Benefits

Even if the wages on a contingent job are comparable to those available to equivalent full-time permanent employees, total compensation may be lower if the contingent job offers fewer (or no) benefits. U.S. employers often have considerable discretion over whether they offer non-full-time workers health insurance, pensions, or other nonmandated fringe benefits. Employers may offer fewer fringe benefits to contingent workers for the same reasons that they pay them lower wages. In addition, the "lumpiness" of fringe benefits may increase the fixed costs associated with hiring. If fringes cannot be prorated to hours or earnings, then part-time or temporary workers who receive fringe benefits may cost the employer *more* per hour to employ.[3]

Reductions in Labor's Influence and Voice in the Workplace

Some observers object to the structure of the labor market that results from the use of contingent work, regardless of its effect on compensation or job security. Because contingent workers often have no permanent association with the employer, firms may treat this labor as the residual factor of production, whose use changes as demand fluctuates.

For those who believe that human labor deserves different treatment than physical capital, this is problematic. Such a situation may create uncertainty and greater economic risk for these workers, as discussed earlier. It may also reduce the ability of workers to organize or exert influence on employer behavior, since employers have fewer fixed investments in these workers. A two-tier labor market could develop, split between core and contingent workers, that might also contribute to social and political splits within the larger society.

Contingent jobs that do not suffer from any of these problems should presumably not be characterized as problematic. Yet even a job in which some of these four attributes are present is not automatically a bad job. Careless discussion of whether contingent work is bad often assumes that the key question is, "Would contingent workers be better off in an identical job with higher compensation and/or less uncertainty?" The answer to this is probably yes for all workers in the labor market. The correct question, however, should be, "What additional compensation would a worker require to be just as well off if placed in a similar full-time permanent job with a single employer?" Workers who need no compensation (or who would even pay) to move from a part-time to a full-time job, or from a temporary to a permanent job, are clearly disadvantaged by contingent work. For them, contingent work lowers their well-being and is problematic.

But other workers require compensation to leave a contingent job.[4] These are workers who want to work only a limited number of hours each week, or who enjoy the flexibility and independence of temporary work or independent contracting. An individual who enjoys the freedom of self-employment as an individual contractor and who turns down offers of permanent employment is clearly better off as a contingent worker than as a permanent worker. Thus, even when contingent jobs provide less in wages, benefits, or job security, some workers still find these jobs preferable to higher wages and more job security because of the other benefits these jobs offer.

The next three sections discuss the three categories of nonstandard work contracts, reviewing the evidence regarding employment growth within these job categories, the characteristics of workers in these jobs, and the effects of these jobs on workers and employers.

Part-Time Work

Part-time work in the United States is officially defined as regularly working less than thirty-five hours per week.[5] Persons who report part-time work on official monthly labor market surveys are asked why they work these hours, and their responses are used to divide up the part-time labor market into those who work part-time for "voluntary" or "involuntary" reasons. Involuntary part-time workers are those who are working part-time for economic reasons: work is slack, materials are in short supply, or they could find only part-time work. Voluntary part-timers are those who indicate that they were looking only for part-time work.[6]

Figure 8.1 graphs the trends in part-time work among women and men, showing the share of the female and male labor force who work part-time and separating them into voluntary and involuntary part-timers. It should be clear from figure 8.1 that there is little overall trend in part-time work among women.[7] Between 26 and 30 percent of the female workforce have worked part-time over the past twenty-five years, with some variance over the economic cycle. Of course, because the total size of the female labor force has grown, many more female part-time workers are in the labor market now than in the past, but their relative share of part-time work has been largely constant. There is a slight downward trend in the share of women reporting voluntary part-time work. About 78 percent of women part-timers were voluntarily working part-time jobs by 1996, down from around 85 percent in 1970. Thus, among women there is no evidence that structural changes in the labor market have led to an increase in part-time contracts over the last fifteen years, but some evidence that fewer women prefer these contracts.

Part-time work in the United States has increased among men, but the share of men working part-time remains relatively low. Since 1968, the share of male part-timers has increased by about four percentage points, from 8.4 percent to 12.4 percent. Furthermore, much of this increase reflects a rise in involuntary part-time employment. The share of voluntary part-timers among male part-time workers has fallen from three-fourths to two-thirds over the past twenty-eight years.

It is important to keep in mind that the majority of *both* male and female part-timers indicate they were seeking part-time work only and are voluntary part-time workers, but the increase in male and female involuntary part-time work is at least consistent with the story that the deteriorating earnings opportunities for less skilled workers are partly due to more of this group being forced into lower-paid contingent work. Nevertheless, involuntary part-time work has grown only slightly faster among less skilled men—the group that has suffered the most from deteriorating wage opportunities in recent years. The share of less skilled male workers (those with a high school degree or less) in involuntary part-time jobs rose about 2.8 percentage points between 1979 and 1993 (from 3.2 to 6 percent), while among skilled male workers this share

Figure 8 1   Share of Part-Time Work

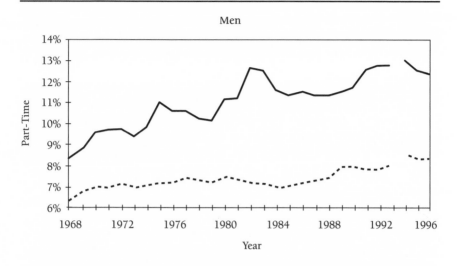

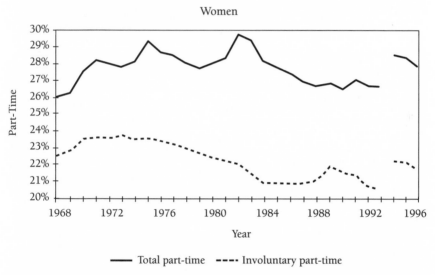

— Total part-time   ---- Involuntary part-time

Sources: 1967 to 1988 in U.S. Department of Labor (1989), table 23; 1989 to 1996 in U.S. Department of Labor, *Employment and Earnings*, January, various issues, table 7 in section entitled Household Data Annual Averages.

Notes: Both plots based on all civilian workers, age sixteen and over, at work in non-agricultural industries. Data between 1993 and 1994 are not consistently defined.

rose 2 percentage points (to 4 percent in 1993.) In short, involuntary part-time employment is not growing much more among the less skilled than among other male workers and cannot be the driving force behind the substantial rises in wage inequality among men.[8]

Columns 1 and 2 of table 8.1 indicate some of the characteristics of all part-time workers and of less skilled part-time workers. The data in these two columns can be compared to the data in columns 5 and 6 on the characteristics of full-time workers who are not in the temporary help services industry. Part-time workers are disproportionately younger, female, and less educated. Not shown here, involuntary part-

Table 8.1   Characteristics of Part-Time, Temporary, and Full-Time Workers, by Main Job Held in 1995 and Skill Level

	Part-Time Workers		Temporary Help Services Workers		Full-Time (Not THS) Workers	
	All	Less skilled[a]	All	Less skilled[a]	All	Less skilled[a]
Percentage						
Female	70.1	69.0	60.4	54.9	43.6	41.1
Black	10.1	12.5	24.6	27.5	11.9	13.7
Hispanic	9.0	12.3	8.5	14.6	9.9	15.1
Under 25	35.3	34.2	20.5	22.1	11.7	14.0
Over 50	14.2	17.9	11.3	13.1	16.4	18.5
Married	47.1	45.6	42.2	41.3	59.5	58.5
Number of children	0.9	0.9	0.8	0.9	0.8	0.8
Percentage with No more than high school degree	46.0	100.0	44.3	100.0	44.9	100.0
College degree or more	17.2	0.0	19.3	0.0	26.6	0.0
In poor families	14.3	19.6	19.6	26.3	4.7	7.8
Percent part-time	100.0	100.0	27.2	28.2	0.0	0.0
Average hourly earnings	$11.29	$9.61	$10.09	$8.72	$14.04	$10.82

Table 8.1   *Continued*

	Part-Time Workers		Temporary Help Services Workers		Full-Time (Not THS) Workers	
	All	Less skilled[a]	All	Less skilled[a]	All	Less skilled[a]
Median hourly earnings	$7.08	$6.25	$7.24	$6.13	$11.50	$9.13
Average hours per week	21.7	22.1	36.2	35.8	43.3	42.5
Average weeks per year	36.7	35.2	32.6	30.4	47.8	47.1
Average weeks unemployed	3.2	4.3	8.5	11.1	1.6	2.1
Percentage						
With employer-provided health insurance	21.0	17.8	23.6	17.2	67.2	59.1
With health insurance coverage	78.3	71.8	66.7	58.9	84.6	77.4
With employer-provided pension	15.7	12.3	8.9	5.3	53.5	43.7

Sources: Data for columns 1, 2, 5, and 6 come from the 1996 March CPS. Data for columns 3 and 4 come from combining the 1995 and 1996 March CPSs, to increase the number of observations.

[a] Less skilled workers are those with only a high school degree or less.

time workers are more likely to be male, younger, black, and less skilled. There are strikingly few differences between less skilled part-time workers and all part-time workers other than their lower wage levels.

Columns 1 and 2 of table 8.2 show the industry and occupational location of all part-timers and of less skilled part-timers. As noted earlier, most firms that use part-time workers face either variable client demand or client demand during nonstandard work hours. Part-time workers are thus heavily clustered in sales and service occupations, in wholesale and retail trade, and in professional services industries.[9] Four

Table 8.2   Occupation and Industry Status of Part-Time, Temporary, and Full-Time Workers, by Main Job Held in 1995 and Skill Level

	Part-Time Workers		Temporary Help Services Workers		Full-Time (Not THS) Workers	
	All	Less skilled[a]	All	Less skilled[a]	All	Less skilled[a]
Occupational distribution						
Managerial, professional and technical	20.8	6.1	16.7	6.4	32.4	10.4
Sales	17.5	19.8	3.7	2.1	10.2	9.3
Clerical	18.7	15.5	37.5	29.2	15.0	15.1
Service	27.2	36.2	7.8	9.6	11.3	15.6
Blue-collar	15.8	22.2	34.2	52.7	31.2	49.7
Industry distribution						
Agriculture, mining, construction, fishing, and forestry	4.8	6.9	0.0	0.0	8.5	12.5
Durable and nondurable goods	4.8	5.7	0.0	0.0	20.5	26.0
Transportation, communication, and utilities	3.3	3.5	0.0	0.0	7.8	8.2
Wholesale and retail trade	34.2	40.6	0.0	0.0	18.3	22.1
Finance, insurance, and real estate	4.1	3.5	0.0	0.0	6.7	5.0
Business and repair services	5.6	6.7	100.0	100.0	5.0	5.1
Personal services	6.2	8.8	0.0	0.0	2.6	3.6
Entertainment and recreation	3.2	3.0	0.0	0.0	1.5	1.4
Professional services	32.0	19.5	0.0	0.0	23.0	12.5
Public administration	1.8	1.8	0.0	0.0	6.0	3.6

Sources: Data for columns 1, 2, 5, and 6 come from the 1996 March CPS. Data for columns 3 and 4 come from combining the 1995 and 1996 March CPSs, to increase the number of observations.

[a] Less skilled workers are those with only a high school degree or less.

major studies of firm use of part-time labor all conclude that the primary reason firms hire part-time workers is to resolve scheduling problems (Nollen, Eddy, and Martin 1978; Bureau of National Affairs 1988; Zeytinoglu 1992; and Houseman 1997). In the three older studies, few employers indicate that they hire part-time labor to save on compensation costs. In the most recent of these employer surveys, conducted in 1996, Susan Houseman (1997) finds that 21 percent of employers hire part-timers to save on wage and/or benefit costs, and that 54 percent offer part-time jobs in part to meet their employees' wishes for part-time hours. (In this survey, firms were allowed to give multiple reasons for the use of part-time work.) Overall, employers say that part-time workers are best suited for jobs involving discrete tasks that are necessary to meet peak demand problems. Employers believe that part-timers are less suited for managerial and professional jobs or for blue-collar jobs, and this belief is reflected in the occupational mix of part-time workers.

In contrast to research based on direct survey questions asking employers why they hire part-time workers, a variety of studies attempt to estimate the determinants of part-time employment within a firm. This work indicates that higher quasi-fixed costs of hiring, as well as a greater compensation differential between part-time and full-time workers, increase the likelihood that a firm uses part-time work (see Montgomery 1988a, 1988b; Ehrenberg, Rosenberg, and Li 1988; and Houseman 1997). This finding suggests that employers may indeed be avoiding higher labor costs by using part-time workers, even if they do not say so directly in surveys.

Increases in the cost of mandated benefit payments, such as social security, unemployment compensation, and disability and workers' compensation payments, should also increase the relative cost of part-time workers to a firm, since their entire salary is usually subject to such taxes. There is no research on this issue for part-time workers, although the increases in FICA taxes over the past twenty-five years have clearly not decreased the overall use of part-time work. Mark Montgomery and James Cosgrove (1993) find that the relative use of part-time workers is much lower in child-care centers that offer more extensive nonmandated fringe benefits, such as health insurance and vacation days, particularly if they are offered to all staff.

Although most evidence indicates that scheduling demands are the most important reason employers use part-time work, compensation studies suggest that employers who do use part-timers pay them differently. Virtually all of the evidence supports the standard wisdom that part-time jobs pay lower wages than full-time jobs. For instance, the majority of minimum-wage workers in 1990 were in part-time jobs (Card and Krueger 1995, table 9.1). Row 13 of table 8.1 shows that the median hourly wage among part-time workers was $7.08 per hour—62 percent of the wage earned by full-time workers (see column 5).

Part-time workers not only earn less but tend to have less experience and less education. Controlling for both human capital characteristics and for the selectivity of workers between part-time and full-time work, most researchers find that human capital attributes explain a significant amount of the part-time/full-time wage differential, but not all of it (see Nakamura and Nakamura 1983; Simpson 1986; Ehrenberg, Rosenberg, and Li 1988; Main 1988; Ermisch and Wright 1993; and Lettau 1995). Rebecca Blank (1990a) has also controlled for the self-selection of workers into work, as well as the selection into part-time and full-time work among those who choose to work. With this fuller selectivity adjustment, her results are notably different from those of earlier studies: part-time wages, particularly for professional and managerial jobs, are somewhat *higher* than for full-time jobs for women. In Houseman's (1997) employer survey, 75 percent of the employers say the hourly pay costs of part-time workers are the same as full-time workers *in comparable jobs* (an important caveat). For men, part-time jobs continue to pay less even after fully accounting for labor market choices. Part-time involuntary workers also make less in wages, even after personal and job-related characteristics are controlled for.

Studies on the effect of part-time work on the probability of fringe benefit receipt are completely unambiguous. Every estimate suggests that part-timers are less likely to receive fringe benefits, whether based on raw comparisons or controlling for all possible differences between part-time and full-time workers.[10] Employers appear far more likely to exclude part-time workers completely from fringe benefit plans than to include them in some prorated fashion. Only 21 percent of part-time workers report that they receive health insurance through their employer, compared to 67 percent of full-time workers, and only 16 percent receive a pension, compared to 54 percent of full-time workers (see column 1 of table 8.1). Of course, many part-timers do receive health coverage from other sources (most typically through the employment of other family members), so that the share of part-timers with health insurance coverage is only six points lower than the share of full-timers with coverage.

Ultimately, it is impossible to give a simple yes or no answer to the question, "Are jobs that offer part-time hours bad jobs?" The appropriate answer is clearly, "It depends." Few part-time jobs are explicitly unstable with respect to the four negative attributes listed earlier. In fact, most are permanent jobs offered by the firm and held by a series of workers over time. The recent BLS survey of short-term jobs found that only 5 to 11 percent of all part-time workers held jobs that were not permanently available (Polivka 1996a).[11]

There is evidence, however, that part-time work offers lower total compensation to many workers. Whether this is a signal of problems depends on the other perceived benefits of part-time work. Many teenage workers or married female workers with young children clearly view part-time work as a preferred labor market option that has more benefits than costs. Similarly, the relatively small number of professional and managerial workers who are able to negotiate part-time jobs with their employers appear to face few short-term employment disadvantages from these jobs.[12] On the other hand, some number of part-time workers—particularly involuntary part-time workers—clearly find themselves disadvantaged in these jobs and would prefer an equivalent full-time job if it were available. The incidence of involuntary part-time work is increasing among workers at a slow rate but does not appear substantially higher among less skilled workers.

Temporary Help Services Employees

A second category in the contingent workforce are those workers explicitly hired for short-term and temporary jobs. Some of these workers are hired directly by employers, and others are employed by temporary help services (THS) firms. Unfortunately, most of our information covers only the latter group—those employed through temporary agencies. Using the recent BLS survey data, Houseman (1997) estimates that only 1.1 percent of all wage and salary workers are agency temporaries, while 3.4 percent are direct temporary hires by the company. I know of no other data on short-term direct hires, however, and this section focuses primarily on THS employees.

Since 1982, the BLS has collected data on temporary help services workers from two sources. The current employment statistics survey asks employers in different industries (including a "help supply services industry") about the number of their employees, while the current population survey (CPS) asks workers about their industry of employment.[13] The data from these two sources are not consistent. In particular, the establishment data find a substantially larger count of THS workers than the worker survey and show faster growth in this category over time. There are at least two reasons for this data divergence. First, in 1995 about 22 percent of THS workers were registered with more than one temporary help agency, a practice that would lead to an overcount from the estab-lishment survey. Second, a number of workers under the aegis of a tem-porary help agency report their industry of employment as where they are currently working rather than as temporary help services. Thus, the es-tablishment data provide an overcount of THS workers, while the CPS worker-based survey provides an undercount of these workers.[14]

Figure 8.2, which graphs both the establishment and CPS data on temporary help services workers from 1982 to 1996, shows a sharp rise

Figure 8.2   Temporary Help Services as a Share of All Employment

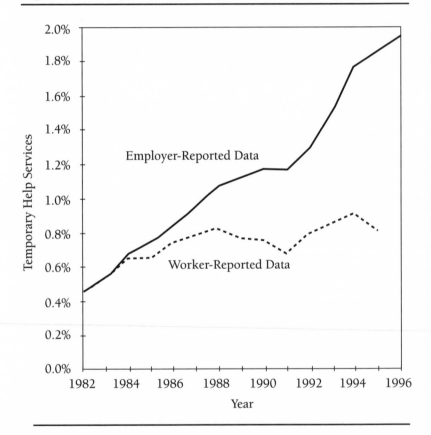

Sources: Employer data provided by Bureau of Labor Statistics. All employees in SIC 7363, help supply services, as a share of all nonfarm employees. Worker-reported data tabulated from March CPSs. All workers, sixteen to sixty-five, indicating their main industry in previous year was SIC 736, personnel supply services, as a share of all workers. These data are noisier owing to small annual samples.

in the number of workers included in this industry over the past decade, from 0.5 percent of the labor force to 1.9 percent of employed workers in the establishment data, and from 0.5 to 0.8 percent of employed workers in the CPS data. For a ten-year period, this is rapid growth, regardless of which series is used.[15]

Given our particular concern with changing labor market opportunities for less skilled workers, it is worth investigating whether the growth in THS employment has been greater among the less skilled. Tabulations from the CPS data indicate that the share of workers with a high school degree or less in THS jobs has increased from 0.5 to 0.8 percent, the same share that prevails among all workers.

Columns 3 and 4 of table 8.1 describe the characteristics of all workers and of less skilled workers who report they are in the temporary help services industry.[16] Compared to full-time workers (columns 5 and 6), THS workers tend to be younger, are much more likely to be black, and are more likely to be female, although in the aggregate they are less female than part-time workers. Only 27 percent work part-time, an indication that there is not a high overlap between THS workers and part-time workers.

Columns 3 and 4 of table 8.2 describe the occupational breakdown of temporary help services workers. Not surprisingly, a disproportionately large number are in clerical occupations, and fewer are in professional and managerial jobs. There are very few THS workers in the two occupations heavily represented by part-time workers, sales and service, and there are slightly more blue-collar THS workers than there are in the full-time permanent labor market.

Given the rapid growth in THS employment, it is worth asking which workers are moving into THS jobs. Columns 1 and 2 of table 8.3 show the breakdown of THS workers by occupation, gender, and education level in 1984 to 1985 and 1994 to 1995. Column 3 shows the growth in THS employment in each of these categories. Over this decade, almost all categories of THS workers grew rapidly, but male-dominated blue-collar THS jobs showed particularly strong growth. As a result, the share of female THS workers and of THS workers in clerical and service occupations decreased. Lewis Segal and Daniel Sullivan (1995) suggest that fully half of the decline in manufacturing employment between 1991 and 1993 may have been offset by an increase in the use of temporary and leased workers on blue-collar jobs. Much of this growth was not among the least skilled, however, but among those with at least some post-high school training.

The rising share of temporary help services workers supports the story about growing use of contingent workers. But as with part-time

Table 8.3　Growth in the Temporary Help Services Industry

	% of THS Employment 1984–1985	% of THS Employment 1994–1995	% Change in Employment 1984–1985 to 1994–1995
Occupation			
Managerial, professional, and technical	24.3	16.7	3.0
Sales	2.8	3.7	98.1
Clerical	43.6	37.5	29.0
Service	15.5	7.8	−24.6
Blue-collar	13.7	34.2	274.3
Gender			
Female	76.7	60.4	18.1
Male	23.2	39.6	154.8
Education level			
Less than high school	12.5	12.1	45.1
High school degree	40.5	32.1	18.8
Some post-high school	27.3	36.4	99.9
College or more	19.8	19.3	46.1
Total	100.0	100.0	49.9

Sources: Data from the 1985 to 1986 and 1995 to 1996 March CPS, using information on main job in previous year.

work, the issue should not be overstated. At present, less than 2 percent of the overall workforce is employed by temporary help firms. In addition, we need to ask what work in the temporary help services industry means and whether these jobs exhibit any of the four negative attributes of contingent work.

A large share of employers use temporary workers at some point over the year. In Houseman's (1997) employer survey in 1996, 46 percent of firms report using agency temporaries during the previous five years, while 38 percent report doing their own short-term hiring for temporary jobs.[17] In this survey, firms facing more variable product demands are more likely to use temporary workers, an indication that these workers are used to meet variable demand schedules. Consistent with this finding is evidence that THS employment changes seem to lead the business cycle; perhaps THS workers are hired when demand is changing (Segal and Sullivan 1995; Abraham 1988). (A nice distinction with part-time work is that most employers who use part-timers face daily or weekly variation in demand across nonstandard hours. Employers who use THS workers typically face more seasonal or project-oriented variation in demand.)[18] In addition, about one-fifth of employers use temporary help agency workers as a way to screen candidates for permanent hiring (Houseman 1997).

This evidence on demand variability is consistent with the theory that increasing global competition is driving more employers to maintain a smaller group of core workers. If competition is fierce, firms want to move as quickly as possible to meet demand shocks. The use of temporary workers may allow them to do this without some of the fixed training and employment costs that a larger group of permanent workers requires.

The wages paid to temporary help agency workers are lower on average than the wages received by full-time permanent workers. Table 8.1 shows that the median THS worker receives $7.24 per hour, 63 percent of the wage received by full-time workers. Because THS workers tend to be younger and less skilled, however, it is important to look at the wages for workers of equivalent skills, controlling for human capital characteristics.

Wage regressions for THS workers generally indicate that THS workers are extremely heterogeneous and that their relative wage situation depends on their occupation. One cannot assume that temporary workers are paid less than equivalent permanent workers, although some of them appear to face this problem. Using data on THS workers from Israel, Yinon Cohen and Yitchak Haberfeld (1993) find that temporary bookkeepers are paid more than regular employees, controlling for human capital characteristics, while temporary clerks are paid less. There were lower returns to human capital investments for temporary workers in some occupations, but not in others. Segal and Sullivan (1995) also find evidence that only some THS workers receive lower wages. They run wage regressions among all workers in the United States, controlling for a range of personal characteristics and including a dummy variable for THS workers. They find that white-collar temporary workers earn slightly more than nontemporary workers, while pink-collar temporary workers earn about 10 percent less. Blue-collar temporary workers earn 34 percent less than their permanent counterparts. Workers who move into temporary jobs from permanent jobs experience a wage increase in white-collar occupations and a wage decrease in blue-collar and pink-collar occupations. In Houseman's (1997) employer survey, 62 percent of the employers say that the hourly pay of agency temporaries is higher than that of regular employees in comparable positions.

Fringe benefits among THS workers have been less thoroughly explored. Most of the available evidence suggests that, like part-time workers, THS workers are far less likely to have access to health and pension plans. A 1987 BLS survey of temporary help services workers found that only about one-fourth received health insurance benefits from employers, and only 2 percent had access to pensions (Williams 1989). My tabulations in table 8.1 indicate that 24 percent of temporary workers report receiving health insurance through their employer, while 9 percent report receiving some pension assistance. These percentages are far below the share of full-time permanent workers receiving fringe benefits.

If one asks whether THS workers are accurately characterized as problematic contingent workers, there is again no simple yes or no answer. In a survey of THS workers, 38 percent said they had been offered a full-time permanent job and turned it down (National Association of Temporary Services 1994). The recent BLS survey suggests that between 39 and 66 percent of temporary help agency workers do not believe their job with the agency is permanent, while 67 percent of THS workers indicate they would prefer a more traditional work environment. As with part-time work, it is clear that at least some workers prefer these jobs, even as others do not (Polivka 1996a, 1996b).

Independent Contracting, Employee Leasing, and On-Call Workers

In the final category of contingent work, firms directly arrange for particular jobs to be completed by workers outside the firm. They may lease employees from another firm or business services agency, sign contracts with independent service providers, or place certain workers "on-call" for work when needed. Bringing in a carpet-layer or an electrician is a form of direct short-term contracting. So is hiring a management consultant or an architect for a specific project. Another form of outside independent contracting is to hire outside firms to provide a permanent stream of services, such as signing a contract with a maintenance firm to service the copier machine or hiring a lawyer for on-call legal consultation.

Has this form of contingent employment increased in recent years? We have limited data on the share of jobs filled by workers in these categories. These jobs are not readily separated out of more aggregate employment categories in U.S. government data. For instance, there is information on the self-employed, among whom a certain share are independent contractors; others, however, are shop owners and not part of the contingent workforce. Similarly, there is information on total employment within the business services industry, which includes some amount of contracting work. But business services also include many job categories that supply goods and services routinely purchased by firms as a product input; these are not typically considered independent contracting.

A few employer surveys have tried to measure the use of independent contractors. In Houseman's (1997) survey, 44 percent of all employers report using contract workers over the previous five years and 27 percent report using on-call workers. Katharine Abraham and Susan Taylor (1993) look at a special survey, appended to regular BLS establishment questionnaires in thirteen industries, that asked about the use of contracted services in five areas, ranging from janitorial services to computer services. Their data indicate that the use of contracted services in all five areas grew between 1979 and 1987. About 20 to 25 percent of the establishments contracted out some of these services. Among those firms that contracted out janitorial services, most hired contractors for 100 percent of their needs; the implication is that firms contracted out either all or none of these services. In contrast, there was a wide range in the extent to which firms contracted out computer services.

Abraham and Taylor estimate the determinants of contracting out among firms. They find that janitorial services are more likely to be contracted out in high-wage firms, consistent with the theory that labor cost savings motivate contracting out. But this is not true in other areas, such as accounting services, where the high-wage firms appear less likely to hire outside accountants. There are similar differences along other dimensions as well. More cyclical or seasonal industries are less likely to contract out janitorial or machine maintenance services, but more likely to contract out accounting services. This finding suggests that contracting is used for very different reasons for different tasks, even within one establishment. Finally, the results indicate that economies of scale may be important. Larger firms are less likely to contract out services, evidence that jobs may be contracted out when there are economies of scale in providing the service. For small firms with limited demand, it may be cheaper to hire an outside contractor for some tasks than to maintain permanent staff to do those tasks in-house.[19]

In the recent BLS survey, 7.3 percent of the workforce report that they are independent contractors or that they work for such firms. Another 1.6 percent of workers say they are on-call to a particular firm. In general, these workers are somewhat older and more likely to be white and male than other workers. They work on a heterogeneous mix of jobs that are more likely to be in executive and administrative, sales, and precision production occupations. They are also more likely to be in construction, services, or finance and insurance, and less likely to be in manufacturing or wholesale and retail trade. Of course, this onetime survey provides no information on changes in this category over time (Cohany 1996).

The limited information available suggests that the data on independent contractors show much of the same heterogeneity as the data on THS and part-time workers. Many of these workers are entrepreneurial types who enjoy the independence and variety of consulting work. The BLS estimates that 3.8 percent of all independent contractors believe their job is not permanent; only 17 percent say they would prefer a more traditional job contract. On-call workers show somewhat less satisfaction with their arrangements. Between 17 and 35 percent of on-call workers believe their jobs are temporary, and 62 percent would prefer a more traditional job contract (Polivka 1996a, 1996b).

Cross-National Evidence on Contingent Jobs

Interest in contingent work is not confined to the United States. In fact, the use of nonstandard hours and nonpermanent jobs has been discussed more in many European countries than in the United States. Countries as diverse as the Netherlands and Spain have recently changed their labor laws to make it easier for employers to hire workers on shorter hours or for limited time periods.

In general, the United States has experienced a smaller increase in part-time work than many other countries. Table 8.4 shows part-time work as a share of total employment in 1979 and 1995 in a number of OECD nations. In virtually all countries, part-time workers grew as a share of the workforce; in some countries, such as the United Kingdom

Table 8.4   Part-Time Employment in Selected OECD Countries

	1979	1995
United States	16.4	18.6
Canada	13.8	18.6
Japan	15.4	20.1
Austria	7.6	13.9
Belgium	6.0	13.6
Denmark	22.7	21.6
Finland	6.7	8.4
France	8.1	15.6
Germany	11.4	16.3
Greece	NA	4.8
Ireland	5.1	11.3[a]
Italy	5.3	6.4
Netherlands	16.6	37.4
Norway	27.3	26.5
Portugal	7.8	7.5
Spain	NA	7.5
Sweden	23.6	24.3
United Kingdom	16.4	24.1

Source: OECD, *Employment Outlook* (July 1996), table E.
[a]1994.

and the Netherlands, this growth was quite large (see Thurman and Trah 1990; Houseman 1995; Gornick and Jacobs 1994; and Nakamura et al. 1995).

Data on temporary work are harder to come by, although a few special surveys in some countries provide some guidance. A. S. Bronstein (1991) suggests that five million workers in the European Community were in temporary jobs in 1988 and cites evidence of growth in this number over the 1980s. Bernard Casey et al. (1989) discuss the use of temporary employment in Germany and the United Kingdom in the 1980s.

The biggest cross-national difference between the United States and many other nations is the level of social protection available to workers on nonstandard labor contracts. In comparison to their U.S. counterparts, temporary or part-time workers in other countries are much more likely to have health insurance (typically through a national health insurance system rather than through their jobs) and pensions (also more likely to be nationally provided). They are more likely to have access to some amount of unemployment compensation when laid off, and their level of income protection if they become unemployed for long periods of time is typically greater. In addition, many European countries explicitly limit temporary and part-time work, allowing firms to hire contingent workers only in special circumstances or for particular types of jobs.

How Many Contingent Workers Are There, and How Many Are in "Bad Jobs"?

By making a few assumptions, it is possible to arrive at a very rough estimate of the size of the contingent workforce. Columns 1 and 3 of table 8.5 show estimates for 1995 and 1985, among all workers and among less skilled workers. One of my assumptions is that all part-time and THS workers are contingent workers. It is more difficult to know how to measure outside contractors. A maximal estimate would count all persons in the business services industry. A more reasonable estimate would count perhaps 75 percent of business services workers as contingent workers. This leads to an estimate of the size of the contingent workforce of between 27 and 28 million in 1995, largely driven by the size of the part-time workforce.[20] While these numbers are larger than those estimated for 1985, as a share of the total labor force they are almost identical in both years, indicating that about 22 to 23 percent of the labor force is on nonstandard contracts.

Column 3 of table 8.5 repeats these estimates among less skilled workers only (those workers with only a high school degree or less). Perhaps surprisingly, the incidence of contingent work in this population is quite similar to that in the overall population. In both 1985 and 1995, about 22 to 24 percent of the less skilled labor force were in contingent jobs.

How many of these contingent workers might be considered "at risk" or in problematic contingent jobs? This is an even more difficult number to arrive at. Table 8.5 presents a guesstimate of such a number in columns 2 and 4. I include all involuntary part-time workers at a minimum, and at a maximum also include 25 percent of other part-time workers (who may be seeking part-time work only because of household or time constraints, but who may be seriously disadvantaged by the lower compensation these jobs provide). I include 40 percent of all THS workers at a minimum (since 60 percent of THS workers plan to continue working in temporary

Table 8.5   Estimated Size of the Contingent Labor Force, by Skill Level (in Thousands)

	All Workers		Less-Skilled Workers[a]	
	Total	"Problem"	Total	"Problem"
Part A. Based on Main Job Held in 1995				
Temporary help Services	1,012	405–678	400	160–268
Part-time (Not including THS)	21,787	4,489–8,813	9,960	2,748–4,551
Business Services (Not including THS or part-time)	4,031–5,375	806–1,075	1,797–2,395	359–479
Total	26,380–28,174	5,700–10,566	12,157–12,755	3,213–5,298
Percentage of labor force	21.7–22.8	4.6–8.5	22.1–23.1	5.8–9.6
Part B. Based on Main Job Held in 1985				
Temporary help services	711	284–476	359	144–241
Part-time (Not including THS)	19,524	4,824–8,499	11,852	3,655–5,704
Business services (Not including THS or part-time)	3,011–4,015	602–803	1,689–2,252	338–450
Total	23,246–24,250	5,710–9,778	13,900–14,563	4,137–6,395
Percentage of labor force	21.6–22.5	5.3–9.0	22.7–23.6	6.7–10.4

Notes: In columns 1 and 3, THS and part-time jobs are the total (nonoverlapping) number of such jobs reported in the March 1996 or March 1986 CPSs. Business services counts 75 percent (minimum) to 100 percent (maximum) of all remaining business services jobs.

In columns 2 and 4, the THS minimum represents 40 percent of all THS jobs and the maximum represents 67 percent of all THS jobs. The part-time minimum represents all involuntary part-time workers, and the maximum also includes 25 percent of all remaining part-time workers. Business services includes 20 percent of all business services jobs shown in column 1.

[a] Less skilled workers are those with only a high school degree or less.

jobs for at least six months [National Association of Temporary Services 1994]), and 67 percent of all THS workers at a maximum (the proportion who would prefer more traditional work contracts, as cited earlier). Determining the extent of constraints among other contingent business services providers (independent contractors) is impossible. It seems unreasonable to assume that a large share of self-employed consultants are doing this involuntarily; thus, I assume that only 20 percent of these workers would prefer permanent work.[21]

The results suggest that 25 to 40 percent of all contingent workers may face some constraints in their jobs that make them less desirable than equivalent permanent full-time jobs. This percentage represents between 5 and 9 percent of all workers in both 1985 and 1995. Among the less skilled, the numbers are only slightly higher—between 6 and 10 percent of all less skilled workers in 1985 and 1995.

The two striking conclusions of table 8.5 are that there is little trend over time in contingent work, and little difference between the overall labor force and the less skilled labor force. Between 5 and 10 percent of all workers appear to be in jobs that may cause them serious constraints because of the nonstandard nature of their job contract. While the problems with these jobs may present valid policy concerns, there is little evidence that contingent work itself is the driving force behind changes in the less skilled labor market, or that its share of the labor market is increasing rapidly over time.

Two alternative calculations on "problem" contingent jobs can be made utilizing data from the recent BLS survey. If we add the number of workers who are in short-term or impermanent jobs (3.4 million workers) to the number of workers in permanent jobs who are involuntarily working part-time (another 3.1 million), then 5.3 percent of employed workers are in "problem" jobs. Alternatively, by adding the number of workers in nontraditional work arrangements (this does not include part-time work) who would prefer traditional work to the number of involuntary part-time workers, we come up with 5.7 percent of all employed workers.[22] Both of these estimates are on the low side but within the range of my estimate in table 8.5 that 5 to 9 percent of the workforce are in problem jobs.[23]

Policy Issues

This chapter has made it clear that nonstandard work contracts are growing slowly over time. Forms of contingent work besides part-time work, however, still compose a relatively small share of the labor market. "Problem" contingent jobs—those in which workers face serious economic problems because of their lower compensation or greater job insecurity—appear to represent only about one-quarter of all jobs with nonstandard contracts. For this reason, policies aimed at limiting contingent work or improving the wages and benefits of contingent workers might make sense only if targeted at those contingent workers who are seriously constrained by their jobs. Certainly there is little evidence that it is the contingent sector of the economy that is most affected by changing sectoral demands. The fact that contingent workers (at least in part-time and THS jobs) are more likely to be female than male underscores this finding, since it is less skilled men who have experienced the greatest decline in their labor market prospects over the last fifteen years.

On the other hand, "problem" contingent jobs are held by 5 percent or more of the workforce, more than six million workers. Nonstandard work contracts may be particularly constraining to the blue-collar male workers who have moved from permanent to temporary jobs, or to both the women and men involuntarily employed part-time. There are a variety of policy options that would offset or limit the problems that contingent work may be creating in these workers' lives.

It is worth noting that a wide variety of labor market policies influence the incentives of employers to use contingent workers. A number of tax, employment, and labor regulation laws may encourage the use of contingent workers by exempting part-time, temporary, or leased workers and independent contractors from their provisions. Employers do not have to make contributions to social security, unemployment, workers' compensation, or health insurance for temporary workers or independent contractors. Making it even more difficult, each federal employment or labor statute has its own definition of "employee"; as a result, some contingent workers may be covered by some laws and not by others. The report of the recent Commission on the Future of Worker-Management Relations (1994) discusses these problems extensively and calls for a standardized definition of "employee" based on the economic reality of the worker-firm relationship, including as covered employees all workers with long-term attachments to the firm, whether part-time or under long-term leasing or contracting arrangements. These legal changes would presumably lessen the incentive for employers to force workers into contingent categories purely to avoid legal obligations and would instead ensure that employers use contingent labor only to achieve flexibility and efficiency goals.

In addition to this sort of legal reform, a variety of other policies related to contingent work are often discussed.

Supplementing Benefits Through the Public Sector

Probably the most common problem across the range of contingent jobs discussed in this chapter is their lack of fringe benefit coverage, particularly the lack of health insurance and private pension funds. The problem of providing medical care to the growing uninsured population in the face of rising medical insurance costs has no easy answer, but it is certainly a key question for many contingent workers. Many of the health reform proposals in recent years would allow workers not covered by insurance on their job to purchase public or private insurance at rates that reflect broad risk-pooling. Some of the proposals would also provide tax subsidies to lower-income workers who needed to purchase this insurance, offering public cost-sharing like that provided by many employers. Policies of this sort would go a long way toward reducing the many health insurance inequities between contingent and noncontingent jobs.

The problem with pension coverage for contingent workers is presumably somewhat less acute, given the social security system of publicly funded retirement benefits as well as the availability of individual retirement investment options, such as IRAs. A scheme under which the government subsidizes private pension investments for lower-wage workers (at a level similar to that provided by most firms that contribute to their workers' pension funds) might make pension availability more equitable between contingent and noncontingent workers.

The cost of such public subsidies to workers in contingent jobs would be the higher taxes and public spending that such programs require. It is also worth noting that such programs would be unlikely to target only contingent workers as defined in this chapter. Indeed, any scheme to provide health insurance and pension subsidies to those who do not receive them through their employer is likely to affect many more permanent full-time employees who do not receive such benefits than contingent workers.

Mandating Benefits by the Private Sector

The alternative to supplementing benefits for workers who do not receive them from their employer is to mandate that employers provide such benefits to all workers, whether in contingent or permanent positions. Such a mandate would increase the costs associated with employing part-time workers, temporary workers, and outside consultants—as well as the cost of low-skilled workers in general, since this group is generally less likely to be in jobs that provide extensive fringes. A mandate would presumably result in two changes: it would decrease the demand for these workers in aggregate as they become more costly to employ, but employers that currently utilize temporary workers or outside contractors would pull these jobs in-house, increasing the demand for permanent workers. Given an increase in cost for these jobs, one would expect that the increased number of permanent full-time jobs would be less than the loss in contingent jobs.

The negative effects of such mandates on workers are twofold. Given that a majority of contingent workers *prefer* their current jobs over equivalent permanent full-time jobs, many of them would be worse off if forced to transfer into a permanent full-time job. Second, some of these workers would not have the option of moving to a permanent full-time job and would become unemployed as the overall demand for contingent jobs declined.

On the other hand, two kinds of workers would benefit from such a policy. Some involuntary contingent workers would find full-time permanent employment of the sort they prefer, and some contingent workers would retain their jobs, but with more extensive fringe benefit compensation.

The magnitude of gains and losses is hard to estimate in the absence of any research on the impact of mandated benefits on contingent employment. Certainly the more extensive the mandates, the more losers and the fewer winners are likely to result. It is worth noting that the strong political opposition to employer benefit mandates in the United States (evident throughout the recent health care debates) makes this option more difficult to implement than the previous option of providing public subsidies to contingent workers who have no fringe benefits.

Training and Skills Investment

To the extent that some contingent work provides less on-the-job training and a lower return to education or experience (hence less incentive to invest personally in skills), some workers who spend several years in the contingent part of the labor force may be less prepared to compete in a labor market that increasingly rewards skill. Increased availability of subsidies and loans for training or retraining, particularly those aimed at low-income workers, would provide opportunities for contingent workers who want to move into more permanent jobs but are viewed by employers as too limited in their experience or skills.

Limiting the Use of Contingent Work

Many European countries, with more regulated labor markets, explicitly regulate or even forbid the use of temporary workers except in very specific circumstances. Many countries have job severance requirements that make it difficult for firms to make temporary contracts with their workers. Other rules limit the use of part-time work. While many European countries have loosened such restrictions in the last decade, they are still much more prevalent abroad than in the United States, where, outside of certain unionized settings, such restrictions are almost unknown. Some observers, concerned with the growth of the contingent work sector of the economy, have called for limits on the share of a firm's workforce that can be under temporary or outside contract.[24] One can imagine similar limits on part-time jobs as well.

The discussion of contingent work in this chapter should make it clear that imposing uniform restrictions on all firms would be deeply inequitable. To the extent that scheduling and demand variability problems drive much of the use of contingent work, some employers have a much higher demand for contingent workers than do others. Determining the appropriate level of contingent work regulation for different industries and occupations would be a complex and difficult task.

In addition, because many contingent workers prefer these jobs to permanent full-time employment, such regulation could make many in the targeted population worse off. I can see no way to eliminate the problematic contingent jobs while keeping those that impose no costs on workers, largely because these differences are often less a function of the jobs than of the workers' circumstances.

Within the labor market model in the United States, where regulation of voluntary contracts between workers and employers is limited, any policy proposal to limit contingent work would raise major political opposition. In the U.S. political and social environment, it is not clear whether workers or employers would be more strongly opposed. Without better evidence of substantial harm to contingent workers than is presently available, such a policy seems too draconian a response.

Unemployment Assistance to Contingent Workers

The unavailability of unemployment insurance (UI) to self-employed contractors and to many part-time or temporary workers who work limited hours or switch jobs frequently may exacerbate the economic uncertainty associated with contingent work. One option is to expand the pool of workers who qualify for unemployment insurance. It may also be useful to provide more extensive short-time unemployment insurance to workers who seek full-time permanent jobs but can only find part-time work.

As most economists are quick to point out, expanding such assistance could create incentives for these workers to spend more time unemployed. Particularly among the self-employed, it may be hard to differentiate between those who can't find contracting work and those who do not try very hard to find work (although this problem is hardly absent in the current UI system). On the other hand, expanded UI availability would raise the well-being of those workers who do become unemployed and are newly eligible for these funds. Whether the net balance of costs and benefits would be positive or negative is hard to determine a priori.

Summary of Policy Issues

While a number of policies might limit the problems associated with contingent work, it is not clear from existing evidence whether the benefits of any of them would outweigh the costs. The evidence that a substantial share of contingent workers are relatively satisfied in their jobs suggests that they might receive windfall gains if contingent jobs are improved. On the other hand, the workers who are clearly quite disadvantaged in contingent work would greatly benefit from some of the policies discussed here.

Given limited evidence that the problems of contingent work have become markedly worse in recent years, policy options that involve major costs should probably be viewed with skepticism. New research, along the lines outlined in the next section, might provide a better sense of which contingent workers should be targeted by any policy, and of what the effects of some of these policies might be. In the short run, the only policy suggestion I would seriously recommend is ensuring better health insurance coverage for all workers—contingent and noncontingent—who are not provided with insurance coverage through their work. The reasons to improve health insurance coverage, however, are only slightly related to the problems of the contingent workforce per se, and much more related to the current large market failures in the health care market in the United States.

Research Questions

It should be clear from the review in this chapter that there are a substantial number of research question to which we currently have no answers and little data with which to explore them. In outlining five major areas of research interest, I would emphasize that to conduct this research we need more extensive employer and worker data on the use of nonstandard labor contracts.

How Extensively Are Nonstandard Contracts Used Outside of Part-Time Work?

The new BLS data collected in early 1995 provide the best available measure of the magnitude of temporary hiring, independent contracting, and the use of on-call workers. While these point-in-time numbers greatly enhance what we already know about this group of workers, it is important to collect information on this phenomenon over time, including data on changes in the characteristics of workers in these jobs and on the types of work being done through independent contracting.

In addition, the current measures of temporary help services employees in the CPS seem inadequate. As noted earlier, these data identify fewer THS workers than are reported in establishment surveys, and the category includes more than just employees of temporary help firms.

How Much Employment or Income Instability Actually Accompanies Contingent Work?

It is far from certain that, as many commentators assume, any job that is not permanently attached to a firm must create economic uncertainty for the person who fills it. We have no information on the extent to which THS workers or independent contractors face economic uncertainty because of the nonpermanent nature of their job contracts. The heterogeneity among these workers suggests that some persons regularly earn as much as they desire, while others face economic difficulties. Longitudinal data tracking employment, earnings, and overall household income, with a large enough sample of nonpermanent workers to look separately at their economic and family characteristics, would provide much better information on the effect of nonpermanent jobs on people's economic well-being.

To What Extent Are the Lower Wage and Fringe Benefits of Many Contingent Jobs Offset by the Advantages of These Jobs?

Data on a broader range of job characteristics and on workers' evaluations of those characteristics would be useful. These data should ask explicitly about hours flexibility, job hierarchies, employment and earnings uncertainty, as well as the standard questions on wage and nonwage compensation. This information would allow researchers to look more closely at the "compensating differentials" issues involved in part-time, temporary, and independent contracting jobs.

What Is the Job Progression Among Workers on Nonstandard Contracts?

One of the best measures of the problem (or nonproblem) of nonstandard work contracts is the question of whether such jobs form a discrete segment of the labor market. If people work nonstandard contracts at times when they have high demands on their time outside the workplace (such as when they are in school or when they have small children), this may not be a problem if they are able to move easily back into standard labor market contracts and into jobs with higher human capital returns and fringe benefits. On the other hand, if workers who move into contingent jobs become stuck in them, then we would view those jobs with much more concern. While there is research on dynamic patterns in part-time work, virtually no work has been done on dynamic labor market patterns among workers in other forms of contingent work.

How Do Different Countries Compare in How Their Social Assistance Programs or Mandated Benefits for Contingent Workers Affect the Use of These Workers?

The claim that increases in fringe benefit costs and changing competitive structures in the labor market are driving the rise in contingent work can perhaps best be tested through cross-national comparisons. Different countries impose different costs on employers who hire contingent workers. Different countries have also faced different sectoral shifts in demand. These cross-national differences can provide the background data for more complete research on the determinants of the use of contingent work.

This chapter was written as part of the project "Demand-Side Strategies Affecting Low-Wage Labor Markets." Support was provided by the Russell Sage Foundation. Leslie Moscow provided excellent research assistance. Thanks are due to Edward Gramlich, Colleen Heflin, Anne Polivka, and attendees of the project conference for useful comments.

Notes

1. For more information on the results of this BLS survey, see the series of articles in the *Monthly Labor Review* (October 1996).
2. The reasons for these wage differences are only poorly understood. One of the more common explanations is that high-wage employers are paying efficiency wages to employees in jobs that cannot be easily monitored. But this does not explain why such employers also pay above-average wages in other more easily monitored positions, such as clerical or janitorial work.
3. A theory of compensating differentials suggests that contingent workers who receive lower wages (all else being equal) could receive a higher fringe benefit package. The fact that many of these jobs include *both* lower fringes and lower wages suggests that firms are not simply trading off nonwage and wage compensation on these jobs.
4. More precisely, if the compensation a worker requires to be as well off in permanent work as in similar contingent work is *greater than* the compensation differential between these jobs, then he or she is better off in contingent work.
5. For a more extensive recent review of the literature on part-time work, see Blank (1990b) or Tilly (1990). For a further review of the trends over time in part-time work, see Levenson (1995). Hotchkiss (1991) explores the accuracy of defining part-time work as less than thirty-five hours.
6. Stratton (1994) indicates that "involuntary" part-time workers are indeed different from voluntary part-timers in their propensity to move into full-time work.
7. Changes in the current population survey questionnaire created a data discontinuity between 1993 and 1994 in figure 8.1.
8. These calculations are from tabulations of the 1980 and 1994 March CPS data that ask about workers' main jobs in 1979 and 1993. Data inconsistencies make it difficult to do valid comparisons after 1993.
9. Part-timers are particularly prevalent in certain medical care and educational categories within the professional services industries.
10. See Bureau of National Affairs (1988), Ehrenberg, Rosenberg, and Li (1988), Blank (1990a), and Houseman (1997). These studies typically use only very gross measures of fringe benefit availability, ones that indicate only whether part-timers have access to pensions and health benefits. Large differentials in access, however, almost surely mean large differentials in the dollar value of fringes.
11. The range reflects different definitions of what constitutes permanent work.
12. Evidence indicates that female workers who move into part-time work from full-time work tend to move back into full-time work quite quickly (Blank, forthcoming). This movement is consistent with a story that says women use part-time work during the times in their lives when household demands are higher. Tilly (1992) discusses this phenomenon of high-skilled women working short-term part-time positions as "retention" part-time work, driven by the desire of employers to keep high-quality employees.
13. Until 1989, BLS collected separate information on temporary help services (old SIC 7392); more recently, this category was combined with a residual

category to create a new help services category (new SIC 7363), which has been available in a consistent form since 1982. Since 1989, the National Association of Temporary Services has provided estimates of THS employment within this larger help services category (Steinberg 1994). In figure 8.2, I use the aggregate help services category (SIC 7363) and refer to these workers as THS workers. The estimated NATS series on THS workers averages 94 percent of the more aggregate BLS series from 1990 to 1993 and moves in an almost identical way.

The CPS tapes provide information only on the aggregate industry SIC 736—personnel supply services—of which 86.3 percent is composed of SIC 7363. I use the question asking about industry of "main job last year."

14. See Polivka (1996a) for a further discussion of this data inconsistency.

15. I have not been able to find any definitive reason for the growing divergence between these two series over time. As temporary help agencies become more common, double registration of workers across agencies may have increased. And as THS workers are more commonly used for extended periods of time within firms, worker tendencies to misreport their industry may have grown as well.

16. The data on THS workers in tables 8.1, 8.2, and 8.3 are tabulated from the March CPS of 1995 and 1996 and based on workers who report themselves as working in the temporary help services industry on their main job in the previous year. I use two years of data in order to expand the sample.

17. In a 1981 survey, Mangum, Mayall, and Nelson (1985) find that 69 percent of firms use temporary help services or limited-duration hires in one or more jobs over the year.

18. A few recent papers (Golden and Appelbaum 1992; Laird and Williams 1995) estimate the determinants of the size of the temporary help services industry using monthly time-series data. These results also generally indicate that demand factors are the primary reason firms use THS workers.

19. These results are also consistent with tabulations by Murphey (1989), who uses related data, and with the estimates of Houseman (1997).

20. I ignore any additional self-employment, outside of the business services industry, and have no good way of measuring leased employees, on-call workers, or direct temporary hires.

21. There is much greater uncertainty in the estimates of THS and business services workers in table 8.5, both because of data problems and because we know less about the extent of worker difficulties in these jobs. It is worth noting, however, that even doubling both of these categories would still result in similar conclusions, since it is the large group of part-time workers who dominate the estimates in table 8.5.

22. Data for the first calculation were provided by Anne Polivka at the Bureau of Labor Statistics. The second calculation is based on data in Cohany (1996, table 5) and in Polivka (1996b, table 9).

23. Other recent estimates of contingent work have been made by Spalter-Roth and Hartmann (1995) and Belous (1989). Spalter-Roth and Hartmann base their definition of contingent work on how many employers a worker had over the year, and on whether the worker worked full-time or year-round. Their estimates suggest that 16 percent of all workers are in contingent (and by their de-

finition, problematic and unstable) jobs, and another 13 percent are "questionable"—hard to classify as to whether their jobs are stable or not. As an estimate of all contingent work, their numbers are lower than mine, but their interpretation of "problem jobs" makes their estimate of problematic contingent work much higher than mine. The biggest difference in their numbers and mine, their inability to separate involuntary from voluntary part-timers, leads them to count more part-time work as problematic and to categorize a substantial amount of part-year employment as contingent work. Belous estimates there were twenty-nine to thirty-six million contingent workers in 1979 (based on a smaller labor force). Belous both double-counts workers (many workers are both part-time *and* in the business services industry, for instance) and includes all self-employed in his count.

24. For instance, Hartmann and Lapidus (1989) call for regulating the quantity of temporary work in the same way home work is regulated.

References

Abraham, Katharine G. 1988. "The Role of Flexible Staffing Arrangements in Employers' Short-Term Adjustment Strategies." In *Employment, Unemployment, and Hours of Work,* edited by Robert A. Hart. London, England: George Allen and Unwin.

Abraham, Katharine G., and Susan K. Taylor. 1993. "Firms' Use of Outside Contractors: Theory of Evidence." Working Paper 4468. Cambridge, Mass.: National Bureau of Economic Research.

Appelbaum, Eileen. 1989. "The Growth in the U.S. Contingent Labor Force." In *Microeconomic Issues in Labor Economics,* edited by Robert Drago and Richard Perlman. New York: Harvester Wheatsheaf.

Belous, Richard S. 1989. *The Contingent Economy: The Growth of the Temporary, Part-Time, and Subcontracted Workforce.* Report 239. Washington, D.C.: National Planning Association.

Blank, Rebecca M. 1990a. "Are Part-Time Jobs Bad Jobs?" In *A Future of Lousy Jobs?* edited by Gary Burtless. Washington, D.C.: Brookings Institution.

———. 1990b. "Understanding Part-Time Work." In *Research in Labor Economics,* vol. 11, edited by Laurie Bassi and David Crawford. Greenwich, Conn.: JAI Press.

———. Forthcoming. "The Dynamics of Part-Time Work." In *Research in Labor Economics,* edited by Solomon W. Polachek. Greenwich, Conn.: JAI Press.

Bronstein, A. S. 1991. "Temporary Work in Western Europe: Threat or Complement to Permanent Employment?" *International Labor Review* 130(3): 291–310.

Bureau of National Affairs. 1988. "Special PPR Report: Part-Time and Other Alternative Staffing Practices." *Bulletin to Management* 39 (June 23).

Callaghan, Polly, and Heidi Hartmann. 1991. *Contingent Work: A Chart Book on Part-Time and Temporary Employment.* Washington, D.C.: Economic Policy Institute.

Card, David, and Alan B. Krueger. 1995. *Myth and Measurement: The New Economics of the Minimum Wage.* Princeton, N.J.: Princeton University Press.

Casey, Bernard, Rudiger Dragendorf, Walter Heering, and Gunnar John. 1989. "Temporary Employment in Great Britain and the Federal Republic of Germany." *International Labor Review* 128(4): 449–66.

Cohany, Sharon R. 1996. "Workers in Alternative Employment Arrangements." *Monthly Labor Review* 119 (October): 31–45.

Cohen, Yinon, and Yitchak Haberfeld. 1993. "Temporary Help Service Workers: Employment Characteristics and Wage Determination." *Industrial Relations* 32(2): 272–87.

Commission on the Future of Worker-Management Relations. 1994. *Report and Recommendations.* Washington, D.C.: U.S. Department of Labor (December).

Ehrenberg, Ronald G., Pamela Rosenberg, and Jeanne Li. 1988. "Part-Time Employment in the United States." In *Employment, Unemployment, and Labour Utilization,* edited by Robert A. Hart. London, England: George Allen and Unwin.

Ermisch, John F., and Robert E. Wright. 1993. "Wage Offers and Full-Time and Part-Time Employment by British Women." *Journal of Human Resources* 28(1): 111–33.

Golden, Lonnie, and Eileen Appelbaum. 1992. "What Was Driving the 1982-1988 Boom in Temporary Employment?" *American Journal of Economics and Sociology* 51(4): 473–93.

Gornick, Janet C., and Jerry A. Jacobs. 1994. "A Cross-National Analysis of the Wages of Part-Time Workers: Evidence from the United States, United Kingdom, Canada, and Australia." Working Paper 113. Syracuse, N.Y.: Luxembourg Income Study.

Hartmann, Heidi, and June Lapidus. 1989. "Temporary Work." In *Investing in People, Background Papers,* vol. 2. Washington, D.C.: U.S. Department of Labor, Commission on Workforce Quality and Labor Market Efficiency.

Hotchkiss, Julie L. 1991. "The Definition of Part-Time Employment: A Switching Regression Model with Unknown Sample Selection." *International Economic Review* 32(4): 899–917.

Houseman, Susan N. 1995. "Part-Time Employment in Europe and Japan." *Journal of Labor Research* 16(3): 249–62.

———. 1997. "Temporary, Part-Time, and Contract Employment in the United States: New Evidence from an Employer Survey." Kalamazoo, Mich.: W. E. Upjohn Institute for Employment Research.

Laird, Karylee, and Nicolas Williams. 1995. "Employment Growth in the Temporary Help Industry." University of Cincinnati. Unpublished paper.

Lettau, Michael K. 1995. "Compensation in Part-Time Jobs Versus Full-Time Jobs: What If the Job Is the Same?" Washington, D.C.: Bureau of Labor Statistics.

Levenson, Alec R. 1995. "Where Have All the Part-Timers Gone? Recent Trends and New Evidence on Dual-Jobs." Working Paper 95-1. Santa Monica, Calif.: Milken Institute for Job and Capital Formation.

Main, Brian G. M. 1988. "Hourly Earnings of Female Part-Time Versus Full-Time Employees." *Manchester School of Economic and Social Studies* 56(4): 331–44.

Mangum, Garth, Donald Mayall, and Kristin Nelson. 1985. "The Temporary Help Industry: A Response to the Dual Internal Labor Market." *Industrial and Labor Relations Review* 38(4): 599–611.

Montgomery, Mark. 1988a. "Hours of Part-Time and Full-Time Workers at the Same Firm." *Industrial Relations* 27 (Fall): 394–406.

———. 1988b. "On the Determinants of Employer Demand for Part-Time Workers." *Review of Economics and Statistics* 70 (February): 112–17.

Montgomery, Mark, and James Cosgrove. 1993. "The Effect of Employee Benefits on the Demand for Part-Time Workers." *Industrial and Labor Relations Review* 47(1): 87–98.

Murphey, Janice D. 1989. "Business Contracting-Out Practices: Evidence from a BLS Survey." Washington, D.C.: Bureau of Labor Statistics.

Nakamura, Alice, Dallas Cullen, John Cragg, and Rob Bruce. 1995. "Labor Market Change and Canada's Unemployment Insurance and Provincial Welfare Programs." Edmonton, Canada: University of Alberta. Unpublished paper.

Nakamura, Alice, and Masao Nakamura. 1983. "Part-Time and Full-Time Work Behavior of Married Women." *Canadian Journal of Economics* 16 (May): 229–57.

Nardone, Thomas, and Anne E. Polivka. 1989. "On the Definition of 'Contingent Work.'" *Monthly Labor Review* 112 (December): 9–16.

National Association of Temporary Services. 1994. *1994 Profile of the Temporary Workforce.* Alexandria, Va.: NATS.

Nollen, Stanley D., Brenda B. Eddy, and Virginia H. Martin. 1978. *Permanent Part-Time Employment.* New York: Praeger.

Organization of Economic Cooperation and Development (OECD). 1996. *Employment Outlook.* Paris, France: Organization of Economic Cooperation and Development.

Polivka, Anne E. 1996a. "Contingent and Alternative Work Arrangements, Defined." *Monthly Labor Review* 119 (October): 3–9.

———. 1996b. "Into Contingent and Alternative Employment: By Choice?" *Monthly Labor Review* 119 (October): 55–74.

Segal, Lewis M., and Daniel G. Sullivan. 1995. "The Temporary Labor Force." *Economic Perspectives* (March-April): 2–19.

Simpson, Wayne. 1986. "An Analysis of Part-Time Pay in Canada." *Canadian Journal of Economics* 19 (November): 798–807.

Spalter-Roth, Roberta, and Heidi Hartmann. 1995. "Contingent Work: Its Consequences for Economic Well-Being, the Gendered Division of Labor, and the Welfare State." Discussion Paper. Washington, D.C.: Institute for Women's Policy Research.

Steinberg, Bruce. 1994. *The Temporary Help Industry: Annual Update.* Alexandria, Va.: National Association of Temporary Services.

Stratton, Leslie S. 1994. "Are Involuntary Part-Time Workers Indeed Involuntary?" University of Arizona. Unpublished paper.

Thurman, Joseph E., and Gabriele Trah. 1990. "Part-Time Work in International Perspective." *International Labor Review* 129(1): 23–40.

Tilly, Chris. 1990. *Short Hours, Short Shrift: Causes and Consequences of Part-Time Work.* Washington, D.C.: Economic Policy Institute.

———. 1992. "Dualism in Part-Time Employment." *Industrial Relations* 31(2): 330–47.

U.S. Department of Labor. 1989. *Handbook of Labor Statistics.* Washington: U.S. Government Printing Office.

Williams, Harry B. 1989. "What Temporary Workers Earn: Findings from New BLS Survey." *Monthly Labor Review* 112 (March): 3–6.

Zeytinoglu, Isik Urla. 1992. "Reasons for Hiring Part-Time Workers." *Industrial Relations* 31(3): 489–99.

Part IV

National Differences

Chapter 9

The Collapse in Demand for the Unskilled: What Can Be Done?

Stephen Nickell

In the United States, the poor are getting poorer. In Germany,[1] by contrast, the poor are getting richer. Britain is in between. The rich, on the other hand, are getting richer in all three countries.

Across the OECD, changes in technology and trade patterns have led to a significant decline in the demand for workers without skills. This fact is at least partly responsible for the wage changes in the three countries discussed in this chapter. So we are left with something of a puzzle. Given that shifts in technology and trade patterns are much the same in all developed countries, how is it that the lowest-paid in the United States are doing so badly whereas those in Germany are doing so well? Figure 9.1 illustrates the size of the gap. It appears that throughout the 1980s the real wages of bottom decile male workers in Germany gained on those of workers in a similar position in the United States by an enormous 4 percent per annum. In what follows, I shall address this puzzle, because an understanding of how Germany achieves this outcome may shed some light on the question of what might be done to solve the low pay problem in the United States.

Unfortunately, the solutions indicated by pursuing the comparison with Germany tend to be rather long-haul. So we must also consider what might be done in the short run. Again utilizing evidence from other OECD countries, I investigate demand expansions, public employment/job creation, across-the-board switches away from payroll/income taxes toward excise taxes (VAT), and finally, low-wage job subsidies, minimum wages, and negative income tax systems. I begin, however, by comparing the United States with Britain and Germany.

Figure 9.1　Growth in Real Wages of Low-Paid Workers over the 1980s (Annualized Percentage Change)

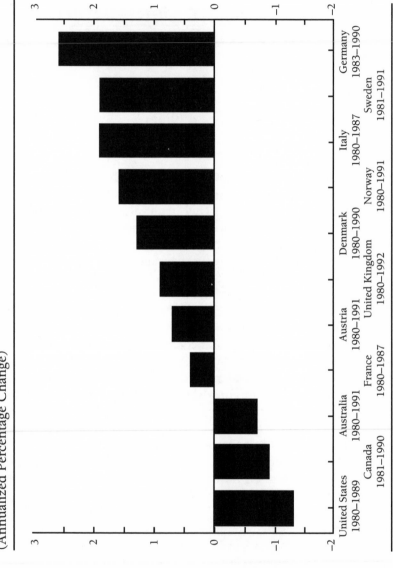

Source: OECD, *Employment Outlook* (1993, ch 5).

The United States, Britain, and Germany: An Overview

The economies of the United States, the United Kingdom, and Germany are worth comparing because, while Germany has an unskilled *unemployment* problem that is no worse than that in the United States, the low-pay problem is more or less nonexistent in Germany. For example, bottom decile U.S. men receive about one-half of the pay of bottom decile Germans on a Purchasing Power Parity (PPP) basis (see Freeman 1995, 66). The male decile 9 to decile 1 earnings ratio in Germany is around 2.3 and stable compared with 3.3 and rising in the United Kingdom, and 5.6 and rising in the United States. The situation is similar, although not quite as diverse, for women.

Germany has the largest economy in Europe with a GDP per capita of around $18,500 in 1992. This compares with $16,000 in the United Kingdom and $22,000 in the United States, so the United States is about 19 percent "richer" than Germany. Curiously, this is almost precisely accounted for by differences in the annual hours worked per adult—1,272 in the United States compared with 1,047 in Germany. In other words, Americans work around 21 percent more.

Table 9.1 gives a brief picture of the three economies over the last thirty years. Productivity growth is lower now than in the 1960s in all three countries, although Germany has fallen back relatively more, perhaps not surprisingly, because in the 1960s it was still making a rapid recovery from its wartime collapse. Also, it is clear that Germany has taken far more of its productivity growth in the form of leisure than the other two countries have. Nevertheless, Germany remains very well represented in the high-technology sector, despite recent worries in this regard (see Audretsch 1995). Overall, Germany compares favorably in terms of growth and dynamism despite having a generally higher level of "disruption" (for example, higher rates of immigration, the problems associated with absorbing East Germany). So whatever labor market rigidities it might have, these do not seem to have had an important adverse impact on the German level of prosperity and technical advance.

The United States, Britain, and Germany: Unemployment and the Distribution of Wages

Table 9.2 sets out the overall unemployment rates in the three countries. In both Britain and Germany, unemployment rose sharply at the beginning of the 1980s, so that for the last fifteen years the German rate has been comparable to that in the United States, with the U.K. rate being

Table 9.1   Some Economic Performance Statistics, 1960 to 1994

A. Productivity Growth (%)

	Output per Worker			Output per Worker-Hour		
	1960 to 1973	1974 to 1979	1980 to 1994	1960 to 1973	1974 to 1979	1980 to 1992
United States	1.78	−0.12	1.01	2.15	−0.95	2.01
Germany	4.18	2.64	1.48	4.97	4.23	2.36
United Kingdom	2.86	1.25	1.68	4.02	3.32	2.91

B. Hours, Full-Time Manufacturing Workers, 1990

	Annual Hours	Holidays/52	Hours per Week
United States	1904	0.09	40.0
Germany	1643	0.16	37.6
United Kingdom	1769	0.13	38.8

C. Annual Hours per Worker

	1970	1979	1993
United States	1889	1808	1776
Germany	1949	1764	1588

D. Value-Added in High-Technology Industry

	% Manufacturing		% GDP	
	1979	1988	1979	1988
United States	20.8	24.4	4.8	4.7
Germany	16.5	20.3	5.6	6.3
United Kingdom	15.0	19.7	3.7	3.9

Sources: (A) Centre for Economic Performance, OECD dataset; Gordon (1995), table 2; (B) Bell and Freeman (1994); (C) OECD (1994a, table B); (D) Bean and Crafts (1995).

rather higher. In table 9.3, we see how these rates break down by skill level. The general picture indicates that the movements in unskilled unemployment rates are not dissimilar in the United States and Germany, but that the unskilled rate for men has risen further in the United Kingdom. On the other hand, unemployment rates among the skilled have risen substantially in both Germany and the United Kingdom but have

Table 9.2   OECD Standardized Unemployment Rates

	1955 to 1959	1960 to 1967	1968 to 1973	1974 to 1980	1981 to 1995
United States	4.9	4.9	4.6	6.7	6.9
Germany	3.2	0.6	1.0	2.7	6.0
United Kingdom	2.1	2.6	3.4	5.2	9.9

Sources: Layard et al. (1994, annex table A3); OECD (1994a).

Notes: OECD standardized rates in Germany are substantially lower than the rates reported in German official statistics because the latter exclude various categories of workers (for example, the self-employed) from the denominator.

Table 9.3   Unemployment Rates by Skill (Percentage)

	1971 to 1974	1975 to 1978	1979 to 1982	1983 to 1986	1987 to 1990	1991
United States[a]						
Total (male)	3.6	5.5	5.7	7.3	5.0	5.8
High education[b]	1.7	2.2	2.1	2.7	2.1	2.8
Low education[c]	5.3	8.6	9.4	12.8	9.8	11.0
Ratio	3.1	3.9	4.5	4.7	4.7	3.9
Total (female)	4.6	6.3	5.7	6.7	4.5	5.2
High education	2.2	3.1	2.8	3.1	2.1	2.8
Low education	6.6	9.3	9.8	12.5	9.3	10.9
Ratio	3.0	3.0	3.5	4.0	4.4	3.9
Germany[d]						
Total (male)		2.8	3.4	6.3	4.9	3.8
High education[e]		1.5	2.0	3.3	2.9	2.1
Low education[f]		5.2	7.6	13.9	12.1	10.0
Ratio		3.5	3.8	4.2	4.2	4.8
Total (female)		4.9	5.6	8.5	6.9	4.8
High education		1.5	2.9	5.8	5.4	3.7
Low education		6.6	7.9	12.8	11.8	8.8
Ratio		4.4	2.7	2.2	2.2	2.4

(*Table continues on p. 302.*)

Table 9.3   *Continued*

	1971 to 1974	1975 to 1978	1979 to 1982	1983 to 1986	1987 to 1990	1991
United Kingdom[g]						
Total (male)	2.9	4.4	7.7	10.5	7.5	10.0
High education[h]	1.4	2.0	3.9	4.7	4.0	5.7
Low education[i]	4.0	6.4	12.2	18.2	13.5	17.4
Ratio	2.9	3.2	3.1	3.9	3.4	3.1
Total (female)	2.7	4.6	6.7	8.7	5.9	6.8
High education	3.1	3.6	4.2	6.4	4.3	4.5
Low education	2.6	4.8	7.3	9.4	6.8	7.9
Ratio	0.8	1.3	1.7	1.5	1.6	1.8

Sources: For the United States, Bureau of Labor Statistics, *Handbook of Labor Statistics* (1989, table 67), *Statistical Abstract of the United States* (1993, table 654). For Germany, Buttler and Tessaring (1993, table 3). For the United Kingdom, General Household Survey data tapes.

[a] Data refer to individuals aged twenty-five to sixty-four.

[b] Four or more years of college (15.7 percent of labor force in 1970, 28.2 percent in 1991).

[c] Less than four years of high school (37.5 percent of labor force in 1970, 14.5 percent in 1991).

[d] The data have been adjusted to be compatible with the OECD standardized rate. A common multiplier has been used for each category within any one year, but the multipliers differ across years.

[e] Degree (11.3 percent of working-age population in 1976, 15.9 percent in 1989).

[f] No formal qualification (39 percent of working-age population in 1976, 27.8 percent in 1989).

[g] Data refer to individuals aged sixteen to sixty-four.

[h] Passed A levels (18+ examination) or professional qualification or university degree.

[i] No qualifications.

barely moved in the United States. The similarity between unemployment movements among the unskilled in Germany and the United States is critical in any explanation of difference in wage changes at the bottom end. In particular, it rules out simplistic arguments based on German labor market rigidities that may translate incipient adverse wage effects into unemployment increases.[2]

As I have already indicated, the differences in the wage effects are quite startling. In table 9.4, I set out various numbers. In both Britain and the United States, there was a significant jump in the wage premium obtained by high-education groups relative to those with low education. By comparison, the equivalent shift in Germany is small. More stark are the figures for earnings distributions. There was a significant widening

Table 9.4   Aspects of the Earnings Distribution

A. Male Earnings Differentials by Education: Ratio of High- to Low-Education Groups

	Early 1970s	Early 1980s	Late 1980s
United States	1.49	1.37	1.51
Germany		1.36	1.42
United Kingdom	1.64	1.53	1.65

B. Earnings Dispersion (Males)

	1975	1979 to 1981	1985 to 1986	1987 to 1988	1989 to 1990
United States					
D9/D5	1.93	1.95	2.09	2.10	2.14
D5/D1	2.44	2.44	2.63	2.63	2.63
D9/D1	4.71	4.76	5.50	5.53	5.63
Germany					
D9/D5			1.65	1.65	1.65
D5/D1			1.45	1.41	1.39
D9/D1			2.39	2.32	2.29
United Kingdom					
D9/D5	1.66	1.72	1.85*	1.91	1.96
D5/D1	1.43	1.47	1.59*	1.61	1.64
D9/D1	2.37	2.53	2.94*	3.08	3.21

C. Earnings Dispersion (Females)

	1975	1979 to 1981	1985 to 1986	1987 to 1988	1989 to 1990
United States					
D9/D5	1.97	1.98	2.11	2.11	2.15
D5/D1	2.13	2.00	2.16	2.27	2.27
D9/D1	4.17	3.96	4.56	4.79	4.88
Germany					
D9/D5			1.60	1.58	1.58
D5/D1			1.56	1.50	1.50
D9/D1			2.50	2.37	2.37
United Kingdom					
D9/D5	1.72	1.71	1.80*	1.84	1.92
D5/D1	1.47	1.43	1.50*	1.56	1.58
D9/D1	2.52	2.45	2.70*	2.87	3.03

(*Table continues on p. 304.*)

Table 9.4 *Continued*

D. Male Earnings Deciles (Deflated by CPI)

	United States			Germany			United Kingdom		
	D1[a]	D5[a]	D9[a]	D1	D5	D9	D1	D5	D9
1980	100	100	100				100	100	100
1981	98	98	99				101	102	106
1982	95	96	101				100	103	108
1983	93	95	100	100	100	100	100[b]	106[b]	112[b]
1984	89	96	101	103	104	105	101	108	116
1985	89	96	103	110	107	109	101	109	117
1986	91	98	105	114	111	113	104	113	123
1987	88	97	104	119	115	115	105	116	128
1988	90	97	104	123	119	120	107	119	135
1989	89	95	104				108	121	138
1990							107	121	138

E. Female Earnings Deciles (Deflated by CPI)

	United States			Germany			United Kingdom		
	D1	D5	D9	D1	D5	D9	D1	D5	D9
1980	100	100	100				100	100	100
1981	97	98	100				101	102	109
1982	96	100	104				100	103	108
1983	95	101	105	100	100	1001	105[b]	109[b]	115[b]
1984	93	102	107	107	105	107	107	111	117
1985	96	103	109	119	111	112	108	113	119
1986	94	105	113	124	115	119	111	117	127
1987	95	108	116	134	120	121	113	121	129
1988	95	108	116	143	125	126	116	126	139
1989	95	108	119				118	128	147
1990							118	130	147

Sources: (A) OECD (1993, table 5.6) and Davis (1992); (B) and (C) OECD (1993, table 5.2); (D) and (E) OECD (1993, table 5.3).

[a] D9, D5, D1 are the upper limits of the deciles of the earnings distribution.

[b] Measurement changed, so not comparable to previous numbers.

in the 1980s in both Britain and the United States, but no corresponding change in Germany. Furthermore, the differences in the real income changes are dramatic: the poor are rapidly getting richer in Germany, and rapidly getting poorer in the United States. The spread of the wage distribution differs widely across countries as well, particularly in the bottom half, where the D5/D1 ratio in the United States is almost twice that in Germany.

Overall, two questions are worth investigating. First, why are the changes for low-wage earners in the United States relative to Germany so dramatically worse on the wage front when they are no better on the unemployment front? Second, how can the German wage distribution be so compressed relative to the U.S. wage distribution without the unemployment experiences of those at the bottom end being any worse? It is to be hoped that answers to these two questions may shed some light on how we might attack the low-wage problem in the United States.

Why Have Low-Wage Workers Done So Much Better in Germany Than in the United States?

Wage determination in Germany would certainly militate against large falls in unskilled wages relative to skilled wages. The system is dominated by industry unions whose wage agreements are extended to non-union firms within each region. However, given the fall in the relative demand for unskilled workers across the OECD, if unions maintain the relative wages of the unskilled, we must face the question as to why unskilled unemployment rates have not worsened dramatically, or at least no more dramatically than in the United States. And to answer this, we must look more closely at supply and demand.

Supply and Demand

Francine Blau and Lawrence Kahn (1994) have looked at supply and demand by skill level for all three countries and come to a number of interesting conclusions. First, they find that the relative demand shift against unskilled workers was slightly less severe in the United Kingdom and Germany than it was in the United States. However, they also argue that the relative *supply* shift in favor of skilled workers is *much* stronger in the United States than in Britain and Germany. Thus, on a pure demand-and-supply basis, relative wages should have shifted more against the unskilled in the latter two countries. Blau and Kahn hold wage-setting institutions responsible for the fact that this has not happened. However,

Table 9.5   1979 to 1990 Public-Sector Employment Growth per Capita (Annual Percent)

United States	0.2
Germany	0.2
United Kingdom	0.1
European Community	0.6

Source: OECD (1994b, table 1.1)

Note: These figures represent growth in public-sector employment normalized on the working-age population (sixteen to sixty-four).

this conclusion still leaves unexplained the fact that German unskilled unemployment is no worse than that in the United States.

One problem with the Blau and Kahn analysis of Germany is that education level is measured by years of schooling. Since most of German postcompulsory education takes place outside school (vocational training is provided by employers), the years of schooling measure is unsatisfactory. It is worth looking at these questions in more detail.

On the demand side, it is possible that the German public sector has been used to mop up the excess supply of unskilled workers. In fact, although we have no information on public-sector employment growth by skill, we see from table 9.5 that the rise in public-sector employment in all three countries has been particularly small and is unlikely to have had a significant impact either way.

Another possibility is that the particularly low growth in labor supply in Germany has led to less downward pressure on wages, particularly at the bottom end. In table 9.6, we see that while both the male and female labor forces have increased faster in the United States than

Table 9.6   Growth in the Labor Force

	Men			Women		
	1975 to 1979	1979 to 1983	1983 to 1991	1975 to 1979	1979 to 1983	1983 to 1991
United States	1.8	0.9	0.9	4.3	2.5	2.1
Germany	0.0	0.8	0.4	0.8	1.2	1.7
United Kingdom	0.1	−0.2	0.0	1.7	0.2	1.9

Source: OECD (1994b, statistical annex, tables G, H).

in either Germany or Britain, the overall difference was actually smaller in the 1980s than in previous periods. Furthermore, the overall increase in the United Kingdom is lower than (men) or comparable with (women) Germany. So it is hard to believe that it is these differences that are generating the dramatic differences in real wage growth at the bottom end.

A third possibility is that tax rates on labor have changed in such a way as to allow real consumption wages to rise in Germany without serious adverse effects on labor costs and hence employment. Table 9.7 reports some of the numbers that are not consistent with this story since the relevant German tax rates have not changed significantly. However, we do know that the Germans tend to make more use of active labor market programs, so could these have made all the difference? In table 9.8, we see that much more is spent on both labor market training and direct job creation or subsidized employment in Germany than in the United States. However, the measured impact of these policies in Germany does not appear to be very great, according to Laurence Bellman and Hartmut Lehmann (1990). For example, they find no impact of un-

Table 9.7   Tax Rates

A. The Marginal Tax Wedge (%)				
	1978	1981	1985	1989	1991 to 1992
United States	44.3	50.4	48.1	38.2	38.5
Germany	66.0	64.3	67.5	66.3	63.8
United Kingdom	51.6	51.9	54.6	49.9	50.4

B. Average Payroll and Income Taxes (%)		
	1976 to 1980	1986 to 1990
United States	34	35
Germany	41	42
United Kingdom	32	29

Notes: The overall tax wedge includes payroll taxes, personal income taxes, and consumption taxes and is taken from OECD (1994c, table 9.1). Payroll plus income taxes are equal to (labor costs ÷ posttax wages) − 1. They therefore include employers' pension contributions and are computed from the CEP OECD dataset.

Table 9.8   Active Labor Market Programs, 1990

	Labor Market Training		Direct Job Creation/ Subsidized Employment	
	1	2	1	2
United States	0.11	0.9	0.01	0.4
Germany	0.38	2.5	0.17	0.4
United Kingdom	0.23	1.1	0.02	0.1

Source: OECD (1993, table 2B1).

Notes: 1 = expenditures as percentage of GDP; 2 = annual inflow as a percentage of labor force.

employment training on the flow out of unemployment, although they do find a small positive effect of direct job creation on the outflow from short-term unemployment. Again, however, job creation does not appear to have a large enough effect to have the sort of significance to influence unskilled employment.[3]

The final and most obvious explanation for the difference between German wage and unemployment shifts on the one hand and the U.K. and U.S. changes on the other, is that the relative supply shift in favor of the skilled has kept pace with the relative demand shift in Germany but not in the other two countries. Detailed econometric evidence that sheds light on this hypothesis is not available. However, we do have some information on supply shifts, as presented in table 9.9. Insofar as these numbers tell us anything, they indicate that the rate of growth of the supply of skills slowed down in the United States and the United Kingdom during the 1980s, but that no such slowdown was apparent in Germany. Although these numbers are consistent with our hypothesis, they are hardly decisive. On the other hand, they are reinforced by the undoubted fact that the German education and training system makes it easier for the great mass of the working population to assimilate new skills and respond to shifts in the pattern of demand. This is probably the key factor. The very high level of education and training of the vast majority of German workers enables them to respond flexibly to demand shifts. As a consequence, in Germany, in contrast to Britain and the United States, we do not find a large number of workers who simply cannot cope with the demands placed upon them by technological change.

In order to pursue this issue, we should note that it relates to the second question asked earlier.

Table 9.9 The Changes in the Supply of Skilled Workers

A. Relative Supply of College-Educated Workers

	Percentage of Population or Labor Force			Growth Rates	
	1970	1980	1990	1970 to 1980	1980 to 1990
United States	10.8	16.6	21.5	4.4	2.6
Germany	6.0	7.4	9.4	3.6	3.5
United Kingdom	8.0	12.0	18.3	7.0	4.3

B. Supply of Qualified Workers

	Percentage of Workforce with a Qualification			Growth Rates	
	1[a]	2[b]	3[c]	2/1	3/2
Gemany	61.0	65.8	72.2	1.3	1.3
United Kingdom[d]	45.3	57.0	69.7	2.9	2.5
United Kingdom (A-level plus)	16.1	24.8	35.8	5.1	4.7

Sources: (A) OECD (1993, table 5.7); (B) Abraham and Houseman (1994, table 9) for Germany, General Household Survey data tapes for the United Kingdom.

Notes: The German vocational qualifications are typically of a far higher standard than those in the United Kingdom. Indeed, it may be argued that only A-level or higher qualifications in the United Kingdom are comparable in quality with those in Germany. (A-levels are national examinations taken at age eighteen.)

[a] 1976 in Germany; 1971 to 1974 in the United Kingdom.

[b] 1982 in Germany; 1979 to 1982 in the United Kingdom.

[c] 1989 in Germany; 1987 to 1990 in the United Kingdom.

[d] Males only.

How Can the Lowest-Paid Workers in Germany Earn So Much and Keep Their Jobs?

As already noted, German men in the bottom wage decile seem to earn around *twice as much* as American men in a similar position, and yet they are no more likely to be unemployed. One possibility worth investigating is that the German education system produces a much more compressed distribution of human capital than do either the British or U.S. system. Detailed evidence in favor of this compression hypothesis is provided in table 9.10. Under the assumption that the

Table 9.10   International Test Scores

A. Distribution of Scores in International Mathematical Tests
of Thirteen-Year-Old Pupils, 1963 to 1964 (%)

Score (out of 70)	United States	Germany	United Kingdom
<5	22	8	24
6–30	62	59	49
31–51	14	30	22
>51	1	3	5
Mean score	16	25	19
cv (sd/mean)	82	53	88

B. Scores in International Mathematics Tests for Thirteen-Year-Old Pupils, 1990

Score (out of 100)	United States	Germany	United Kingdom
Average	59.5	70.8	55.3
Top decile	89.3	93.3	82.7
Bottom decile	32	50.7	29.3

C. Percentage of Employees at Various Levels of Literacy,
by Literacy Type, 1995

Literacy Level[a]	United States			Germany		
	Prose[b]	Document	Quantitative	Prose	Document	Quantitative
4/5	24.8	22.7	27.1	15.5	22.4	27.6
3	34.0	33.9	32.5	40.5	41.6	45.2
2	26.2	25.6	24.5	33.3	30.7	22.9
1	15.0	17.8	15.9	10.7	5.3	4.3

Sources: (A) and (B) Prais (1994); (C) OECD (1995, tables B-1a, B-1b, B-1c).

[a] Level 1 is the minimal level; level 5 requires a very high degree of sophistication.

[b] "Prose," "document," and "quantitative" refer, respectively, to the ability to extract information from text, from displays, and of a numerical kind.

Swiss education system, which is similar in style to that in Germany, produces results comparable to those of the German system, it is clear from these tables that German children are better, on average, at mathematics than British and American children at age thirteen. More important, the variation in mathematics ability is far smaller in Germany, and the lower part of the ability range is vastly superior. In panel (C) of table 9.10, information on a completely different talent, literacy, reinforces this impression. While the proportion of employees at the top level of literacy is not dissimilar in the United States and Germany, the numbers with minimal levels of literacy are substantial in the United States and considerably smaller in Germany. Thus, in all aspects of literacy, ability is significantly more compressed in Germany than in the United States.

Sigmund J. Prais and Karin Wagner's (1985) description of a detailed comparison of mathematics tests in Germany and Britain reinforces this evidence. They compare the results of Hauptschule tests in Baden-Württemberg with comparable results in tests given by the Assessment of Performance Unit of the British Department of Education and Science. Their findings indicate that the average Hauptschule pupil is as good as the average English pupil. This finding may not seem very compelling until it is realized that the German Hauptschules take only pupils in the bottom 50 percent of the ability range. The top 50 percent of German pupils go to a Gymnasium (top 25 percent) or a Realschule (26 percent). To emphasize the higher variance, it is worth noting that in 1963 to 1964, the average English grammar school pupil (top 20 percent) scored better than the average German Gymnasium pupil.

More generally, as Prais and Wagner (1985) make clear, the German school system is geared to maintaining high standards for the bottom half of the ability range. In German schools, as in Swiss and Dutch schools, basic standards in language, arithmetic, and practical work are set for *all* to attain, and instructional time and resources are used to bring all pupils to an acceptable level of achievement. As R. G. Luxton, a principal schools inspector, notes, the consequence is that Germany's "standard of achievement, especially of the less academic," is higher than Britain's, specifically "achievement in classroom lessons, in homework, in exercise books, and in the acquisition of appropriate qualifications" (quoted in Prais 1994, 200).

Germany's school system has its impact on the transition to work. Christoph Buechtemann, Juergen Schupp, and Dana Soloff (1993) for twelve years followed a sample of pupils coming to the end of their compulsory schooling in 1978 to 1979 in Germany and the United States. After twelve years, some 80 percent of German youth had attained either a vocational training certificate or a degree. All but 1 percent of the remainder had received some formal post-secondary education or training. In the United States, there is mass higher education, so that some 52 percent of U.S. school leavers were at some point enrolled in higher education, compared with only 16 percent in Germany. However, 31 percent of U.S. school leavers received no formal training or education after leaving school, and 46 percent gained no certificate or degree.

So far then we have a picture of a German education and training system that trains a high proportion of the German work force to a significant level of skill—a far higher proportion than in the United States or the United Kingdom. How does this system contribute to a level of productivity high enough at the bottom end to sustain such high wage levels? The answer to this question is best understood by looking at some of the matched plant studies in the *National Institute Economic Review* (for example, Steedman and Wagner 1987). The skills of the supervisors in German metalworking plants raise the productivity of unqualified operatives far above that of their counterparts in (technologically) comparable U.K. plants. However, it is more instructive to look in detail at the service sector, where most of the unskilled jobs are located, in order to see how the same kind of thing happens.

Sigmund J. Prais, Valerie Jarvis, and Karin Wagner (1989) compare the British and German hotel industries by looking at matched samples of hotels in the two countries. These hotels turn out to have almost identical occupancy rates (54 percent in Britain, 57 percent in Germany) and to provide a comparable quality of service. The hotels in both countries employ a considerable number of unqualified staff (mainly chambermaids) who would almost certainly be in the bottom decile of the pay distribution. In Germany, however, 35 percent of employees possess vocational qualifications in hotel work or related activities, compared with 14 percent in Britain. Average productivity is vastly higher in German hotels, which employ 0.25 person-days per guest night relative to 0.49 person-days per guest night in Britain. Much of this productivity advantage arises from the fact that housekeepers are much more effective in organizing and utilizing unskilled chambermaids in Germany than they are in Britain. And German housekeepers appear to be effective simply because most of them have been properly trained (on a three-year program). It is this type of evidence that demonstrates clearly how the high quality of schooling and subsequent training available to, and utilized by, the vast bulk of German young people tends to raise productivity all the way down to the bottom of the ability range. As a result, the productivity distribution is compressed relative to the United Kingdom and the United States, even though average labor productivity in some service sectors in the United States may be higher than in Germany (see McKinsey Global Institute 1993).

The overall conclusion to be drawn from the German experience of the decline in demand for the unskilled, compared to the experiences of the United Kingdom and the United States, is straightforward. A strong emphasis in the schooling system on sustaining a high level of performance by those in the bottom half of the ability range, combined with a comprehensive system of vocational training, mitigates many of the adverse consequences of a shift in demand away from the unskilled. Furthermore, the training system cannot operate successfully without a schooling system that provides effective preparation.

What are the lessons to be drawn from the German experience? Obviously, in the long run a shift in the focus of the education system towards the bottom half of the ability range is the key. In both the United States and the United Kingdom, the current system is excellent for the top half but tends to leave the bottom end floundering. However, since we cannot expect either the United Kingdom or the United States to revise its entire education system along German lines over any reasonable time horizon, we must now concentrate on getting the low-skilled closer to the middle using demand-side policies. Some approaches along these lines are considered in the next section.

Expanding the Demand for the Unskilled

Since the late 1960s, it is clear that the equilibrium unemployment rate in the United States has risen slightly. The evidence also suggests that much of the increase in this equilibrium rate is due to the shift in relative demand against the unskilled (see Juhn, Murphy, and Topel 1991, or compare the U.S. numbers for 1971 to 1974 and 1987 to 1990 in table 9.3). By contrast, in Britain and Germany over the same period unemployment rates have risen significantly among the skilled as well as the unskilled, an indication that some of the causes of the rise in the equilibrium rate are more or less neutral in regards to skill (see Nickell and Bell 1995).

In the United States, therefore, it is hard to see how any general demand expansion could possibly be sustained without generating inflationary pressure arising from the skilled labor market. This constraint suggests that an aggregate demand expansion biased in favor of the unskilled might be more feasible. How this would be achieved is another matter. It may be possible to focus the demand expansion on certain low-skill industries (construction?), but such an approach is very hit and miss and could go disastrously wrong. A more targeted approach would be to institute a direct job creation program for the unskilled. The problem is, what would they do? If they did something useless, it could rightly be objected that isolating unskilled individuals in obvious large-scale make-work schemes is not acceptable. If they did something useful, on the other hand, they might displace other unskilled workers operating in substitute areas. This problem raises the issue of the effective "cost per job." In practice, it has been found that direct job creation can be useful for small and precisely targeted groups, such as the long-term unemployed, who can thereby be reintegrated into the labor force. However, more general large-scale programs have not typically been found to be valuable (see, for example, de Munnik 1992; OECD 1993, 66–67; Calmfors and Skedinger 1995, 104–5). Given the problems of directly expanding demand, the obvious alternative is to consider policies that attempt to lower the price of labor in general and unskilled labor in particular.

Cutting Taxes on Labor Across the Board

Both the OECD (1994b, 1994c) and Edmund Phelps (1994) suggest that reducing payroll taxes is a good idea; the shortfall could be made up by increasing VAT. Thus, Phelps argues, "in continental Europe, where the sum of payroll and income taxes bears down very hard on employment, such a substitution of tax instruments would achieve a major gain in employment and some gain in the general level of real wage rates as well" (1994, 28). Presumably, since the sum of payroll and income taxes is not insubstantial in the United States, the same switch would be worth trying there as well.

The general argument for this switch is that since payroll taxes apply only to labor income and consumption taxes apply to all (spent) income, a switch from the former to the latter raises the reward for working relative to not working and thereby reduces unemployment.[4] How big is this effect? The crucial factor is the extent of nonlabor income, which is not subject to payroll tax. It is arguable that, for the typical person at risk of unemployment, this nonlabor income is extremely small. For example, in 1987 to 1988, only 7 percent of unemployment entrants in Britain had savings of more than £3,000 (see Layard, Nickell, and Jackman 1991, table A6), a sum that would produce an annual interest income of around 10 percent of the unemployment benefit. So it may be that this tax-switching effect is simply too small to have any noticeable effect.

Turning to the more general question of whether cutting any of the taxes on labor would have any impact on unemployment, the cross-country evidence suggests that, in the long run, we cannot expect much from this quarter. The results set out in OECD (1990, annex 6A) clearly indicate that these taxes are shifted onto labor and that cutting them affects employment only in the short run. Most of the numerous time-series studies on individual countries are conveniently summarized in Layard, Nickell, and Jackman (1991, 210) and OECD (1994c, 247). The results might be described as "all over the place." The problem with trying to pin down these tax effects through short time-series studies is that it is very hard to discriminate between quite long-lasting temporary effects and permanent effects. At the end of their exhaustive discussion in OECD (1994c, ch. 9), the authors conclude that "an overall cut in labor taxes *without* compensating increases in other taxes could have a beneficial effect on labor markets," and that "changes in the mix of taxes by which governments raise revenues can be expected, at most, to have a limited effect on unemployment" (p. 275). Not very compelling conclusions.

Overall, therefore, we cannot expect much to be achieved by changing tax rates across the board.

Cutting Taxes on Low-Paid Labor

As already noted, the German education system devotes considerable efforts to bringing those at the bottom of the ability range up as close as possible to the middle. If it is not possible to do this through the education system, an alternative is to use the tax/benefit system to mimic the outcome—that is, to focus tax cuts or subsidies on the low-paid to raise both their incomes and their employment. The main issues have been extensively discussed by Adrian Wood (1994 ch. 10), Edmund Phelps (1994), and Patrick Minford (1994). Nevertheless, a number of points are worth emphasizing here. The two main approaches involve either subsidizing low-wage jobs or subsidizing low-wage individuals, or more generally, low-income households. The standard public economics response to these two possibilities is to note first that it is irrelevant to the incidence of the subsidies whether they are paid to employers or employees, and second, that subsidizing low-income households is preferred because such programs precisely target the poor. Indeed, the evidence suggests that the overlap between low-paid individuals and low-income households is not great (see Layard, Piachaud, and Stewart 1978, for example). This is the view taken by Minford (1994).

This conclusion, however, ignores one particular aspect of the low-pay problem with which we are faced. The problem is not just one of poverty but also of absence of work. Having access to money but not to work is damaging to the self-esteem of most people and socially corrosive. For good or ill, in Western societies there is a strong relationship between personal fulfillment and market work. As a consequence, it may be desirable to have a system in place that provides private-sector jobs for low-skill individuals at a reasonable wage. One way of doing this is to fix a minimum wage (for prime-age adults) and then to subsidize employers in order to provide an adequate supply of jobs at this wage. The subsidy could be of the tapering kind suggested by Jacques Dréze and Edmond Malinvaud (1994).

This proposal has a number of advantages. If it creates jobs at reasonable wage levels for the unskilled, the unemployment benefit system can be structured to pressure the unemployed to take these jobs. The subsidy system is not attached to individuals, so there is none of the stigma associated with schemes in which individuals of a given type "carry" subsidies with them to employers. On the other hand, it has to be recognized that such subsidized jobs reduce the incentive to acquire training. This effect, however, could be offset by training subsidies. The major drawback to the proposal is the expense. Because subsidized minimum-wage jobs are not exclusively taken by the poor (for example, they may be taken by spouses of higher earners), this scheme costs more than subsidizing low-income households.

Summary and Conclusion

In the United States, the poor are getting poorer, whereas in Germany they are getting richer. Indeed, workers in the bottom decile of the male earnings distribution in Germany earn twice as much as their equivalents in the United States. Yet the unemployment rate of the unskilled in Germany is much the same as in the United States, as is the nonemployment rate. So are there any lessons in the German experience?

First, compulsory schooling in Germany is focused on bringing *all* pupils up to an acceptable level of achievement. As a consequence, the variation in attainment among schoolchildren is substantially lower in Germany than in the United States. Moreover, some 80 percent of German youth attain either a vocational training certificate or a university degree, and 19 of the remaining 20 percent receive some type of formal post-secondary education or training. By contrast, around 31 percent of U.S. school leavers receive no other formal training or education after leaving school, and 46 percent gain neither a certificate nor a degree.

So the education and training system in Germany trains a far higher proportion of the workforce up to a significant level of skill than the U.S.

system does. One of the consequences is that the skills of supervisory-level workers in Germany raise the productivity of unqualified workers in both manufacturing and the service sector. The relatively compressed wage structure is thus sustained without excessive unemployment at the bottom end.

There are obviously some lessons here for raising the pay of those at the bottom end of the U.S. earnings distribution. Applying them would take a very long time, however, even if to do so were politically feasible. So what of the alternative demand-side policies that could be introduced over a reasonable period of time?

There are two approaches—direct demand expansion, or tax cuts and job subsidies. Demand expansion focused on the unskilled and job creation programs are not very effective unless they are used for small and precisely targeted groups, such as the very long-term unemployed. Tax cuts and job subsidies hold out more hope if they can be concentrated at the bottom end of the pay distribution. Standard public finance suggests that negative income tax schemes are the most efficient for alleviating poverty. However, if it is desirable to focus on the provision of work, then a combination of minimum wages and job subsidies could be effective in providing reasonably paid jobs for the unskilled.

This chapter was prepared for the Russell Sage Foundation Conference on Labor Demand Policies and Low-Skilled Workers, New York, New York, June 26–27, 1995. I am grateful to Brian Bell and Daphne Nicolitsas for assistance in its preparation, to the Economic and Social Research Council for research support, and to Richard Freeman, Peter Gottschalk, Philip Harvey, and other conference participants for helpful comments on an earlier draft.

Notes

1. Both here and elsewhere, Germany is taken to mean West Germany.
2. Nonemployment rates among the unskilled are also similar in Germany and the United States. Thus, according to the German Socio-Economic Panel, the 1984 to 1990 average nonemployment rate among those over twenty-five in the working-age male population in Germany who have no qualifications is 31.6 percent. The equivalent number in the United States (less than four years of high school) is 32.5 percent. The German group represents the bottom 12 percent of the working population in education terms, and the U.S. group the lowest 15 percent, so they are almost exactly comparable.
3. For example, the annual flows in and out of unemployment in Germany are around 7 percent of the labor force, whereas the annual flow into all job cre-

ation/job subsidy schemes is a mere 0.4 percent of the labor force, and this figure includes a substantial amount of displacement.

4. This is the non-labor-income argument. Hoon and Phelps (1995) provide a real interest rate argument, which we do not consider here.

References

Abraham, Katharine G., and Susan N. Houseman. 1994. "Earnings Inequality in Germany." Working Paper 94-24. Kalamazoo, Mich.: W. E. Upjohn Institute for Employment Research.

Audretsch, David B. 1995. "The Innovation, Unemployment, and Competitiveness Challenge in Germany." Discussion Paper 1152. London, England: Centre for Economic Policy Research.

Bell, Linda, and Richard Freeman. 1994. "Why Do Americans and Germans Work Different Hours?" Working Paper 4808. Cambridge, Mass.: National Bureau of Economic Research.

Bellman, Laurence, and Hartmut Lehmann. 1990. "Active Labour Market Policies in Britain and Germany and Long-term Unemployment." Unpublished paper.

Blau, Francine D., and Lawrence M. Kahn. 1994. "International Differences in Male Wage Inequality: Institutions Versus Market Forces." Working Paper 4678. Cambridge, Mass.: National Bureau of Economic Research.

Buechtemann, Christoph, Juergen Schupp, and Dana Soloff. 1993. "Roads to Work: School-to-Work Transition Patterns in Germany and the U.S." *Industrial Relations Journal* 24(2): 97–111.

Buttler, Friedrich, and Manfred Tessaring. 1993. "Humankapital als Standortfaktor: Argumente zur Bildungsdiskussion aus arbeitsmarktpolitischer Sicht." Mitt AB 4, 467–76.

Calmfors, Lars, and Per Skedinger. 1995. "Does Active Labour-Market Policy Increase Employment?" *Oxford Review of Economic Policy* (Spring): 91–109.

Davis, Steven J. 1992. "Cross-Country Patterns of Change in Relative Wages." Working Paper 4085. Cambridge, Mass.: National Bureau of Economic Research.

de Munnik, R. 1992. *Recent Evaluation Studies,* part 2, *The Employment Service,* Rijswijk, The Netherlands.

Dréze, Jacques H., and Edmond Malinvaud. 1994. "Growth and Employment: The Scope for a European Initiative." *European Economic Review* 38(3–4): 489–504.

Freeman, Richard. 1995. "The Limits of Wage Flexibility to Curing Unemployment." *Oxford Review of Economic Policy* 11 (Spring): 63–72.

Hoon, Hian Tech, and Edmund S. Phelps. 1995. "Taxes and Subsidies in a Labor-Turnover Model of the 'Natural Rate.'" Columbia University. Unpublished paper.

Juhn, Chirhui, Kevin Murphy, and Robert Topel. 1991. "Why Has the National Rate of Unemployment Increased Over Time." *Brookings Papers on Economic Activity* 2. Washington, D.C.: Brookings Institution.

Layard, Richard, Stephen Nickell, and Richard Jackman. 1991. *Unemployment: Macroeconomic Performance and the Labour Market.* Oxford, England: Oxford University Press.

———. 1994. *The Unemployment Crisis.* Oxford, England: Oxford University Press.

Layard, Richard, David Piachaud, and M. Stewart. 1978. *The Causes of Poverty.* Royal Commission on the Distribution of Income and Wealth Background Paper 5. London, England: Her Majesty's Stationery Office.

McKinsey Global Institute. 1993. *The McKinsey Global Institute Report on Productivity.* Washington, D.C.: McKinsey and Co. (October).

Minford, Patrick. 1994. "Unemployment in the OECD and Its Remedies." Paper presented at the CEPR/Consorcio Zona Franca de Vigo Conference on Unemployment Policy. Vigo, Spain (September 1994).

Nickell, Stephen, and Brian Bell. 1995. "The Collapse in Demand for the Unskilled and Unemployment Across the OECD." *Oxford Review of Economic Policy* 11 (Spring): 40–62.

Organization for Economic Cooperation and Development (OEDC). 1990. *Employment Outlook.* Paris, France: Organization for Economic Cooperation and Development.

———. 1993. *Employment Outlook.* Paris, France: Organization for Economic Cooperation and Development.

———. 1994a. *Employment Outlook.* Paris, France: Organization for Economic Cooperation and Development.

———. 1994b. *The OECD Jobs Study,* part 1, *Evidence and Explanations.* Paris, France: Organization for Economic Cooperation and Development.

———. 1994c. *The OECD Jobs Study,* part 2, *Evidence and Explanations.* Paris, France: Organization for Economic Cooperation and Development.

———. 1995. *Literacy, Economy, and Society, OECD/Statistics Canada.* Paris, France: Organization for Economic Cooperation and Development.

Phelps, Edmund S. 1994. "A Program of Low-Wage-Employment Tax Credits." Working Paper 55. New York: Russell Sage Foundation.

Prais, Sigmund J. 1994. "Economic Performance and Education: The Nature of Britain's Deficiencies." *Proceedings of the British Academy* 84: 151–207.

Prais, Sigmund J., Valerie Jarvis, and Karin Wagner. 1989. "Productivity and Vocational Skills in Services in Britain and Germany: Hotels." *National Institute Economic Review* (November): 52–74.

Prais, Sigmund J., and Karin Wagner. 1985. "Schooling Standards in England and Germany: Some Summary Comparisons Bearing on Economic Performance." *National Institute Economic Review* (March): 53–77.

Steedman, Hilary, and Karin Wagner. 1987. "A Second Look at Productivity, Machinery and Skills in Britian and Germany." *National Institute Economic Review* (122): 84–95.

Wood, Adrian. 1994. *North-South Trade, Employment and Inequality: Changing Fortunes in a Skill-Driven World.* Oxford, England: Clarendon Press.

Index

Boldface numbers refer to figures and tables.